ENCYCLOPEDIA OF ANIMALS

p

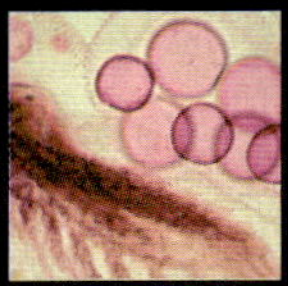

A WORLD FULL OF ANIMALS 6

SIMPLE ANIMALS 10

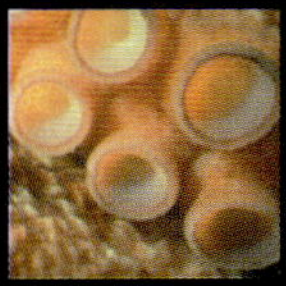

WORMS, SNAILS & STARFISH 40

INSECTS & OTHER ARTHROPODS 70

FISH 100

Contents

A WORLD FULL OF ANIMALS

Boa constrictor

The world teems with animals. Almost everywhere we look, creatures are going about their daily lives. On a walk through the countryside we see birds high in the sky. Insects buzz around the flowers. Mice and voles scamper through the undergrowth. Rabbits race across fields. Worms burrow in the soil under our feet. Even in a busy city, pigeons flock and cockroaches scuttle.

Mushroom

These are a tiny selection of the kinds of animals that live on Earth. No one is sure exactly how many there are. Nearly two million kinds, or species, have been studied and identified by scientists. But many remote mountains, rainforests, coastlines and deep seas remain to be explored. The total number of animal species on Earth may be 10 million, 20 million or even more. Most of them are likely to be small insects such as beetles.

EVOLUTION

Evolution is when living things change or adapt to their surroundings. The world is always changing, as weather and climate alter, seas rise and fall, volcanoes erupt and earthquakes split the land. Living things change too, developing new bodily features and behaviour, so they can survive better in the new and different conditions. But survival is a continuing struggle. It is as if nature chooses or selects which plants and animals will survive, and which will die. This is evolution by natural selection.

Evolution has been happening since life first appeared on Earth some 4 billion years ago. It has meant that some kinds of animals have died out, or become extinct, while others have evolved to take their place. All of this usually happens over a very long time scale, thousands or millions of years. But we have altered the world greatly in the last few hundred years. New types of living things can now be produced in a few weeks or months using the science of genetics. How this will affect nature in the future is very unclear.

Tuatara

THE KINGDOMS OF LIVING THINGS

Scientists used to divide the living world into two main groups, or kingdoms: plants and animals. Today, most experts agree that there are five kingdoms. Two consist of microscopic life-forms, where each individual is just one living cell. One of these kingdoms is Monerans, including the germs known as bacteria.

Manta ray

The other kingdom is Protists. Some protists are like tiny, one-celled micro-animals. They move about and eat food. So they are included at the beginning of this book (pages 12–15). The third kingdom is Plants, such as flowers, trees, grasses, ferns and seaweeds; and the fourth is Fungi, such as mushrooms, toadstools and yeasts. The fifth kingdom, and the largest, is the Animals.

WHAT ARE ANIMALS?

Animals are multi-celled living things that get the energy they need for survival, and the nutrients they need for growth and repair, by feeding on other living things.

Wild bees

Caterpillars

In this way they differ from plants, which capture their energy from sunlight.

Most animals feed by eating or ingesting their food. Carnivores such as wolves eat meat. Herbivores like deer feed on plant parts. Detritivores like worms and millipedes feed on dead and rotting bits of other living things. Omnivores eat almost anything.

Most animals have sense organs such as eyes and ears, so they can detect changes around them. They also have muscles so they can move about, react to changes, find food and avoid danger. However, very simple animals like sponges have few senses and cannot move. Some animals, like mussels and barnacles, fix themselves into position when young and stay put for the rest of their lives.

HOW ANIMALS BREED

The key feature of all living things is that they breed – they produce more of their kind. Animals do this in a huge variety of ways. Many, from butterflies to birds, lay eggs.

Horned grebe

Some, such as mammals, certain snakes and some fish, give birth to babies. A few, such as some flatworms, starfish and jellyfish, can split and grow into two new individuals.

Animals care for their offspring in different ways. Monkeys and apes look after their babies for months, or even years. Most birds spend weeks tirelessly feeding the chicks that hatch from their eggs. Mouthbrooding fish shelter their young in their mouths. The gastric-brooding frog keeps its young tadpoles in its stomach! However, most animals lay or release their eggs, and have nothing more to do with the offspring.

Puffin

Animals live in almost every type of surroundings, or habitat. A waterless desert, an icy glacier, a wave-battered coastline, a deep and pitch-black cave – they are all homes to animals of one kind or another. Each type of animal has features that enable it to survive in its habitat. Glacier grasshoppers can be frozen alive, yet come back to life when thawed out. Desert creatures escape the drought and heat by burrowing underground and staying still or dormant until it rains once more.

Shrimp on a sea slug

Frogs

Stinkbug

HARMFUL, HELPFUL AND USEFUL

Some animals have taken to living alongside people. We have covered much of the world with buildings, roads, factories and rubbish tips. These have become ideal habitats for animals such as cockroaches, rats, mice and gulls. Some animals have become pests. Insects feed on cereal grains and destroy our crops. Some creatures, like flukes and mosquitoes, cause or spread disease.

But we have also found other animals helpful or useful. We have bred farm animals for meat, milk, fur and skins. Working animals pull ploughs and carts or carry goods. Horses, dogs, camels, falcons, frogs and others are used in sports and competitions. For some people, pets are their main companions.

EQUAL ANIMALS

When we talk about "animals and birds", some people think of furry mammals and fluffy chicks. But the animal kingdom contains a gigantic range of creatures – including insects, spiders, snakes, worms, slugs, snails and other less appealing "creepy-crawlies". We may not want to pick them up, but they each have their role to play in nature.

Today, many animal species are in danger of extinction, due to our human activities.

Young male lion

Penguins and chicks

Hagfish

GROUPING ANIMALS

To study and understand the animal kingdom, we need to have some method of grouping or classifying its creatures. Those with important similarities are put together in the same group. The main division is between vertebrates and invertebrates.

Vertebrates are animals with backbones and include fish, frogs and other amphibians, lizards and other reptiles, birds and furry mammals. Invertebrates lack a backbone and include all other animals, from tiny flies to giant squid. This book is organized into sections using the standard system of classifying animals. It begins with simple invertebrates such as sponges and jellyfish. It ends with mammals that have complex behaviour, such as solving problems and using tools. Classification panels give details of how many species are in the group, where they live, what they eat and other information.

The classification system is broadly based on the idea of evolution. For example, all birds are classified together in the group called Aves. They are probably all descended from very early birds that first evolved millions of years ago. So all birds are related to each other. On a wider scale, the first birds probably evolved from reptiles such as the dinosaurs. In this way, relationships spread throughout the animal kingdom.

Backswimmer

It is tempting to see this system as a "ladder of evolution", with simple animals at the bottom and apes, monkeys – and ourselves – at the top. But all animals have amazing adaptations. A penguin might not survive on its own in one of our large cities. But then, we would not survive on our own at the South Pole!

Sheep

We hunt them for "sport", kill them for collections and eliminate them in case they are dangerous. Most of all, we take over their wild places so they no longer have anywhere to live. Habitat destruction is the major threat facing the natural world today. Without these animals, our world would be a far less exciting place.

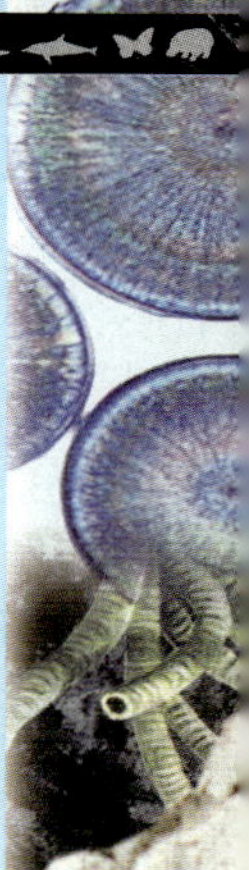

Horned owl

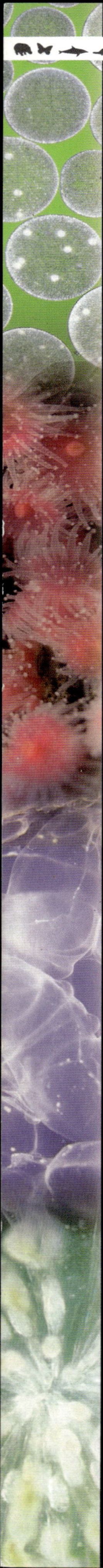

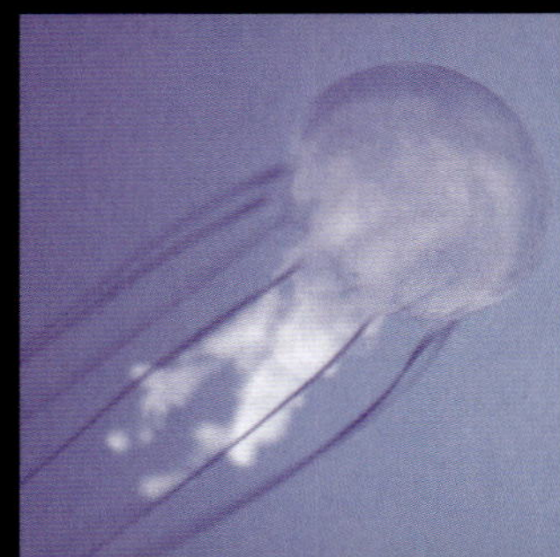

The man-o'-war is a cnidarian—or rather, lots of cnidarians. It is a floating group of cnidarian polyps known as siphonophores.

SECTION 1
SIMPLE ANIMALS

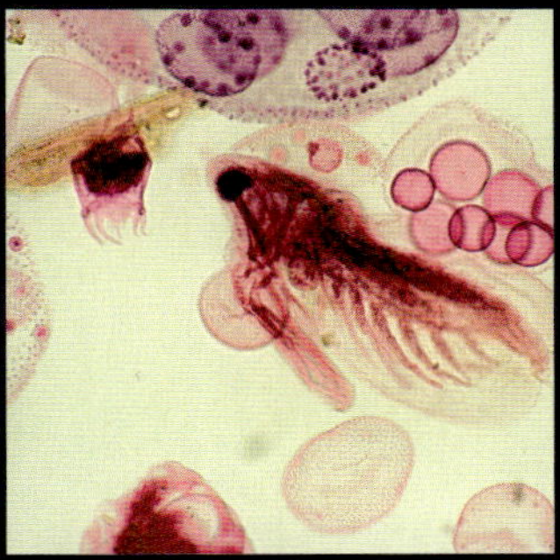

THE SIMPLEST OF ALL LIFE FORMS ARE NOT ANIMALS. They are protists. Each is just a single living cell. Some are like micro-animals, because they eat tiny bits of food. Others are like micro-plants, using the sun's light energy to live and grow. Protists number untold trillions and are the basic food for many tiny animals, especially in the sea, where they form much of the plankton.

A simple animal is a creature with few uncomplicated body parts. The simplest of the life forms we call animals are sponges. Each is little more than a collection of fairly similar cells, with no brain, heart, muscles or similar body parts. Sponges live in rivers and lakes, and on seashores and ocean floors, around the world. Crawling and swimming among them are tiny animals smaller than pinheads, such as water-bears and wheel-animals. Floating above them in the sea are various creatures that resemble bags of jelly. They include comb-jellies and jellyfish, all with long, stinging tentacles.

Close relatives of jellyfish are the sea anemones on the shore, and the anemones' similar but smaller cousins, coral polyps. All of these animals may have few and simple body parts. But they thrive in their millions. Indeed, coral polyps construct the largest animal-made structures on Earth – coral reefs.

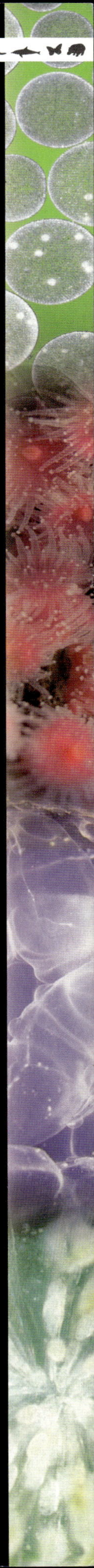

THE MICRO-WORLD OF PROTISTS

PROTISTS ARE VERY SMALL. They are among the tiniest living things, and each is made of just one microscopic cell. An average protist is about 20 times smaller than the dot on this letter 'i'. A very large protist might fit into this letter 'o'. In the deep sea lives a gigantic kind of protist that grows to the size of your finger. Protists are living things, but they are not really animals or plants. They have a separate kingdom (major group) of their own, Protista. However some kinds, called protozoans, are like tiny animals (rather than tiny plants) because they can move around and they eat other living things – especially other protists! They are found in all watery or damp places, including seas, rivers, ponds, soil and on and inside animals and plants. Some kinds cause diseases.

There are many different kinds of protists. Amoebas are shaped like blobs and they can move around by changing shape as they ooze along like plastic bags of jelly. An amoeba feeds by sending out arm-like parts to surround a micro-particle of food, and then merging the arms with its body to engulf the particle. After digesting what it can, the amoeba simply oozes on and leaves the remains behind.

PLASMODIUM AND MALARIA

The protists that cause malaria grow through many stages in their lives. Some are in mosquitoes, some in humans. When a mosquito that does not have plasmodia bites a person who does have them, the mosquito sucks up plasmodia in its meal of blood. Then it bites another person and passes on the parasites.

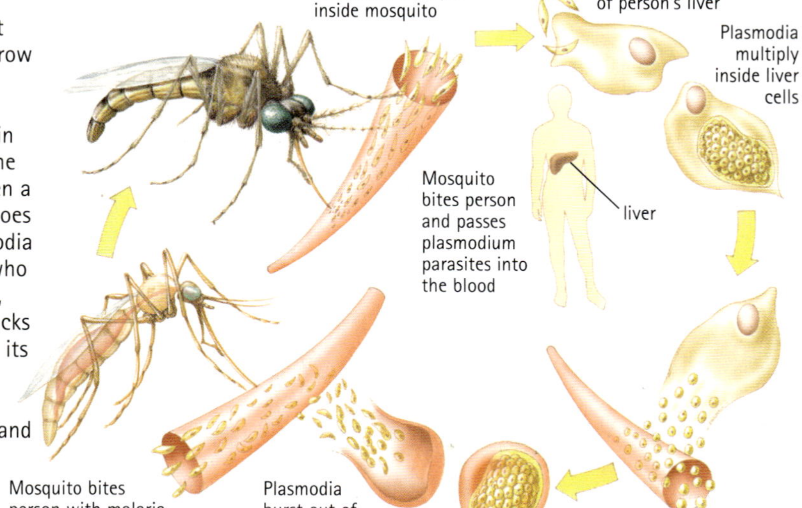

A few types of amoeba are real giants, growing almost to the size of shirt buttons.

Another group of protists is the ciliates, such as stentors and parameciums (pages 16–17). They are known as ciliates because their bodies are covered by a "carpet" of miniature hairs called cilia.

The cilia beat regularly, like rows of miniature oars, to make the protist glide through the water. However, some ciliates, like stentor, cannot move about. They are attached by a stalk to the pond or stream bottom. They beat their cilia to make water currents that bring tiny bits of food to them.

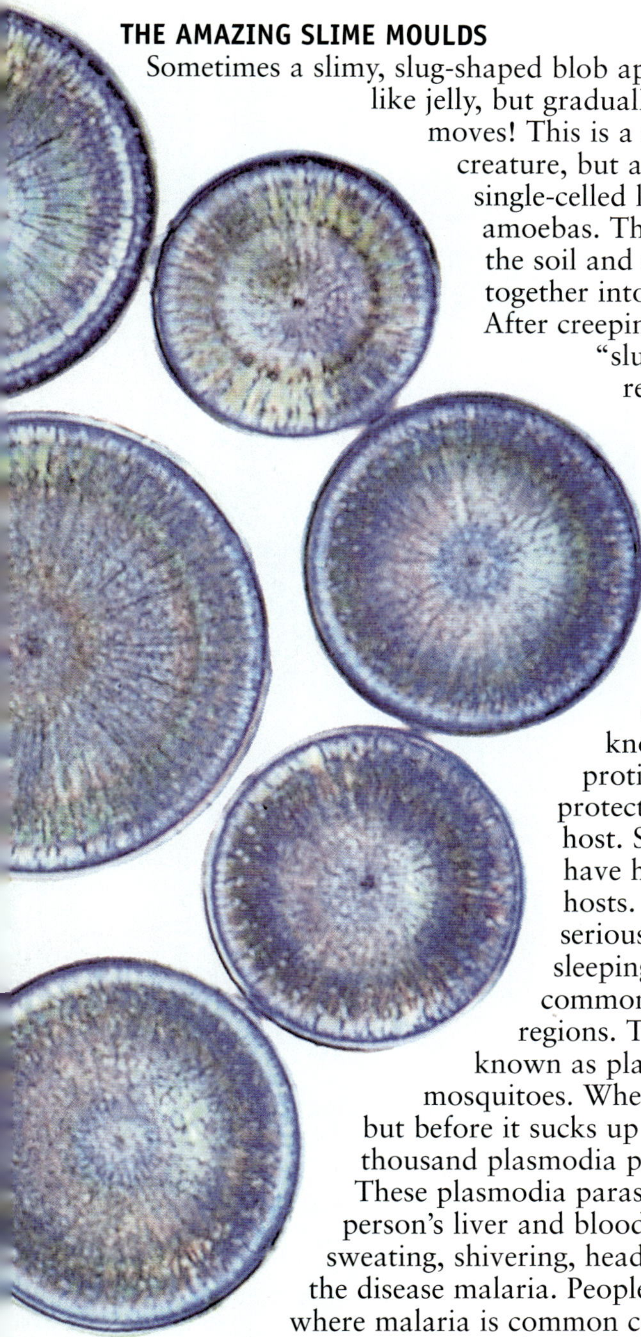

THE AMAZING SLIME MOULDS

Sometimes a slimy, slug-shaped blob appears on an old tree. It looks like jelly, but gradually, over several minutes, it moves! This is a slime mould. It is not a single creature, but a collection of hundreds of single-celled living things resembling amoebas. They normally live separately in the soil and among leaves. They gather together into a slug-like lump to breed. After creeping about for a while, the "slug" grows a stalk that releases tiny, dust-like particles called spores. These blow away and hatch into new amoebas. A large slime mould "slug" can weigh up to 900 g.

PROTISTS AND DISEASES

Many protists are parasites. They thrive on or in other living things, known as the hosts. The protist gains food and protection or shelter from its host. Some parasitic protists have hardly any effect on their hosts. Others cause great harm and serious diseases such as malaria and sleeping sickness. Malaria is common in many warm, tropical regions. The protists that cause it are known as plasmodia. They are spread by mosquitoes. When a mosquito bites a person, but before it sucks up blood, it passes a few thousand plasmodia protists into the person's body. These plasmodia parasites multiply inside the person's liver and blood. Eventually they produce the sweating, shivering, headaches and other symptoms of the disease malaria. People who visit tropical places where malaria is common can take tablets or have injections to prevent them catching it.

◘ Protists come in many shapes. Some are almost perfect spheres, like these diatoms. Others are shaped like bananas or commas.

PROTISTS

(Kingdom *Protista*)
- more than 60,000 kinds or species
- live in water, soil, other damp places and inside creatures and plants
- most are microscopic
- single-celled (body made of only one cell)

Some main groups of protists:

Amoebas
- 16,000 species
- move about and feed by changing shape
- some gather together and are known as "slime moulds"

Ciliates
- 7,500 species
- move and feed by tiny hair-like cilia

Euglenas
- at least 1,000 species
- mainly freshwater
- have one long, whip-like flagellum
- can capture the energy in sunlight, like tiny plants

Parasitic protists
- 5,000 species
- live inside other animals
- some cause diseases, such as malaria, sleeping sickness and dysentery

PROTIST PARTS

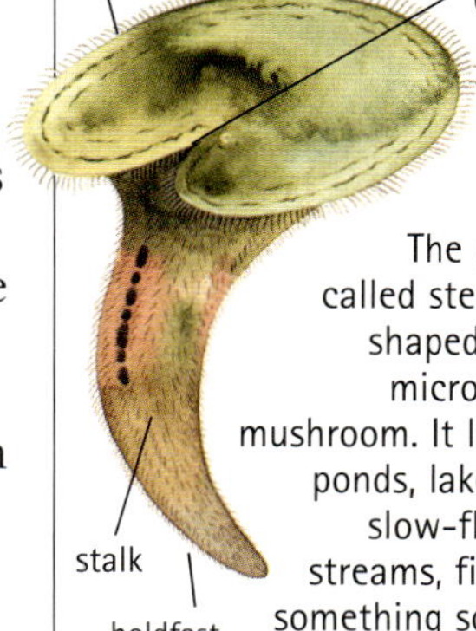

The protist called stentor is shaped like a microscopic mushroom. It lives in ponds, lakes and slow-flowing streams, fixed to something solid by its holdfast. Every now and again it comes loose and wriggles to a new place.

An amoeba is easily small enough to fit onto the head of a pin. It lives in water. It has no proper shape. It can spread out almost flat, extend arm-like parts called pseudopodia, then form into a round ball and roll along.

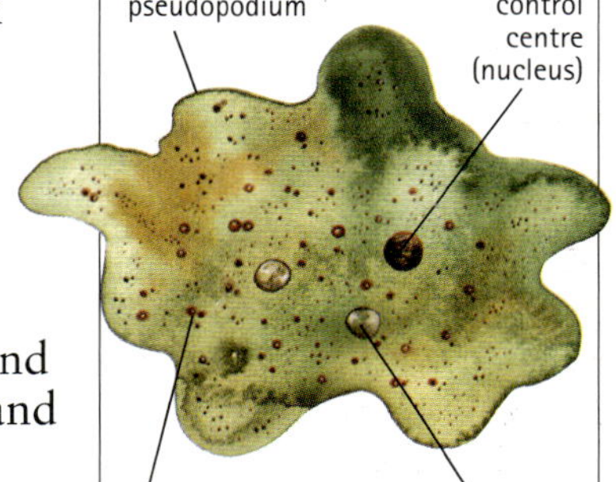

World Watch

More than 200 million people around the world suffer from malaria. And more than two million people die from this disease each year—about one million of them in Africa. The name of the disease, *malaria*, means "bad air". This name came from the time when people thought the illness was spread by bad or stale air. Then it was discovered that malaria was caused by protists too small to see, carried by mosquitoes.

FLOATING PROTISTS

MOST OCEAN CREATURES, EVEN GREAT WHALES, DEPEND ON TINY PROTISTS. These protists live in the upper layers of the sea. They form part of the plankton – a "living soup" of all kinds of tiny plants, animals and other organisms, drifting with the currents. Trillions of plant-like protists trap the sun's light energy and use it to live, grow and multiply. In turn, they are food for millions of tiny animal-like protists. Both kinds of protists are eaten by small sea creatures, such as tiny fish and shrimps, as well as the larvae (young) of bigger animals. These are consumed by larger ocean creatures, and so on, building up the ocean food chains to huge sharks and whales.

SHINY!

Some sea protists can make their own light. At night it makes the waves glow, or the water shine as people or boats pass through. This is often due to *Noctiluca* dinoflagellates. If you disturb water which contains large numbers of these protists they give off enough light between them to make the sea flash! Light production by living things is called bioluminescence.

In a drop of seawater, protists such as foraminiferans (pale and curled like spirals) and radiolarians (blue and ball-shaped) teem in their thousands.

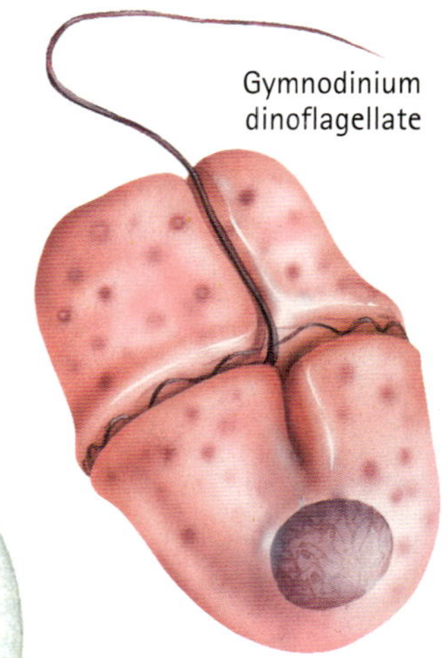

Gymnodinium dinoflagellate

Miliota foraminiferan

GREEN PLANKTON

Much of the plankton can make its own food using sunlight energy. Like trees and other green plants on land, the water-dwelling protists have a green substance called chlorophyll, which absorbs light energy.

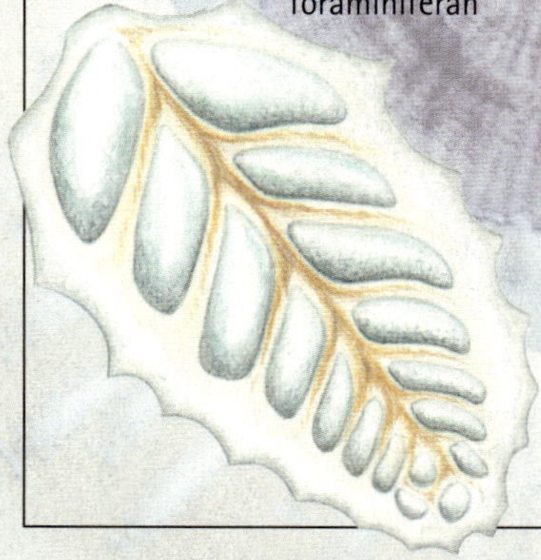

Spiroplecta foraminiferan

Polykrikos dinoflagellate

These members of the green plankton are sometimes called producers, because they produce food for themselves, rather than consuming it as animals do. Because strong sunlight can only shine down about 30 m into the sea, the green plankton have to stay close to the surface to survive.

OILY!

Crude oil, or petroleum, was formed from the remains of billions of tiny plankton organisms that lived millions of years ago. They sank slowly to the seabed in layers. The pressure of more layers above eventually turned them into oil.

Most live concentrated into the top 90 m of the ocean. A few can make weak wriggling movements, but most are at the mercy of ocean currents and they drift about in the endless circulation of seawater.

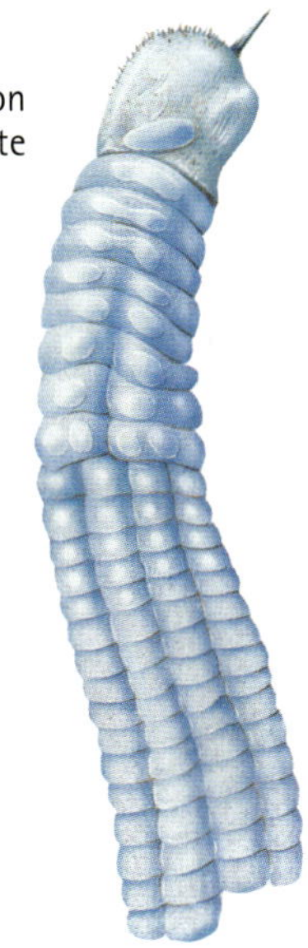

Haplozoon dinoflagellate

DIATOMS

The diatoms are plant-like protists with beautifully shaped, sculpted, and patterned shells. They float in the upper levels of the sea, and also in lakes, as part of the plankton. A diatom's shell is double-layered and made of silica—the main mineral in sand (and also in glass). Some diatoms have ring-like flaps that help them float near the surface.

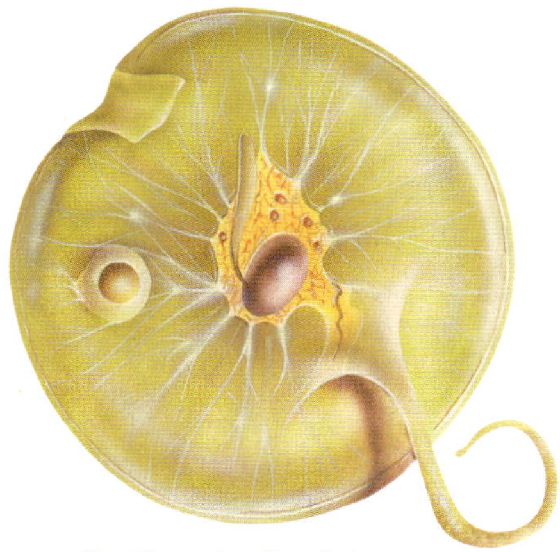

Noctiluca dinoflagellate

RADIOLARIANS

These protists are related to the amoebas shown on the previous page. Like diatoms, they have silica shells.

Rotalia foraminiferan

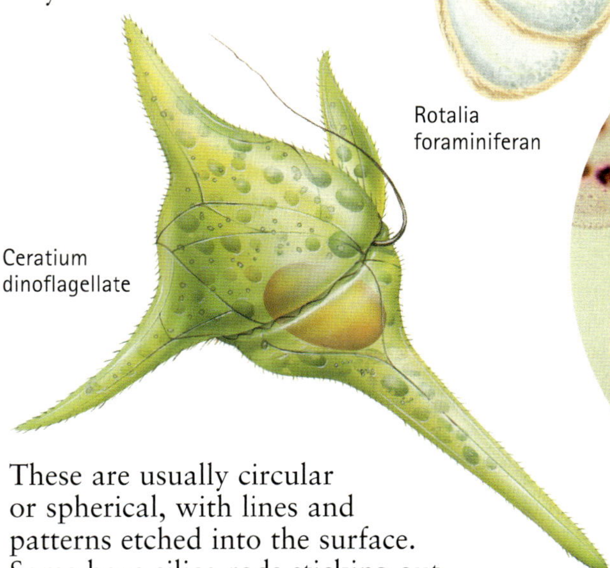

Ceratium dinoflagellate

These are usually circular or spherical, with lines and patterns etched into the surface. Some have silica rods sticking out, like the spokes of a wheel.

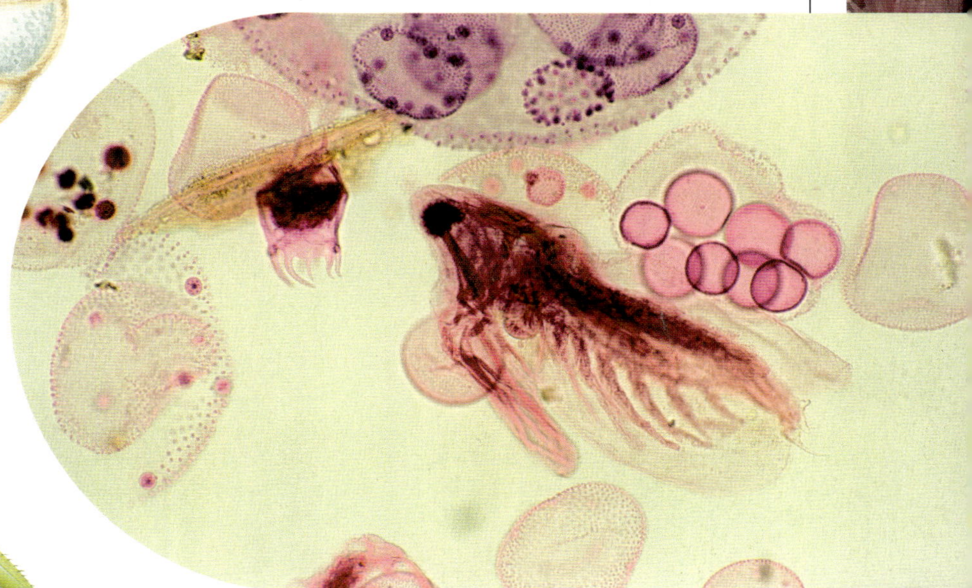

Besides protists, the plankton contains eggs and young forms (larvae) of larger animals such as shrimps and crabs.

FORAMINIFERANS

Another group of amoeba-like protists, the foraminiferans, also live inside shells. However, their shells are usually made of limestone or chalk rather than silica. Foraminiferans are very common in sea plankton, where they float about, feeding on even smaller organisms. A foraminiferan sticks long, thread-like "arms" through the many holes, called foramens, in its shell. It grabs food particles with these arms. A few foraminiferans grow as large as a fingernail.

DINOFLAGELLATES

These plankton protists have long, spine-like projections, which probably help to stop them sinking in the water, and which also deter predators. Some can use the sun's light energy, like plants. Others grab tiny bits of food. In certain conditions, especially a warm springtime, dinoflagellates cause "red tides" along the seashore. They multiply in such huge numbers that their bodies colour the seawater bright red. Some kinds also produce poisons that kill other life forms, such as fish.

SOME KINDS OF FLOATING PROTISTS

Diatoms
- 10,000 species
- live in the sea and in fresh water
- common in plankton
- have glassy, box-like casings

Dinoflagellates
- 2,000 species
- live in the sea and in fresh water
- have two whip-like flagella
- some live inside other creatures, such as corals

Foraminiferans
- 3,000 species
- live in the sea and in fresh water
- have chalky shells with holes
- some capture food, others absorb sunlight

MOSS-ANIMALS

MOSS-ANIMALS OR BRYOZOANS, SOMETIMES CALLED SEA-MOSSES, DO NOT LOOK LIKE ANIMALS AT ALL. As their name suggests, they live in the sea and look more like a patch of moss or a similar plant, or even like a doormat. This is because the tiny moss-animals live together in a group or colony and extend their tentacles, like hundreds of miniature sea anemones (page 32). The tentacles wave in the water and filter floating bits of food, which the moss-animals eat and digest.

▼ Freshwater moss-animals feed on protists such as paramecium, euglena and volvox. Being single cells, these are far smaller than the moss-animal. Sea-living moss-animals eat similar tiny food items such as floating scraps of seaweed, marine protists and also the eggs and larvae (young) of larger animals such as crabs, starfish and worms. The moss-animal grabs its prey with its tentacles, which are covered with microscopic hairs called cilia.

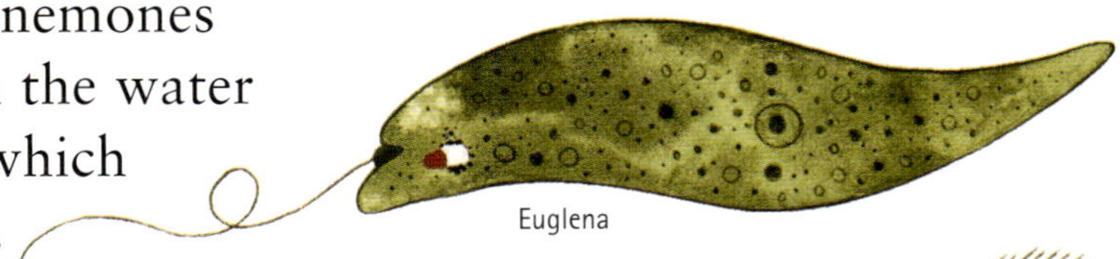
Euglena

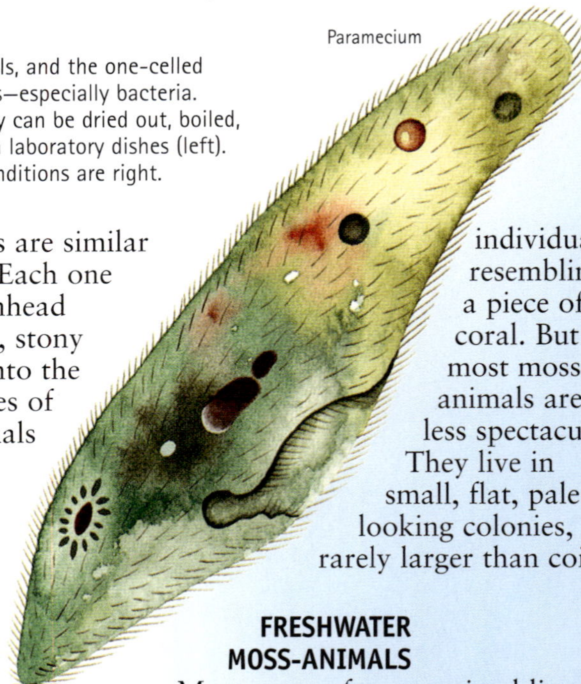
Paramecium

◀ Tiny creatures such as moss-animals, and the one-celled protists, eat the smallest living things—especially bacteria. Some bacteria hardly seem alive. They can be dried out, boiled, frozen and even made into crystals in laboratory dishes (left). Yet they still become active when conditions are right.

In some ways, moss-animals are similar to coral animals (page 36). Each one is tiny, only about half a pinhead across. It lives inside a hard, stony case and puts its tentacles into the water to catch floating pieces of food. Hundreds or thousands of individual moss-animals are connected together into a flat, branching structure which spreads and grows over an underwater object. This object may be a rock or stone, a piece of wood, a large frond of seaweed, or even the shell of another animal like a clam or mussel. In some kinds of moss-animal, the colony grows upwards, like a plant, rooted at the base to a firm object. The cases of neighbouring moss-animals, known as zooids, are cemented to each other. The whole colony may widen like a fan or branch like a twig, and be brightly coloured. It can have millions of individuals, resembling a piece of coral. But most moss-animals are less spectacular. They live in small, flat, pale-looking colonies, rarely larger than coins.

FRESHWATER MOSS-ANIMALS

Most types of moss-animal live in the sea, but a few live in fresh water, especially if it is clean and unpolluted.

INSIDE A MOSS-ANIMAL

A typical moss-animal or bryozoan is about the size of a pinhead. It lives in a hard casing, shaped like a shoebox, that it makes around itself from hard, chalky minerals taken from the water. The bell-shaped ring of feathery tentacles surrounding its mouth filter tiny particles of food, like small algae (plants) and protists, from the water. These food particles are passed down into the mouth and digested in the bag-like stomach. When danger threatens, strong strands of muscle pull the tentacles into the casing and then close and hold down the door-like lid, the operculum.

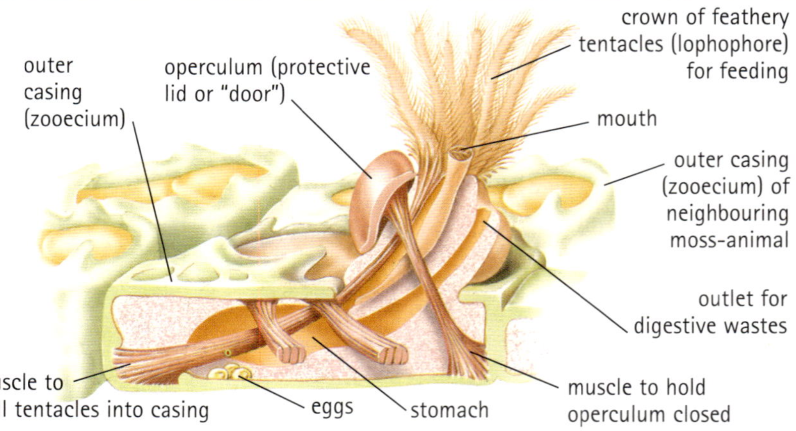

In some kinds the protective case is flexible and jelly-like, rather than hard and stony. In the late summer or autumn, both sea and freshwater moss-animal colonies produce hard, egg-like structures. These survive through the winter and can resist freezing and drying out. The eggs may blow about in the wind, spreading the moss-animals to new places. In the spring they develop into new colonies.

THE ANIMAL CELL

The bodies of all creatures, from moss-animals to blue whales, are made of microscopic units known as cells. A typical animal cell is shown right. A protist is just one, all-purpose cell. A moss-animal is about 5,000 cells. An elephant's body has 100 million million cells.

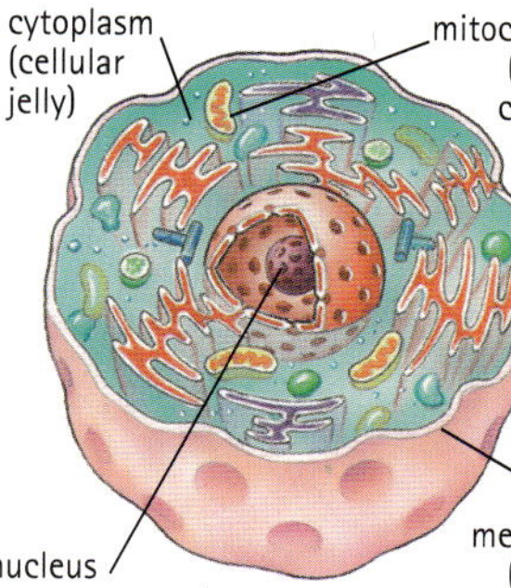

SEA-MAT AND HORNWRACK

The sea-mat is one common kind of moss-animal. It grows on the fronds of kelps and similar brown seaweeds and forms flat, pale, lacy sheets that stand out well against the background of the seaweed frond. Another common type of moss-animal is called hornwrack. It grows about as long as a human hand and is found in deeper water along rocky coasts. Sometimes colonies of hornwrack are washed up on the shore after a storm, and they look like pieces of pale, lacy seaweed.

Moss-animals
(Ectoprocts or Polyzoans)
- about 4,000 species
- aquatic (live in water)
- mostly marine or sea-dwelling
- grow as rooted, branching colonies
- each animal has a bell-shaped ring of tentacles called the lophophore, for feeding
- most individuals are hermaphrodite (have both male and female sex parts)
- breed by releasing tough, egg-like structures

Entoprocts
(Endoprocts or Kamptozoans)
- about 150 species
- aquatic (live in water)
- mostly marine or sea-dwelling
- grow as rooted, branching colonies
- each animal has a C-shaped ring of tentacles for feeding
- breed by releasing tiny, young forms or larvae

Volvox is the main kind of food for freshwater moss animals. It is a protist that lives like a plant, trapping the energy in sunlight to live and grow. Each floating ball is made up of hundreds of volvox protists.

ENTOPROCTS

Entoprocts are another group of tiny creatures, very similar to moss-animals. The largest are only as big as rice grains. They live mainly in colonies and are fixed in one spot. Some grow on stones, others on seaweeds. A few live on other animals, including sponges, worms, crabs and shellfish. Each entoproct has a horseshoe-shaped ring of about 40 tentacles for feeding, a cup-shaped body and a stalk fixing it to its host.

In the warm waters along the coast of South Australia these *Celleporaria* sea-mosses have formed colourful branching colonies on an old piece of wooden jetty.

WATER-BEARS AND WHEEL-ANIMALS

A water-bear has sharp claws on its eight stubby legs, to grip slippery plants or grains of mud and sand. It has mouthparts like sharp needles to pierce and suck food.

WATER-BEARS ARE AMAZING TINY CREATURES, WITH POWERS AS STRANGE AS THEIR APPEARANCE.

A typical water-bear has a plump body and four pairs of stumpy, clawed legs. It also has a faintly bear-like face, which might make it look cuddly – if it were not so tiny. Most water-bears are smaller than the dot on this letter 'i'. They creep about in the soil and dead leaves, among plants such as mosses, in the fresh water of ponds, streams and lakes, and also in the sea. They feed on the sap of plants, or on other creatures even smaller than themselves. Another group of very tiny creatures are wheel-animals. Most look like miniature cups on stalks. They take their name from the ring of microscopic hairs, cilia, around the rim of what looks like the cup-shaped body – which is actually the creature's head. The cilia beat like tiny oars to create water currents, which bring tiny bits of floating food to the animal's mouth.

This is a star-like group or colony of wheel-animals as seen under the microscope.

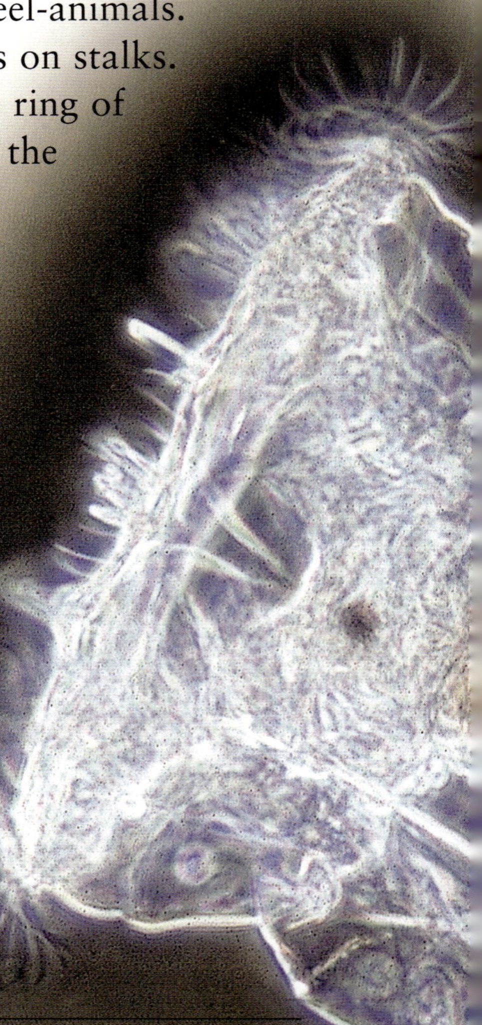

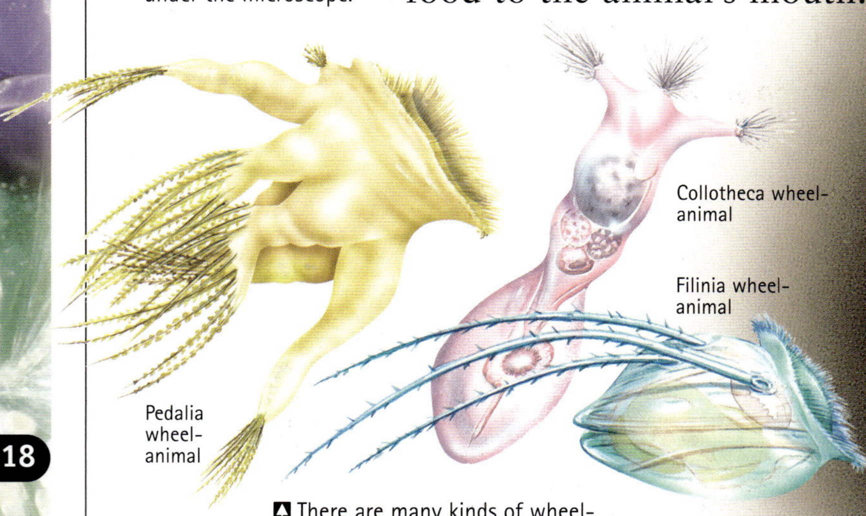

There are many kinds of wheel-animals with different body shapes.

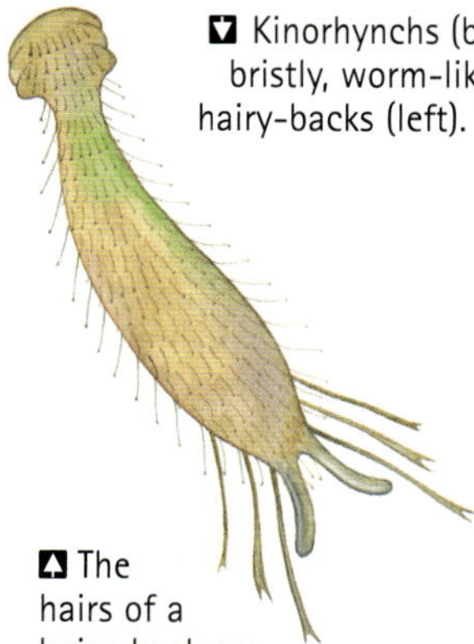

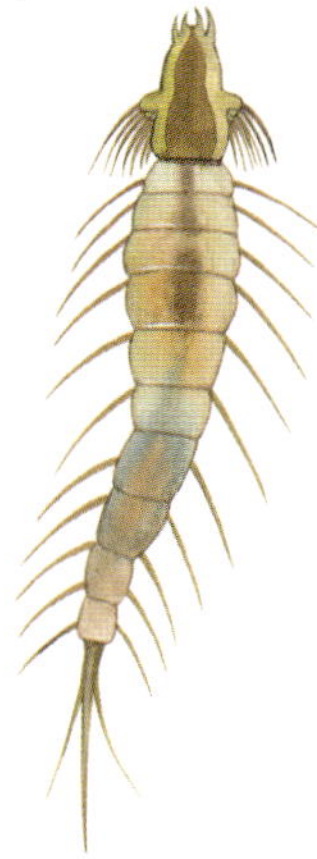

▼ Kinorhynchs (below right) are tiny, bristly, worm-like animals similar to hairy-backs (left). They live in the sea.

▲ The hairs of a hairy-back are really small knobbly outgrowths of the body, called papillae. The head is rounded and the tail forked.

INSIDE A WHEEL-ANIMAL

A wheel-animal has a rounded head like a cup or bowl, a plump body and a claw-like toe for gripping. Around the rim of the head are rings of hair-like cilia. These wave or beat to make a current in the water, which sweeps food into the creature's mouth. Some wheel-animals can swim through the water by means of their beating cilia.

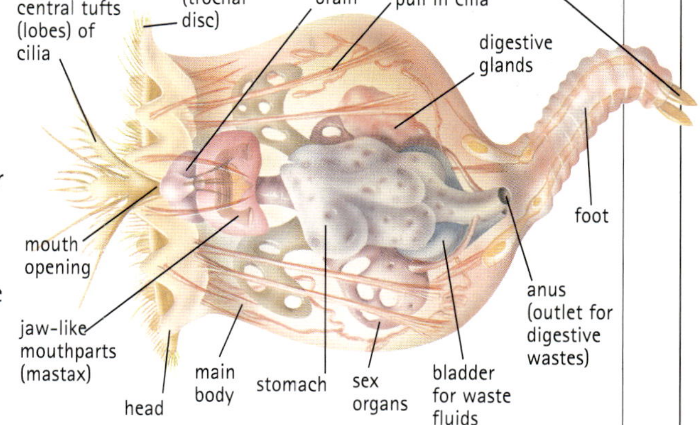

Water-bears are also known as tardigrades, a name that means "slow-steppers". They are very small – from one to 20 could fit on a pinhead. Some live in the sea, between particles of sand and mud. Others dwell in fresh water. But most live in places that are sometimes wet, and at other times dry – like muddy puddles, inside a moss plant or in the rainwater gutters of buildings. They can survive here because, as the dampness dries out, the water-bear turns into a special resting stage called a tun. It simply dries out, shrivels up to about one tenth its normal size and becomes inactive, almost like an egg. This tun stage can survive for many months, even years. When the moisture returns, the water-bear "hatches" out of its tun stage, and carries on living!

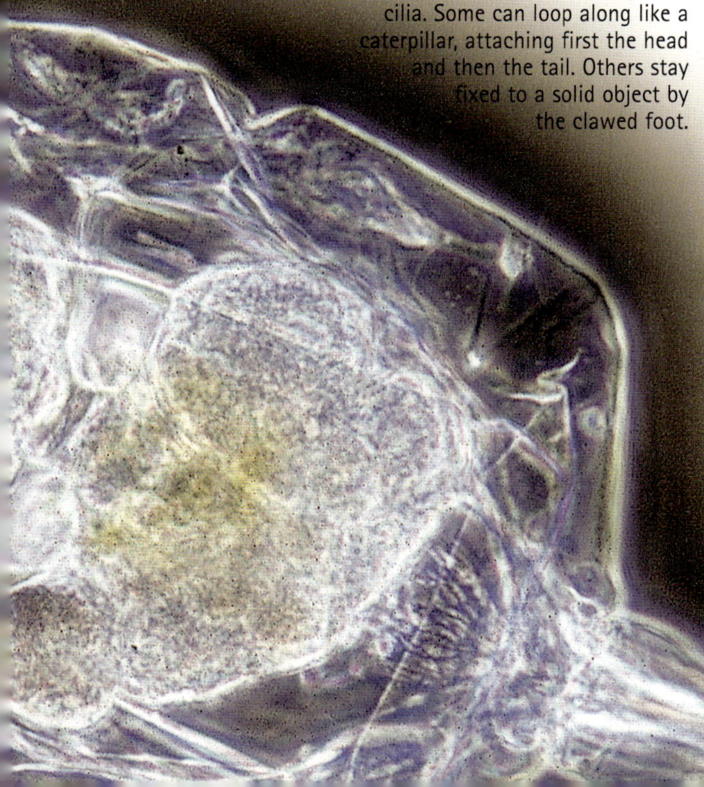

▼ Pieces of food can be seen inside the mouth and stomach of this branchionus wheel-animal. The small dark spot between the brownish food particles towards the centre and the ring of hairs to the far left is the eye spot. This simple type of eye detects the difference between light and dark. A wheel-animal is either male or female. This is a female. The male is only one third the size of the female. He has a shorter body, shaped like a collar. Most wheel-animals swim by waving their cilia. Some can loop along like a caterpillar, attaching first the head and then the tail. Others stay fixed to a solid object by the clawed foot.

A WHEEL HEAD

Wheel-animals are also called rotifers, which means "wheel-carriers". The wheel-like part is the head and mouth of the creature, with its tufts of hair-like cilia. The biggest wheel-animals grow to about 3 mm across, but most kinds are far tinier. Like water-bears, they can survive drying out, and also being frozen or almost boiled, by shrivelling up into a resting stage. The tough-cased, egg-like resting stage of a wheel-animal is known as a cyst.

HAIRY-BACKS

Yet another group of extremely tiny animals are the hairy-backs, also called gastrotrichs. A typical hairy-back has a round, bristly head and a streamlined body with a forked tail. It glides along the bottom of a pond or stream, nosing in the mud to feed on even smaller bits of food such as single-celled plants and tiny protists. Kinorhynchs are similar small animals, resembling worms. They live only in the mud and sand of the sea bed.

Water-bears *(Tardigrades)*
- about 400 species
- microscopic or nearly so
- four pairs of legs, with claws
- live in damp places, some in fresh water, a few in the sea

Wheel-animals *(Rotifers)*
- about 1,800 species
- microscopic or nearly so
- wheel- or crown-like tufts of tiny hairs (cilia) on the head
- live mainly in fresh water, damp places and in the sea

Hairy-backs *(Gastrotrichs)*
- about 450 species
- live in fresh and salty water
- microscopic or small, up to 4 mm
- scaly or hairy body, forked tail

Kinorhynchs
- only about 120 species
- live in sea mud or sand
- small, up to 2 mm
- body divided into about 13 sections or segments

SPONGES

◄ Tiny coral animals (polyps) grow around a sponge's oscule—the main exit hole for water. The tunnels are visible inside the sponge's main body cavity.

SPONGES LOOK MORE LIKE PLANTS THAN ANIMALS. They grow on underwater objects such as rocks or plant stems. They cannot move around, although a few types twitch slightly at the surface when touched. They have no eyes or ears, brain or nerves, heart or blood. But they do catch their own food, by filtering tiny particles from water. The water enters the sponge through thousands of tiny holes, or pores, and then leaves through one of the few big holes. Adult sponges are fixed to the spot, but when they breed, they produce young ones or larvae, which swim actively. Eventually a larva finds a suitable place to settle down and grow into the adult colony of cells we call a sponge.

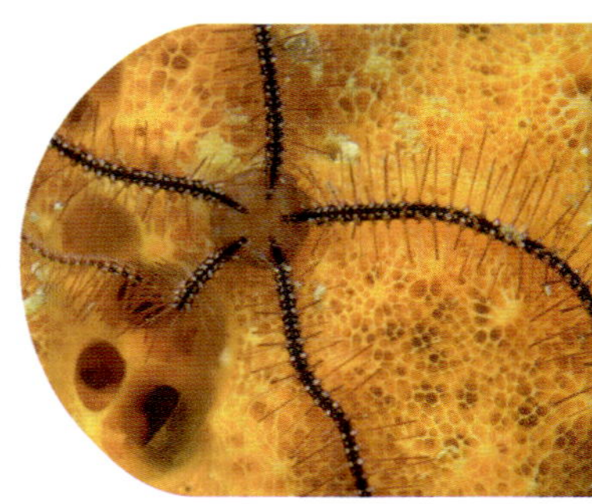

▲ A brittlestar climbs across an orange sponge.

◄ Breadcrumb sponges grow in several colours, including green (upper left). The hymenia sponge is usually blood-red (top right). Some solenia sponges are also red (top left). Column sponges can be purple or blue (centre). Vase sponges are wider, with one large exit hole for water (lower left). The brain sponge is pink (lower right).

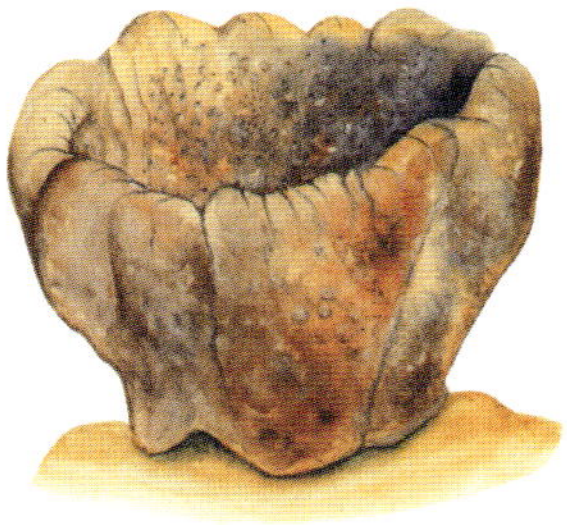

Different types of cup sponge grow in fresh and salt water.

A typical full-grown sponge is not so much one single animal, more a collection or colony of animal-like cells. These form a flask-shaped body surrounding a central cavity. There are many tiny holes or channels in the body wall, linking the cavity inside with the sea water outside. Whip-like flagella on cells lining the cavity beat to make a current of water flow through the channels into the central cavity. The water brings with it tiny bits of food such as protists, tiny seaweeds, and animal eggs and larvae. The water, and the sponge's waste products, pass out through larger channels, oscules, usually at the top.

CLEAN!

A large sponge can sieve water at the rate of a full bathtub every hour. This makes sponges useful in fish tanks and other aquaria. They work as living filters, helping to keep the water clean and clear.

These pink sponges, on an old jetty support, form a network of chambers and holes used by worms, fish and other creatures.

BATH SPONGES

Most bath sponges are now made of plastic foam. But many years ago they were gathered from the sea. The common bath sponge lives on the sea bed, in clear, warm water. It is rather slimy, and is a yellow or purple colour. After it dies, its soft parts rot away to leave its flexible skeleton of fibres and spicules. This skeleton forms the sponge we use in the bath. Its thousands of tiny holes once let the living sponge suck in water. In some areas, such as parts of the Mediterranean Sea, so many bath sponges have been gathered that this animal is now very rare. It takes perhaps 20 years for a new bath sponge to grow.

HOW SPONGES BREED

Like many plants, sponges can reproduce by growing small extra parts, buds, which come away and grow into new sponges. Or they can breed sexually, like animals. Each sponge is both male and female, so it can make both sperm and eggs. An egg and sperm join, or fertilize, and develop into a tiny sponge larva which swims away. It lives in the open sea for a day or two, before settling on the sea bed to grow into a new adult sponge.

HOW DO SPONGES SURVIVE?

Sponges have no obvious defences. They cannot bite or sting. They cannot swim away. So how do they protect themselves? The bodies of many sponges are full of tiny, sharp spikes of hard minerals, such as lime, chalk or silica (the same substance that glass is made from). These spikes, called spicules, make up the sponge's skeleton. They give its body firmness. They also help to deter animals who might try to eat the sponge. In addition, many types of sponges have an unpleasant smell or a horrible taste, which also puts off their predators.

PLACOZOANS

These tiny animals, which grow to the size of an ant, resemble giant amoebas, but their bodies are made up of about 1,000 cells. Placozoans ooze and move like slugs. There are only a couple of species known and both live in the sea.

Sponges *(Poriferans)*
- about 10,000 species
- most live in the sea, a few in fresh water
- many have spiky inner skeletons
- body full of holes
- some grow to 4 m across

Placozoans
- only a few species
- live in the sea
- crawl along like slugs or giant amoebas
- about 3 mm long

COMB-JELLIES

COMB-JELLIES ARE STRANGE, PALE, GHOSTLY SEA ANIMALS THAT ARE SIMILAR IN SOME WAYS TO JELLYFISH. They have mainly see-through or transparent bodies, which are soft and squashy, and they drift or swim with the ocean currents. There are only about 100 different kinds, or species, of comb-jelly, but some of these are amazingly common. They float in their thousands in the upper layers of the sea, as part of the surface plankton. In the twilight zone more than 450 m down, they are even more abundant and drift in huge swarms, millions strong. In fact, in the deep oceans, comb-jellies are some of the most numerous of all animals.

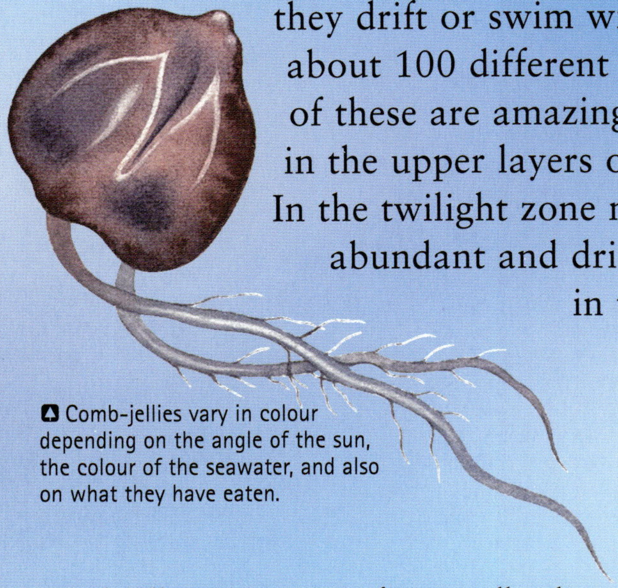

Comb-jellies vary in colour depending on the angle of the sun, the colour of the seawater, and also on what they have eaten.

Comb-jellies range in size from smaller than a baked bean to as long as a human arm. Most are round and ball-shaped or long and slim like sausages. One of the most common kinds is known as the sea gooseberry. It has a pear-shaped body, about the size and shape of a grape, and is completely transparent.

ROWS OF COMBS

Running around the body of a comb-jelly, like stripes, are eight bands or rows of what look like tiny combs – which is how these animals got their name. Each comb is made up of groups of minute hairs known as cilia. These can beat in rhythm, like rows of oars. By beating its cilia, a comb-jelly can swim through the water. Usually it swims straight up or down as part of its daily feeding routine, rising at night and sinking back to the depths by day. But, like many jellyfish, comb-jellies are at the mercy of strong ocean currents.

STICKY TENTACLES

Trailing from the comb-jelly's body are two long, sticky tentacles which dangle in the water. Smaller animals, including tiny shrimps and the young forms of crabs, starfish and worms, become entangled in and stung by these tentacles. The sea gooseberry then brushes its tentacles across its mouth and swallows its prey.

The lampea comb-jelly is one of the sausage-shaped types. The comb-like groups of tiny hairs are on ridges along the sides of the body. In some types of comb-jelly the hairs are fused to each other to form one broad, flap-shaped surface. If a comb-jelly is washed up on the beach, it loses its shape and soon dries out and dies.

GLOWING IN THE DARK

Although most comb-jellies are transparent, if the sun catches them they shimmer in the water with iridescent rainbow colours. At night, some kinds can glow with multicoloured lights. These come from lines of glowing spots inside the comb-jelly, which shine through the transparent body, making the creature visible from a distance. It is possible that the

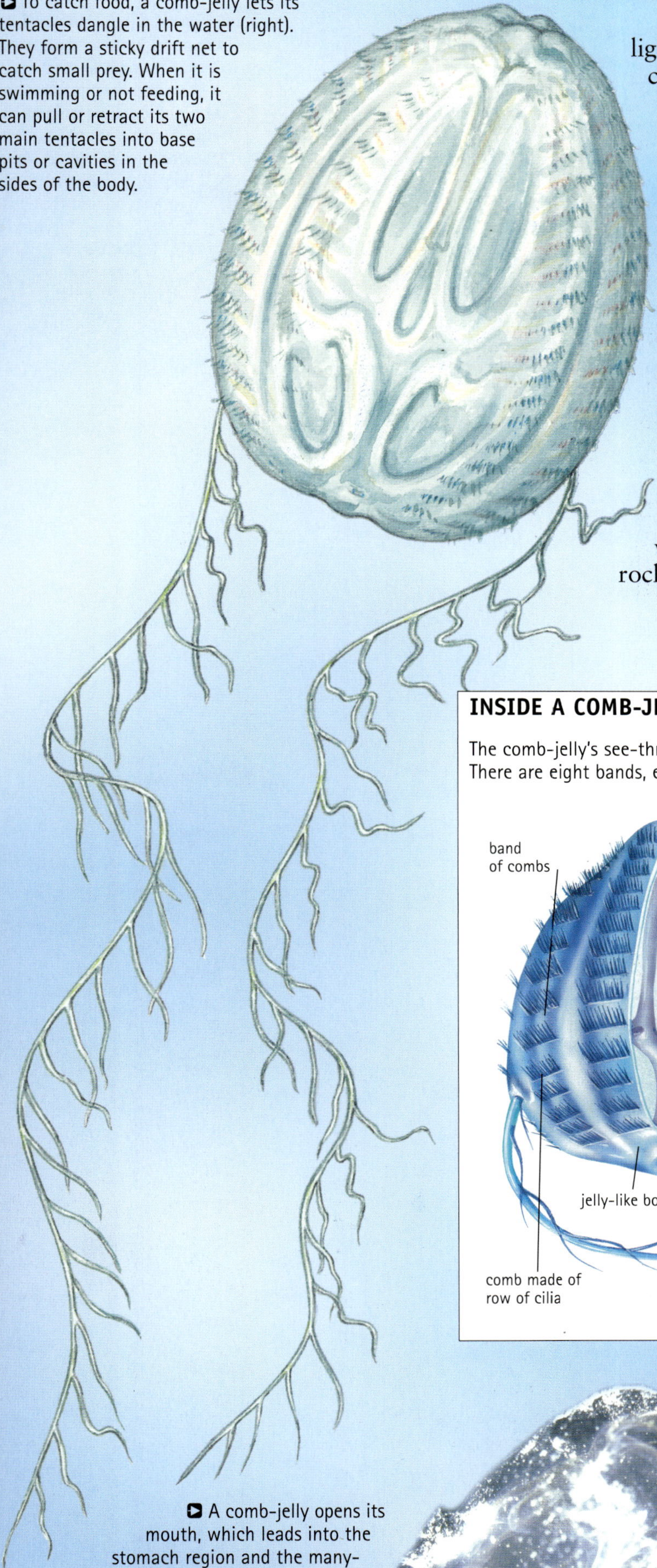

To catch food, a comb-jelly lets its tentacles dangle in the water (right). They form a sticky drift net to catch small prey. When it is swimming or not feeding, it can pull or retract its two main tentacles into base pits or cavities in the sides of the body.

lights attract other animals toward the comb-jelly, which then catches and eats them. (The ability of some creatures to make their own light is known as bioluminescence, page 14.)

VENUS' GIRDLE

Most comb-jellies have rounded bodies. An exception is the remarkable Venus' girdle, which has a lacy, ribbon-like body about the size and shape of a metre ruler. It is like a normal comb-jelly that has been ironed flat! Venus' girdle swims by wriggling from side to side, rather like a snake.

Another unusual comb-jelly is coeloplana, which looks like a slug with a tentacle at each end. It creeps over rocks and seaweeds in search of prey.

INSIDE A COMB-JELLY

The comb-jelly's see-through body contains various chambers and cavities. There are eight bands, each made of a row of tiny hairs or cilia, for swimming.

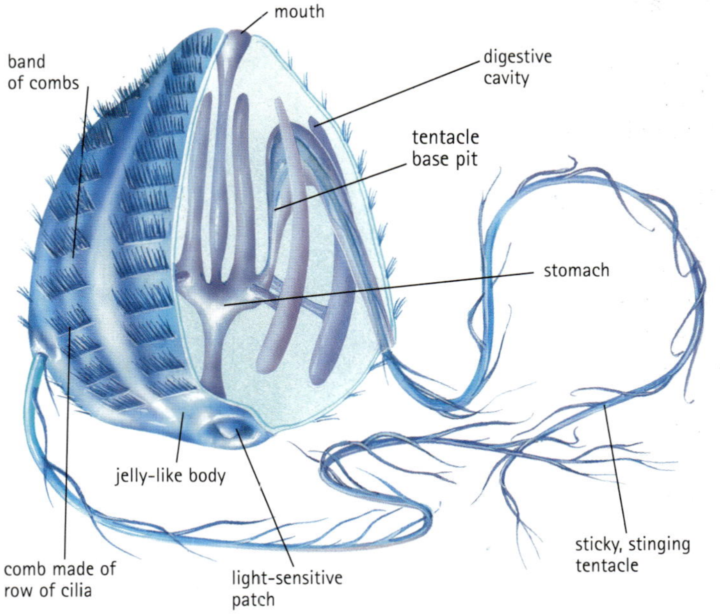

Comb-jellies *(Ctenophores)*
- about 100 species
- most have transparent, rounded bodies
- many have a pair of long tentacles
- live only in the sea
- range in size from 5 mm to more than 90 cm

A comb-jelly opens its mouth, which leads into the stomach region and the many-branched digestive cavities.

THE "NETTLE ANIMALS"

An underside view of a jellyfish reveals the billowing tentacles called oral arms that stick onto prey and pass it into the mouth.

JELLYFISH, SEA ANEMONES AND CORAL POLYPS (THE TINY CREATURES THAT BUILD CORAL REEFS) ALL BELONG TO THE ANIMAL GROUP CALLED CNIDARIANS. This name means "nettle animals". It comes from the tiny stinging cells on the tentacles and other parts of these creatures. The stings are used to capture, paralyse and kill prey; some are strong enough to give a painful sting to humans. However, a few cnidarians have such venomous stings that they can kill people. Cnidarians are also known as coelenterates, which means "hollow gut", because their bodies are almost all stomach, like a hollow bag. Most of these animals live in the sea, and have a circular body shape.

The body of a jellyfish or other cnidarian has a single opening. This is both a mouth, to take in food, and an anus, to get rid of undigested leftovers. It is surrounded by the animal's tentacles. These are usually long and thin, and may number more than one hundred. They are coated with microscopic stinging cells.

The branching stomach cavity and reproductive parts can be seen inside the body of this pencillate jellyfish.

Most cnidarians have soft, squashy, floppy bodies, containing a large, bag-like stomach or gut cavity. The body wall is made of a jelly-like substance. Some types, like the corals, build hard, stony, cup-like skeletons around themselves for protection. Jellyfish have an extra-thick jelly layer which makes up the bulk of the body.

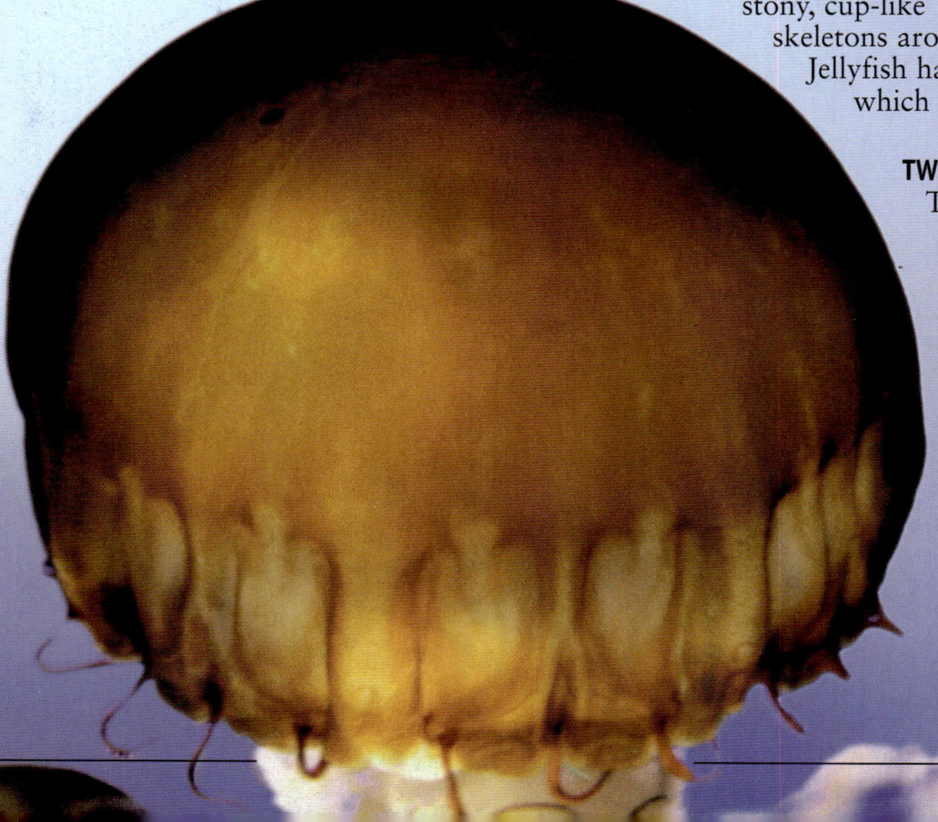

TWO BODY SHAPES

There are two basic types of body plan among the cnidarians. These are the medusa and the polyp. Some cnidarians spend most or all their lives as one form. The jellyfish, for example, are medusas, while coral animals and anemones are polyps. However, some cnidarians are first polyps, then change shape and become medusas – or the other way around.

The soft body or bell of this doughnut jellyfish is buoyed up in the water.

These purple striped jellyfish are hardly visible, as they drift like ghosts in the hazy waters of the sea.

THE POLYP

The typical polyp has a soft, cylinder-shaped body. The long lower part or stalk is attached at its base to a rock, seaweed or other object. At the top of the stalk is the polyp's mouth, surrounded by the ring of grasping, stinging tentacles waving upwards. Sea anemones spend all their lives as polyps. They have no medusa form.

THE MEDUSA

A typical medusa is like a polyp that has had its stalk removed and then been turned upside down. Its body is shaped like an umbrella or bell, with the stinging tentacles dangling downwards from the edges or rim. The mouth is in the middle of the tentacles. A medusa is usually the floating or free-living form, while the polyp is the attached or fixed form. Jellyfish spend most or all of their lives drifting slowly through the oceans, as medusas.

PALE OR COLOURFUL

Some jellyfish, sea anemones and corals are pale or milky white, especially in cooler seas. But many tropical types are beautifully coloured, often in shades of pink, red, yellow and orange.

When the tide is out, anemones on seashore rocks may look like dull blobs of jelly. But as the tide comes in they spread out their flower-like tentacles, which resemble soft, waving plant petals. They are sometimes called "flowers of the sea". But of course, anemones are animals (page 32). Like all their cnidarian cousins, they may look harmless, but they are deadly predators.

INSIDE A JELLYFISH

A jellyfish is mostly a hollow stomach or gut cavity, where its meals are digested and dissolved. It has no proper eyes or ears. But it can detect touch, temperature, patches of light and dark and water currents.

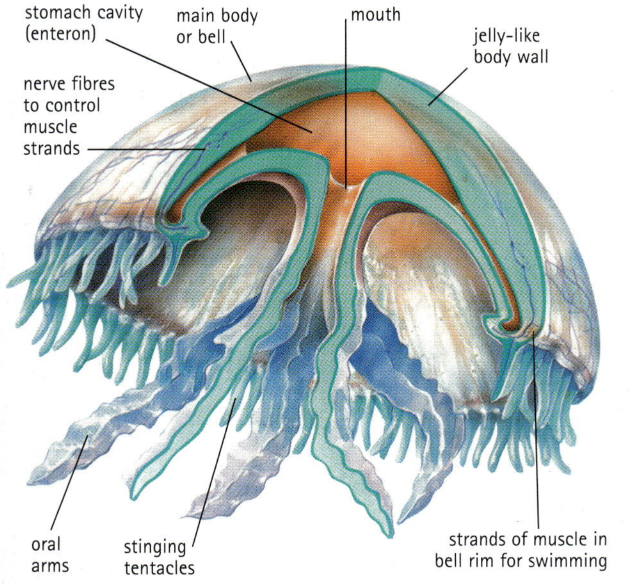

Jellyfish and relatives
(Cnidarians or Coelenterates)

- about 10,000 species
- mostly sea-living, some dwell in fresh water
- have a circular body
- central mouth surrounded by tentacles
- most are soft-bodied, but some (like corals) make hard, stony, protective cases or skeletons

There are two main sub groups:

Anemones and corals *(Anthozoans)*
- about 6,000 species
- live in the sea
- stalk-like body attached at the base, with tentacles above (polyp form)

Jellyfish and hydroids
(Medusozoans)
- about 4,000 species
- most live in the sea, some (like hydras) live in fresh water
- both free-floating medusa and fixed polyps
- a few have stings that are dangerous to humans

JELLYFISH

Haliclystus is a stalked jellyfish that lives in sheltered rock pools, clinging to seaweed.

JELLYFISH RANGE IN SIZE FROM SMALLER THAN THE TIP OF YOUR FINGER, TO GIANTS LARGER THAN A PATIO SUNSHADE UMBRELLA, MEASURING MORE THAN 1.8 m. But most are about the size and shape of a breakfast cereal bowl.

Some types can swim weakly by making pulsing movements of the main body or bell – like opening and closing your fingers. But these swimming motions are weak and most jellyfish are at the mercy of strong ocean currents. They are often washed up helpless onto the shore after a storm. Their floppy bodies collapse, and these creatures soon dry out and die.

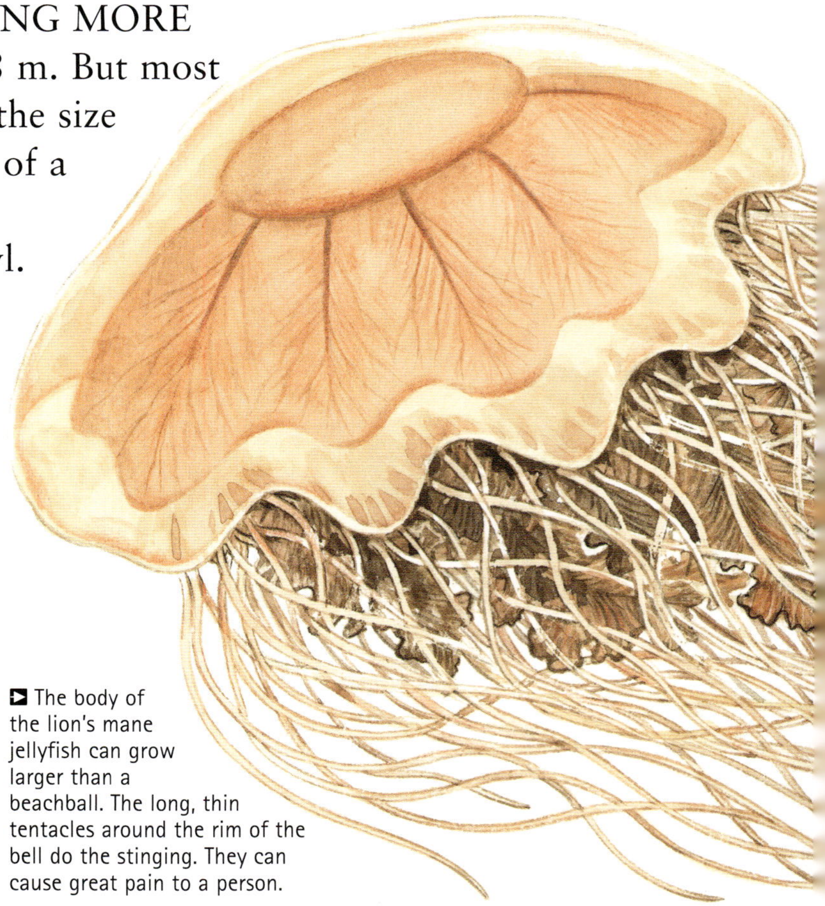

The body of the lion's mane jellyfish can grow larger than a beachball. The long, thin tentacles around the rim of the bell do the stinging. They can cause great pain to a person.

Stauromedusans, or stalked jellyfish, are jellyfish that think they are anemones. There is a stalk on the top of the bell with a sticky end that attaches to a piece of seaweed or sea grass.

SWIMMING JELLYFISH

Around the rim of the jellyfish's main body, or bell, is a ring of muscle fibres. These can be shortened or contracted to squeeze the bell like a purse-string and make pulsating movements, which propel water out of the bell and so push the jellyfish through the water. Usually a jellyfish swims upwards, to rise closer to the surface. When it stops swimming, it sinks down again. Using these movements the jellyfish can follow its prey, the small animals of the plankton, as they rise near the surface at night and sink to mid water during the day.

HOW JELLYFISH BREED

Jellyfish reproduce by releasing tiny young forms, or larvae. These swim off and settle on the sea bed, where they turn into small polyps. At this stage they resemble tiny see-through sea anemones, smaller than this o.

THE CNIDARIAN STING

A jellyfish has thousands of microscopic stinging cells, nematocysts, all along its tentacles. The cell "fires" a barbed dart that carries either a sticky, glue-like substance or a poison (venom). Each stinging cell has a lid covering the dart. Near the lid is a tiny trigger. When a prey animal touches the trigger, the lid springs open and the dart shoots out. Each stinging cell can only be used once, after which it breaks down, is absorbed into the jellyfish's body and replaced by a new stinging cell.

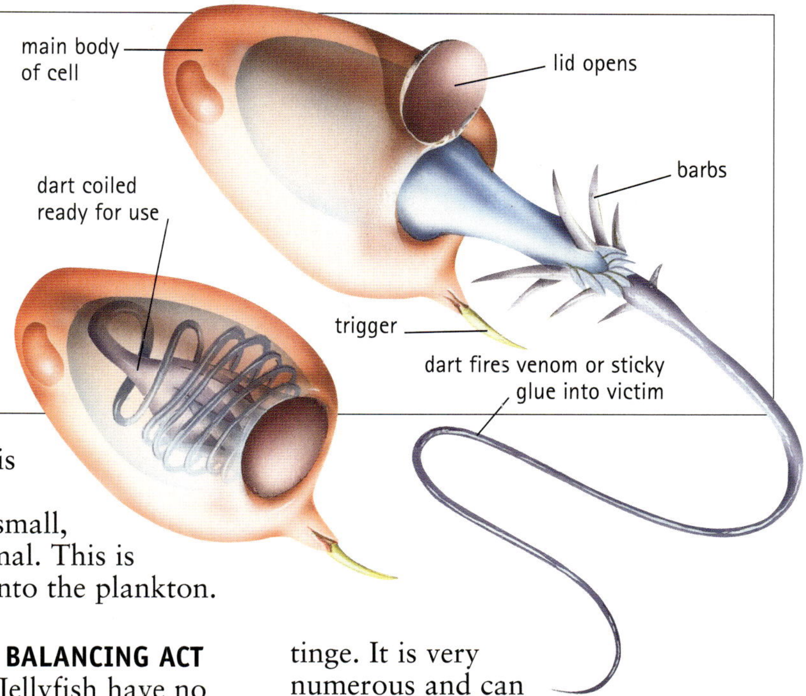

Jellyfish polyps often spend winter in this form. In spring, each polyp form grows "buds". Each bud develops into a very small, star-shaped version of the adult animal. This is released and drifts away into the plankton.

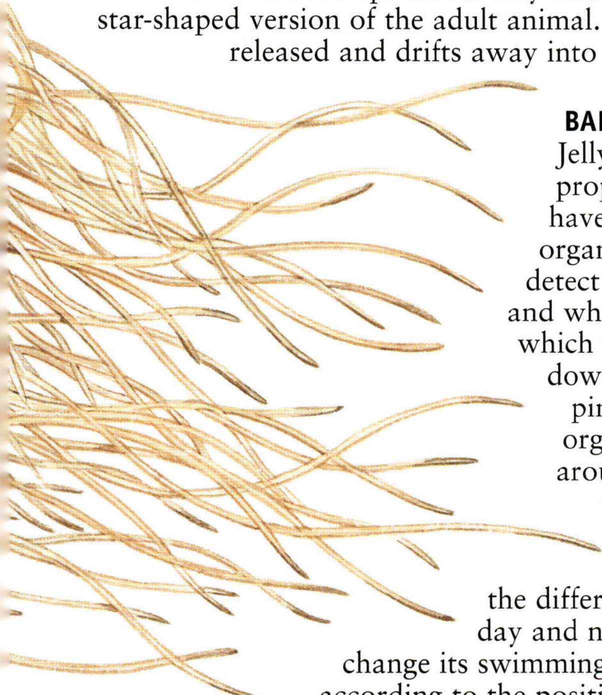

BALANCING ACT

Jellyfish have no proper eyes. But they have special sense organs which can detect light or dark, and which also tell them which way is up or down. These pinhead-size sense organs are spaced around the edge of the bell. The animal uses them to tell the difference between day and night, and also to change its swimming direction according to the position of the sun.

PREDATORS

Even though jellyfish have poisonous stings, some animals eat them. Jellyfish predators include various kinds of fish, squid and especially sea turtles. However, because many jellyfish are pale or transparent this probably makes them harder for predators to see and catch.

FLOATING MOON

The moon jellyfish, aurelia, grows to about 40 cm across and has a bluish tinge. It is very numerous and can be seen in bays and estuaries close to shore, as well as in the open ocean far from land. Moon jellyfish feed on small members of the plankton, such as tiny shrimps and other crustaceans, and also on fish. These get stuck on the stinging cells, the lower surface of the bell, and the frilly oral arms, and are then transferred to the jellyfish's mouth. The moon jellyfish has a fringe of short stinging tentacles and four much longer feeding or oral tentacles. The pink horseshoe-shaped parts in the middle of its main body are its reproductive organs.

◄ The moon jellyfish (aurelia) is one of the most common jellyfish, found in seas throughout the world.

STALKED JELLYFISH

These unusual jellyfish live attached to rocks or seaweeds. They are small, growing only to the size of your little finger. They look like jellyfish that have turned upside down and become stuck by the top of the body, which is underneath. Stalked jellyfish can move to a different place by slowly cartwheeling along. They feed on tiny prey such as worms and copepods.

True jellyfish *(Scyphozoans)*
- about 200 species, all in the sea
- the main form or stage in the life cycle is the free-floating medusa
- the body is circular
- four-part symmetry, with four mouth or oral tentacles and four sets of reproductive organs
- sexes separate—a jellyfish is either female or male

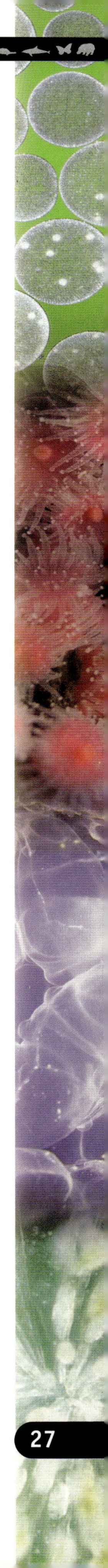

MORE JELLYFISH

PROPER OR TRUE JELLYFISH ARE SHAPED LIKE FLOPPY BELLS OR UMBRELLAS. There are other cnidarians that look like true jellyfish, but are not, although they are close relatives. Some of these jellyfish-like cnidarians have bodies with different shapes, such as boxes or balls. Others, like the man-o'-war, look like a single animal, but each body is really lots of cnidarians all linked together and living as one. These are called colonial cnidarians.

PLASTIC

The peculiar dried-out bodies of the by-the-wind sailor are sometimes found on the beach, after strong winds. Only the skeleton of the disc-shaped float and triangular sail remain. They look and feel like thin plastic.

In true or proper jellyfish, the body is rounded and shaped like an umbrella, and consists of a single cnidarian animal. There are several kinds of similar creatures which are often called jellyfish, but they are not true jellyfish. However, they are still cnidarians, and so close relatives of jellyfish.

BOX JELLYFISH

These jellyfish take their name from the box-like shape of their bodies, which have flat, square sides. Box jellyfish are found only in warm, tropical seas. They have thin, trailing, stinging tentacles, and they feed on small shrimps, fish and other animals floating and swimming in the plankton. The stings of some box jellies are especially powerful and can cause great pain to a person. Also, box jellyfish sometimes gather together in huge swarms, as they drift through the sea. If they are swept inshore by winds and currents, these box jelly swarms can be very dangerous to people swimming and paddling. Swimmers trapped in a swarm of these cnidarians have been stung to death.

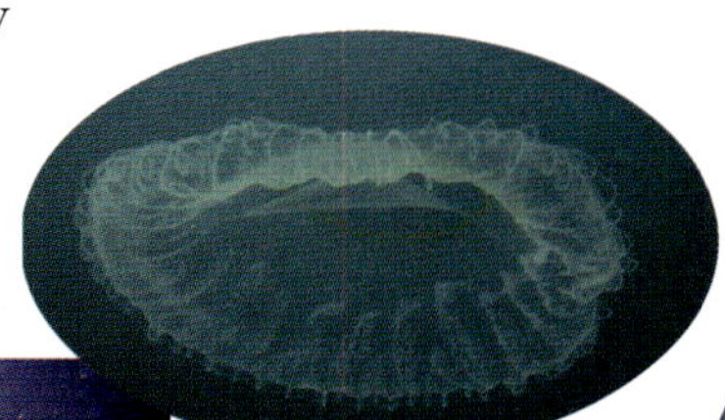

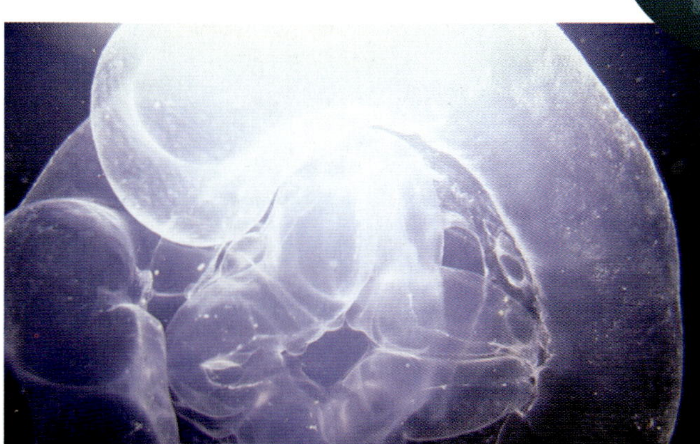

◀▲ True umbrella-shaped jellyfish are very different from the man-o'-war (right).

▶ The man-o'-war is a cnidarian—or rather, lots of them. It is a floating group of cnidarian polyps known as siphonophores.

◀ This massive pink jellyfish floats in the warm waters of the Pacific Ocean, near the Philippines. It looks dangerous, but its venom is not harmful to humans.

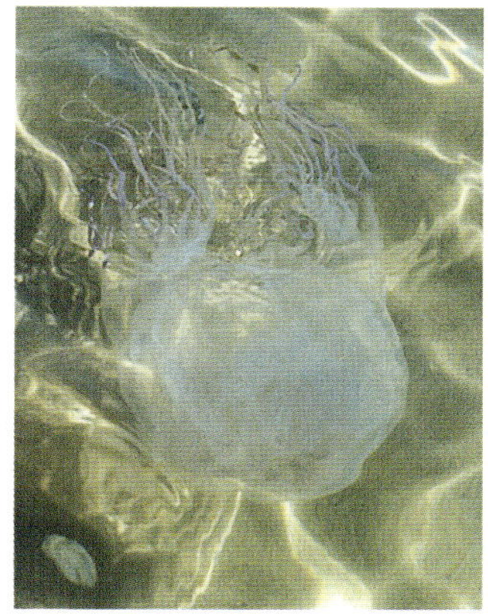

▶ The innocent-looking box jellyfish can inflict extremely painful stings. It is known as the southern sea wasp, or jimble, and is common in Australian waters.

Even when box jellies are stranded on the shore and dead, their tentacles can still produce very painful stings. In some parts of Australia, box jellyfish are a particular hazard and beaches may be closed if a swarm drifts near.

FLOATING COLONIES

Some kinds of cnidarian live in floating colonies. From a distance, they look like a single animal—usually a jellyfish. But they are really hundreds of creatures, polyps, all living together. These jellyfish-like colonies of polyps are known as siphonophores. They usually float at the surface of the ocean.

FLOATING HOTEL

One of the best-known siphonophores, or colonial cnidarians, is the man-o'-war. It is also called the sea bluebottle. It consists of about 100–200 individual polyps, of different shapes and sizes, which all depend on each other.

The bluish-purple, gas-filled, balloon-like float at the top of the colony is one large individual polyp. It catches the breeze, like a sailing ship, to move the colony along. This float polyp buoys up the whole colony of other polyps beneath.

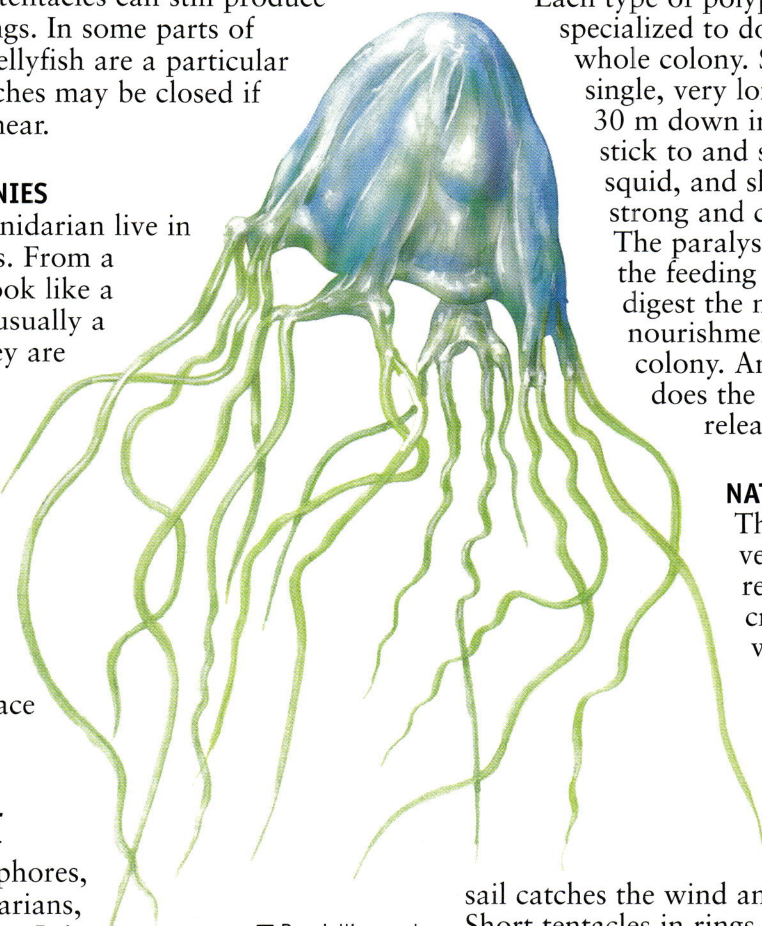

▲ Box jellies such as the sea wasps have more angular, flat-sided bodies than true jellyfish.

FOR THE GOOD OF THE GROUP

Each type of polyp in the man-o'-war is specialized to do a different job for the whole colony. Stinging polyps each have a single, very long tentacle trailing as far as 30 m down into the sea. The tentacles stick to and sting prey such as fish, squid, and shrimps. The venom is very strong and can seriously hurt a person. The paralysed victim is then passed to the feeding polyps. These eat and digest the meal and share the nourishment through the whole colony. Another group of polyps does the job of reproduction, releasing eggs and sperm.

NATURAL SAILING BOAT

The by-the-wind sailor, or velella, is another remarkable colony of cnidarians. Like the man-o'-war, it is a colony of polyps, acting together almost as a single animal. It too has a purplish gas-filled float, but above this is a hard skeleton which acts as a mast to support a thin sail. The sail catches the wind and moves the colony along. Short tentacles in rings beneath the float catch small items of food. By-the-wind-sailors grow as big as your hand and live in huge swarms, especially in the North Atlantic.

JELLYFISH-LIKE CNIDARIANS

Colonial jellyfish *(Siphonophores)*
- members of the hydroid group (see next page)
- body looks like a single creature but is made of many individual cnidarian animals or polyps
- some polyps sting and kill prey
- some digest prey
- some act as floats
- some carry out reproduction

Box jellyfish *(Cubomedusans)*
- resemble true jellyfish but have a more angular, box-shaped body
- have four single or branched tentacles
- extremely strong venom
- include sea wasps

HYDROIDS

THE HYDROIDS ARE CNIDARIANS THAT MAINLY RESEMBLE SEA ANEMONES. Each animal, or polyp, has a stalk-shaped body and a flower-like ring of tentacles. However, some hydroids live as colonies of polyps, almost like a single, large "superanimal". Many of these colonies branch and spread over any solid surface. The man-o'-war and the by-the-wind sailor (pages 28–29) are also hydroids. However, they are unusual, since they are floating rather than fixed, and they resemble jellyfish.

The hydroid obelia grows in many branched groups. The individual animals or polyps are joined by their stalks.

The typical hydroid is a colony of small polyps, each less than about 5 mm tall, all connected and growing together. They attach to and spread over a rock, a frond of seaweed, or even the shell of a larger animal. Such hydroids are often known as sea firs. They are most common on sheltered, rocky seashores. At a glance, they look very much like moss-animals or bryozoans (page 16). But the tentacles of individual hydroid polyps are not covered with tiny hairs or cilia.

INSIDE A HYDROID

Most ponds and streams are home to hundreds of the tiny hydroids called hydras. Each has a stalk-like body with new individuals branching from it, like buds from a plant stem. At the top is a circle of six or eight tentacles around the mouth.

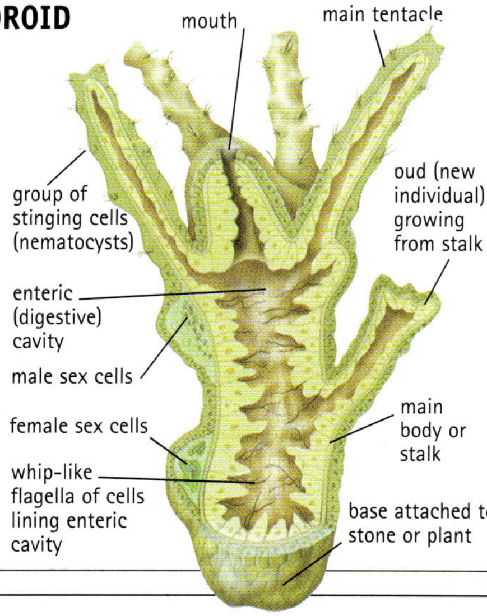

MINI SEA TREES

Some of the best-known colonial hydroids are obelias. Several different species of obelia live along the coasts of the Atlantic Ocean and Mediterranean Sea. Some grow to more than 30 cm in height and have zigzag stalks. Others have branching stems and look like miniature trees.

TWO TYPES OF POLYP

There are two different kinds of polyp in each obelia colony. The feeding polyps live inside hard, protective cups. They stretch out from these when active.

MORE! MORE!

The fresh water hydroid called hydra has amazing powers of recovery and regeneration. If it is sliced in two, each half can grow into a complete animal, regenerating all of its missing body parts. This helps when a piece of a hydra is nipped off by another animal such as a small fish. Hydras have even been turned inside out, yet they still recover and repair their bodies.

Sea firs grow like tiny fir trees and ferns on rocks along the shore below the low-tide line. The branches of the colony bear feeding polyps with their stinging tentacles. Larger sea firs, known as sea ferns and sea hairs, are dried for flower decorations.

The polyp uses its stinging tentacles in the normal cnidarian way to catch tiny animals from the water. Because the polyps are all connected at their stalks or bases, food can easily pass around the colony.

The other kind of polyp is for reproduction. It is flask-shaped and has no tentacles. Tiny medusas, like miniature jellyfish, grow inside each reproductive polyp and are released to swim away in the sea. The medusas produce eggs and sperm, which float in the water. An egg and sperm join to form a tiny larva, which floats in the plankton and then settles and changes into a single polyp. This produces smaller versions of itself attached to its body, like plant buds. In this way the single polyp soon develops into a hydroid colony, and so the life cycle is complete.

IN FRESH WATER

In almost any pond or slow stream, on stones and among the leaves of water plants, live small green or pale brown animals that look like miniature sea anemones. These are hydras. They are not anemones, but hydroids that live in fresh rather than sea water. A hydra feeds in the typical cnidarian way, using its tentacles to catch tiny animals such as water fleas. It can grow buds on its stalk that turn into miniature versions of itself. These eventually separate from their parent and become new individual hydras. This type of reproduction is called asexual or vegetative, because it resembles the way that vegetables and other plants produce buds. Hydras can also reproduce in the usual animal way.

Like corals, hydroids form colourful colonies on reef rocks in tropical and subtropical seas. Some grow over and around sponges and moss-animals, forming crusty coverings with all creatures crammed together.

FIRE CORALS

These colonial hydroids resemble true corals (page 36). Each individual, or polyp, has a hard, chalky casing and a ring of stinging tentacles to catch prey. Fire corals can inflict painful stings on humans. The fire coral known as millepora can resist pounding by waves and often forms the highest parts of coral reefs. Millepora grows in various colours, from white and pink to yellow and orange. It is known as elk's-horn coral due to its antler-like shape.

Hydroids *(Hydrozoa)*

- most are marine, living in the sea
- a few, like hydra, live in fresh water
- most live together in colonies, with connections for passing nutrients among themselves
- some, like hydras, live as individuals
- some colonies, like the man-o'-war, float at the surface of the sea (page 28)
- some, like obelias, live in stalked colonies
- many have powerful stings
- includes the fire corals

SEA ANEMONES

SEA ANEMONES AND CORALS ARE TOGETHER CALLED ANTHOZOANS, OR "FLOWER-LIKE ANIMALS". They form the largest group of cnidarians, with some 6,000 species. Most of these are different kinds of coral, shown on the following pages. More familiar to many people are the sea anemones. These are mostly quite large (for cnidarians). They live singly, rather than in colonies, along coasts and in shallow water. They attach themselves to rocks, plants, shells or other firm surfaces, and usually stay put. Yet sea anemones can move around, by shuffling or gliding on the base of the stalk. If they are in a hurry, they may cartwheel or somersault. A few can even swim, by waving their tentacles or bending their bodies. But usually the only movements we notice are when the anemone's tentacles gently sway in the water – or when they sting and grab their prey.

▲ The dahlia anemone's short stalk is covered with lumps. Bits of gravel, shells and weed stick to these lumps. When the tide goes out and the anemone draws in its tentacles, it looks like a small pebble.

▲ The orange sea anemone has strong, sturdy tentacles around its central mouth.

OLD!

Some sea anemones have lived for as long as people. They have survived in large seawater tanks or marine aquaria, protected and well fed, and with clean unpolluted water, for 70 years or more.

Sea anemones are cnidarians but they have no medusa – the floating, jellyfish-like stage. Anemones live their entire lives as polyps. They resemble hydroids, but most anemones are larger and more heavily built, and they live alone rather than in groups. The stalk is fatter, and the tentacles around the central mouth are shorter and sturdier. Also, many sea anemones are brightly coloured in shades of red, yellow, pink, brown, blue and green. These colours may be warnings to other animals that the anemone is not good to eat and that it can sting with its tentacles.

MULTICOLOURED BEADLETS

One of the most common types is the beadlet anemone. It lives on rocks between the low- and high-tide marks. It is usually bright red, but may be brown, orange or green.

IN DEEPER WATER

Lower down the shore is the snakelocks anemone. It has as many as 200 long, coiling tentacles, usually bright green in colour.

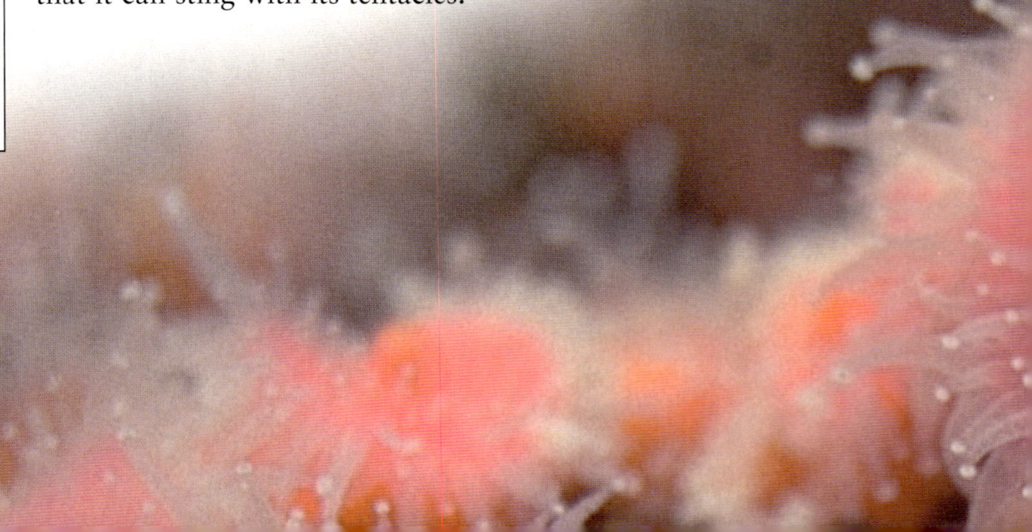

▶ Jewel anemones have pale knobbed tentacles. But their bright, shiny bodies glisten like gem stones in the water.

This type cannot stand being out of water at low tide for as long as the beadlet anemones. The dahlia anemone is another common type, named after the dahlia flower. It is patterned in pink, white and red.

FEEDING AND FOOD

Most sea anemones feed by trapping small fish, shrimps, and similar animals in their tentacles. The stinging cells or nematocysts on the tentacles kill or paralyse the prey. Sea anemones have no eyes, but they can detect touch, and they shoot out their poison stings when their tentacles make contact. They can also detect substances released by the body of any animal they catch and injure. This makes more and more tentacles arch over, to help secure and disable the prey. The nematocyst barbed darts of most common anemones are not large or strong enough to pass into human skin.

An anemone's tentacles are usually arranged in widening rings, based on the number six or eight.

The orange ball anemone has bright, rounded, yellow-orange tips to its pale blue, see-through tentacles.

BIG MOUTH

The mouth of an anemone lies at the centre of its tentacles. It can stretch so wide that the anemone is able to swallow prey almost as big as itself! The meal goes into the large stomach cavity in the stalk, where it is slowly dissolved and digested. Any leftovers are pushed back out later, through the way they came in.

Sea anemones make more of their kind in the same way as hydras, by budding off new individuals from their bodies. Or they can produce eggs and sperm in the usual animal way.

FIGHTING ANEMONES

Sea anemones may not look aggressive. But they try to get the best place in the rock pool. They push and shove against each other in slow-motion trials of strength. They may even try to tip rivals off the rocks into the mud or sand.

LARGEST...!

The biggest sea anemone is a type of discoma. It can reach 60 cm across. It lives among corals on the Great Barrier Reef in Australia.

Anemones and corals
(Anthozoans)

- about 6,000 species, all live in the sea (pages 24–25)
- stalk-like body attached at the base, with tentacles above (polyp form only)
- circular body with tentacles, sex organs, and other parts based on the numbers six or eight

ANEMONES AND PARTNERS

SEA ANEMONES ARE SIMPLE CREATURES. They have no proper brain, only a few nerves to control the movements of their tentacles and stalk. They can only do the simplest actions, such as detecting and eating prey, and gliding along the rocks to a new place. Yet anemones have many "friends" on the seashore. They live in partnerships with other creatures such as fish, shrimps, crabs and worms. These other creatures have thick shells or coatings of body mucus (slime) that protect them from the anemone's stings. Usually, both partners benefit from being together. For example, the anemone feeds on leftovers from the food of its fish friend, while the fish is safe hiding in the anemone's tentacles. This type of helpful partnership in nature is called symbiosis.

Shrimps are at home among anemones.

Symbiosis happens between many types of creatures, such as cleaner fish and bigger fish, and oxpecker birds and cattle. But it is especially common among sea anemones. It has probably evolved gradually, over millions of years.

This tiny porcelain crab is safe among the tentacles of an anemone. It scavenges small bits of food and keeps the anemone clean.

TOLERANT PARTNERS

As a result, the anemone has become used to the presence of another creature in its tentacles. It can detect this partner by the chemical substances that the partner gives off, and so rarely tries to sting it. At the same time, the partner has evolved some kind of protection against the anemone's stings, and is hardly ever hurt.

TYPES OF PARTNERS

Clown or anemone fish, usually striped orange and white, form symbiotic partnerships with anemones. So do various kinds of banded shrimps and crabs. Some hermit crabs allow calliactis sea anemones to live on the large sea snail shell that the crab uses as a mobile home. The anemone gets carried around and probably has more chance of finding prey. Meanwhile the crab is protected by the stinging partner attached to its shell.

The sunstar above is not an anemone friend, but a victim. The large dahlia anemone is slowly pulling the sunstar, a type of starfish, into its mouth.

PLUMOSE ANEMONE

This type of sea anemone can stretch itself tall and thin, or pull down its stalk or column to be shorter and fatter. The anemone pictured here is halfway between these two positions. Plumose anemones occur in many colours, from almost perfect white through cream, yellow and brown to orange and red. They live in seashore pools, especially under rocky overhangs, and on and under breakwaters, piers and jetties. They can catch larger prey, but they mainly feed on tiny bits of floating food filtered from the water by the feathery tentacles.

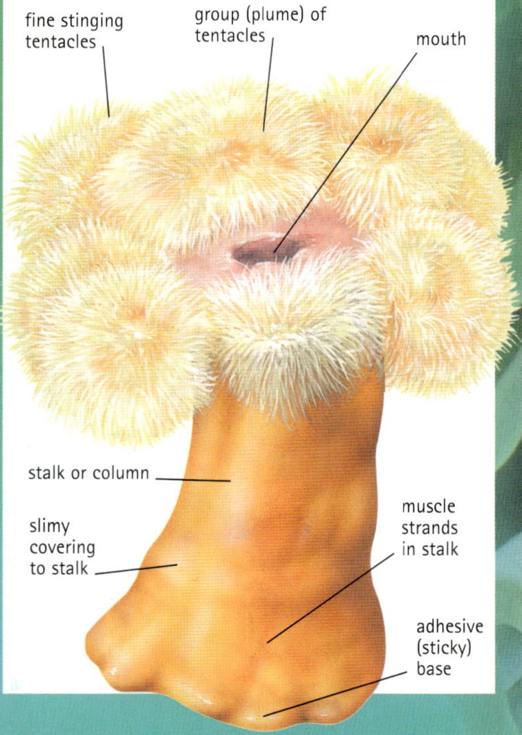

When one catches food, the other can share the leftover bits and pieces. The calliactis anemone is sometimes called the parasitic anemone. But it is not really a parasite, since it rarely does the hermit crab any harm. The two are usually equal partners, so a better name for it would be the symbiotic anemone.

MORE PARTNERSHIPS

Other crabs may grab anemones in their pincers, like underwater flaming torches. The crab waves the anemone, to scare away enemies or to try and sting possible prey. Again, both crab and anemone benefit from the relationship.

Clownfish and their anemone partners are popular in tropical saltwater aquaria. The fish's thick coating of slime protects it against the anemone's stings.

CORALS

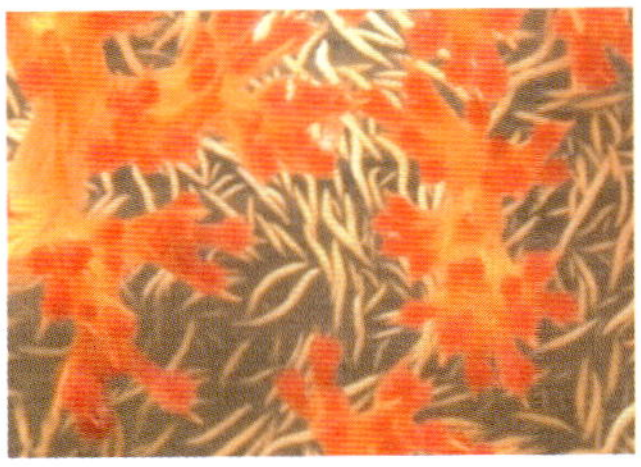

Red-tipped soft corals

THERE ARE MORE THAN 5,000 DIFFERENT KINDS OF CORAL. A coral animal or polyp is usually less than 1 cm tall, and looks like a miniature sea anemone. In fact, corals are very close cousins of anemones (pages 32–33). Most types are found in tropical seas. Some coral polyps live singly, but most live with others of their kind, linked or connected into huge groups or colonies. Some build stony protective casings around themselves. This is how the rocks of a coral reef gradually build up. Sea fans are coral polyps that make tough, horny skeletons which branch into a tree or fan-like shape. The protective cases of soft corals are more like spongy, rubbery jelly.

Some soft corals form colourful, branching, finger-like structures that are tough and leathery.

The reef rocks made by coral polyps have many holes, crevices, caves and overhangs. These are ideal places for larger animals to hide.

Coral animals are cnidarians. They catch their prey with sticky or stinging tentacles, like sea anemones and jellyfish. But, unlike jellyfish, corals do not have a medusa or floating stage in their lives. Like anemones, all coral animals are polyps. In a coral colony, each polyp is connected to its neighbour by living tissue, usually at its base. So the whole colony is joined, almost like one giant multi-animal.

Each polyp can catch its own tiny victims, but the food may then be shared among the nearby members of the colony. This is important because in some corals, certain polyps cannot feed for themselves. Instead, they help to protect or support the colony, by building cases or outer skeletons.

At breeding time, coral animals release clouds of eggs and sperm that drift away in the seawater.

HIDING FROM ENEMIES

In stony corals, each polyp makes a cup-shaped skeleton beneath itself, from rock minerals that it takes out of the sea water. When danger threatens, such as a polyp-eating fish or starfish, the polyp retreats into this protective cup. It emerges again later when the danger is past.

HOW CORALS EAT

A feeding polyp spreads its little tentacles in the sea water. It relies on currents and waves to bring fresh supplies of food, usually with each tide. It catches tiny protists and animals as they drift past. These stick to the tentacles and are then passed to the mouth at the centre, just as in the larger anemones. Many coral polyps come out to feed only at night. This is when sea plankton rise nearer the surface. The polyps wave their shiny tentacles and make a patch of coral rock look like a glistening, multicoloured, living carpet.

BREEDING

When conditions are right, usually on a calm night when the moon is full, all the corals in one area release their eggs and sperm into the sea. These float near the surface in great clouds. Each sperm joins with, or fertilizes, an egg. The fertilized egg develops into a tiny coral larva that floats in the sea for a short time. Then it swims down to the sea bed to find a resting place. The larva sticks itself firmly onto a rock, and grows into a tiny coral polyp, complete with a ring of tentacles. After several weeks, if the single original polyp survives, it has sprouted or budded several new polyps. These remain joined together. As their numbers increase and spread, they gradually form a new coral colony.

This bright, night-time coral reef scene shows various kinds of coral, anemones, sponges and fish such as seahorses and wrasses. By day, most coral polyps withdraw into their protective cases.

INSIDE A CORAL POLYP

A coral animal is like a miniature sea anemone. Its stalk is almost all stomach or digestive cavity. Folds of flesh called mesenteries stick into the cavity, forming a larger surface area for absorbing digested nutrients.

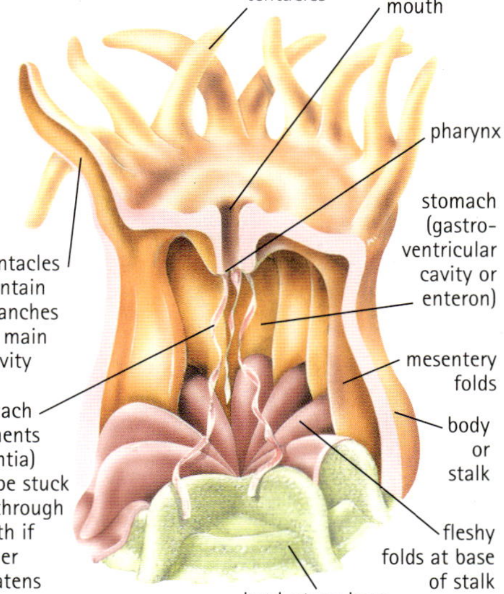

TYPES OF CORAL

- stony or hard corals, usually colonial—some are reef-builders
- soft corals
- gorgonian corals, also called sea fans and sea whips (types of soft coral)

Coral reefs

A CORAL REEF IS A HUGE LUMP OF ROCK MADE BY MILLIONS OF TINY ANIMALS – CORAL POLYPS, AS SHOWN ON THE PREVIOUS PAGE. Reef-building coral polyps make small protective cases, or skeletons, for their soft bodies from chalky minerals they take out of sea water. These cases are shaped like cups, discs or boxes. Each group or colony of coral polyps grows and spreads in its own pattern or shape, as the older polyps form "buds" that grow into new ones. As the older polyp animals die, they leave their empty, stony cases. But more polyps grow above and beside them. In this way, over centuries, thousands of rock-hard polyp cases build up to form the stony, strange and beautiful shapes of the coral reef.

RICH!

Coral reefs are second only to tropical rainforests in the richness and diversity of their wildlife. They are home to half a million different kinds of animal – including one third (more than 7,000) of all fish species.

▲ A colony of soft coral polyps extend their frilly red-tinged tentacles to grasp bits of food.

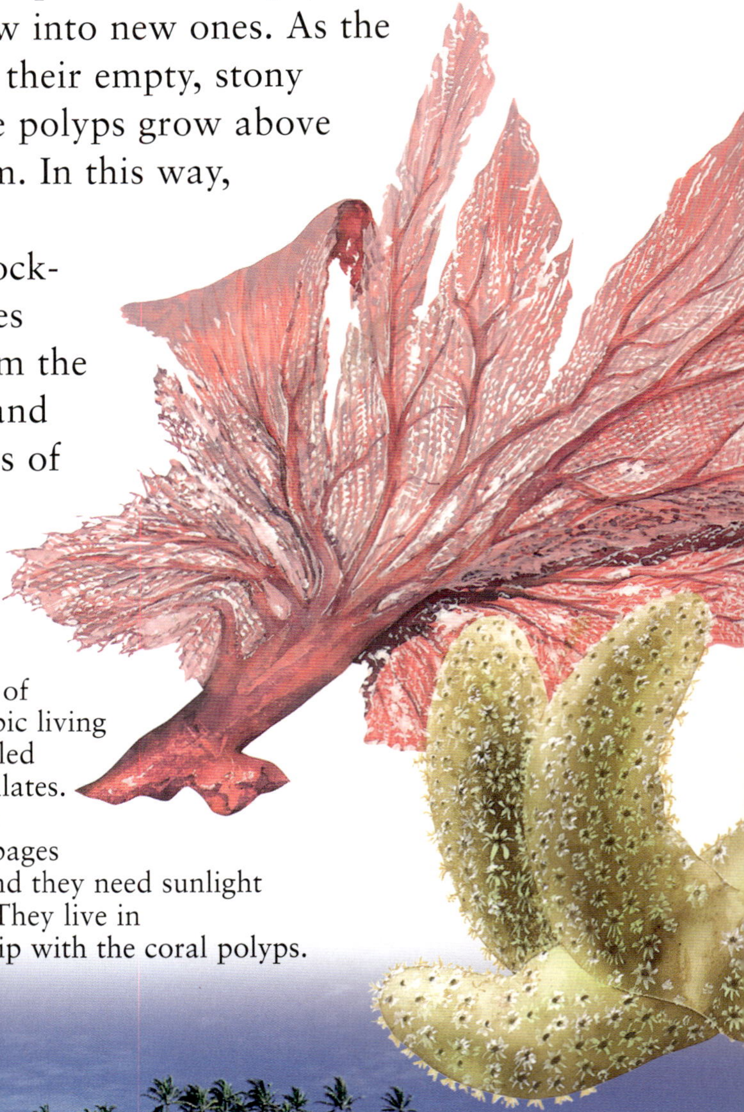

Reef-building coral polyps make the hardest, strongest most massive structures formed by any animals. But they are delicate little creatures. They can only thrive in warm, clear, clean, shallow, sunlit seawater. This is partly because each polyp contains, inside its body, hundreds of microscopic living things called dinoflagellates. These are protists (pages 14–15) and they need sunlight to grow. They live in partnership with the coral polyps.

▼ Coral reefs grow only in shallow tropical or subtropical seas, where the average water temperature is more than about 20°C.

The polyp provides shelter, minerals and raw materials for its protists. In return the protists use the sun's light energy to make food for themselves, which they share with their polyp. So coral polyps need sunlight to survive. This type of helpful partnership is known as symbiosis (page 34).

Corals are usually named after the shapes formed by their thousands of empty skeletons. These build up in patterns according to how the polyps grow and reproduce. The bulges and wrinkles of brain coral look like a human brain!

DIVERSE REEFS

Coral reefs are some of the richest wildlife habitats on Earth. The front of the reef slopes down steeply into the sea, and this is where the wave action is fiercest, especially during storms. But behind the reef ridge or crest, there is usually a shallower, calmer area, protected from the biggest ocean waves. This is the reef flat, or lagoon. The crevices and caves in the reef rocks provide homes for a multitude of fish, shellfish, worms, crabs, shrimp and other animals, and also for plants such as seaweeds.

Gorgonian corals form delicate, lacy, fern-like shapes (left). Finger coral looks like a human hand (below left). There are many different shapes of mushroom corals (below).

PROBLEMS ON THE REEF

Coral animals are quickly affected by any changes to their surroundings. Pollution in the sea, such as oil spills from ships, kills the coral polyps and the many animals that eat them. Another threat is mud and silt from worn-out farm fields and cut-down forests far inland. This is washed into rivers and carried to the sea. The mud makes the water cloudy, so sunlight cannot reach the plant-like protists on which the coral polyps depend. Also, in many parts of the world, the rock-hard coral shapes and patterns are cut away by people, and sold to tourists. This trade is destroying some reefs at an alarming rate.

LARGEST... !

The Great Barrier Reef stretches more than 2,000 km along the coast of Queensland, northeast Australia. It has taken millions of years to reach this size. The Great Barrier Reef is by far the largest structure built by living things (including us!). Many of its 3,000 smaller reefs are now marine parks, where the coral environments are protected.

Corals grow in all colours of the rainbow, like this blue coral from the Caribbean.

THE REEF-EATING STARFISH

Another natural enemy of coral, especially in the Indian and Pacific Oceans, is the crown-of-thorns starfish, which eats polyps. One of these large predators can destroy 4.6 sq m of coral in one year. In some reefs, these starfish have increased hugely in numbers – either as part of a natural cycle, or due to changes made by people.

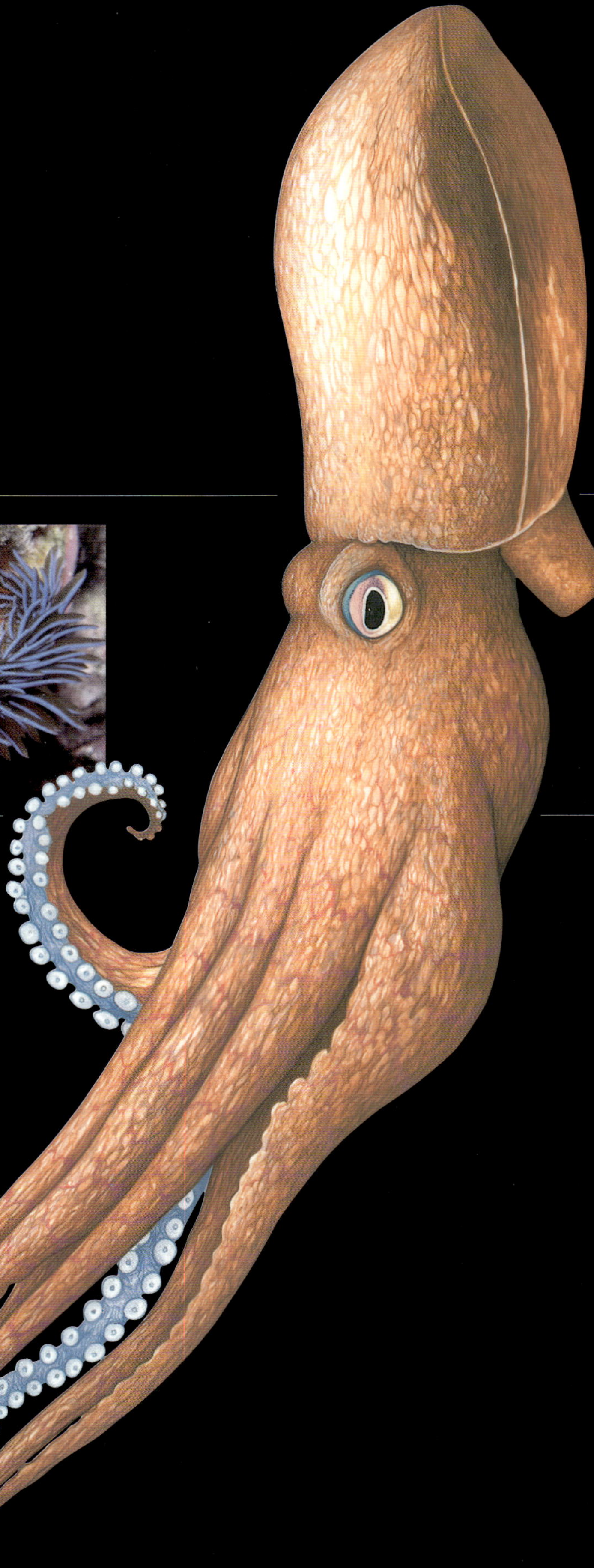

The octopus trails its tentacles behind it as it jets through the water.

SECTION 2

WORMS, SNAILS & STARFISH

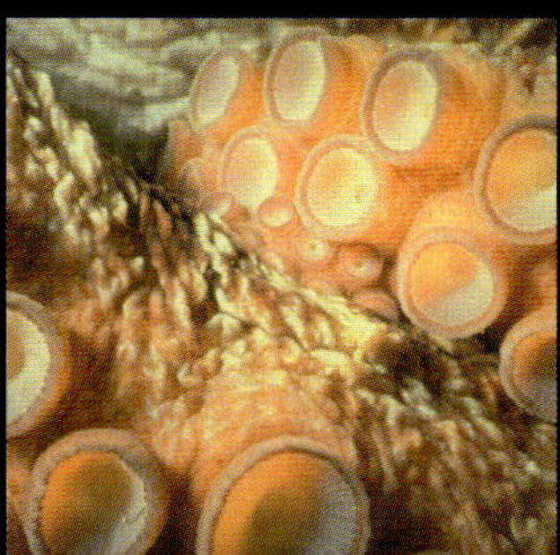

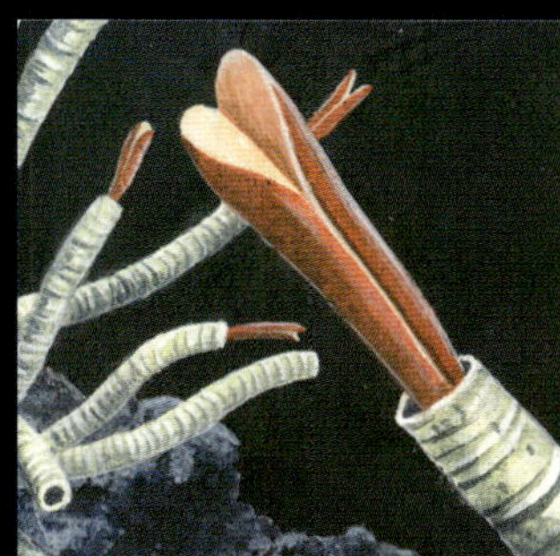

MANY LONG, THIN, SOFT, SLIMY, WRIGGLY CREATURES ARE CALLED WORMS. They are not very appealing to most people. Yet worms are some of the most varied and important members of the animal kingdom. There are at least 20 major groups of worm, ranging from common earthworms that keep the soil fertile, to tiny parasitic worms that cause horrible diseases, to giant tubeworms as thick as your arm living in pitch blackness at the bottom of the sea.

The mollusc group is not well known to many people. Yet it is second only to insects, in the number of different species. Most molluscs have a hard protective shell around the soft body. The group includes limpets and whelks on the seashore, snails in gardens and water snails in ponds. Some molluscs are eaten as food, such as oysters, mussels, scallops and clams. A few, like cone shells, are deadly poisonous. And one of the largest of all animals, the giant squid of the ocean depths, is a mollusc.

Yet another enormous group of sea-dwelling animals is the echinoderms, meaning "spiny-skinned". Starfish, urchins, brittlestars, featherstars and sea lilies are all echinoderms. One of the strangest is the sea cucumber. It looks like an animated sausage eating slimy ooze on the sea bed. If it is attacked, it sicks up sticky threads from its stomach and squirts them out of its mouth!

EARTHWORMS AND LEECHES

The horse leech grows to 30 cm long. It swallows tiny animals whole.

THERE ARE AT LEAST 30 DIFFERENT GROUPS OF WORM-LIKE CREATURES. The main group is the annelids or segmented worms, also called true worms. An annelid worm has a body divided into lots of similar ring-like sections called segments. There are 12,000 species of annelid worms, including familiar earthworms, lugworms and ragworms on the seashore, and leeches. Although these animals are amazingly numerous, we rarely see them because most worms live only in water or under the ground in damp mud, sand or soil. This is because worms absorb oxygen through their thin, moist skin. If the skin dries out, the worm dies. Worms are also soft, slow-moving and vulnerable, so they gain some protection from living in tubes and tunnels.

Most of these tropical fanworms (page 44) are hidden in purple-tinged tubes. Two have spread their spiral yellow feeding tentacles.

DELICIOUS WORMS

Worms have few defences against predators, except their underground lifestyle and ability to breed in great numbers. Birds such as thrushes and blackbirds depend on plentiful supplies of worms for themselves and their chicks. Some birds even trample on the soil to mimic the patter of raindrops, which brings the worms to the surface.

A spiral fanworm's feathery tentacles are covered with sticky mucus, which traps tiny bits of food and flows slowly into its mouth.

Earthworms spend nearly all their lives underground, burrowing in the soil. They push aside some earth and swallow the rest. The earth passes through the worm's gut and nutritious bits like pieces of dead leaves are digested. The remains pass out of the worm's rear end as fine-grained droppings. These are left as curly worm casts at the surface. Millions of earthworms keep soil fertile. They break down and recycle plant and animal remains. Their burrows allow air and moisture into the soil, for plant roots to use, and to help water drain away.

Two earthworms partly emerge from their tunnels on a damp night, to mate. They lie side by side and exchange sperm.

MATING IN THE GRASS

An earthworm has no obvious head. The front or mouth end is slightly more pointed than the rear end, and it has simple detectors that can distinguish between light and dark, but which cannot form an image like proper eyes. One obvious feature of the earthworm is a part called the saddle or clitellum, where several segments seem to be enlarged and fused together. When two worms meet to mate, they put their saddles next to each other. Each earthworm is an hermaphrodite – it has both male and female parts. So each passes sperm to the other, to fertilize its eggs. Each then forms a cocoon of eggs around the saddle. The cocoon slips off and is left in the soil, and baby worms hatch from it.

A leech moves by "looping". It stretches forwards while anchored by its back sucker, and sticks down the front one. Then it detaches the rear sucker, shortens its body, attaches the rear sucker again, and so on.

Sludge worms can survive in stagnant ponds and ditches.

WATER WORMS

The bright red tubifex or sludge worm is a cousin of the earthworm. It lives in fresh water, and is sometimes called the bloodworm because of its colour. The bright red is due to a pigment (coloured substance) that is specialized to take in oxygen from the water, through the skin into the worm's body. The pigment is so plentiful that this worm can live in stagnant water that is very low in oxygen. Hundreds of sludge worms build tubes of sticky mucus in the mud and wave their tails in the water to obtain oxygen.

BIGGEST... !

The world's largest earthworms are giant Gippsland earthworms of Australia. Most are over 90 cm long. But the biggest grow to more than 6.5 m long.

THE BLOOD-SUCKERS

Leeches are like flattened types of worms. They have muscular bodies which can shorten or lengthen, and a sucker at each end. Some leeches prey on smaller worms, insect grubs and similar creatures. Others are parasites, sucking the blood of fish or other animals, including people. The hungry leech clamps itself onto an animal as it passes, perhaps while coming to water to drink. It then rubs its way into the skin with three sets of tiny teeth and gorges itself, sucking in five times its own weight of blood and fluids. The leech can survive for weeks before needing another meal.

ANNELID WORMS

- about 12,000 species
- tube-shaped soft body
- divided into segments

Three main subgroups:

Earthworms
- 3,000 species
- most live in soil or fresh water
- hermaphrodite (each individual is both male and female)
- includes most earthworms, also sludge worms (bloodworms)

Leeches
- 500 species
- many are leaf-shaped
- mostly freshwater, some in the sea or on land
- some are blood-suckers
- hermaphrodite

Bristleworms
Described on page 44

BRISTLEWORMS

BRISTLEWORMS ARE NAMED FROM THE STIFF BRISTLE-LIKE HAIRS, KNOWN AS CHAETAE, STICKING OUT ALL OVER THEIR BODIES. More than half of the types of segmented worms (page 42) belong to the bristleworm group, also called polychaetes. In some types the bristles are attached to paddle-like flaps. Bristleworms live mainly in the sea, and use these flaps as oars, to paddle over the bottom or dig into sand and mud. Some kinds live inside tubes.

Feeding fanworms

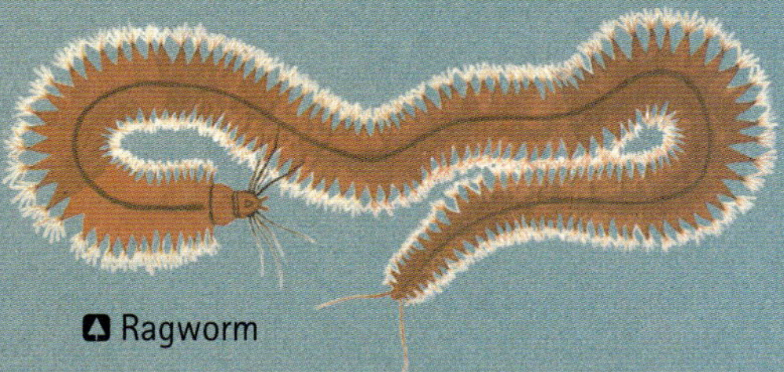

Ragworm

Compared to earthworms, most bristleworms have an obvious head and tail end. The head usually has tentacles, which may look like thin fingers, or be arranged as a frilly ring or a feathery crown. Some types of bristleworms also have simple types of eyes that can pick out shapes. There may be a pair of long thread-like feelers at the tail end.

Bristleworms on the shore include ragworms and lugworms. Ragworms often live in burrows lined with their own hardened mucus (slime), in the muddy silt that collects at the bottom of a rock pool. When the tide is out, the ragworm stays hidden. When the tide comes in, the ragworm emerges from its burrow to feed on the surface of the mud. It can wriggle like a snake, or swim by rowing with its paddle-like flaps.

Ragworms eat a range of food, from dead animals and small creatures such as shrimps to seaweeds. Their strong jaws can easily bite chunks of flesh from a carcass—and even draw blood through human skin. They can also shed their slimy body covering and eat it, to take in the microbes in the slime.

Lugworms hide under the sand in U-shaped burrows. The worm wriggles to make water flow through its burrow, so it can breathe.

FAN-FEEDERS

The main body of a fanworm stays hidden inside a protective tube set into the sea bed, which it builds from mud or sand particles glued together with its own slimy mucus. Fanworms are named for their stiff, feathery feeding tentacles, which they stick out from the top of the tube and spread out like a fan. One of the most beautiful fanworms is the peacock worm. Its tube may be 25 cm long. When safe, it extends the tentacles and waves them in the water. The tentacles are coated with a thin layer of sticky mucus that catches any bits of food floating past. They also work as gills for breathing.

If a fish or other predator swims nearby, the peacock worm whisks in its tentacles and pulls itself down into the safety of its tube. Sometimes peacock worms and other fanworms live in groups, looking like a carpet of flowers. When danger appears, they are gone in a flash, leaving the sea bed looking bare and lifeless.

THE MOUSE WORM

The sea mouse is not a mouse at all, but a type of bristleworm. It grows about 20 cm long. Its plump, humped body is covered with grey-brown, hairy flaps, almost like the fur of a real mouse. Sea mice live mainly on muddy or sandy sea beds, in the Atlantic Ocean and Mediterranean Sea.

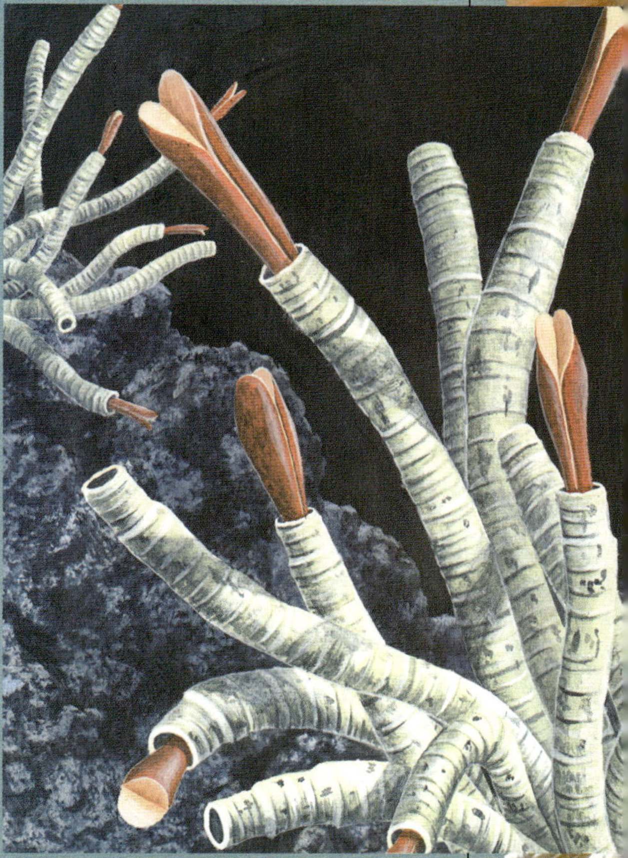

At the bottom of the sea, giant white tubeworms live near vents that pour out scalding, sulphur-rich water. They are 3 m long and as thick as your arm. They take in the sulphur chemicals, and bacteria in their bodies use the chemicals to make food, which they share with the worm.

HARD TUBES

Some bristleworms build much tougher, more rigid tubes from chalky minerals, either in the sand or on rocks. The hard, white, wiggly tubes on seashore weeds and boulders belong to bristleworms called keelworms. When the tide is in, the keelworm pushes its tiny crown of feeding tentacles from the end of the tube, to gather food.

SAND CASTS

Little mounds of sand or mud on the shore are the casts of lugworms. These worms are 15–20 cm long, soft, and thicker at the front end. They feed like earthworms, by eating the sand or mud, digesting any nutrients, and then passing out the remains as the familiar worm cast.

The tubes of peacock worms partly stick up from the sea bed.

(continued from page 43):

Bristleworms
- 8,500 species
- most live in the sea
- body has bristles or flaps
- sexes separate (male or female)
- includes lugworms, ragworms, fanworms, peacock worms, sea mice, scaleworms, catworms

FLATWORMS

FLATWORMS ARE THE SIMPLEST OF ALL WORMS. They are indeed flat and smooth, resembling leaves or ribbons. They lack the ring-like body sections or segments of annelid worms (page 42). There are more than 13,000 species of flatworms. But they are less familiar than earthworms, because most are too small to see easily, while others live in water, and some are parasites inside other animals. Most free-living flatworms are found in the sea, among weeds or the pebbles on the shore. Some live in fresh water and a few in damp soil.

◀ Free-living flatworms or turbellarians often look like leaves. They live as predators, hunting even smaller creatures, or scavenging on corpses. The many-branched intestine and the mouth area under the centre of the body are visible through the thin skin.

Flatworms that can move around freely, rather than being parasites inside animals, are called turbellarians. The freshwater turbellarians, or planarians, are streamlined animals, with an obvious head and tail end. Some species even have several small eyes around the front end, while others have two larger eyes on top of the head. Some also have a pair of feelers on the head, to help them feel objects and detect scents as they move about.The underside of a flatworm is covered in tiny hairs, cilia, which wave smoothly to and fro to glide the worm along.

SHRINK!

Some flatworms can reproduce by splitting themselves into two. Each half then regrows the missing portion and two separate flatworms result. They can also feed on themselves if food is in short supply, absorbing their own bodies and gradually shrinking in the process.

▼ Flatworms in the sea are larger and more varied than the freshwater species. Some are brightly patterned or coloured.

Many freshwater planarians have an obvious head end with eyes.

Flatworms can also move by rippling their muscular undersides. Many feed on smaller animals, or on the dead bodies of other creatures. When some flatworms find food, they push part of their gut out from the body, then slowly suck the food and gut inside again.

FLATWORMS OF POND AND STREAM

Planarians are common in ponds and streams all around the world. They hide among pebbles and weeds by day, and are mostly only fingernail-sized or smaller, so are seldom seen. They are active mainly at night. In the dark water, they glide smoothly along the surfaces of plants, or slither across submerged logs and stones. Sometimes they slip upside down along the underside of the water's surface, feeding on creatures trapped by the surface film.

Large tropical flatworms crawl through dead leaves in rain forests.

Different types of these free-living flatworms are suited to particular freshwater habitats. The crenobia planarian lives in cold upland streams. It has ear-like feelers and a pair of large eyes. The polycelis planarian is also found in running streams. It has many tiny eyes around the edges of its head. The dugesia planarian has a triangular head with two large eyes on the top. It lives in ponds and streams, but cannot cope well with fast currents.

INSIDE A FLATWORM

Flatworms have very simple bodies. On the outside is a layer of cells called the epidermis. On the inside there is another layer of cells, the endodermis, arranged in tubes to form the intestine (gut or digestive tract). The only way in and out of the intestine is the mouth, which may be at the head end, the tail end, or part way along the underside. In between the epidermis and the intestine are masses of cells called the parenchyma. These make up the flatworm's muscles, glands, nerves and reproductive organs.

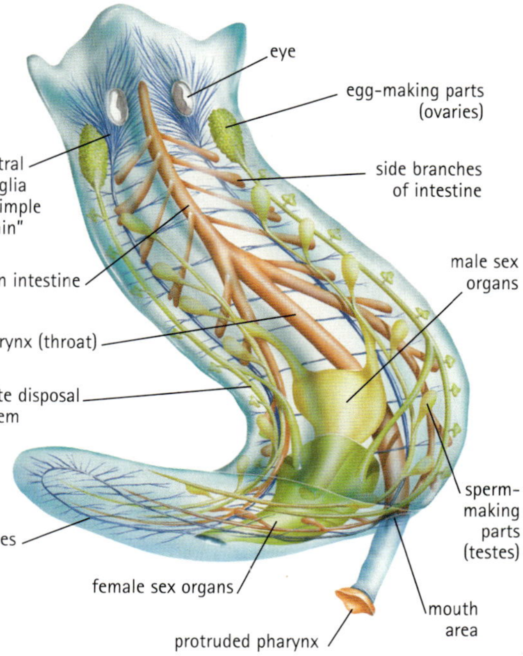

HOW FLATWORMS BREED

Most flatworms are hermaphrodites. This means each has both male and female sex organs. So any two flatworms can come together and mate, each passing on sperm to the other. Each of the pair then goes on to develop and lay its eggs.

The eggs are sticky when first laid, and are attached beneath stones or underwater logs. After a few weeks, the eggs hatch out into tiny baby flatworms that gradually grow into adults. This is quite different to parasitic flatworms (page 48), where the young forms or larvae often differ in shape from the adults.

Flatworms *(Platyhelminthes)*
- 25,000 species
- live in water or damp places, or inside other animals
- soft, flattened, leaf-like body
- no body sections or segments
- most are hermaphrodite (male and female)
- some free-living, some parasitic

Divided into three groups:

Flukes and Tapeworms
Described on pages 48–49

Free-living flatworms *(Turbellaria)*
- most in the sea, some in fresh water, a few on land
- most less than 2 cm long
- head end has dark eyes

Gnathostomulans
- 100 species
- live in the sea
- small (up to 1mm)
- tiny and worm-like

FLUKES AND TAPEWORMS

FLUKES AND TAPEWORMS ARE FLATWORMS (PAGE 46) THAT MOSTLY LIVE AS PARASITES, ON OR INSIDE OTHER ANIMALS AND PEOPLE. Many flukes can live both inside their host – in its intestine, liver, or heart – and on or under its skin, gripping by special leech-like suckers. Tapeworms live right inside their host's gut, for months at a time. The host is not always aware of the worm's presence, but it may feel ill since the worm steals its nutrition or damages its body parts. Tapeworms tend to live in larger mammals. Flukes live in nearly every kind of animal, from insects and crabs to fish, reptiles, birds and mammals.

Most flukes are leaf-shaped and about 2.5 cm long, although some are more rounded, like other worms. At the front end, the adult fluke has a sucker which it uses to hang on to its host. There may be another sucker farther down its body, to give the fluke extra sticking power.

The outside of an adult fluke is covered with slimy mucus. This protects it from the host's body fluids and digestive juices, which would otherwise attack and kill it. The adult fluke feeds by sucking up the blood and other fluids from its host animal. One kind of fluke lives inside the bodies of frogs and toads. When the host returns to water to breed, the flukes release their eggs into the water as well. Then the tiny fluke larvae attach themselves to the frog's tadpoles, infecting the next generation of amphibians.

LONG!

Tapeworms can grow very long. One kind found in whales may reach 20 m in length. Tapeworms have been a problem for people as long as there have been people. Ancient Egyptians suffered from these parasites.

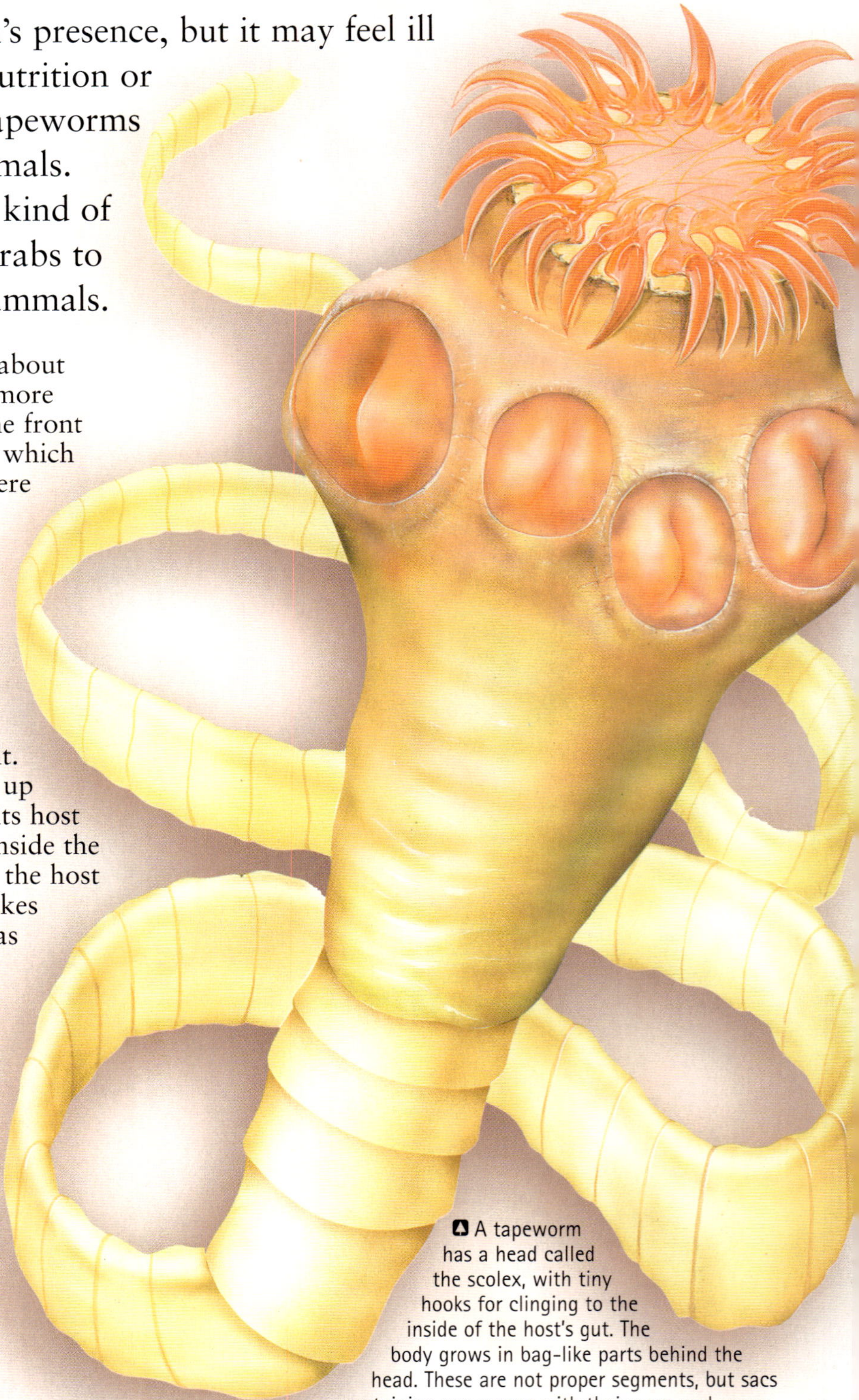

A tapeworm has a head called the scolex, with tiny hooks for clinging to the inside of the host's gut. The body grows in bag-like parts behind the head. These are not proper segments, but sacs containing sex organs with their eggs and sperm.

The liver fluke is a flatworm that burrows into the livers of animals such as sheep.

A COMPLICATED LIFE

Many kinds of flukes have complicated life cycles. They live on or in different hosts at different stages of their lives. Some flukes even move from one host to another four times. Typically, a fluke would spend most of its adult life in the body of a large vertebrate animal such as a fish, reptile, bird or mammal. But it transfers its eggs or larvae to the body of an invertebrate, such as a snail or a slug, when it breeds.

FLUKE DISEASES

Liver flukes infest the livers of sheep and cattle and cause disease. As an adult, the liver fluke feeds on blood in the sheep's liver. Its eggs pass out with the sheep's droppings and lie in the pasture. They only develop further if they hatch near a water snail. When the young or larval fluke finds a snail, it burrows in and lives there for a while. Then it leaves the snail and attaches itself to plants at the water's edge. If a sheep eats a plant with one of these larvae on it, the sheep becomes infected, the fluke larva grows into an adult, and the cycle is complete.

This fluke is less than 1 mm long. It lives in the blood of many animals.

TROPICAL DISEASE FLUKES

Bilharzia or schistosomiasis is a tropical disease caused by a blood fluke called schistosoma. These flukes live inside the veins near the host person's intestine or bladder. The eggs are released near the gut, and some pass out of the host's body with the faeces. If they get into water, they can infect the second host, a type of water snail. After developing inside the snail, the next stage of fluke larva escapes into the water. If these larvae end up on a human, they burrow into the skin and enter the blood.

TAPE-LIKE WORMS

Tapeworms get their name from the tape- or ribbon-like bodies of the adult worms. The body is flat and can be very long—as much as 9 m or more, looped back and forth several times inside the host's intestine.

LIFE CYCLES OF FLUKES AND TAPEWORMS

Many flukes infest two, three or four hosts during the different stages in their lives. For example, certain kinds of flukes live inside a person, in the intestine, liver or bladder. They produce tiny eggs, which pass out in the host person's urine or faeces. Only if the eggs find their way into a host (such as the correct type of snail) do they develop into larvae. Then this host must be eaten by the right type of fish, for the next stage to happen. Finally a person eats the poorly cooked fish and takes in the fluke larvae, which mature into adults.

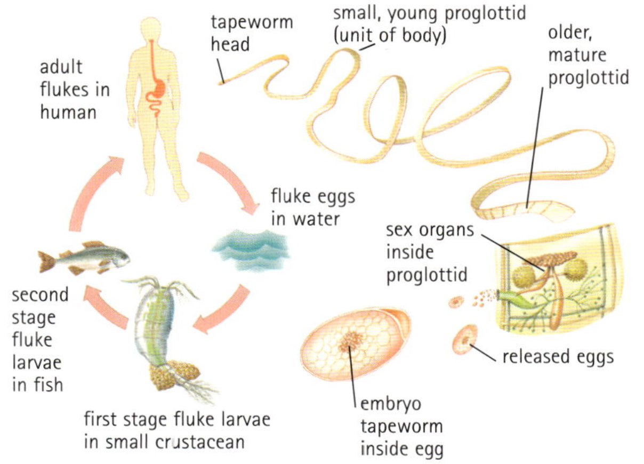

Most tapeworms live as parasites inside the intestines of large carnivorous animals, including people. At the front end, the tapeworm secures itself to the gut wall of its host with hooks and suckers. The tapeworm has no mouth or gut of its own. It feeds by absorbing nutrients through all the surfaces of its body. It has plenty of food all around it, provided by its host.

People badly affected by tapeworms become very thin, even though they eat normally. This is because the worms "steal" their food. One kind of human tapeworm has the pig as a second host. Another species infects cattle. If someone eats pork or beef infected with tapeworm larvae, he or she may become infected. In the past, the pork tapeworm was a common human parasite due to eating raw or under-cooked pork. Cooking or curing the meat kills any tapeworm eggs or larvae.

FLATWORMS (continued from page 47):

Flukes *(Trematoda)*
- parasites, some causing diseases in animals and people
- most small, less than 5 cm
- leaf-shaped body

Tapeworms *(Cestoda)*
- parasites in animals and people
- long, 9 m or more
- ribbon-shaped
- tiny head with hooks
- no mouth or intestine
- egg bags look like segments

ROUNDWORMS

ROUNDWORMS ARE FOUND ALMOST EVERYWHERE, IN VAST NUMBERS. Most are tiny and live in water or soil, so we rarely notice them. Others are parasites and cause disease and suffering. They include eelworms, hookworms, threadworms, filarial worms and a host of other species. A typical roundworm has a long body that tapers towards each end, is round like a tube, and does not have sections or segments. Roundworms are also known as nematode worms.

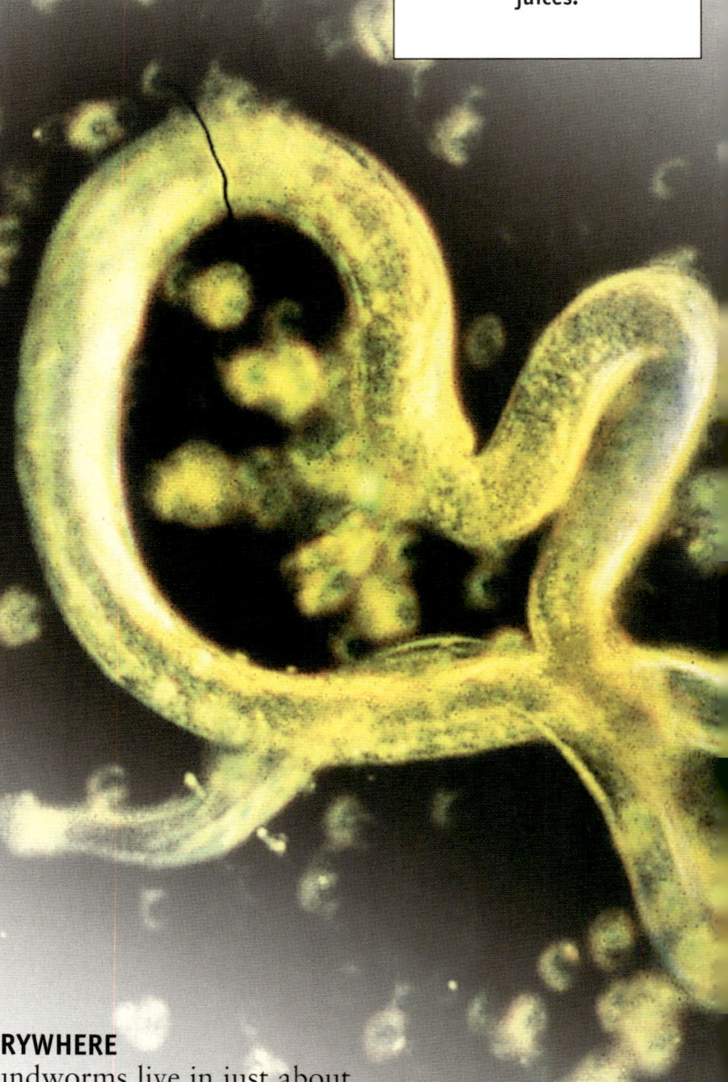

The strongyloides roundworm is a parasite in sheep. It bores through the skin into the blood and ends up in the intestine.

SO MANY!

Some kinds of roundworms are found in such vast numbers, they are hard to imagine. One rotting apple may have 90,000 roundworms inside it. More than 20 million roundworms have been found in one wheelbarrow-load of seaside mud. Some soil roundworms are predators of even tinier creatures, sucking their juices.

About 20,000 different kinds of roundworms or nematodes have been discovered. But the true number is probably far higher – perhaps half a million. Because they are so plentiful, roundworms are very important in the balance of nature. By feeding on dead and decaying animals and plants, they help to break these down and return the goodness to the soil, recycling vital nutrients. Tiny roundworms living between grains of sand at the seaside feed on bacteria, and by doing so, help to keep the beaches clean!

EVERYWHERE

Roundworms live in just about every habitat on the planet. Most are so small that we cannot see them. Free-living (nonparasitic) roundworms are usually less than 1–2 mm long. A single spadeful of garden earth may contain 0.5 million.

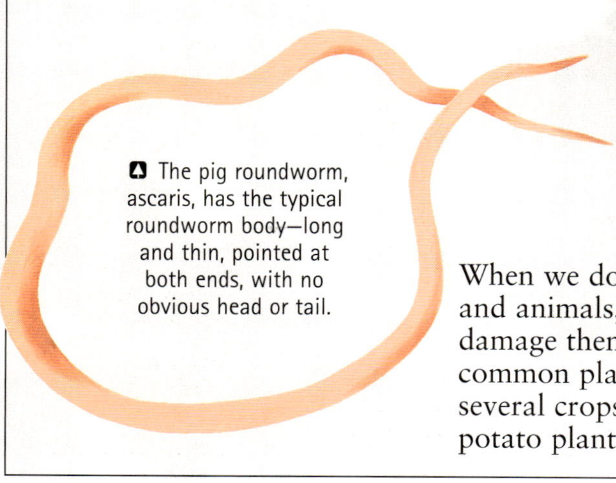

The pig roundworm, ascaris, has the typical roundworm body—long and thin, pointed at both ends, with no obvious head or tail.

When we do notice roundworms is when they are parasites in plants and animals, and cause enormous damage. Roundworms not only do damage themselves. They may also carry viruses that infect the host. A common plant parasite is the eelworm, which attacks the roots of several crops, notably potatoes, tomatoes and sugar beet. A single potato plant may have 40,000 eelworms infesting its roots.

◀ The threadworm (pinworm) is a common human parasite. It is harmful in large numbers.

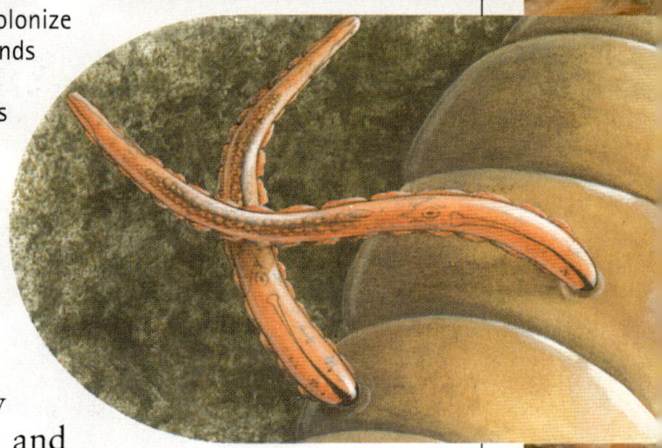

▶ Some types of roundworms colonize plants and ruin crops. Certain kinds cause hard swellings known as galls. Others puncture plant cells and suck out the sap. Still others infest animals of all kinds. No creature is safe, even other worms. These tiny roundworms are eating their way into an earthworm.

THE DREADED HOOKWORM

Hookworms are particularly harmful parasitic nematodes. They are among the most common causes of human illness, affecting more than 1,000 million people, especially in tropical Asia. Newly hatched hookworms burrow through the skin of a person and get into the bloodstream. They then travel around the body and settle in the intestine, where they feed and grow. They have a very weakening effect on people. Children, especially, suffer from anaemia (shortage of red blood cells). An infected person becomes pale and weak, and the legs and abdomen swell. If not treated quickly with drugs that kill the worms, death may result.

FILARIAL WORMS

Another unpleasant tropical parasite in humans is the filaria roundworm, wucheria. It gets into the body's lymph tubes and glands, which carry fluids around the body and fight germs. As the worms grow and multiply, they block the lymph system and cause terrible swellings, especially in the limbs, known as elephantiasis.

The filiaria roundworm is spread by flies and mosquitoes. The worm's young are released by the mother and make their way to the surface blood vessels. When a mosquito bites the person's skin, it takes up the filaria with the blood. The worm grows inside the mosquito's head. Then, when the mosquito bites another person or animal, the worm enters through the wound and infects the new host. Some roundworms have several hosts in their lives, as flukes do (page 48).

GIANT ROUNDWORM

The Guinea worm, another tropical parasite, lives in humans and may grow more than 90 cm long. It causes pain and disfigurement, and ulcers develop when the worms release their eggs through the skin.

Roundworms *(nematodes)*
- 20,000-plus species
- all habitats
- most are free-living, some are parasites
- body rounded, but without segments
- many are tiny
- largest are up to 90 cm

THE LIVES OF PARASITES

Many kinds of roundworms, flukes, tapeworms and other worms live as internal or endo-parasites. They obtain shelter and nutrients from their hosts, and usually cause harm in return. The life of a schistosoma parasite (a fluke, page 48) is shown here. Worms are suited to the parasitic way of life. Their thin, flexible bodies can squeeze through the host's blood vessels, intestines, and other parts. A worm can also absorb nutrients and oxygen easily through its thin skin.

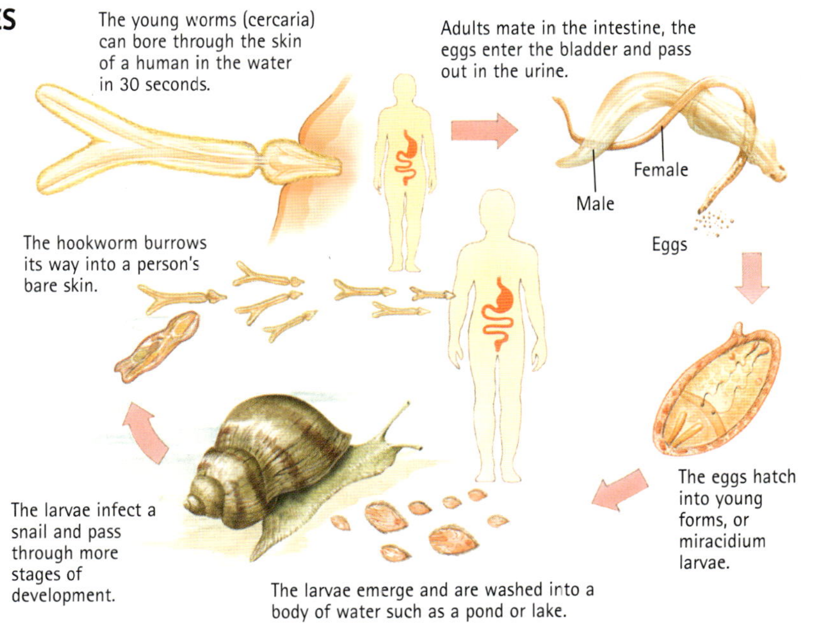

OTHER WORMS

BESIDES THE MAIN GROUPS OF WORMS (SEGMENTED WORMS, FLATWORMS, AND ROUNDWORMS), THERE ARE MANY OTHER TYPES OF WORMS. They include ribbon worms, spoon worms, arrow worms and acorn worms. They are not necessarily close relatives of the main worms, or of each other. But all have the main worm feature – a long, wriggling body.

Ribbon worms live among rocks and stones on the shore and under the sea. They hunt tiny animals for food.

Ribbon worms or nemerteans live mostly in the sea. They have soft, slimy bodies that are slightly flattened towards the head, and range in length from 0.5 mm to 9 m. Some ribbon worms are black or dark, others are brightly striped or banded. Most are predators.

Horsehair worms or hair worms often live in groups and look like a mass of living, writhing hair. They often coil themselves almost into knots. Adults live in damp soil or water and do not feed at all. They just reproduce their kind. The young horsehair worms live as parasites, inside the bodies of insects and similar hosts.

LONGEST!

The longest known animal is a type of ribbon worm – the bootlace worm. It often grows to 4.5 m long, but incredible lengths of 30 m have been recorded.

SPINY-HEADED AND PEANUT WORMS

Spiny-headed worms are all parasites and live inside larger animals, especially fish. Their mouthparts are equipped with spiny hooks, which they use to attach themselves to their hosts.

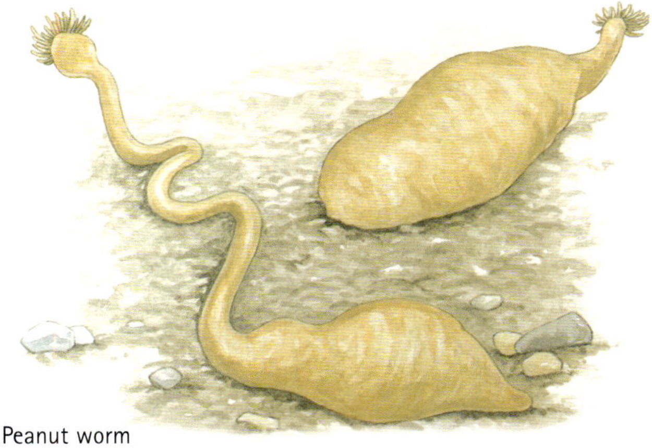

Peanut worm

Peanut worms are cylinder-shaped, with a flexible stalk-like proboscis at the top that can be extended or pulled back inside the body. The proboscis has frilly tentacles at the end, which are used for feeding. Peanut worms range from pinhead size to more than 70 cm long.

SPOON WORMS

Spoon worms include some of the strangest of all animals. Most have pear-shaped bodies, with hooks and a proboscis at the head end. They live in the sea, either in mud burrows or crevices in the rocks. In one kind, the bonellia spoon worm, the female has a body about 15 cm long. But her enormous proboscis is 90 cm in length, and is forked at the end. She is vivid green in colour. Yet the male is almost microscopically small compared to the giant female. Bonellias are quite common in the Mediterranean Sea.

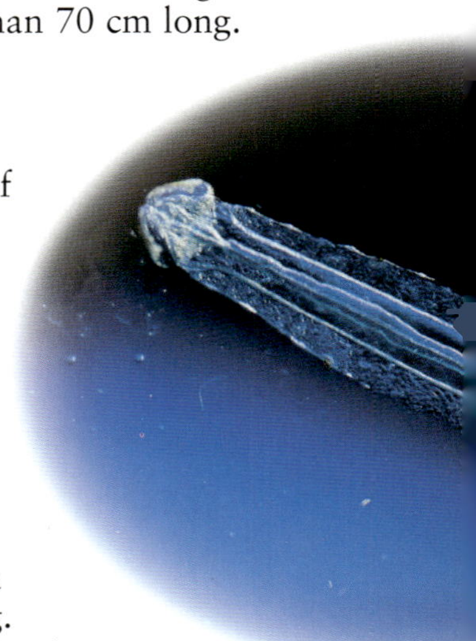

Arrow worms live in the tropical oceans in huge numbers. They feed mainly on smaller animals of plankton, including fish fry.

Spiny-headed worms

Arrow worms

ARROW WORMS

Arrow worms are transparent, arrow-shaped animals about 2.5 cm long, with small "fins" at the sides and tail. They live in the upper layers of the sea and hunt small fish and animal plankton such as copepods, using spines near the mouth to grasp their prey.

BEARD WORMS

Beard worms live in the ocean depths, in tubes almost buried in the mud. They have long, thin bodies, just a "matchhead" wide, but 90 cm or more long. At the front is a beard-like tuft of as many as 100 tentacles. They have no stomach or intestine, absorbing nutrients through the body surface.

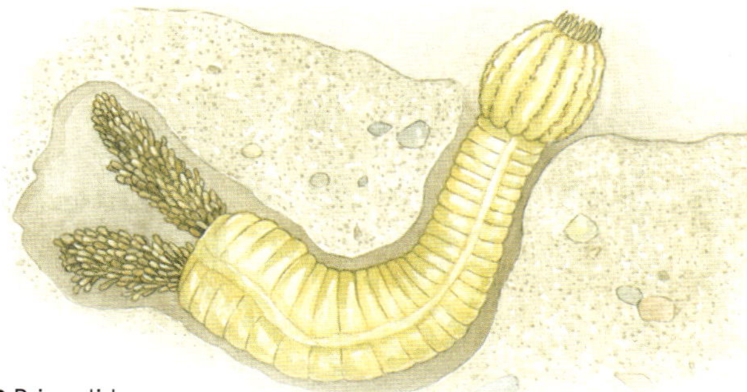

Priapulid worm

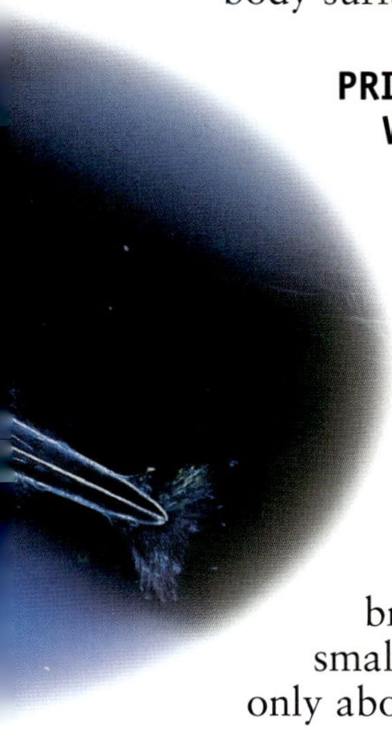

PRIAPULID AND HORSESHOE WORMS

Priapulid worms burrow in the mud on the sea bed or shore. They resemble the peanut worms, but the stalk-like proboscis at the head end has a ring of teeth rather than tentacles. Priapulid worms have frilly appendages on the tail. These probably work as gills for breathing. This is one of the smallest of all animal groups, with only about ten known species.

Horseshoe worms are another very small group in terms of numbers of species. But the worms themselves can be very abundant in muddy sand. They live in tubes which they make for themselves. Some kinds burrow into limestone rocks. The animal itself is long and worm-like, but at its top or head end it has a fan-like swirl of tentacles. When feeding, only the spreading tentacles can be seen at the top of the tube.

ACORN WORMS

Acorn worms live in burrows in mud and sand on the sea bed. They are found mainly in shallow water near the coast. They range in size from about 2.5 to 50 cm long. Between the proboscis and the rest of the body is a distinct collar. In some, the proboscis is short and looks like an oak tree's acorn. Acorn worms are very fragile creatures, and when they are out of their burrows, they easily fall to pieces!

TONGUE WORMS

Tongue worms are parasites, living inside the nose passages and lungs of mammals, birds and reptiles. The tongue worm has no obvious features except for its head end, which has five finger-like parts sticking out. The middle one of the five has the tongue worm's mouth at its tip.

Horsehair worm

Ribbon worms *(Nemertea)*
- 900 species
- most are marine
- long and ribbon-shaped
- sexes separate in most species

Horsehair worms *(Nematomorpha)*
- 250 species
- water or damp soil, some marine
- long and hair-like
- sexes separate

Spiny-headed worms *(Acanthocephala)*
- 1,000 species
- parasitic
- spiny mouthparts

Peanut worms *(Sipuncula)*
- 350 species
- marine, in sand and mud
- cylinder-shaped
- mouth with frilly tentacles

Spoon worms *(Echiura)*
- 150 species
- marine, in burrows in mud or sand
- sausage- or pear-shaped
- long, finger-like proboscis

Beard worms *(Pogonophora)*
- 100 species
- marine, in the deep sea
- beard-like tentacles on head
- sexes separate

Arrow worms *(Chaetognatha)*
- 70 species
- marine, in plankton
- long, transparent body, with flaps or fins
- most are transparent
- extremely numerous

Priapulid worms *(Priapula)*
- 10 species
- marine, live on the sea floor
- tube-shaped

Horseshoe worms *(Phorona)*
- 20 species
- marine
- live in hard tubes
- have head tentacles

Tongue worms *(Pentastoma)*
- 100 species
- mainly parasites of reptiles, mammals, and birds
- four short tentacles around head end

Acorn worms *(Hemichordata)*
- 100 species
- marine, on the sea floor, mostly in burrows
- finger-like proboscis on head

THE RANGE OF MOLLUSCS

SNAILS AND SLUGS, AND SEA CREATURES SUCH AS WHELKS, COCKLES, CLAMS AND MUSSELS, ARE ALL MOLLUSCS. So are octopuses, squid and cuttlefish. Indeed, there are nearly 100,000 species of mollusc, making up the second largest group of animals after insects and other arthropods. They vary greatly in size and shape, but all have soft bodies, and many have hard shells. Most molluscs move about on a large, flat pad, called the foot. The head of a mollusc often has soft, bendy tentacles, used for feeling its way about or grasping food. The main mollusc groups are described on the following pages.

The bright colours and patterns of tropical sea slugs warn that they are bad to eat. The knobs and frills help in breathing.

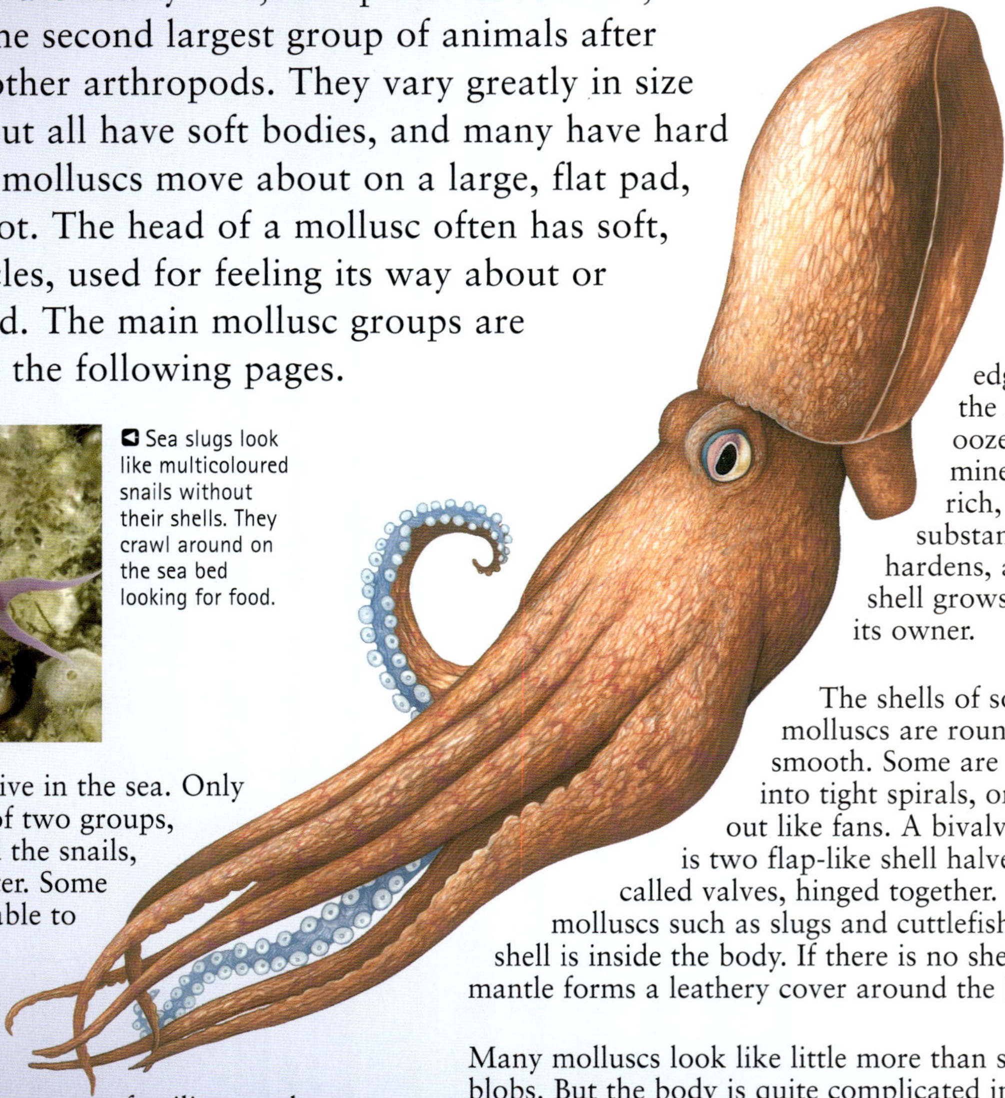

The octopus trails its tentacles behind it as it jets through the water.

Sea slugs look like multicoloured snails without their shells. They crawl around on the sea bed looking for food.

Most molluscs live in the sea. Only certain species of two groups, the bivalves and the snails, live in fresh water. Some snails are even able to live in damp conditions on land. There are seven main groups of molluscs. The three most familiar are the gastropods such as snails, limpets and winkles; the bivalves such as mussels, clams, oysters and razorshells; and the cephalopods such as octopuses, cuttlefish, nautiluses and squid.

All molluscs have a large, cloak-like part around the main body, called the mantle. In many molluscs, this makes a hard, protective shell on the outside, which the creature can withdraw into, to avoid danger. The shell grows as the edges of the mantle ooze a mineral-rich, liquid substance. This hardens, and the shell grows with its owner.

The shells of some molluscs are round and smooth. Some are coiled into tight spirals, or spread out like fans. A bivalve's shell is two flap-like shell halves, called valves, hinged together. In molluscs such as slugs and cuttlefish, the shell is inside the body. If there is no shell, the mantle forms a leathery cover around the body.

Many molluscs look like little more than squishy blobs. But the body is quite complicated inside, containing many of the usual important parts such as a brain, heart and kidney. Muscles can pull and squeeze the body into almost any shape.

Scallops are bivalve molluscs, which means they have two shell parts. The scallop can snap its shell shut to swim jerkily.

Tusk shells have long, curving, tapering shells that look like elephants' tusks. The shell is open at both ends. The tusk shell lives half buried, head-down in the sand. It feeds by spreading its thread-like tentacles into the sand.

THE MOLLUSC'S RADULA

One special feature of molluscs is a file-like "tongue" called a radula, covered in rows of hard teeth. The mollusc uses this to scrape away at its food, perhaps tiny seaweeds covering a rock, or lettuces in the garden. Not all molluscs feed in this way, however. Squid and octopuses are active predators, tearing up prey with a beak-like mouth.

THE MOLLUSC'S FOOT

The mollusc's large, muscular, pad-like foot is used for many tasks. Squid and octopuses have developed the foot into tentacles to catch prey. A limpet uses its sucker foot to cling to rocks. A snail slides about on its foot. A clam's foot is like a strong finger that pokes and digs into the sand or mud. A razorshell's foot is so powerful, it can dig the animal down into the seashore mud, almost as fast as a person could dig with a spade.

FOOD FROM MOLLUSCS

All over the world, people like to eat molluscs – favourites include oysters, clams, cockles, mussels, scallops, abalones, winkles, octopus and squid. They are usually an important source of food in coastal places and on islands. Some molluscs have become rare or endangered as a result of being over-collected for food.

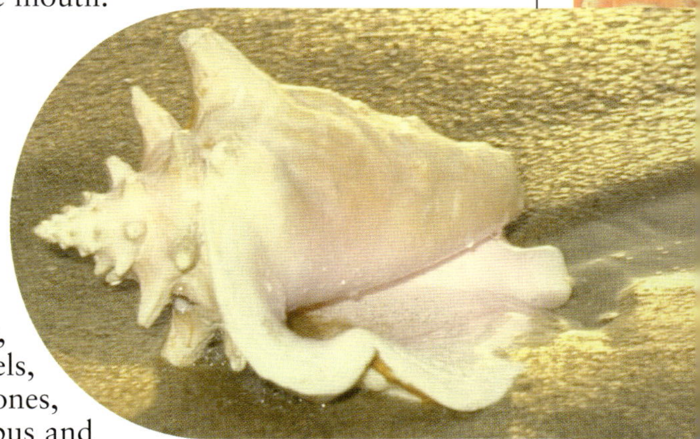

Many mollusc shells are incredibly beautiful, especially when wet from the sea. The tropical conch shell is especially attractive. Empty, it has been used as a trumpet to make sounds for thousands of years. However, the souvenir trade in mollusc shells endangers many species (page 60).

Chitons are oval in shape and have a shell divided into eight arched plates, making them look as if they are protected by chain-mail armour. The alternative name for this group is "coat-of-mail shells". They graze on the film of seaweed covering rocks in shallow water along the coast. Chitons can curl up tightly if dislodged from their rocks.

MOLLUSCS

- up to 100,000 species
- most live in the sea, some in fresh water, a few on land
- soft body in cloak-like mantle
- many have hard shell around body
- many have large, muscular base or foot
- some have flexible tentacles

Main groups of molluscs:

Tusk shells
- 350 species
- marine
- burrow into sand
- single shell shaped like elephant's tusk

Slugs and snails
- 70,000 species
- marine, freshwater and land-living
- most have a single shell, often coiled
- head has tentacles
- glide on muscular foot

Bivalves
- 20,000 species
- most are marine, some freshwater
- hinged shell of two parts (valves)
- foot rounded, not flattened
- most burrow, or live attached to rocks

Squid and octopuses
- 650 species
- live in the sea
- long tentacles around mouth
- large eyes, big brains
- hide in rocks or swim in the sea

Chitons
- 550 species
- live in the sea, on rocks on the shore, or in shallow water
- body oval and domed (like a woodlouse), with eight plates
- no eyes

Mussels are fixed to seashore rocks by strong, stringy byssus threads.

SLUGS AND SNAILS

Some sea slugs have large hair-like tentacles on their backs. These can carry stings or horrible-tasting fluids.

LAND SNAILS AND SEA SNAILS, LAND SLUGS AND SEA SLUGS, ALONG WITH LIMPETS AND WHELKS, ARE ALL GASTROPODS – MOLLUSCS WITH SOFT, SQUIDGY BODIES. The name gastropod means "stomach-foot", because these molluscs seem to slide along on their stomachs. But it is really the same muscular foot possessed by all molluscs. Many snails and limpets have a hard shell, so gastropods are sometimes called univalves (meaning "one shell"). A slug's soft body is exposed.

Few molluscs are more familiar than the common garden snail. After a heavy rainstorm, snails emerge as if from nowhere in the damp conditions. They rasp their way through many kinds of leaves and plant bits on the ground.

When a gastropod slides along the ground, its large, flat stomach-foot spreads out underneath. Muscles in the foot ripple backwards and forwards. Land snails and slugs ooze a trail of slime to ease the way forward and reduce friction.

THE SHELL'S TRAPDOOR

On the back of the foot, most sea snails and some land snails have a flap called an operculum. When danger threatens, the snail retreats into its shell and pulls the operculum over the opening, like closing a trapdoor, for protection.

LARGEST... !

The biggest snail is the African giant snail. Its huge shell can be almost 25 cm across.

Many gastropods have four tentacles on the head. Two are feelers that help them to find their way by touch. The other two are often stalks with eyes at the tip. But many gastropods have no eyes at all.

SHELLS AND SURVIVAL

Snails seem to live everywhere, not only in all parts of the oceans, but in almost all habitats on land. Like all molluscs, the snail needs plenty of moisture to survive. So land snails stay in or near moist places. If the weather is too cold or too dry, the snail makes a seal of slime over its shell entrance. This hardens into a kind of temporary door. In the autumn, in temperate regions, many snails settle down for the winter in this state. As it gets warmer in the spring, the snail breaks open the seal and emerges again. In hot, dry weather, snails also seal themselves in their shells and wait for cooler, moister conditions. Surviving heat or dryness like this is called aestivation.

MALE AND FEMALE

Snails are hermaphrodite, which means that each animal is both male and female at the same time. When they mate, each snail passes sperm into the body of the other snail. Each partner goes on to develop and lay a clutch of leathery eggs. There may be dozens of eggs in a single clutch.

JELLY BABIES !

Water and pond snails lay their eggs in a string or blob of jelly, usually stuck to the stem of a water plant or stone. The jelly helps to protect the eggs from being eaten, and also stops them drying out if the water level in the pond or stream changes. In an aquarium tank water snails often lay their eggs on the glass. This allows a clear view of the tiny baby snails developing inside.

Slugs like this keeled slug have a great appetite for all kinds of plants, including potatoes. The keeled slug often burrows under the soil, especially to eat plant roots and to hide during the day.

Eventually many tiny snails hatch. Except for their size, they look very like the adults, each with its tiny shell. It takes about two years for a snail to reach maturity.

Most snails are little bigger than cherries. But a few, such as the giant ram's-horn snail of ponds and lakes, can be 10 to 15 cm across.

SLUGS

Slugs are like snails that have lost their protective shells, although some slugs do have small shells inside their bodies, just under the skin of the back. Some even have a tiny shell on the back. To protect themselves, slugs produce large quantities of very sticky slime, which puts off many predators. The slime also helps to stop the slugs from drying out. However, some birds, such as thrushes, and some mammals, including hedgehogs, can cope with this slime. They eat large numbers of slugs. Song thrushes can even tackle snails. They bash the snail against a hard object, like a stone, until its shell breaks open. Then they quickly eat the tasty flesh inside.

This Indonesian sea slug can swim by undulating its cape-like foot. The gills are tall, yellow and spiky. Sea slugs eat seaweeds and small animals such as sea mats and corals that coat rocks.

SLUGS AT SEA

The marine relatives of snails and slugs include some of the most beautiful of all sea creatures. Like land slugs, sea slugs are mostly without shells. Many of them have feathery gills and bodies covered with amazingly bright, almost glowing patterns and colours. There are sea slugs in shades of orange, pink or blue, and with tufts of vividly brilliant gills on their backs. The bright colours warn predators that they should be left alone. Sea slugs taste horrible, and some even have poisonous stings on their backs.

GROUPS OF SLUGS
(continued from page 55):

Land and freshwater snails, slugs
- 20,500 species
- on land and in fresh water
- spiral or coiled shell (not in slugs)

Sea slugs
- 1,250 species
- mostly slug-like, lacking shells
- bright colours
- frilly gills

Sea slugs are also called nudibranchs. This yellow-spotted red nudibranch is from the seas around the Philippines.

SEA SNAILS AND LIMPETS

MANY KINDS OF SNAILS LIVE IN THE OCEANS. In fact, there are more than twice as many sea-living snail species as there are land and freshwater species combined. These sea snails include whelks, limpets, top shells, winkles (periwinkles), cowries, cone shells and many others, especially in tropical seas. All of these have a one-piece, usually coiled, shell, and are gastropods (page 56). Also included in this large group are the sea hares, which look more like a combination of a slug with a hare's long ears.

Slipper limpets tend to attach themselves to their own kind. They also change sex with age. The oldest, near the base of the pile, are females. The uppermost are males.

Cowrie shells have been used as trinkets since prehistoric times. They may have been an early form of money.

There are about 55,000 kinds of sea snails. Many land snails are drab grey or brown, but many sea snails are stunningly colourful, although their brightness fades after death. Some sea snails live along the coast, in the rock pools and shallows. Others live on the very deepest ocean floor in pitch darkness. Land snails have lungs to breathe air. Sea snails have gills to breathe in water, like fish.

Marbled cone shell

The chocolate-lined top shell is one of many top shells with very fine lines on the shell.

LIMPETS AND ABALONES

When the tide goes out, limpets can be seen clinging to rocks or other surfaces, where they graze on seaweeds. The limpet's soft body is completely protected from predators such as birds and fish by its hard, cone-shaped shell, which it pulls down tight onto the rock. The muscular foot clamps down hard, with such force that it is very difficult to pull a limpet from its resting place. When the tide comes in again, the limpet lifts its shell slightly and slides over the rocks, searching for seaweeds.

The common spider conch from the Indian and Pacific region has long shell projections like the legs of a spider.

It scrapes and pulls these into its mouth with its toothed tongue. When the tide begins to fall, the limpet returns to its "home base" on the rock.

ABALONES

Abalones are like big limpets. They live among beds of kelp seaweed in South Africa and California, and grow up to 20 cm across. They are a great seafood delicacy, not only with people, but also with many animals, including sea otters, seabirds, seals and sea lions.

Green sea hare

WINKLES AND WHELKS

Winkles or periwinkles are among the commonest of the sea snails, visible on seashores all over the world. When a winkle retreats inside its shell, it closes the "door" – a plate called the operculum.

Whelks are larger than winkles, with a sturdy, spiral shell that can grow up to 10 cm long. A whelk is a carnivore. Its sharp-toothed tongue or radula is on a flexible stalk, the proboscis. The whelk uses this to probe and rub its way through the shell of a victim, such as an oyster or mussel, to get at the flesh.

MORE TYPES OF SNAILS (continued from page 55):

- Top shells, turban shells, limpets, violet sea snails, winkles, spire shells, conches, necklace shells, moon shells, whelks, oysters drills, turret shells, cone shells, augers

Whelks are also known for their egg cases. These are the spongy, papery objects found washed up on the beach, and sometimes called seawash balls. Each compartment is an egg about 1 cm across. The female glues the eggs into a fist-sized mass as she lays them in shallow water. The first young to hatch feed on the others!

SEA HARES

These odd creatures look like land slugs with large "ears". But like sea slugs, they have feathery gills, and bright patterns and colours. Like their namesakes on land, they graze on plants. If in danger, they release a coloured substance or dye into the water.

Limpets cling tightly to rocks at low tide.

DEADLY!

Cone shells in the Indian and Pacific Oceans have radula teeth which are like tiny, hard "darts". These are fired like miniature harpoons at the prey. The dart injects an incredibly powerful venom that can kill a fish – or even a human.

The dog whelk eats other molluscs, such as mussels, especially when they are dead. It uses its sensitive breathing tube or siphon to detect the smell of rotting flesh in the water.

SEASHELLS

THE VARIETY OF SHAPES AND COLOURS IN SEASHELLS FROM AROUND THE WORLD IS AMAZING, MAKING THESE SOME OF NATURE'S MOST BEAUTIFUL AND INTRICATE OBJECTS. Most seashells are the hard homes made by various kinds of molluscs (mainly sea snails) when they were alive. After the sea snail has died, all that remains is its shell, and this may get washed up on the beach. But most shells are fairly brittle, and get broken by the action of the waves. Even on a beach, wind, waves, rain and sand gradually crack and wear the shells into fragments. Finally they are ground up and the chalky minerals are recycled.

The abalone or ear shell is valued for its pearly lining and as a food.

World Watch

Should people collect seashells? Taking one or two that have been washed up on the beach may seem to do no harm, since the original animals have passed away. But collecting the living animals for their shells is having devastating effects on many species. Abalones are some of the many molluscs that have been over-collected in certain parts of the world. The very survival of this beautiful creature is threatened.

Strawberry topshell

Some shells, such as scallops, cockles, mussels, oysters and razorshells, belong to bivalved molluscs. In life, these shell parts are joined in pairs, at a hinge, but they often get washed up as single items on the shore. The insides of some shells, especially those of some bivalves, are lined with mother-of-pearl. This is a smooth, shiny substance that shines with a pearly sheen.

TOWER SHELLS

Tower shells are long, tapering spirals. A common species on the European coast is the auger shell, which can grow to 5 cm in length.

TOP SHELLS

Some of the most colourful sea snail shells are top shells. European top shells are quite small, from about 2.5 cm in height. But many are patterned with glorious streaks or zigzag markings.

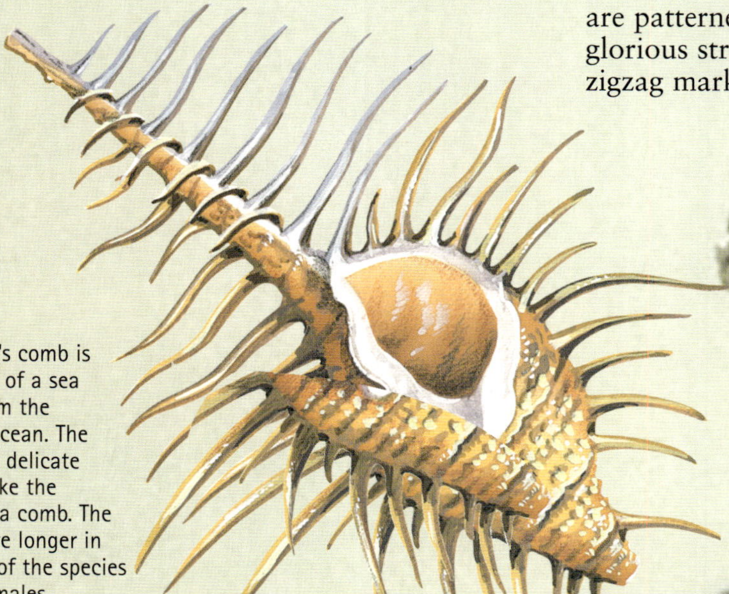

Venus's comb is the shell of a sea snail from the Pacific Ocean. The shell has delicate spines, like the teeth of a comb. The spines are longer in females of the species than in males.

Their coloured backgrounds may be cream, orange, red or grey-green, depending on the species. Some tropical top shells are much larger, reaching well over 15 cm in height, and are even more colourful in bright hues of red and pink or vivid green and blue.

Lampshell shells look like bivalve molluscs, but belong to a different animal group, the brachiopods.

COWRIES

Cowries have perhaps been prized for longer than any other seashells. Cowrie necklaces have been found in the tombs of Ancient Egypt.

The largest and most impressive cowries live in the warm seas of the tropics. The tiger cowrie of the Indian and Pacific Oceans, for example, grows to 10 cm or longer. Its shell is beautifully blotched in orange or brown on a cream background. Cowries are smaller and much less common in temperate regions such as northern Atlantic shores. The spotted cowrie shell can sometimes be found on sandy beaches.

CONCHES

The conches are some of the largest of all sea snails. In North America, a "conch" is usually a queen conch, common off the coast of Florida. Queen conches are valued not only for their shells but also as seafood and fish bait.

Spider conch shell

Conch shells are among the most prized of all shells with collectors, because of their delicate patterns and colours and their glossy sheen.

Screw shell

Harp shells have intricate ridges, grooves and stripes.

Like other seashells, they may be burned to make lime minerals, or ground up to make porcelain. Sadly, queen conches have been collected in such numbers that they have become quite scarce.

The largest sea snail shell is that of the trumpet conch of Australia, which can be over 75 cm long and 90 cm across the spines. The smallest seashells are almost microscopic, even when the animal is fully grown.

BIVALVE MOLLUSCS

The breathing tubes or siphons of a giant clam are cone shaped.

BIVALVE MEANS "WITH TWO VALVES". Bivalve molluscs have a shell in two halves, called valves. The valves are usually joined together by a flexible hinge, so that in most species, the animal can open and shut them rather like a small suitcase. The soft, fleshy body of the bivalve mollusc is inside, protected by the hard shell, which few predators can lever or crack open. Most of the creatures we call "shellfish" belong to this group. They are shelled, but are not fish! They are well known because they are eaten as seafood. Examples are cockles, mussels, oysters, scallops and clams.

The file shell's tentacles filter food from the water.

Most bivalve molluscs cannot move around easily, and some are stuck to their rocks. So they let the water bring food to them, by filtering out edible particles. The water is sucked into the body through a tube called a siphon. Inside, food is filtered by the comb-like or feathery gills, which also take in oxygen. The water leaves through another siphon.

BIVALVES GALORE

Cockles have pale, rather rounded shells, with furrows radiating outwards. They live in sand and mud on the lower shore, using the muscular foot to burrow down below the surface. Mussels stick themselves to rocks and breakwaters (groynes) with strong threads called byssus threads. This means they are not rolled around and damaged by the waves. At low tide they are exposed to the air, but they keep their shells tightly shut and are soon covered again as the tide returns. Oysters have grey shells, which are irregular and flaky or scaly. They are highly prized as seafood in many parts of the world. They are farmed on boards or fences in some estuaries, so that natural populations can be left alone.

Scallops can swim away from danger by quickly opening and closing their shells, and squirting out water. The tiny dots around the mantle are eyes.

BORING INTO WOOD AND ROCK

Some bivalves use their hard shells to make holes, even drilling into wood or soft rock. Piddocks and shipworms have shells with rough surfaces, which they use to rub and grind away at rock or wood. Eventually, the mollusc has dug a small burrow for itself, where it can live unmolested by predators. A colony of shipworms (left) can cause great damage to wooden boats and breakwaters.

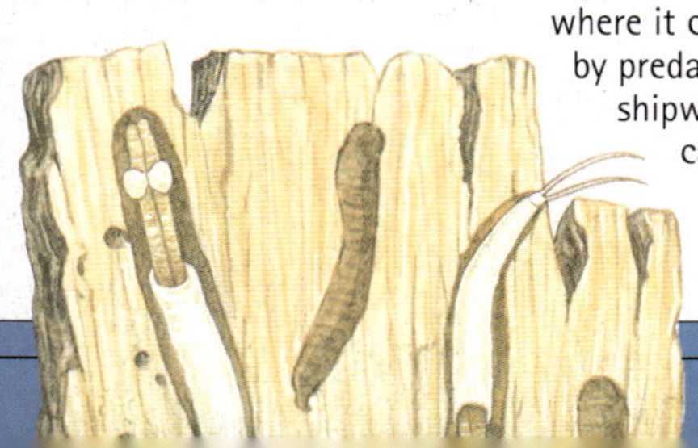

Scallops are among the few bivalves that can move fast. They swim by flapping the two valves of the shell open and shut. As in many bivalves, the mantle forms a fleshy covering to the edges of the valves. It may have waving tentacles and tiny eyes.

Razor or pod shells often turn up on the beach. They are named after the old-fashioned barber's "cut-throat" razor, because of their narrow, rectangular shape, up to 20 cm long. They burrow into the lower shore.

The cockscomb oyster is a red oyster that looks like a cockerel's comb.

FRESHWATER BIVALVES

Although most bivalves live in the sea, some have adapted to life in fresh water, mostly in rivers or lakes. One of the largest is the swan mussel, which can grow to more than 20 cm long. It is common in muddy lakes or slow rivers. The pearl mussel is another large species, and is famous for its pearls. Pearl mussels prefer large, fast, sandy rivers, with soft water.

The pea mussel really is the size of a pea, and is very common in rivers. Most bivalves are either male or female, and breed by casting their eggs and sperm into the water, to mix and develop. Pea mussels are hermaphrodite (both male and female). The tiny young develop inside the mother-father, and are born fully formed.

WHAT ARE PEARLS?

In oysters and many other molluscs, the fleshy, shell-forming mantle makes a special substance called nacre, which lines the inside of the shell. It forms a smooth, white, mother-of-pearl lining called the nacreous layer. A foreign substance, such as a bit of grit or a tiny parasite, may enter the shell. If the mollusc cannot get rid of it, it is gradually covered in nacre. This builds up in thin layers until the grit is completely wrapped in a ball of shiny white nacre – a pearl. The finest pearls come from pinctada pearl oysters, which live in the Pacific Ocean. The world's largest pearl came out of a giant clam. It was 12 cm across.

OPEN WIDE!

Some animals are able to break into the hard shells of bivalve molluscs. Birds such as the oystercatcher have hard, chisel-like beaks to lever open mussel and oyster shells. A big lobster may be able to use its larger, crushing pincer to crack the shell. The walrus opens the shell with its tusk.

LARGEST...!

The giant clam, tridacna, lives in the Pacific Ocean. It is the world's largest bivalve. Its shells can be over 120 cm in length and it weighs as much as 330 kg.

The razor shell (razor clam) uses its muscular foot to burrow into the seabed. It pushes the foot, like a pink finger, down into mud. The foot tip swells to anchor itself, then the razor shell shortens the rest of the foot to drag itself and its narrow shell deeper.

Like all bivalves, giant clams usually stay open to feed–clamping shut when danger threatens.

ANOTHER GROUP OF MOLLUSCS:

Bivalves
- 20,000 species
- most are marine, some freshwater
- hinged shell of two parts, called valves
- finger-like foot
- most burrow, or live attached to rocks

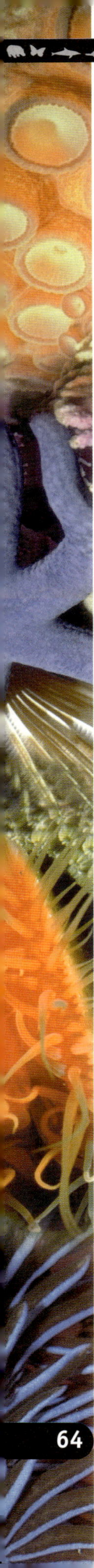

SQUID, OCTOPUSES AND CUTTLEFISH

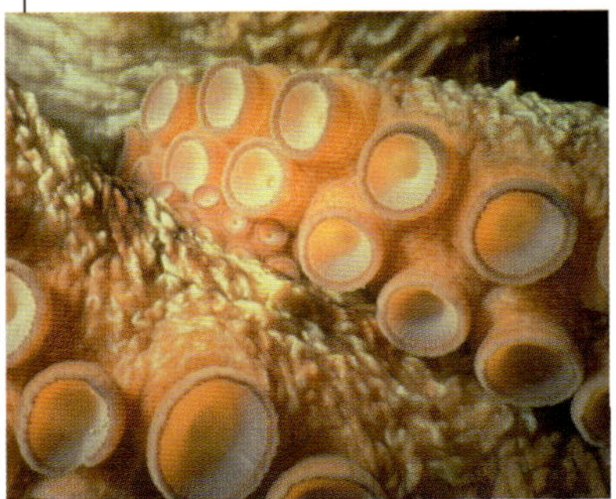

Octopus tentacles are covered in suckers, which they use to hold their prey and to move over the rocks.

THE MOST FASCINATING OF ALL MOLLUSCS ARE SQUID AND OCTOPUSES. They are called cephalopods, a name that means "head-footed", because their molluscan foot is at the head end and has lots of long tentacles. They have the typical mollusc's soft body, but only the squid has a shell, which is small and rod-shaped, and inside the body. These creatures are fierce predators. Squid swim very fast, and octopuses hide away in caves and holes in the rocks. Squid and octopuses can squirt out an ink-like liquid if they are attacked. This makes the water cloudy, allowing the mollusc to escape to safety.

The pearly nautilus may s t on a rock to rest (top), or float slowly in mid water with its tentacles pulled in (above).

The paper nautilus or argonaut looks like the pearly nautilus, but it is really a type of octopus. The female makes a thin, papery shell to shelter herself and her eggs, and sometimes her much smaller male partner.

Squid are narrow and streamlined, with flap-like fins at one end to keep them steady in the water. They have large eyes and good vision, to track their prey in the ocean. To catch food, they use a long pair of tentacles, which have adhesive suckers at the end. They have eight shorter tentacles too, also with suckers. Squid move slowly by rippling their fins, or dart suddenly using a kind of jet-propulsion, squirting water rapidly out of the siphon (breathing tube).

Some kinds of squid can produce lights inside their bodies. They have special body parts to create the light, and some can even direct the light like a torch. This is very useful in the dark depths of the sea.

CUTTLEFISH

Cuttlefish are like small, flattened squid, with a fin running around all sides of the body. Even more than squid, they are the chameleons of the sea, able to change colour and pattern in a split second.

LARGEST... !

The giant squid of the ocean depths is the largest mollusc, and also the largest animal without a backbone. It reaches a maximum length of about 17 m from the tip of its outstretched tentacles to its tail end. Its eyes are the largest in the animal kingdom, at more than 40 cm across. The smallest squid are only about 1 cm long.

A cuttlefish holds its tentacles together for streamlining as it swims.

The skin of a cuttlefish is patterned with tiny spots of different colours – yellow, red, brown and black. The animal can control the size of these by muscles, and make many different shades by mixing the amounts of each colour.

The blue-ringed octopus of the Indian and Pacific region is only small, but has a very poisonous bite. The rings on its body glow bright blue if it is threatened.

OCTOPUSES

An octopus has a sack-like body, large eyes, and eight long tentacles used for catching prey. Like other cephalopods, its beak-like mouth is hidden in the middle of the ring of tentacles, where they join the body. Octopuses have complicated behaviour and are often said to be the most intelligent invertebrates. They can recognize different shapes, choosing the correct one to obtain food. They can also remember simple tasks, such as how to open a food box.

The common octopus of the Atlantic varies in size, but can reach about 90 cm in body length, with a tentacle spread of 3 m. Octopuses are rarely seen. They spend most of the day holed up in crevices in the rocks. They come out mainly at night, to hunt for other molluscs, crabs and similar prey. They also scavenge for dead meat.

THE NAUTILUS

Only one kind of cephalopod has a proper external shell like other molluscs. This is the nautilus, which has a shiny shell curled over its body. It swims along the sea bed, using its 35 or so tentacles to find prey. Unlike its cousins, it cannot squirt ink to hide and escape danger.

CEPHALOPOD MOLLUSCS

Octopuses, squid and cuttlefish
- 650 species
- marine
- streamlined shape (squid and cuttlefish)
- ten tentacles in squid and cuttlefish, eight in octopus

Nautiluses
- 6 species
- marine
- large spiral shell
- many tentacles

STARFISH AND SEASTARS

Sun star

STARFISH AND THEIR RELATIVES ARE CALLED ECHINODERMS. This means "hedgehog skin", and many of them are indeed very spiny. These creatures are numerous and widespread, but they all live in the sea, so many are unfamiliar. They have a body built around a radial plan, like the spokes of a wheel, rather than the bilateral or two-sided bodies of other animals. They also have tiny, flexible tube feet that end in suckers, for walking and feeding. As well as starfish, this group includes feather stars, sea lilies, sea urchins and sea cucumbers.

Sea lily (crinoid)

Most groups of sea animals have a few species adapted to life in fresh water or even dry land. Echinoderms do not. These creatures are quite large, and many are brightly coloured and easy to see, especially as they are slow-moving.

MANY ARMS

Many species of starfish have five arms, but some have seven, and others as many as 14. The upper side of the body usually has small, hard plates or spines embedded in the skin, for protection. Underneath, each arm has rows of tiny tube feet, like miniature sucker-ended fingers. The arms bend so that the starfish can glide across the sea bed.

Starfish are flat, and have arms that spread out from the centre in a star-like pattern.

ARMED!

If a starfish is damaged and loses part of an arm, it can re-grow the missing piece again. The new part is often slightly smaller. Sometimes it branches into two, giving a six-armed starfish!

POISONOUS CORAL-EATER

The crown-of-thorns starfish eats small coral animals called polyps. Sometimes these starfish gather in such large numbers that they eat away an entire coral reef. They are covered with sharp, poisonous spines as defence.

The Pacific blue star has five arms. Like its relatives, it is a slow-motion but very effective predator.

Starfish are very strong and can prise open the shells of clams and other bivalve molluscs. When attacking its victim, the starfish arches over it and clamps a couple of arms onto each side. It then pulls with great strength and stamina. As the two parts of the mollusc's shell begin to gape, the starfish turns its stomach inside out, through its mouth and into the gap in the shell. It then begins to digest the prey's flesh. Eventually, the shell opens wide and the starfish completes its meal.

SOME TYPES OF STARFISH

Common starfish are indeed common. They sometimes gather in huge numbers over about 2.5 square kilometres of sea bed, moving slowly as they feed on bivalves and other molluscs, worms, crabs and also other echinoderms. These vast marauding columns of starfish leave a trail of dead and dying sea bed animals in their wake.

Starfish look harmless, but they are all predators.

The sand star lives on fine sand, where it often lurks, half buried. It has a beautiful star shape, and its five arms are edged with spines. The common sun star is bright red, with as many as 14 short arms, spreading out sun-like from its large central disc. Its prey includes the common starfish.

WRITHING ARMS

The brittlestar (shown on page 20) is indeed brittle. Parts of its long, delicate arms often break off. The five arms spread out from a small central disc, and can loop back on themselves as the creature writhes speedily across the sea bed.

Most brittlestars live below the tide zone, in deeper water. They can sometimes be found piled up in huge heaps, with 1,000 individuals on just a few square metres of the sea bed. Most brittlestars feed by gathering up small edible items from the mud, or by filtering them from the water. The common brittlestar of the Atlantic and Mediterranean regions is a filter-feeder. It lives in dense colonies, with each animal waving its spiny arms to catch anything edible that may float past.

FEATHERY ARMS

Feather stars are similar to starfish and have feathery arms, used for both feeding and swimming. Many have ten arms, but some species may have almost 200! Feather stars grasp onto rocks or seaweeds and can also creep about. They feed by waving their arms in the water to filter out edible particles.

LILIES IN THE SEA

Sea lilies are close relatives of feather stars and feed in a similar way. Each animal is attached by a stalk to the sea bed, usually deep in the ocean. The stalk may be more than 90 cm long. They look like flowers on stalks, hence their name.

This starfish is humped over its prey, dissolving and absorbing its flesh.

ECHINODERMS

- 6,250 species
- live in the sea
- five-rayed (spoked) body plan
- inner skeleton, often spiny
- tiny tube-like feet

Three of the main groups:

Starfish
- 1,500 species
- flat and star-shaped
- usually five arms (sometimes more)

Brittlestars
- 2,000 species
- flat and star-shaped
- usually five arms (sometimes six, or branched)
- arms long and brittle

Feather stars and sea lilies
- 625 species (mostly feather stars)
- either swimming (feather stars) or stalked (sea lilies)
- feed by filtering seawater

SEA URCHINS AND SEA CUCUMBERS

Sand dollars take their name from their resemblance to coins, being round and flat or disc-shaped. They move around just below the surface of the sand.

SEA URCHINS, SAND DOLLARS AND SEA CUCUMBERS ARE ECHINODERMS, LIKE STARFISH (PAGE 66). They have the same echinoderm feature of tiny tube feet, and many species bristle with spines. These are for protection, but sea urchins also tilt their spines to move along, as if on stilts. Some types of urchins have poison-tipped spines.

These sea squirts are barrel-shaped, with jelly-like bodies. They feed by filtering tiny creatures from the water as it flows through them. Other types are shaped like tiny tadpoles and live inside a "house" that they build from jelly-like material.

Sea urchins and sand dollars have rounded bodies, either ball-shaped, or flattened. The scientific name for their group is the echinoids, which means "hedgehog-like". It refers to the spiny covering of many species. Echinoids, like starfish, have a five-rayed body plan. But the arms are curled up and over and joined at the top to make the ball-like body. Urchins use their spines to lever themselves along slowly, and they can also climb by using their very long and flexible tube feet.

Sea urchins feed by grazing on seaweeds and small animals, such as moss-animals, that grow on the surfaces of underwater rocks. Some urchins, known as heart urchins, have a more streamlined and almost heart-like shape. This helps them to burrow beneath the sand. One type is known as the sea potato. Its brownish, potato-shaped empty shell, known as a test, is sometimes washed up on beaches.

SEA CUCUMBERS

Sea cucumbers are named after their warty, sausage-shaped bodies, which look similar to a cucumber. Unlike most other echinoderms, sea cucumbers have soft bodies, although the skin is tough and leathery. The mouth is surrounded by tentacles, which can be pulled back inside the animal. Sea cucumbers have three rows of tube feet and crawl slowly along the sea bed.

When disturbed or attacked, some sea cucumbers can shoot out parts of their insides, including their stomach and intestine. This sticky mass entangles and puts off most predators, even lobsters. The sea cucumber then re-grows the missing parts.

SQUIRTS IN THE SEA

Sea squirts are not echinoderms, but members of a group called the tunicates. They resemble blobs of jelly, and live stuck to rocks or seaweeds along the tide zone and in the shallows. They are called sea squirts because, when the tide has gone out to leave them exposed on the shore, they sometimes squirt out jets of water.

The rosy feather star (near right) waves its filter-feeding arms to catch tiny bits of food. The sea potato or sand urchin (on the sand) is a hairy-looking urchin that lives in a burrow under the beach. Lancelets (below) are long, pale creatures that filter-feed in sea bed sand and gravel.

Sea squirts or tunicates have very special features. These include a main nerve or nerve-cord, and a stiff tube called a notochord—a very simple version of our own backbone.

▲ The largest kind of sea cucumber, the stichopus sea cucumber, lives in seas around the Philippines. It can grow more than 90 cm long and nearly 15 cm wide.

These creatures may bridge the gap between the two great groups of animals, the invertebrates (animals without backbones) and the vertebrates. A sea squirt larva looks like a tadpole and has a very simple rod-like version of the backbone, called a notochord, inside its body. But this breaks down as the larva grows into an adult.

Lancelets are fish-like creatures that also possess a notochord. However, unlike fish, they have no proper backbone, jaws, eyes or fins. They live half-buried in sand or gravel, filtering food from the water. Lancelets grow to about 10 cm long, and can swim weakly if they need to escape from a predator. They live in shallow water, in temperate and tropical seas.

MORE ECHINODERMS
(continued from page 67):

Sea urchins and sand dollars
- 950 species
- ball-shaped body, may be spiny
- no arms

Sea cucumbers
- 1,150 species
- body long and sausage-shaped
- no arms
- tentacles around mouth

Other sea creatures:

Tunicates *(sea squirts)*
- 1,400 species
- attached to rocks or swimming
- tadpole-like young or larvae

Lancelets
- 25 species
- small, about 10 cm
- fish-shaped body
- no eyes or fins

▼ Sessile sea squirts look like see-through bottles attached to the rocks (below). Flask-shaped planktonic sea squirts swim and drift along (below right). Some sea cucumbers have frills and flaps along the body (bottom, in the sand).

Most moths fly at night.

SECTION 3 INSECTS & OTHER ARTHROPODS

THERE ARE AT LEAST 5 MILLION DIFFERENT KINDS, OR SPECIES, OF ANIMALS. And at least 80 out of every 100 species are insects. They range from tiny gnats and fairy flies, almost too small to see, to fist-sized beetles, and moths with wings as long as your hands. Three key features of insects help to make them so successful, widespread and diverse. These are: a hard outer body casing (exoskeleton), wings for flying and six legs with flexible joints for fast running.

Other animals have a tough outer body casing and jointed limbs, too. They include eight-legged spiders and scorpions (arachnids), and multi-legged centipedes and millipedes. Most insects do not live in the sea. But another huge group of joint-limbed creatures does – crustaceans such as crabs, lobsters, prawns, shrimps and krill. Most people are not familiar with creatures of the open ocean. So they rarely see one of the world's most numerous kinds of animal – the small flea-like crustaceans known as copepods.

All of the above creatures belong to the animal group known as arthropods. This name means "jointed legs". The arthropod's body casing and limb design have allowed this group to conquer all the Earth's habitats – from high mountains, hot springs and salty lakes, to dark caves and the deepest seas.

THE WORLD OF BUGS

Social insects live in groups, often in huge nests like this termite mound. Other social insects are ants, bees and wasps.

THERE ARE PROBABLY MORE THAN TEN MILLION DIFFERENT KINDS, OR SPECIES, OF ANIMALS. Of these, possibly nine out of ten are bugs and other insects. The insects belong to a larger animal group known as the arthropods, which means "joint-limbed". The leg has rigid sections linked by flexible joints – similar to our own arms and legs. Insects and other arthropods also share another main feature – a hard outer covering to the body, called the cuticle. It forms a protective casing known as an exoskeleton, which covers the arthropod's body like a suit of armour. Ants, beetles, bugs, cockroaches, flies, fleas, bees and other insects, which all have six legs, are arthropods. So are the eight-legged arachnids such as spiders and scorpions, the multi-legged centipedes and millipedes, and crustaceans such as crabs, lobsters and shrimps. For every human being alive today, there are probably at least one million insects and other arthropods.

Dragonflies are among the biggest flying insects.

Arthropods are mostly small. But they affect people the world over. Some are harmful. Termites eat away wooden buildings and bridges. Locusts devastate vast areas of crops. Wasps annoy us with their stings, and lice with their blood-sucking bites. Poisonous spiders and scorpions can cause great pain, even death. Serious diseases are spread by some arthropods, such as malaria by mosquitoes, plague by fleas and Lyme's disease by ticks.

INSIDE AN INSECT

An insect's body is divided into three main sections – head, thorax (chest) and abdomen. Most insects have three pairs of legs and one or two pairs of wings, all attached to the thorax. (The worker ant, as shown here, lacks wings.)

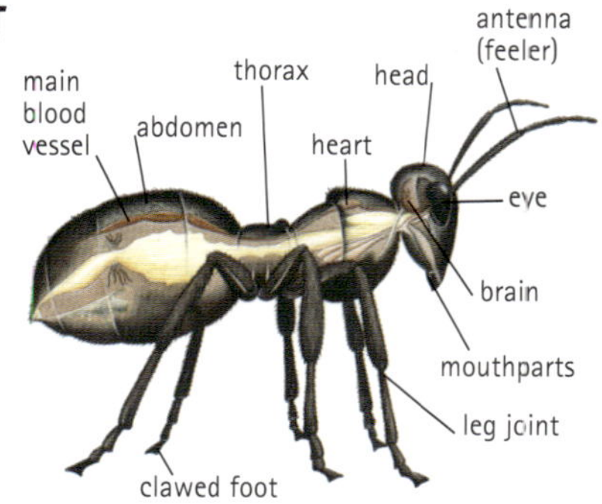

Mites are tiny arthropods related to spiders. Some live in soil. Others are parasites and suck blood from animals.

USEFUL ARTHROPODS

Some arthropods are useful to both people and plants. Bees make honey and carry pollen for flowers. Predatory insects such as lacewings eat plant pests such as aphids (which are also arthropods). Silkworms are really moth caterpillars that spin silk. Dung beetles help to recycle animal droppings. Small flies called fruit flies, drosophila, have been used as insect "guinea pigs" to unlock the secrets of how genes work.

SENSES

Most arthropods have keen senses, especially sight, smell and touch. Each eye is made of a cluster of separate units, each with its own lens. This design is called a compound eye. Arthropods cannot see as much detail as we can, but most are excellent at detecting small movements, and many insects can see different colours.

Arthropods use their feelers or antennae to smell and even "taste" the air or water around them, detecting tiny particles of scents and odours. The antennae and the tiny hair-like bristles on the body and legs can also detect the slightest touch and movements such as wind or water currents.

THE CUTICLE

An arthropod's cuticle is like a thick, stiff outermost layer of the skin. It forms a rigid casing, the exoskeleton, to support the soft inner parts of the body.

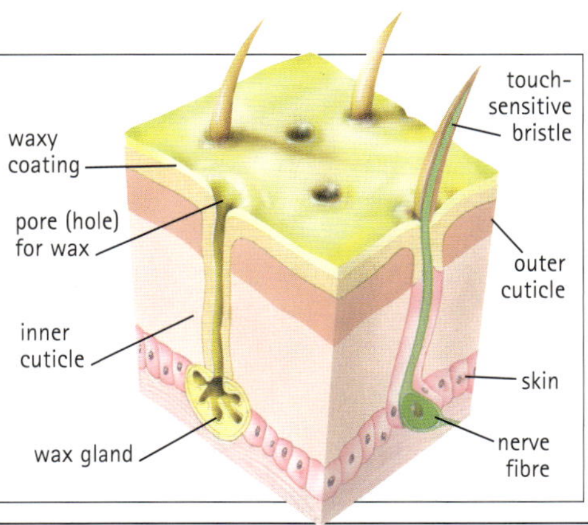

Grasshoppers and crickets have powerful chewing "jaws". In most insects these move from side to side rather than up and down.

WHERE INSECTS LIVE

Insects are found in almost every corner of the Earth, on land and in the air—in forests and grasslands, deserts, marshes and wetlands, streams and lakes, even high on mountains and glaciers, and deep in pitch-dark caves. Our parks and gardens, and even our houses, also buzz and crawl with insects. They include houseflies and ants, fleas on pets, and silverfish in dark cupboards. Insects have not colonized the sea itself, although they live on coastal land.

OTHER ARTHROPOD HABITATS

Spiders, scorpions, centipedes and millipedes thrive mainly in warmer countries, especially among the dead leaves of the tropical forest floor and high above among the tree leaves. Most crustaceans, from tiny copepods to huge crabs and lobsters, live in the sea. Some, like crayfish and water fleas, dwell in fresh water. A few, like woodlice, can survive in damp places on land.

Insects
- more than one million species
- body divided into three main parts
- three pairs of legs
- most have two pairs of wings
- live on land and in fresh water

Crustaceans
- 43,000 species
- body divided into three main parts
- many have a hard, shell-like casing
- several pairs of legs
- two pairs of feelers
- most live in the sea

King Crabs
- 5 species
- heavy, rounded outer shell
- long tail spine
- large eyes
- live in the sea

Arachnids
- 80,000 species
- body divided into two main parts
- four pairs of legs
- jaws with fangs
- most are land-living

Centipedes
- 3,000 species
- body long and flattened
- one pair of legs per body segment
- long feelers
- jaws with fangs
- run fast
- live on land

Millipedes
- 10,000 species
- body long and rounded
- two pairs of legs per body segment
- short feelers
- walk slowly
- live on land

AN ARTHROPOD'S COVERING

The arthropod's body is covered by the cuticle, which is thin and light, yet strong and tough. It is made mainly from a substance called chitin. In land arthropods such as insects, the cuticle has a waxy, waterproof covering. In order to grow, an arthropod must shed its cuticle, and grow a new, bigger one underneath. This process is known as moulting or ecdysis.

BEETLES AND WEEVILS

BEETLES AND THEIR SMALLER COUSINS, WEEVILS, MAKE UP THE LARGEST SUB-GROUP OF INSECTS. They are called the Coleoptera. There are almost half a million known kinds, or species, of coleopterans, making up about one third of all animal species. And hundreds of new species are found each year. Most insects have two pairs of wings, but in beetles the front two have become hard and strong, like a shield over the top of the body. They are called wing cases, or elytra. The wing cases form a protective covering for the delicate second pair of wings. These are folded under the wing cases when the beetle is at rest. As it takes off, the beetle lifts the hard wing cases and then unfurls its thin wings, which it flaps to fly away. Beetles are the most widespread of all insects. They live in almost every habitat and region of our planet except the sea. Some are almost microscopic, others are nearly as big as a fist.

The great diving beetle must come to the surface every few minutes to gather air to breathe. It has strong mouthparts and can bite hard.

STRONGEST... !

The strongest insect is the rhinoceros beetle, also called the hercules beetle. It can lift and support more than 800 times its own weight.

A typical weevil has a long trunk-like snout. Some weevils are pests, eating wheat and flour, or crops such as apples, carrots, nuts and clover.

Beetles are not only incredibly numerous, they are also extremely varied. The familiar red spotted ladybirds that we see in parks and gardens are brightly coloured to warn other animals that they taste horrible. Predators such as birds soon learn to avoid these small beetles.

Tiger and ground beetles are active hunters, with large eyes for seeing prey and long legs for racing after it. One kind of green ground beetle, the bombardier, can squirt a spray of stinging chemicals from its rear end at an attacker.

Green tiger beetles are truly the tigers of the insect world. They stalk and then rush after victims, killing them with a bite from the strong, fang-like jaws.

WEEVILS

Weevils form the largest sub-group of beetles, with more than 60,000 species. They feed on seeds, fruits and flowers. A weevil has a long, curved snout (called the rostrum), which looks like a tiny elephant's trunk.

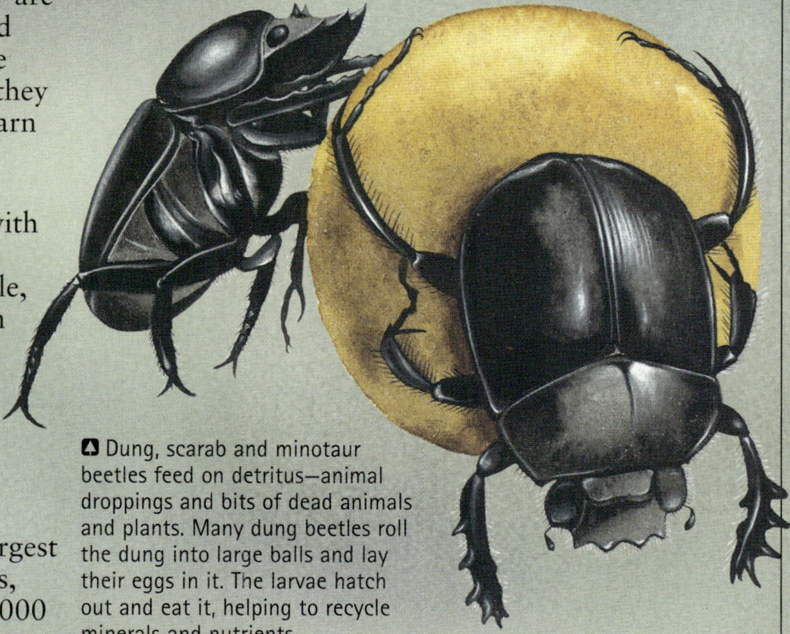

Dung, scarab and minotaur beetles feed on detritus—animal droppings and bits of dead animals and plants. Many dung beetles roll the dung into large balls and lay their eggs in it. The larvae hatch out and eat it, helping to recycle minerals and nutrients.

NIGHT LIGHTS

On hot summer nights, flashes of pale green or yellow light can sometimes be seen among trees, or on the forest floor. These are fireflies and glow worms. They are not flies or worms, but kinds of beetle. Fireflies flash to attract each other in the mating season. Their wormlike larvae also give off light, to warn predators such as shrews that they have a nasty taste and should be left alone.

Old beams and other wooden objects often have round holes we call woodworm. These are the work of the furniture beetle. The adult beetles lay their eggs on wood (trees or furniture). When the larvae hatch from the eggs, they tunnel into the wood, feeding on it as they go. These larvae change into adults, which eat their way out and fly away.

Female fireflies and glow worms have no wings and small wing cases, showing the segmented main body or abdomen underneath. The males are much smaller and fly to the females.

The surface of the wood is marked with their small, round flight holes, and inside is a network of tunnels and powdered wood. The larvae of longhorn and deathwatch beetles also tunnel through wood, eating and weakening it as they go.

NATURE'S UNDERTAKERS

Sexton or burying beetles are the undertakers of the natural world. They have a keen sense of smell and are attracted to rotting bodies, such as dead birds or small mammals such as mice and rats. First the beetles mate, then they set to work to bury the corpse, by digging out the soil beneath it. They then lay their eggs in a chamber dug into the soil next to the body. When the larvae hatch, they feed on the decaying flesh of the corpse.

HEAVIEST... !

The heaviest insect is a kind of beetle, the goliath beetle of Africa. It can weigh up to 108 g, which is almost as heavy as two ordinary hen's eggs.

WATER BEETLES

Some beetles live in fresh water. Diving beetles use their hairy legs as oars to row themselves through the water. The larva of the great diving beetle is a fierce predator, catching tadpoles and small fish with its sharp, curved jaws. Whirligig beetles swirl about like tiny wind-up toys on the surface of a pond. Each eye is divided into two parts. One part looks up into the air, the other down into the water.

Beetles and weevils
(Coleoptera)
- almost 500,000 species
- front wings are hard wing cases
- biting mouthparts to eat small animals or plant food
- most are active, fast runners

BUTTERFLIES AND MOTHS

AFTER THE BEETLES, THE SECOND LARGEST SUB-GROUP OF INSECTS IS THE BUTTERFLIES AND MOTHS, WITH ABOUT 175,000 SPECIES. They live wherever there are trees and flowers, being most numerous in tropical parts of the world. They are known as Lepidoptera, a name that means "scaly winged", because their large, papery wings are covered with tiny scales. The bright patterns on the wings are made by different colours and patterns of scales, like a living mosaic. There are a number of differences between moths and butterflies. Most moths are active at night; butterflies usually fly by day. Most moths are dull browns and greys; many butterflies are brightly coloured. Most moths have feathery feelers (antennae); butterflies have thin, club-ended feelers.

The peacock butterfly has large patches on its wings that look like eyes and are called "eye spots". When the butterfly is in danger, it opens its wings to reveal the eyes, which frighten away predators.

Clearwings are day-flying moths. They look more like butterflies, with their bright colours and slim bodies.

Blue morpho butterfly

Butterflies and moths are insects which go through a drastic change in body shape as they grow up. This is called complete metamorphosis. The life cycle begins when an adult male and female mate, often flitting about in a courtship flight. The female usually lays her eggs on the food plant – the plant that the caterpillars will eat when they hatch. She places them carefully, either in groups or singly, on the undersides of leaves. For the brimstone butterfly (see the box, opposite), the caterpillars' food plant is buckthorn. In fact, caterpillars do little else except eat. After growing and moulting its skin several times, each caterpillar changes into an inactive, hard-cased chrysalis. This seems to rest for a few weeks, or even through the winter.

A butterfly or moth, like this large white butterfly, has a long, tube-shaped mouth. This is normally coiled up under the head. To sip nectar from deep in a flower the butterfly straightens its mouth and uses it like a drinking straw to sip up the sugary fluid.

World Watch

During the 19th century, butterfly and moth collecting became a popular hobby. Millions of brightly coloured specimens were killed, dried and put on display in glass cases. This made some species of butterflies and moths extremely rare. Many are now protected by law. But illegal collecting continues in some places, especially tropical regions. The large, bright butterflies are sold to collectors and tourists.

▶ Moths usually have hairy, plump bodies. The feathery antennae of a male moth can pick up the female's scent from more than 1 km away.

The outside of the chrysalis doesn't appear to change, but inside the body breaks up into a kind of thick, living soup. This re-forms into the wings, legs, feelers and other parts of an adult butterfly or moth. The adult emerges from the chrysalis case and flies away to search for its own food, usually the sweet, sugary fluid called nectar in flowers.

Some butterflies and moths migrate long distances as adults, to avoid dry or cold seasons and find more sheltered places. In North America, monarch or milkweed butterflies fly south in late summer from Canada to Mexico. This journey of more than 3,200 km can take up to four months. In southeast Australia, bogong moths shelter in caves in the cool uplands during the hot, dry summer, and return to the lowlands to breed in the autumn.

LARGEST... !

The giant agrippa moth has the biggest wingspan of any insect, up to 30 cm from tip to tip. The birdwing butterfly of New Guinea is second. Its wingspan is about 28 cm.

Butterflies and moths
(Lepidoptera)
- 175,000 species
- adults have four wings, often colourful
- adult has long, tubular mouth
- most feed on flowers
- larvae are leaf-eating caterpillars

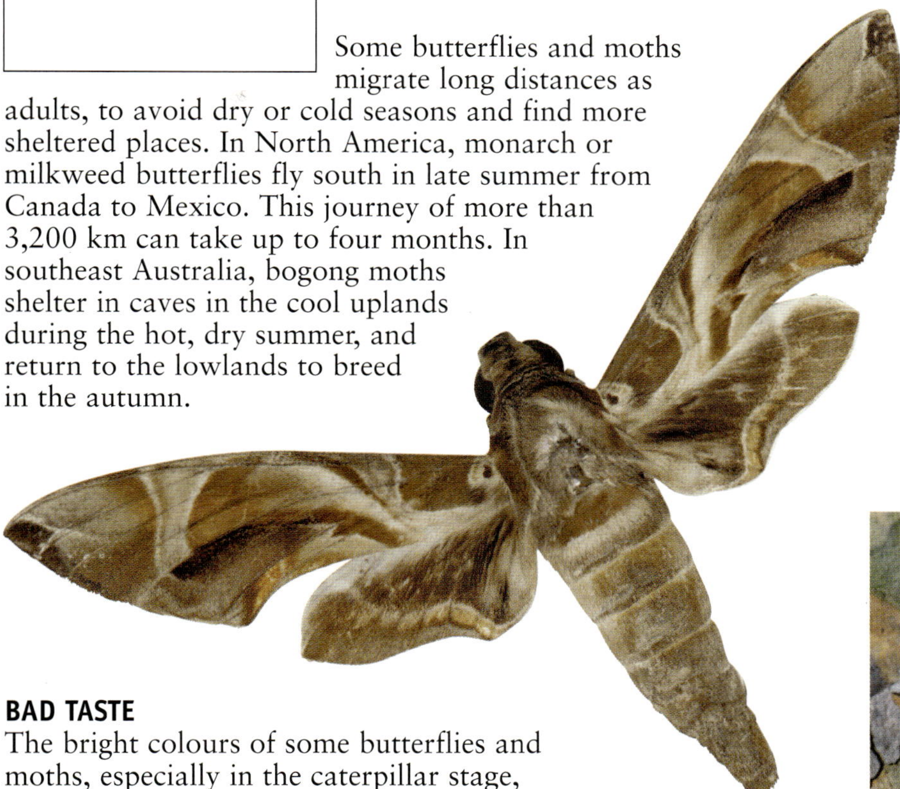

▲ Moths usually hold their wings out sideways at rest.

▲ The hawkmoths, like this elephant hawkmoth, are fast and powerful flyers with narrow, V-shaped wings.

BAD TASTE

The bright colours of some butterflies and moths, especially in the caterpillar stage, warn animals who might try to eat them that they taste horrible. Others are brightly coloured to attract mates.

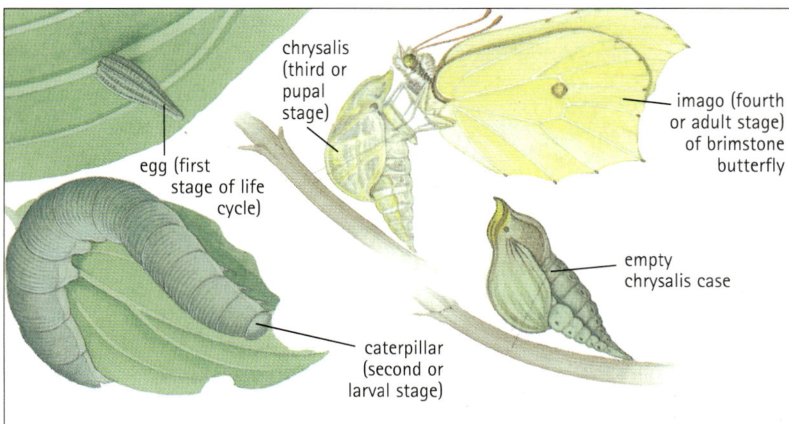

THE LIFE CYCLE OF A BUTTERFLY

When a young butterfly or moth hatches from its egg, like this brimstone, it is a long, worm-shaped creature called a caterpillar, grub or larva. This crawls, eats and grows, moults its skin, eats and grows again, and so on, moulting perhaps seven times. Then it sheds its last skin, forms a hard case around itself and becomes an inactive chrysalis or pupa. Inside this case the creature's body undergoes amazing changes. Finally the adult butterfly emerges from the case, stretches its crumpled wings and flies away. These changes in body shape while growing up are called complete metamorphosis.

BEES, WASPS AND ANTS

BEES, WASPS AND ANTS MAKE UP THE THIRD LARGEST SUB-GROUP OF INSECTS. They are known as Hymenopterans. They include the familiar honeybees and bumblebees, as well as carpenter bees, many kinds of wasps and hornets with their dangerous stings, black and red ants, and army ants, which march through tropical forests in columns. They also include more than 100,000 species of tiny parasitic wasps that live on and in plants or other animals.

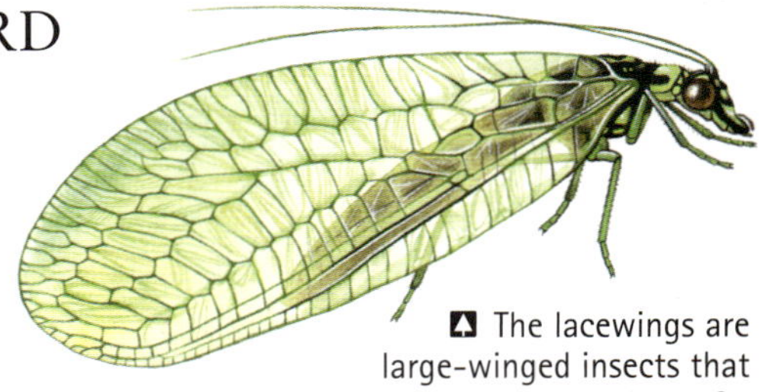

▲ The lacewings are large-winged insects that prey on smaller, soft-bodied bugs such as aphids.

Ants, wasps and bees are the main kinds of social insects. They live together in colonies or nests, helping each other by doing different tasks such as fetching and distributing food, cleaning, or defending the colony from attack. Some bumblebees live in colonies of only a few individuals, perhaps four or five. A typical wasps' nest numbers 2,000 individuals. A honeybees' nest or hive has up to 50,000 members.

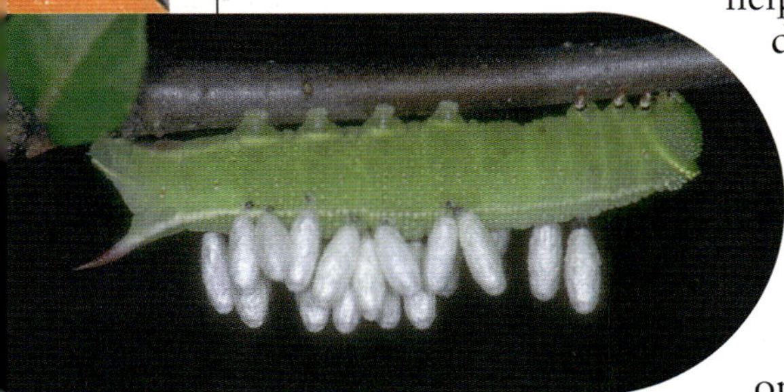

▲ This sphinx moth caterpillar is host to maggot-like parasitic wasp larvae, which will eat it alive.

Driver ants and army ants have no permanent nests. They march through the forest in columns half a million strong, killing and eating anything in their path and setting up a bivouac camp for their overnight stop.

▼ Ants follow an invisible trail of scent, or pheromone, as they forage for food.

◀ The female great wood wasp has a long, sharp "sting", which is really an egg-laying tube or ovipositor. She drills through tree bark to the grub of a wood-boring wasp within and lays an egg in it. When this egg hatches, the wasp larva feeds on the host larva, slowly killing it and finally emerging as an adult wood wasp.

QUEEN AND WORKERS

In a typical wasps' or bees' nest, there is just one female who lays eggs. She is the queen. A queen honeybee lays up to 1,500 eggs each day. She is looked after by female workers. Some of these workers, called forager workers, fly off to collect food, mainly pollen and nectar, from flowers.

As well as laying eggs, the queen bee also controls the colony by preventing workers from developing into queens themselves. Her mouthparts produce a special chemical called queen substance, which spreads through the nest. If she dies, the queen substance fades away. Then some of the grubs, developing in their six-sided compartments, or cells, in the nest, develop into young queens. Others develop into male bees or drones.

◀ Bees gather nectar and pollen from flowers, chew and predigest it and "sick" it back up as honey. This feeds the grubs (larvae) in the nest.

The young queens and drones mate. One new queen takes over the existing colony. The others fly off to found fresh colonies elsewhere. Wild bees nest in holes in trees and rocks. Honeybees have been domesticated in hives for more than 3,000 years.

INSECTS WITHIN INSECTS

Some parasitic wasps lay their tiny eggs on or inside the bodies of other insects. Even the eggs of insects are not safe from attack by these tiny wasps. The smallest of all insects are called fairy flies. About ten would fit on a pinhead. But they are not flies; they are minute wasps. They lay their eggs inside the eggs of other insects. When the grubs hatch out, they are surrounded by the nutritious contents of the egg, which they consume before emerging.

Bees and wasps like this common wasp have four wings. But the two wings on each side are hooked together so they flap up and down as one.

TERMITES

Termites have the largest and most complicated colonies of any insect. There may be more than five million in one nest, all controlled by a king and queen. Worker termites fetch and carry food, and special soldier termites with large jaws guard the colony. The queen termite lays 30,000 eggs each day, and she can live for 15 years!

LACEWINGS AND ANT-LIONS

Lacewings take their name from their delicate wings. The adults have a weak, fluttery flight and are often attracted to lighted windows at night. They and their pincer-jawed larvae eat smaller creatures such as bugs. Adult ant-lions look similar to lacewings and are found mainly in warm countries. The ant-lion larva digs a cone-shaped pit in loose soil or sand and waits at the bottom. When a small insect tumbles into the pit, the ant-lion slides the sand, and the prey, down into its huge jaws.

Bees, wasps, and hornets make their nests from chewed wood, which dries as thin paper.

These bumblebees have opened a cell in their nest to clean the pupa. Like butterflies, hymenopterans go through four stages in their lives—egg, grub or larva, the pupa in its cocoon or case, and the adult.

Bees, wasps and ants *(Hymenoptera)*
- at least 130,000 species
- four thin wings, joined on each side
- chewing mouthparts
- ants mainly wingless
- many can sting
- many feed from flowers

Termites *(Isoptera)*
- 2,250 species
- live in large colonies
- workers are wingless
- feed on rotting wood
- live mainly in warm countries

Lacewings and ant-lions *(Neuroptera)*
- 5,000 species
- lace-like veins in the large wings
- larvae and adults catch and eat other insects
- live mainly in warm countries

FLIES

THE COMMON HOUSEFLY IS A WELL-KNOWN, BUZZING NUISANCE IN THE KITCHEN OR AT A PICNIC. It is a member of the insect subgroup called the true or two-winged flies, Diptera. The group has more than 90,000 species around the world. It includes gnats, midges and mosquitoes, craneflies, horseflies, botflies, hoverflies, fruitflies, bluebottles, greenbottles and dungflies. The main feature of all these flies is that they have just one pair of proper wings, rather than the usual two pairs of most insects. The second or rear pair are small, thin, and club-shaped. Called halteres, they help the insect to balance as it flies.

▲ Dungflies roll animal droppings into balls and lay their eggs in it, so the maggots (larvae) can feed on it when they hatch.

TWO-WINGED OR TRUE FLIES

The two-winged or true flies are the supreme aerobats of the insect world. Not only can a hoverfly hover in mid-air, it can also fly sideways and backwards. The wing of a fly or similar insect is a thin flap that contains no muscles. The fly moves its wings by changing the shape of its thorax, the part of the body where the wings are attached. It does this by using muscles inside its thorax to make the wings click up and down. The wings are attached to the body by rubbery hinges, which make them bounce back up at the end of each down stroke. Using this method, most insects can beat their wings more than 300 times a second. Some midges and hoverflies flap them more than 1,000 times a second. The speed of the flapping creates a droning, buzzing or whining sound.

▲ Different types of biting midges suck the blood of many animals, especially mammals and birds, but also amphibians and even insects.

BITING!

Mosquitoes, gnats and midges bite people to suck their blood. But only the females do this. They need the concentrated nourishment from blood to help their eggs develop. Male mosquitoes and midges feed harmlessly on nectar from flowers.

WHAT FLIES EAT

Many flies eat very different foods in their young or larval stage than they do in the adult stage. Hoverflies are expert flower-feeders. They especially like the flat flowers of plants in the carrot family. Yet their larvae eat aphids and other bugs, or dung, or even survive as "guests" in the nests of ants and wasps, feeding on the debris and rubbish.

Midges and mosquitoes bite us to suck our blood. They can be a great nuisance and spread diseases such as malaria and yellow fever (pages 12–13), especially in wet and marshy areas where they breed. They lay their eggs on the surface of ponds and pools.

The clusters of tiny, waxy eggs stick together and float on the surface like miniature rafts. Then the comma-shaped larvae hatch out and swim down into the water by wriggling, to feed on tiny plants and animals.

The five species of tsetse fly (Glossina) live in Africa. They feed by sucking the blood of people and animals such as cattle, but as they feed they spread microscopic protists called trypanosomes. These breed in the blood of a person and cause a serious disease called sleeping sickness.

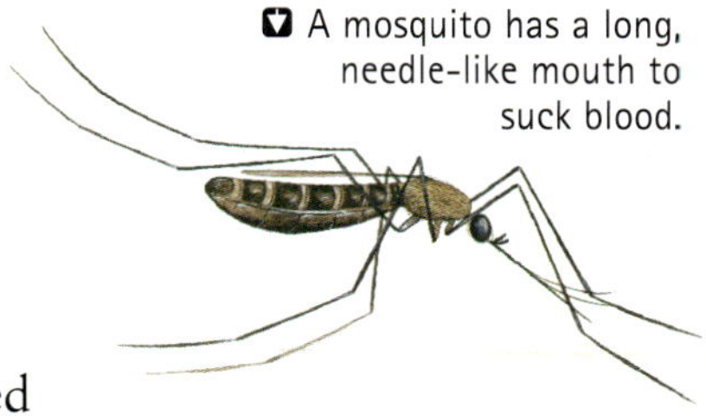

A mosquito has a long, needle-like mouth to suck blood.

HORSEFLIES

The large, powerful horseflies can inflict painful bites on people, cattle, and horses with their blade-like mouthparts. The wounds itch, bleed and swell up, but horseflies rarely spread disease. Their larvae also bite fiercely and suck the body juices from worms, grubs and other small, soft-bodied animals.

FLESH-EATING GRUBS

Some kinds of fly, such as the botfly of tropical America and the tumbu fly of Africa, lay their eggs on the skin of large animals, including people. The maggots or larvae of some species burrow through the skin and eat the living flesh beneath. They can cause serious infections.

The sheep nostril fly really does lay its eggs inside the nose of a sheep. Its larvae live and feed in the nose passages, and can bore their way through to its eyes and brain.

DRIBBLING ONTO ITS FOOD

The housefly buzzing around the kitchen may have fed last on rotting garbage or animal droppings. It dribbles saliva (spit) from its sponge-like mouthparts onto its food to make it dissolve into a liquid. Then it paddles around in and sucks up this "soup". Germs stick onto its legs and mouthparts. Then it buzzes off – and may land on your meal! Houseflies can spread various illnesses, including diarrhoea and food poisoning.

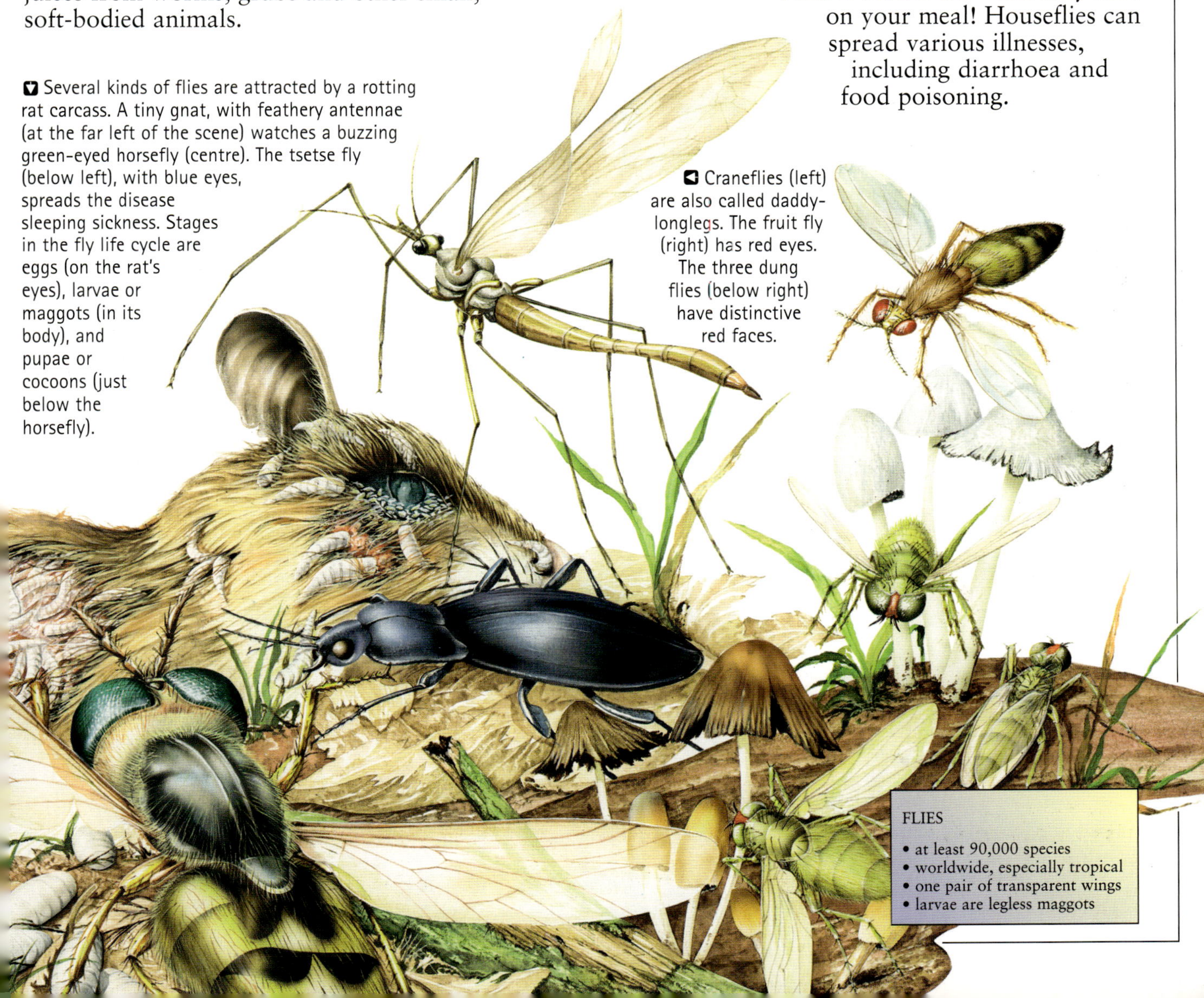

Several kinds of flies are attracted by a rotting rat carcass. A tiny gnat, with feathery antennae (at the far left of the scene) watches a buzzing green-eyed horsefly (centre). The tsetse fly (below left), with blue eyes, spreads the disease sleeping sickness. Stages in the fly life cycle are eggs (on the rat's eyes), larvae or maggots (in its body), and pupae or cocoons (just below the horsefly).

Craneflies (left) are also called daddy-longlegs. The fruit fly (right) has red eyes. The three dung flies (below right) have distinctive red faces.

FLIES

- at least 90,000 species
- worldwide, especially tropical
- one pair of transparent wings
- larvae are legless maggots

DRAGONFLIES AND DAMSELFLIES

A dragonfly has its legs together in a basket-like trap to catch prey in flight.

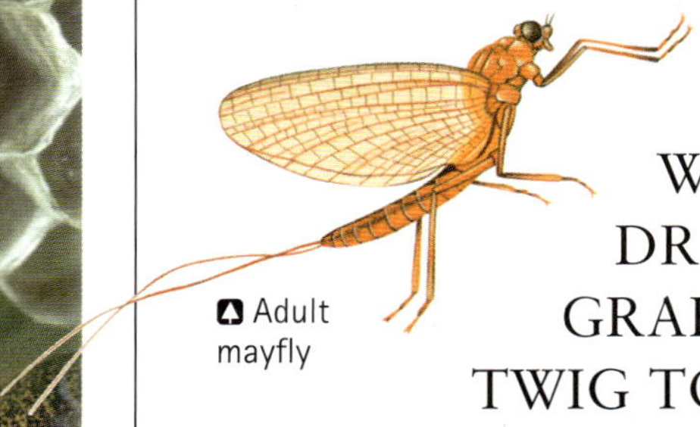

Adult mayfly

WITH WHIRRING WINGS, A DRAGONFLY DARTS FROM ITS PERCH NEAR THE POND GRABS A TINY GNAT IN MID-AIR AND RETURNS TO THE TWIG TO EAT. There are some 5,000 species of dragonfly and damselfly, known as Orthopterans. Each has a long, slender body, two pairs of long, large, vein-patterned wings and very big eyes for seeing prey. Damselflies are usually smaller and slimmer than dragonflies, and their flight is slower and less direct. The dragonfly is one of the champion insect flyers, able to cruise at around 5 km/h, dart ten times faster in a short burst, then stop almost at once and hover. Dragonflies and damselflies usually hunt over ponds, swamps and slow rivers. In fact, these are the places where they grow up. The young stages of these insects, called larvae or nymphs, live underwater. They grow and develop for up to five years in the water, depending on the species, before climbing out, shedding their skins and becoming adults.

Damselflies hold their wings over their backs at rest. Males and females link together at breeding time to form a "mating chain" that may be five or six damselflies long!

All the insects shown here have one feature in common. Their young, or larvae, live in fresh water – often for two years or more. The larvae are usually brown or grey and creep around in ponds, lakes, streams and swamps. Dragonfly larvae are large, and like their parents they are very strong hunters. They feed by grabbing other water creatures, such as tadpoles and even small fish, with their enormous pincer-like jaws. The larva sheds or moults its skin many times. Finally it climbs up a reed or plant stem, and the adult crawls out of its last larval skin. Its wings spread and harden, and its body becomes slim and colourful. Then the adult dragonfly dashes off to catch its first victim, in the air rather than in the water.

KEEP OUT!

An adult male dragonfly takes over a length of riverbank or lakeside as his breeding territory. He defends it fiercely by chasing off other males that stray nearby. He may even fly at people walking past to get a good look and make sure they are not rivals.

The stonefly has two long feelers on its head and two long tail filaments. It is a weak flyer and usually crawls over plants and rocks near water.

The emperor dragonfly has a blue patterned body and wings 10 cm across. It holds them out to the sides while resting.

When a female appears, he holds her behind her head using his tail claspers, and she swings her abdomen forward to mate with him.

MAYFLIES

A mayfly lives for a year or more as a larva in a stream or river, eating tiny plants and other bits of food. It sheds its skin up to 25 times – a record for an insect. Then it crawls up a plant stem into the air and sheds its skin twice, first becoming a winged sub-adult, and then a proper adult, able to breed. Yet after all this, the adult mayfly lives for only a few hours. It has just enough time to breed before it dies. Adult mayflies often emerge in swarms on the same day. They "dance" over the water as they mate, and the females lay eggs by dipping their rear ends below the water's surface. Some adult mayflies have such tiny mouths that they could not feed even if they had time!

STONEFLIES

Stoneflies also have short lives as adults, usually just a week or two. Yet they also spend a year or more as water-dwelling larvae. Stonefly nymphs dwell in clear, gravelly, fast-flowing streams.

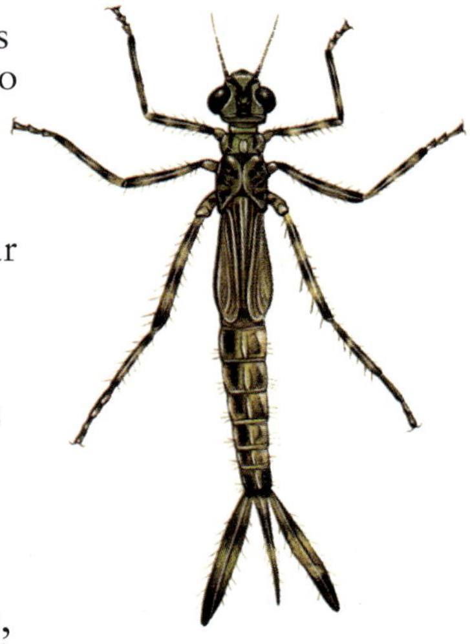

A mayfly larva has three tail filaments, which help it swim. It has small, non-flapping wings.

Stoneflies grip the stony stream bed with their strong hooked legs, to prevent themselves being swept away in the current. Adult stoneflies resemble adult mayflies, but they have two tail filaments rather than three, and when at rest, they hold their thin, veined wings flat over their bodies.

Dragonflies and damselflies *(Orthoptera)*
- about 5,000 species
- two pairs of large, long, transparent, veined wings
- big eyes
- young (nymphs) live in water
- adults often fly near water

Mayflies *(Ephemeroptera)*
- about 2,000 species
- delicate veined wings, usually two pairs
- three thin or fan-shaped tail filaments
- young (nymphs) live in water
- adults very short-lived

Stoneflies *(Plecoptera)*
- about 3,000 species
- flattened body
- two thin or fan-shaped tail filaments
- young (nymphs) live in water
- adults live along river banks

Caddisflies *(Trichoptera)*
- about 6,000 species
- young (nymphs) live in water, often in protective cases
- adults hairy, with four wings
- live near fresh water

Caddisflies are usually active at night.

CADDISFLIES

Adult caddisflies have slightly hairy wings and bodies, like some moths. They are seldom seen far from water, where their larvae live inside tube-shaped cases built from whatever is common in the pond or stream. Some caddis larvae even use tiny empty snail shells as mobile homes.

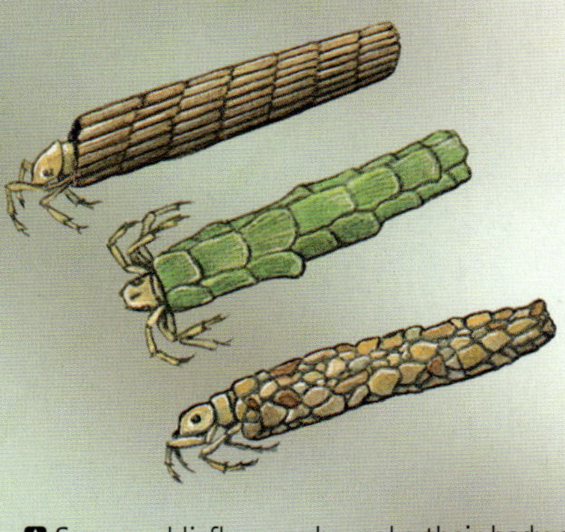

Some caddisfly nymphs make their body cases from snipped-off lengths of plant stems (top). Others use bits of water plant leaves (centre) or tiny pieces of gravel (bottom).

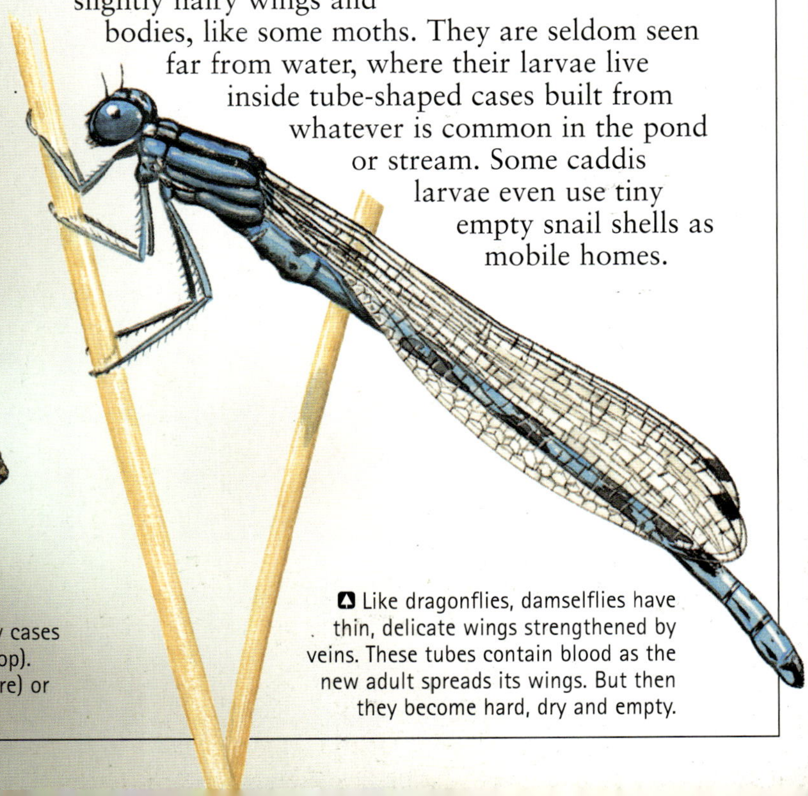

Like dragonflies, damselflies have thin, delicate wings strengthened by veins. These tubes contain blood as the new adult spreads its wings. But then they become hard, dry and empty.

BUGS

In certain seasons, usually summer, female aphids do not lay eggs, but give birth to fully formed babies, or nymphs. This allows them to reproduce very quickly.

THE WORD "BUG" IS OFTEN USED FOR ANY TYPE OF INSECT, OR FOR ANY OTHER KIND OF CRAWLING CREATURE. However, bugs are really a distinct subgroup of insects, known as Hemipterans. There are some 70,000 species of bug. They all share the usual insect features of six legs, a three-part body and four flapping wings, but they also have a feature unique to the group – a mouth like a needle, specialized for piercing and sucking liquids and juices. Some bugs are predators. Assassin bugs and bedbugs, and water bugs such as pondskaters and backswimmers, feed on the blood and body fluids of other animals. Other bugs are plant-feeders, such as leafbugs, cicadas and aphids.

Leaf hoppers and frog hoppers are small bugs that suck sap from plant stems and buds. The nymphs surround themselves with a bubbly froth called "cuckoo spit", for protection from the hot sun and predators.

Several kinds of bug live on or under the water. Pondskaters skim around on the surface, hunting for flies and other insects that have fallen in. The pondskater senses the ripples made by the struggling prey and speeds over to bite and suck out its body juices. Backswimmers and water boatmen row themselves through the water using their hairy legs. They have very strong mouthparts for catching tiny pond creatures and can even give a person a painful bite. The water scorpion is a large bug that captures prey with its pincers. The long tail is not a sting, but a snorkel – a tube through which the water scorpion breathes as it hangs just below the surface.

Cicadas are large bugs that make loud, shrill chirping sounds.

CALLING TO ATTRACT A MATE

Some insects use sounds to attract mates. And some of the loudest insect sounds are made by male cicadas. Their piercing, high-pitched calls are heard in many of the warmer parts of the world. The noise comes from the sides of the cicada's thorax or body, which flick in and out, like shaking a metal sheet to and fro very rapidly. Adult cicadas live and feed in trees. But their young, or nymphs, develop in the soil, feeding on the sap of plant roots. They are among the longest-lived of all insects. Some cicada nymphs stay underground for more than 20 years, before emerging and shedding their skins to become adults.

The backswimmer's front four legs touch the water's surface, to detect tiny ripples made by prey.

The earwig's tail pincers, or cerci, are used to capture prey, fend off enemies, and hold the partner when mating. They are curved in males (right) and straight in females.

Green leaf bug

After crawling from its old split skin, the cicada's crumpled wings soon expand.

INSIDE AN INSECT'S LEG

The leg of an insect or other arthropod is like a long, slim tube made of several sections. The casing, or exoskeleton (page 72), is thin between the sections to allow the leg to bend, moved by several muscles inside.

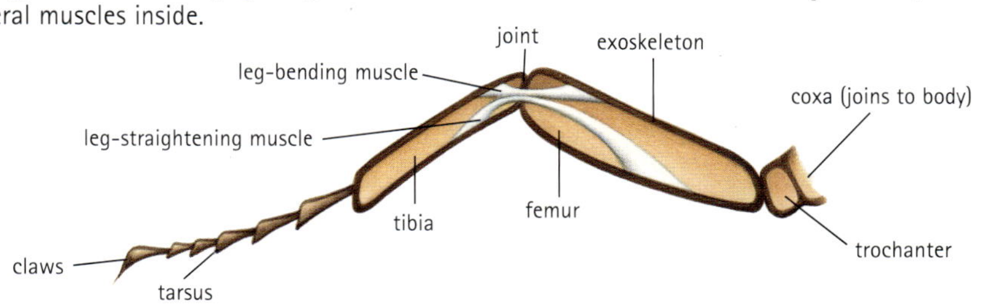

This tropical cockroach is camouflaged to resemble dead leaves on the forest floor. Cockroaches were one of the first kinds of insect to appear on Earth, more than 300 million years ago.

APHIDS

The greenflies and blackflies that become pests in the garden during summer are bugs called aphids. They are mostly very small, at just a few millimetres long. They suck sap from flowers such as roses, fruits such as currants, vegetables such as cabbages and lima beans, and many other plants.

Aphids have amazing powers of reproduction. They spend the winter as eggs. The first aphids to hatch in spring are females. They can produce young without having to mate with a male first. This method of breeding is known as "parthenogenesis." It allows aphids to reproduce very quickly and build up large swarms. In late summer, females produce some male babies, too. These mate with the females, which lay eggs to live through the winter.

COCKROACHES

Cockroaches look like bugs, but belong in their own insect subgroup. They are among the toughest of all insects, and with their strong chewing mouthparts can survive on almost any scraps of food. They also reproduce quickly and may become serious pests. Cockroaches live in almost all land habitats, from icy mountains to deep caves or the dead leaves and soil of tropical forests.

True bugs *(Hemiptera)*
- about 70,000 species
- beak-like mouthparts for piercing and sucking
- many have narrow bodies

Cockroaches *(Blattodea)*
- 3,700 species
- long, low, flattened body
- long feelers
- hard front wings protect rear wings underneath
- fast-running

Earwigs *(Dermaptera)*
- 1,200 species
- flattened body
- pincer-like tail

EARWIGS

Earwigs will hide in any dark hole or crevice, and will burrow in soil or crawl under tree bark. They eat a range of plant and animal foods, including harmful grubs. The female is a caring parent. She cleans her eggs and protects her young.

Many bugs, like these blackspot leaf bugs, are coloured or camouflaged to match their surroundings.

Some bugs show parental behaviour, which is rare among insects. This female shieldbug guards her eggs against predators.

CRICKETS AND GRASSHOPPERS

Crickets, like this green bush cricket, and mantids usually live singly.

CRICKETS AND GRASSHOPPERS HAVE LONG, POWERFUL BACK LEGS FOR LEAPING AND JUMPING, USUALLY TO ESCAPE PREDATORS. They belong to the insect sub-group known as Orthopterans. Most have camouflaged bodies, coloured and patterned to blend in with their surroundings. As they leap, they may spread their two rear wings in a flash of whirring colour. The young or larvae of crickets and grasshoppers look like small versions of the adult, except that they do not have wings. The wings grow gradually, each time the larva sheds its skin. This type of development is known as incomplete metamorphosis, and the larvae are called nymphs. There is no pupa or chrysalis stage (page 77). Other insects that grow like this include cockroaches, bugs, dragonflies, termites, mantids, earwigs and stoneflies.

Grasshoppers have large, fan-like rear wings. When these are not in use they are folded and protected by the smaller, harder front wings.

The rasping and chirping of crickets and grasshoppers are familiar sounds in hot weather. The male insects "sing" to warn others off their territory or to attract a mate. Crickets and the similar katydids rub the comb-like front wing veins together to make the noise. Grasshoppers and locusts rub their back legs against the front wing veins. Each leg has a row of hard pegs that make the wing vibrate. One kind of cricket, the mole cricket, lives in a burrow rather than on grass stems and plants like most crickets and grasshoppers. To make its song even louder, it digs a mating burrow with the entrance shaped like a double funnel.

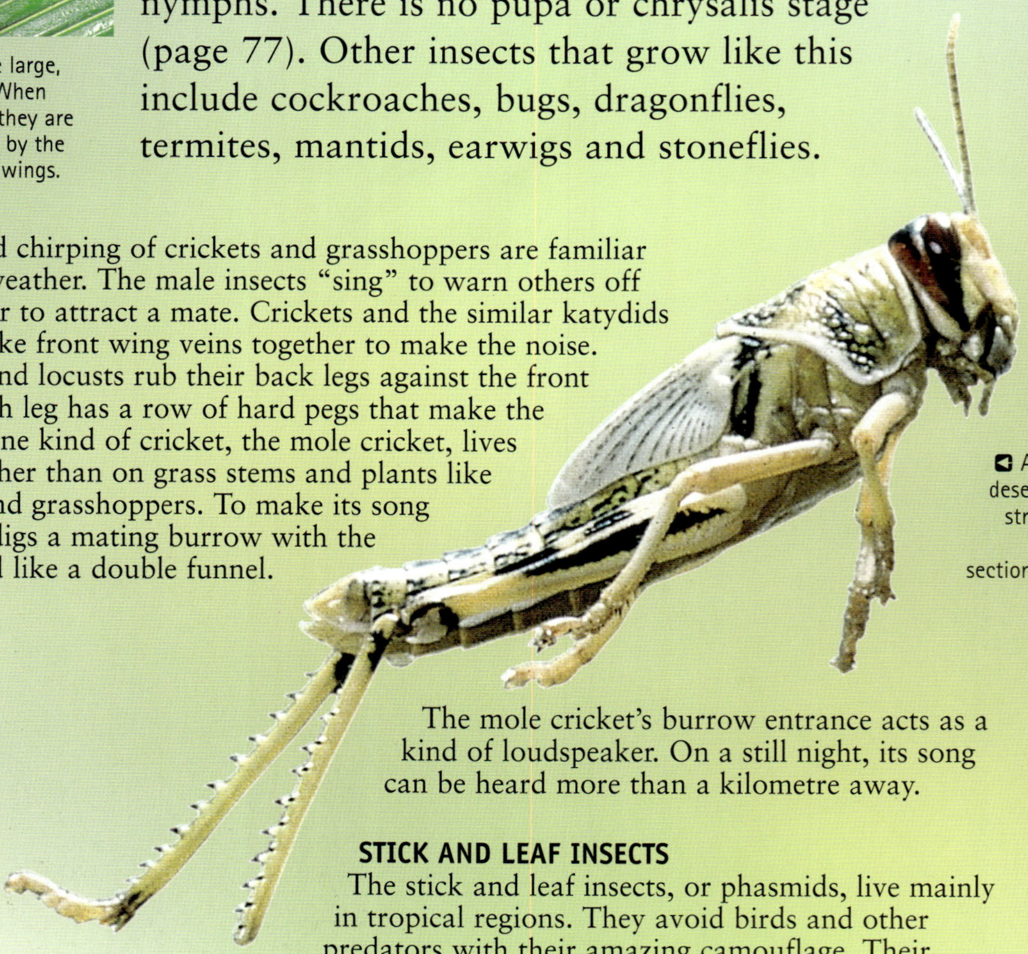

A leaping desert locust straightens each leg section in turn.

The mole cricket's burrow entrance acts as a kind of loudspeaker. On a still night, its song can be heard more than a kilometre away.

STICK AND LEAF INSECTS

The stick and leaf insects, or phasmids, live mainly in tropical regions. They avoid birds and other predators with their amazing camouflage. Their bodies look like thin sticks or twigs, or like flat leaves.

A stick insect spreads its large, fan-like rear wings.

Leaf insects (shown here on the leaves) are extremely well camouflaged in both appearance and behaviour. They move and sway to mimic a leaf being blown by the wind. Stick insects (at the top) hold out their legs at the same angles as the twigs around them.

Most of them are green or brown, to match the plants on which they feed. Some leaf insects even have V-shaped patterns on their bodies resembling the veins or ribs of a leaf. Others have brown edges, patches or blotches, so that they look like old or damaged leaves.

LONGEST... !
The longest insects are some kinds of stick insect. They grow to 35 cm from head to tail.

NO MALES NEEDED

Some kinds of female stick insect do not need to mate with a male before laying eggs. In some species males are hardly ever found. This kind of breeding is called parthenogenesis.

A grasshopper (left) has shorter antennae or feelers than a cricket (below).

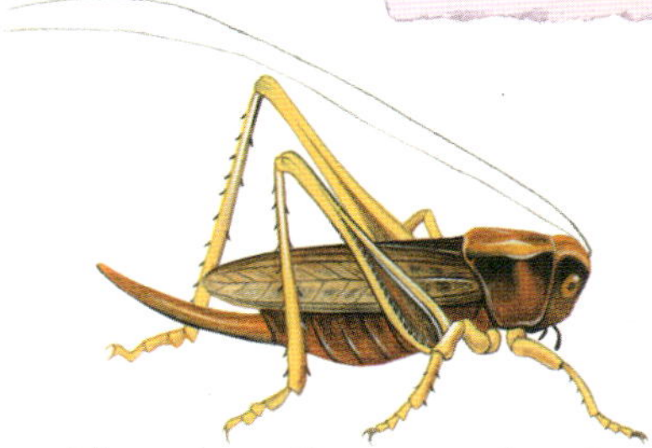

MANTIDS

Mantids are fierce hunters. They catch and eat other small animals, such as large insects and spiders, grabbing them with their spiny, pincer-like front legs. The mantis has large eyes and excellent vision. It sits patiently on a plant or flower, waiting for a suitable victim to come near. Then it strikes, too fast for us to see, and grabs the prey in its spiny "arms". When some kinds of mantid breed, the female eats the male just after they mate, or even while mating. In other species there are no males. The females reproduce by parthenogenesis.

The praying mantis is named for its waiting-to-pounce posture, with front legs folded as if in prayer.

Crickets, locusts and grasshoppers
(Orthoptera)
- 20,500 species
- long, strong hind legs for jumping
- small, hard front wings
- large, fan-like rear wings
- feed on plants

Stick and leaf insects
(Phasmatoidea)
- 2,500 species
- live mainly in the tropics
- resemble leaves, twigs or sticks
- even the eggs are camouflaged, to resemble plant seeds
- large, fan-like rear wings
- eat plants

Mantids
(Mantodea)
- 1,800 species
- live mainly in warmer countries
- triangular head with big eyes
- large front legs with pincer-like claws
- eat mainly other insects

FLEAS, LICE AND OTHER INSECTS

The louse has hook-shaped, gripping legs with very strong claws. It clings to the skin or hair and resists being brushed off or washed away. In tropical regions, lice spread diseases such as typhus and relapsing fever.

FLEAS AND LICE ARE TINY, WINGLESS INSECTS THAT ARE PARASITES. They feed on other animals, called their hosts, either by sucking their blood or by chewing their skin or feathers. Fleas have sideways-flattened bodies and can slip easily among fur or feathers. They pierce the flesh of the host using their sharp, needle-like mouthparts. Most fleas are parasites of mammals. Humans, rats, cats, dogs, rabbits, bears, porcupines, beavers and many others each have their own particular flea species. Other fleas are parasites of birds, especially those that live in burrows, such as puffins, where the flea larvae can develop in warm safety. A flea escapes danger by leaping with its long, powerful back legs. These have a special click mechanism that stores energy and then releases it suddenly, like a spring-loaded lever. The average flea measures just a few pinheads across, but it can jump more than 30 cm – about 100 times its own length. For its size, the flea is the world's greatest animal athlete!

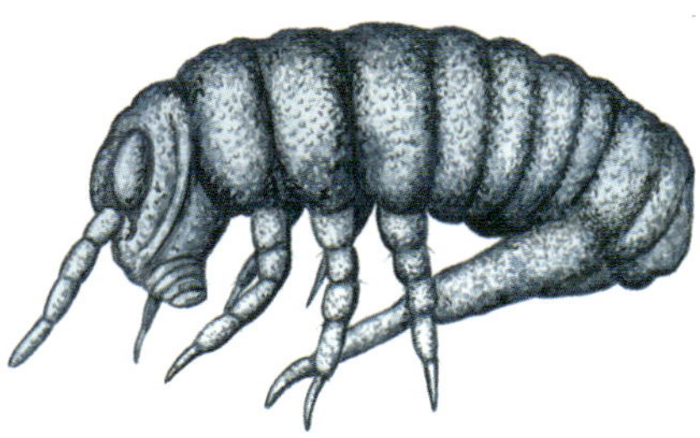

The springtail has a long, lever-like tail. This is normally hooked under the main body. When released, it springs downwards and flicks the insect into the air.

A human louse sucks the blood of its host. The blood gradually fills the front of the louse's abdomen, turning it dark red.

OLDEST... !
The first insects were probably springtails. Fossils in 400 million-year-old rocks have been found.

A louse clings on to its host using its sharp claws. Its flattened body lies close to the skin, making it very difficult to remove. Like fleas, there are different kinds of lice for different animals, including humans, dogs, guinea pigs, elephants, seals, warthogs and hummingbirds! The human louse is about 2 mm long, and its bite causes an itchy lump. The female glues her eggs to human hairs. The eggs look like tiny grains of salt and are called "nits".

SILVERFISH

This is one of the simplest or most primitive of all insects. It has no wings, but very long antennae and a three-forked tail. It is found in kitchens and food stores, coming out at night to feed on scraps. The silverfish is so-named because of its silvery colour and its bendy, fish-like movements.

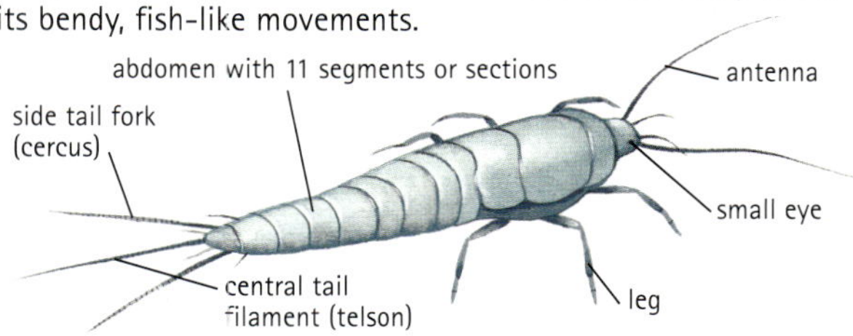

BARKLICE AND BOOKLICE

In addition to the lice described above, which are sometimes known as sucking or parasitic lice, there are two other groups of lice. Barklice are small and active, living on the bark of trees, among leaves or in birds' nests. They feed mainly on tiny plants and moulds.

▲ Thrips are tiny, fly-like insects with two pairs of hairy or feathery wings. They can breed fast to form huge swarms that ruin farm crops.

Booklice are similar and are sometimes found in old houses and buildings. They usually feed on mould, but they also eat the starchy paste used in the glue that binds the pages of old books.

THRIPS

The thrips are among the smallest of all insects. They have feathery or fluffy wings and can fly quite well. Most feed on plants, and especially on the flowers. They can multiply quickly and eat the flowers of wheat, onions, carrots and fruits such as apples and oranges. In warm, thundery weather they may take to the air in great swarms, crawling on our skin and in our hair and eyes. They are sometimes known as thunderflies or thunderbugs.

SPRINGY TAIL

Springtails are also very small insects, the longest being no more than 5 mm. They are named after the spring-like structure on the tail. If a springtail is disturbed, it flicks this down to jump away. Springtails are so different from other insects that they have their own major sub-group (or sub-class), Collembola.

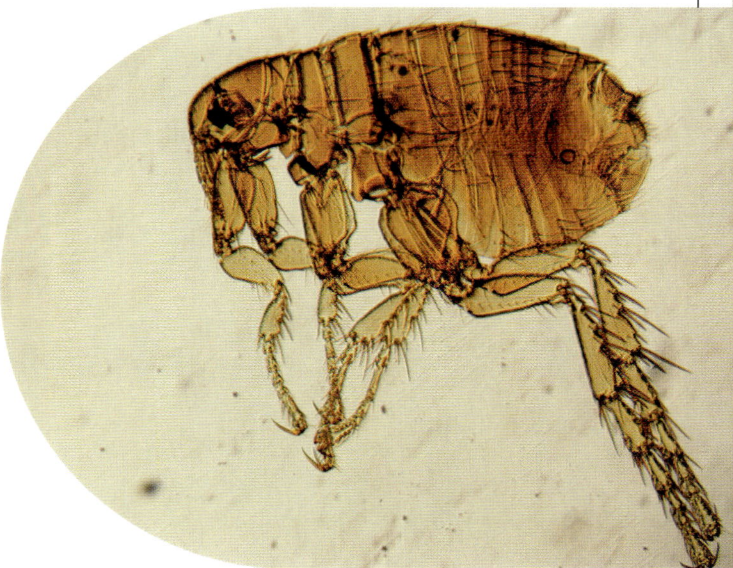

▲ A flea's back legs are more than twice as long as its front and middle legs. The needle-like mouthparts are between the front legs.

Springtails are among the most abundant and widespread of all insects. They live in their millions in the soil, among dead leaves and moss, and in rotting wood. Some kinds are pests because they eat farm crops such as cereals and clover. Others live on sandy beaches, around rock pools on the shore, and even at the surface of the stagnant, polluted water in ditches.

Fleas *(Siphonaptera)*
- 1,800 species
- very small
- wingless
- body flattened sideways
- powerful jumpers
- blood-sucking parasites of mammals and birds

Lice *(Phthiraptera)*
- 3,500 species
- very small
- wingless
- parasites of other animals

Booklice and barklice *(Psocoptera)*
- 2,000 species
- resemble lice but more active
- some eat paper and book bindings

Thrips *(Thysanoptera)*
- 5,000 species
- tiny
- resemble flies with hairy wings

Bristletails and silverfish *(Thysanura)*
- 600 species
- wingless
- shiny flat body, long antennae
- bristly two- or three-pronged tail

Springtails *(Collembola)*
- 2,000 species
- very small
- wingless
- spring-lever tail for leaping
- live in damp habitats, including surfaces of ponds and streams

CRABS, LOBSTERS AND SHRIMPS

Common shore crab

INSECTS ARE THE MOST COMMON ANIMALS ON LAND. But they do not live in salty water. Instead, another group of arthropods occupies the oceans – the crustaceans. They include crabs, lobsters, shrimps and barnacles. The shrimp-like krill eaten by great whales are crustaceans. So are the small creatures called copepods, which teem in such vast swarms that they are the most numerous animals in the sea. Some crustaceans, such as water fleas and crayfish, live in fresh water. A few, like woodlice, live on land.

Like all crustaceans, the slipper lobster grows by shedding or moulting its old carapace (shell). The new one underneath enlarges and then hardens.

For many people, the most familiar crustaceans are crabs. There are thousands of crab species, from giant spider crabs with pincers as long as your arm, to tiny porcelain and pea crabs that would fit in this o. A typical crab has a flattened body covered by the hard, shell-like carapace. The abdomen (rear part of the body) is small and tucked under the shell at the back. There are ten limbs – one pair of large pincers and four pairs of walking legs. Most crabs live in the sea, but a few dwell in rivers and lakes. The common shore crab is very hardy and can live in both salt and fresh water, and even out of water for a few hours.

THE HERMIT'S HOME

The front end of a hermit crab has the typical hard crab carapace and pincers, and two pairs of large walking legs. But the rear of its body is soft and twisted. This is because a hermit crab lives in the abandoned shell of a sea snail, such as a whelk. It holds the shell from inside with its two pairs of smaller rear legs. When the hermit crab grows too big for its shell, it has to "move house". It finds a larger shell, and quickly slides its body backwards into the new home.

CRAYFISH AND LOBSTERS

Crayfish and lobsters are like elongated crabs with the rear body part, the abdomen, held out straight at the rear like a tail, rather than tucked underneath.

The red-banded cleaner shrimp lives on coral reefs. Its bright colours advertise the service it provides—picking tiny parasites and pests off larger animals such as fish. The shrimp gets a meal and the fish gets cleaned.

The middle body part of crayfish and lobsters, the thorax, has four pairs of walking legs with a pair of very large, strong pincers or claws at the front. In some types of lobster one pincer is bigger and designed for crushing, while the smaller one is sharper for cutting and snipping.

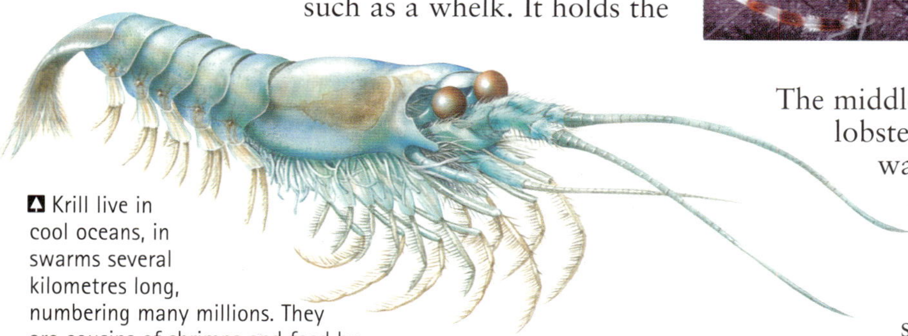

Krill live in cool oceans, in swarms several kilometres long, numbering many millions. They are cousins of shrimps and feed by filtering the tiny plankton from seawater.

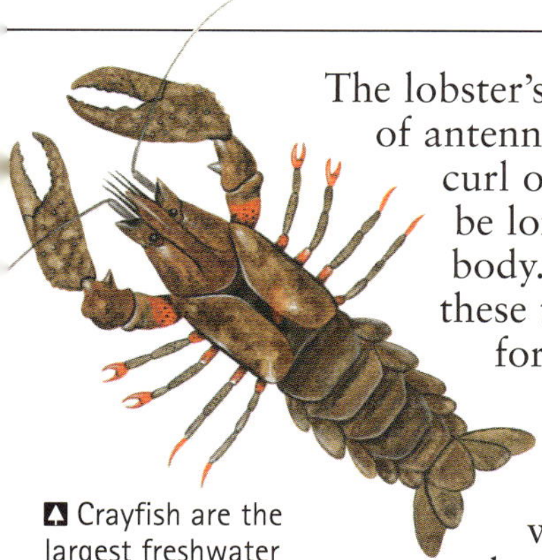

▲ Crayfish are the largest freshwater crustaceans. Like their cousins, lobsters, they feed at night. By day they hide in a lair, in a hole or under a stone.

The lobster's head has two pairs of antennae. The larger pair curl out in front and may be longer than the whole body. The lobster uses these to feel among rocks for food such as shellfish, which it crushes with its pincers. A lobster is well protected. Its head and thorax are covered by a thick, rigid carapace. The abdomen has a series of jointed plates, one for each segment. It can also defend itself with its powerful pincers.

SHRIMPS AND PRAWNS

Shrimps and prawns are like small, lightly built lobsters. Shrimps can crawl well but prawns usually swim by rowing with the five pairs of paddle-shaped limbs under the abdomen. The shrimp has a body flattened from top to bottom, while the prawn is flattened from side to side. They eat anything they can find, including dead animals. When alive they are almost transparent and well camouflaged against the rocks and sand. They only turn pink when cooked!

BIGGEST... !

The Japanese giant spider crab is the largest crustacean and the largest living arthropod. Its body is the size of a dinner plate, and it can measure 3.5 m across its outstretched claws.

▲ Some crabs, like the robber crab, live partly on land. This powerful crustacean can even climb up trees near the shore.

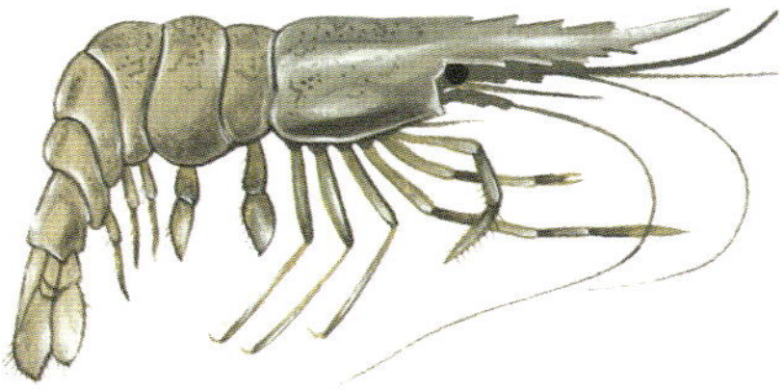

◄ Prawns use their delicate pincers to search through mud and sand for anything small and edible.

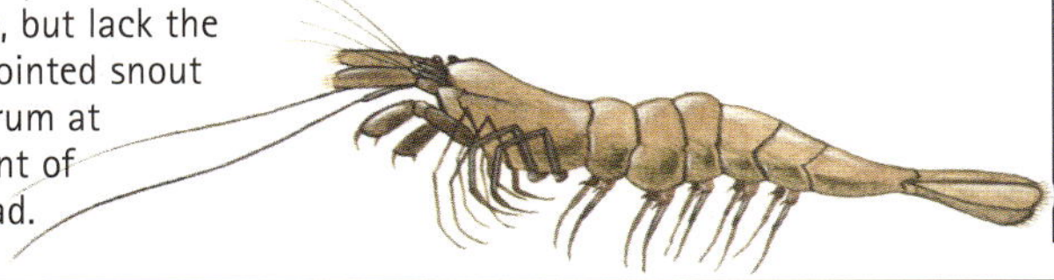

► Shrimps are similar to prawns, but lack the long, pointed snout or rostrum at the front of the head.

CRUSTACEANS

Main groups include:

Crabs
- 5,700 species
- most live in the sea
- round, flattened body, hard shell
- four pairs of walking legs
- one pair of pincers

Lobsters and crayfish
- 400 species
- most live in the sea
- long body
- four pairs of walking legs
- one pair of pincers

Shrimps and prawns
- 2,000 species
- most live in the sea
- long body
- swim and crawl well

All of the above are in the main crustacean group Decapoda, meaning "ten-limbed".

Krill
- 90 species
- swim in the open sea
- resemble shrimps
- live in gigantic shoals

BARNACLES AND OTHER CRUSTACEANS

▲ Acorn barnacles coat rocks along the seashore and in shallow water. They are preyed on by whelks, starfish and fish. Some species can survive above the high-tide level, with the occasional spray from waves.

WHEN THE TIDE IS OUT, AN ACORN BARNACLE HARDLY LOOKS LIKE AN ANIMAL AT ALL. Its pyramid-shaped shell, cemented firmly to a rock, has a tightly shut door at the top. But when the tide comes in, the door opens and the barnacle extends its long, feathery, fan-like limbs into the water. These beat regularly with a grasping motion to pull tiny bits of food towards the barnacle's mouth. Many other kinds of small crustaceans live along seashores and in the open oceans. The adults look very different, resembling shrimps, fleas or mussels. But their young forms or larvae are all very similar. These billions of small crustaceans make up much of the ocean plankton.

A barnacle begins life as a tiny egg which hatches into a vaguely shrimp-like larva. This drifts and swims as part of the plankton for a few days. In shallow water, it finds a firm place like a rock where the waves break at low tide. The larva sticks its head to the rock with its own natural glue and grows several hard, chalky plates around its body. Finally it changes into the adult barnacle, which feeds by kicking its feathery limbs to create water currents that draw food particles into its shell. Sometimes barnacles cause problems when they settle to live on a ship's hull, a buoy or an undersea cable. They also attach to large sea animals such as whales, sharks and turtles. They may live there for 20 years or more.

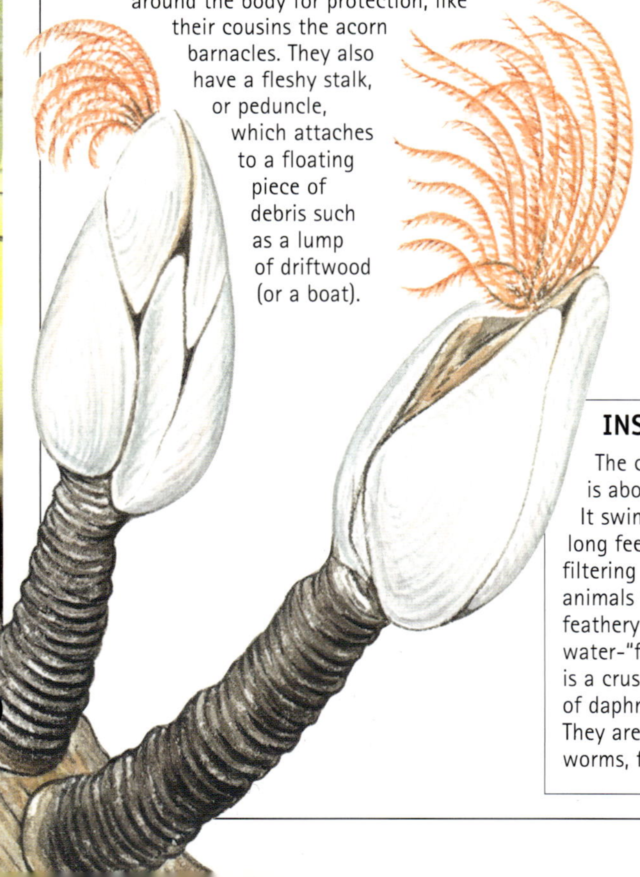

▼ Goose barnacles have shell-like plates around the body for protection, like their cousins the acorn barnacles. They also have a fleshy stalk, or peduncle, which attaches to a floating piece of debris such as a lump of driftwood (or a boat).

▲ Woodlice can only survive in damp places, such as among dead leaves or under tree bark. This is because the covering, or cuticle, over the jointed body shell is not waterproof. If a woodlouse is exposed to the hot sun, it dries out and dies.

INSIDE A WATER-FLEA

The common water-flea, daphnia, is about the size of this letter 'O'. It swims jerkily by rowing with its long feelers (antennae), and feeds by filtering microscopic plants and animals from the water with its feathery legs. Although it is called a water-"flea", it is not a true flea – it is a crustacean. There are thousands of daphnia in even the smallest pond. They are important food for small worms, fish and shellfish.

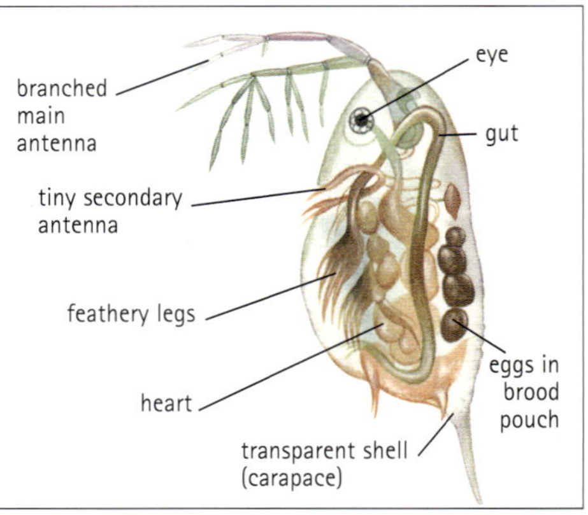

TOUGH!

The eggs of brine and fairy shrimps are very hardy. They can survive being deep-frozen or even boiled. The adults can cope with great heat too. Some live in hot springs where the water is a scalding 71°C.

Brine shrimps are food for crabs and flamingoes.

LIVING UPSIDE DOWN

Fairy shrimps and brine shrimps have rows of feathery or brush-like limbs along each side of the body. They swim slowly – and upside down – by waving these limbs. These delicate-looking crustaceans rarely grow longer than your finger, and most are much shorter.

Fairy shrimps have no defences against predators, partly because they live in places where predators are uncommon. They inhabit temporary pools, such as puddles of rainwater, where animals like fish cannot survive. When the pool dries out, the adult fairy shrimps die, but they leave very tough eggs in the mud. These hatch when the pool fills again. Brine shrimps can survive in the extremely warm and salty water of salt lakes and coastal lagoons.

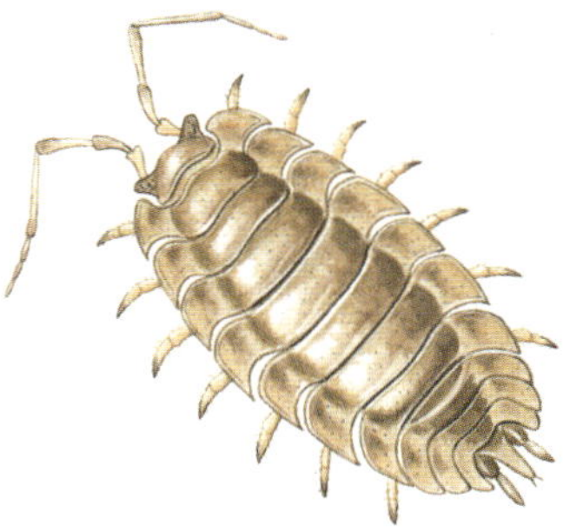

The oniscus woodlouse is very common and lives in woods, parks and gardens.

THE MOST COMMON CRUSTACEANS

The open seas are the main home of copepods and ostracods, although some kinds are found in ponds and lakes. Copepods resemble slim woodlice with very long feelers. They are among the most numerous creatures found in plankton, and many kinds of sea creatures depend upon them for food. Ostracods look like tiny versions of mussels or clams. They are sometimes called mussel shrimps or seed shrimps, and are more at home on the sea floor, where they filter food from water or mud. The largest kinds are just 5 mm across.

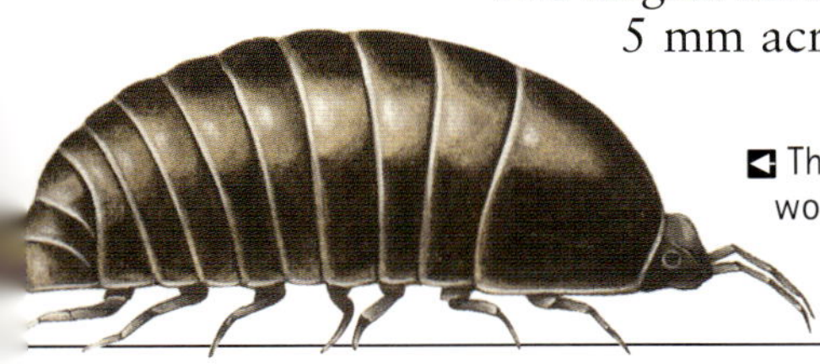

The pillbug is a woodlouse that can roll up into a ball for protection.

Some ostracods release substances into the water that glow with a greenish-yellow light. This may be a signal that breeding time has arrived. Or it may serve to confuse predators, such as shrimps.

WATER-FLEAS AND FISH LICE

Water-fleas have large, feathery antennae, which they use to row through the water. As they move, they both feed and breathe using their legs, which work as gills (page 102) to take in oxygen and as sieves to gather food. Fish lice are not true lice, but louse-shaped crustaceans. They are blood-sucking parasites on fish and other water-dwellers.

MORE CRUSTACEANS
(continued from page 91):

Barnacles
- 1,000 species
- live in the sea
- feather-like legs
- some have shells and attach to rocks
- some are parasites

Ostracods
- 5,700 species
- most live in the sea
- very small
- oval body enclosed in hinged shell

Copepods
- 8,400 species
- most live in the sea
- shrimp-like body
- long feelers
- largest are coin-sized
- swim jerkily

Water-fleas
- 480 species
- mainly freshwater
- long branched feelers for rowing
- bob up and down

Fairy shrimps and brine shrimps
- 175 species
- fairy shrimps live in freshwater pools, brine shrimps in salty water
- long body
- feathery legs for swimming and feeding

Tadpole shrimps
- 15 species
- live in freshwater pools
- shell-like covering at front, long forked tail
- up to thumb-sized

Amphipods
- 3,600 species
- most live in the sea
- small and shrimp-like
- narrow body
- includes freshwater shrimps, sandhoppers, and beach-fleas

Isopods
- 4,000 species
- most live in the sea
- flattened body
- seven pairs of legs
- includes woodlice

SPIDERS

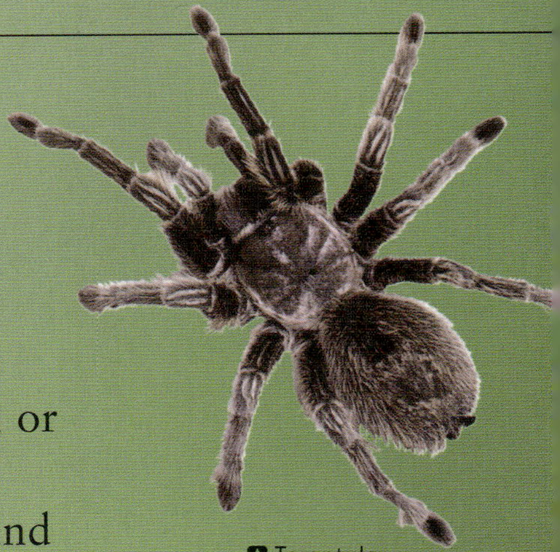

Tarantula

SPIDERS ARE MEMBERS OF THE ARTHROPOD GROUP CALLED ARACHNIDS. The main feature of an arachnid is that it has eight legs, unlike an insect which has six, and a crustacean which has ten or more. Other arachnids include harvestmen, scorpions, ticks and mites. With some 80,000 species, arachnids form the second largest group of arthropods, after insects. Like insects, they are mostly land-living, although a few kinds of spiders and mites inhabit fresh water. Unlike insects, they lack wings. Most arachnids are predators or hunters, but some mites and ticks are parasites of other animals. Arachnids live all over the world, in a wide range of habitats.

Some spiders, like the Costa Rican orb-weaver, build an extra-visible zigzag area of silk in the middle of the web. This is called the stabilimentum.

Spiders have one important ability that sets them apart from most other arthropods, including other arachnids. They make a kind of silk thread using special parts at the rear of the body, called spinnerets. Spider silk is used for various purposes – to spin protective cocoons around the eggs, to make a parachute for a baby spider so that it can blow in the wind to a new place, to act as a safety line in case the spider loses its footing and falls, to line a burrow or tunnel, to wrap up and subdue prey before it is eaten, and to weave webs for catching prey.

Bird-eating spiders have ve large mouthparts, or chelicera with sharp fangs. They al have long palps (which lo like a front pair of legs) f touching and tastir

Spider silk is one of the strongest materials known. It can take more strain than a steel thread of the same thickness. Different sorts of silk are used for different purposes. Cocoon silk is thick and smooth, while web silk is like sticky, coiled elastic.

Huntsman spiders live in tropical forests. They are large and strong enough to catch prey by force, and do not spin webs.

HIDDEN DANGER

Trapdoor spiders live in burrows, using their silk to make a hinged, door-like covering to the entrance. The trapdoor spider detects vibrations in the ground as a suitable small creature passes by. Or it lays silk threads as tripwires that the creature touches. The spider then darts out of its burrow and bites the victim with its large fangs, which all spiders possess. It injects poison and drags its meal down into the burrow, closing the trapdoor behind.

MAKING A WEB

A common type of web is the orb web. It is roughly circular with radial threads like spokes in a wheel. First, the spider must choose a suitable place with twigs the correct distance apart. The spider sets out the top frame and makes a couple of radial threads (1). Next comes the rest of the frame and more radial threads (2), then the last of the spoke-like radials (3). These are all made from a strong, tight, non-sticky type of silk. The spider then works around in a spiral from the outside towards the centre, spinning a much looser, elastic, sticky silk to snare its prey (4).

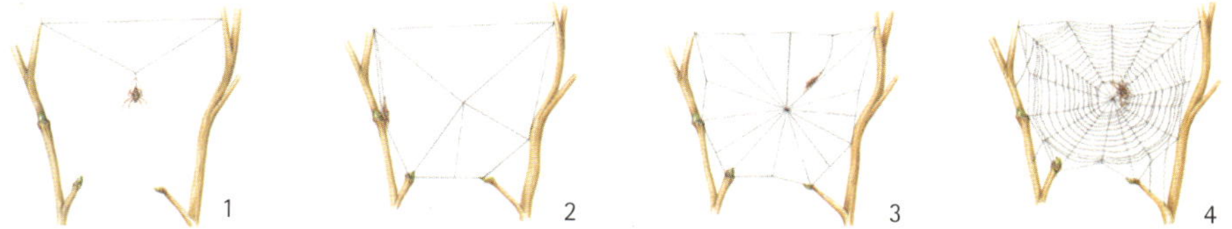

LARGEST... !

The largest spider is the goliath bird-eating spider, Theraphosa leblondi, of South America. It measures 28 cm across its legs. It catches other spiders, and also lizards, birds and small mammals like mice!

This yellow agriope orb-web spider has wrapped a moth in silk thread to eat later. If the spider has plenty of food, it may leave the victim tied up but alive, hidden in the fork of a nearby twig.

WEBS GALORE

Web-spinning spiders make all shapes and sizes of webs. Some are woven in amazingly precise geometric patterns. Others are a tangle of threads in a dark corner. But when a victim hits the web, the silk threads quickly entangle it. If the web is badly damaged, the spider eats the silk and recycles it to spin another one.

POISONOUS SPIDERS

All spiders have poisonous bites. But only about 30 species have fangs strong enough, and poison powerful enough, to harm people. The most deadly are the black widows, Latrodectus, that live in many warm countries, the Australian funnel-web spiders and the Brazilian huntsman.

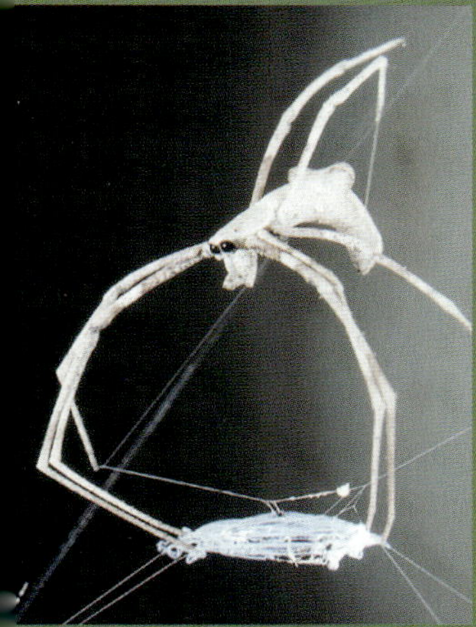

The net-casting spider spins a small web and holds it out with its three front pairs of legs. The web is a net ready to throw over the prey. This spider's huge eyes watch for victims and see where to cast the net.

Wolf spiders do not make webs. They run quickly across soil, rocks and tree bark after their prey, using their extra-long legs. Since they have no home base, the female wolf spider carries her whitish silk egg cocoon under her body.

ARACHNIDS

- members of the arthropod group
- about 80,000 species
- adult has eight legs

Spiders
- 50,000 species
- worldwide, all habitats
- body has obvious waist
- make webs from silk

SCORPIONS AND OTHER ARACHNIDS

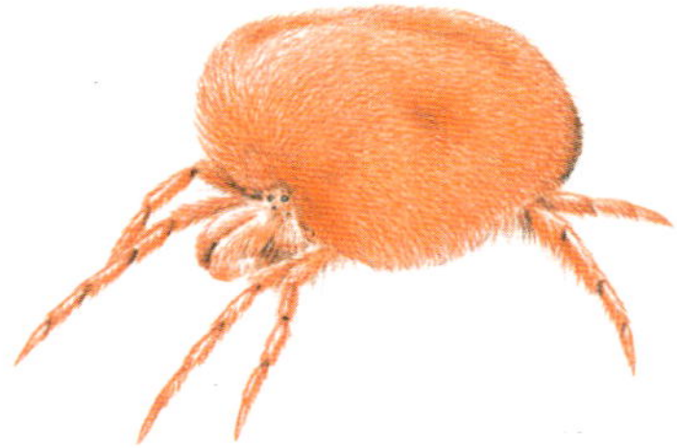

The giant red velvet mite is one of the biggest mites, at about 15 mm long. It lives in the dry terrain of Africa, where it hunts tiny worms and insects, and scavenges on dead plants and animals.

A SCORPION'S LONG BODY AND LARGE PINCERS MAKE IT LOOK LIKE A SMALL LOBSTER. But the scorpion's eight legs show that it is an arachnid, not a crustacean. The sting at the end of its long, arching tail is occasionally used to paralyse prey, but is mainly for self-defence. Several kinds of scorpion can inflict very painful stings on larger animals and people, and a few are even fatal. Although scorpions have from four to eight eyes, like spiders, their sight is poor. But this is not important since most scorpions hide by day, squeezed into a rocky crevice or wedged under a stone or log. At night they come out and detect prey mainly by feeling vibrations in the ground. A scorpion grabs its victim using its large pincers, or pedipalps. It may sting the prey to stop it struggling, before tearing it to pieces using its strong, claw-like mouthparts called chelicerae.

HEAVIEST... !
The heaviest and largest arachnids are tropical scorpions from India and West Africa. Some species grow up to 25 cm long. They look ferocious, but their stings are rarely more painful than a wasp's sting.

False scorpions or pseudoscorpions, are tiny arachnids – only as long as this letter 'm'. They look like miniature scorpions, but lack the stinging tail and are quite harmless to humans. False scorpions walk backwards as well as forwards, and often wave their large claws in the air. They live among dead leaves and moss, and under bark.

TICKS AND MITES

There are about 32,000 species of ticks and mites, which are the smallest arachnids. Some mites are less than 0.2 mm long. Both mites and ticks look like small, fat spiders.

A false scorpion uses its pincers in the same way as its larger relative, to grab prey.

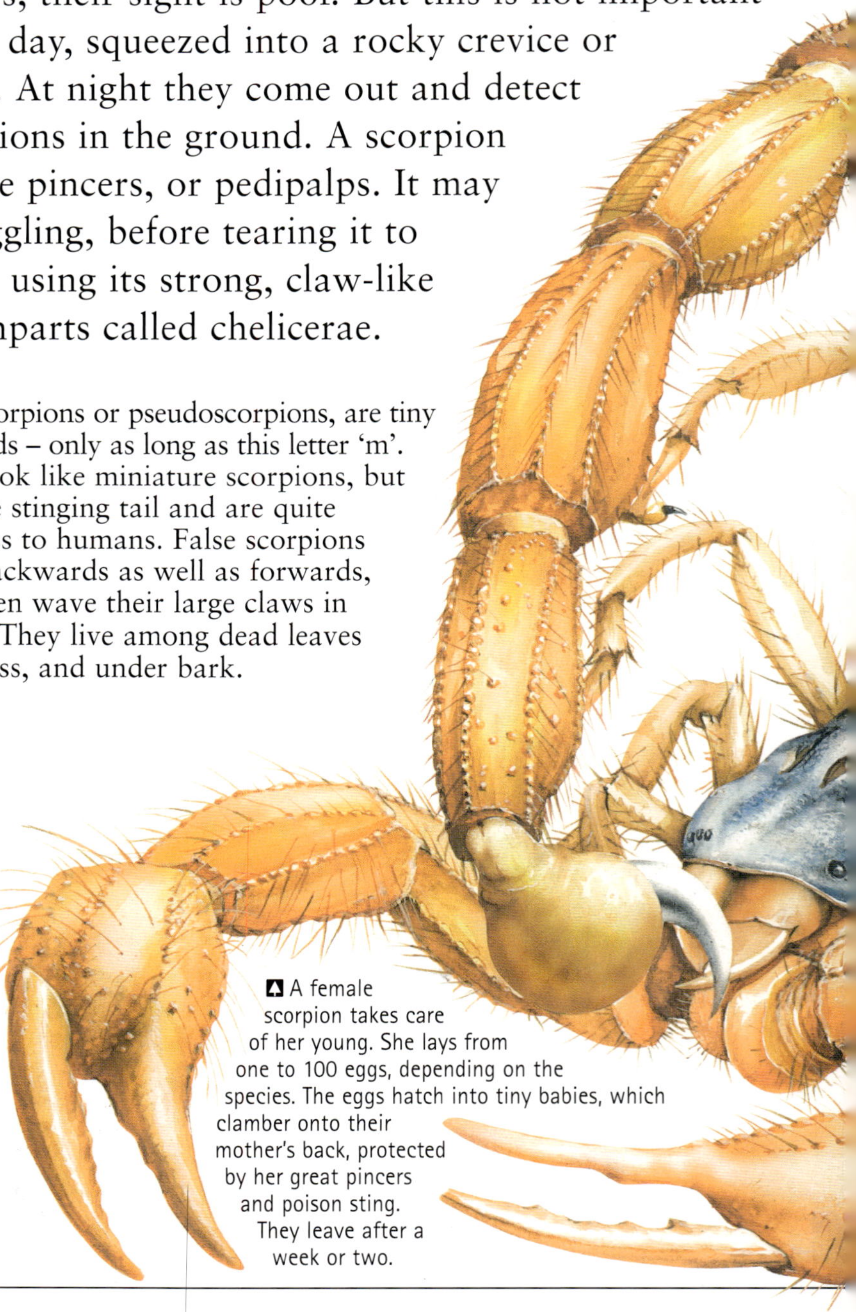

A female scorpion takes care of her young. She lays from one to 100 eggs, depending on the species. The eggs hatch into tiny babies, which clamber onto their mother's back, protected by her great pincers and poison sting. They leave after a week or two.

DEADLY!

One of the most dangerous scorpions is the fat-tailed scorpion of North Africa. Its venom is as strong as a cobra's. The durango scorpion of Mexico and Central America is also deadly. It kills up to 1,000 people each year.

All ticks are parasites of larger animals such as mammals, birds and reptiles. They bite into the skin and suck the host's blood. Some ticks spread diseases, such as Rocky Mountain fever and Lyme disease (spread by deer ticks). Some mites are also parasites. They infest plants and animals, including humans, sucking their fluids. Others feed on food and skin flakes in dust.

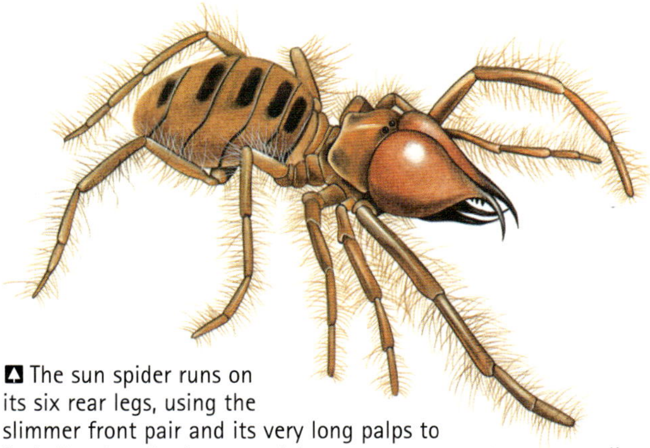

▲ The sun spider runs on its six rear legs, using the slimmer front pair and its very long palps to feel vibrations in the ground. It can outpace most prey, even lizards.

Some people are allergic to dust mites, or rather, to their dry, powdery droppings. They may develop breathing problems such as asthma. Mites also infest food stores, especially dry foods such as grains, flour, or bran. The flour mite lives all over the world and causes immense damage in food stores. Yet other kinds of mites catch small insects and other prey.

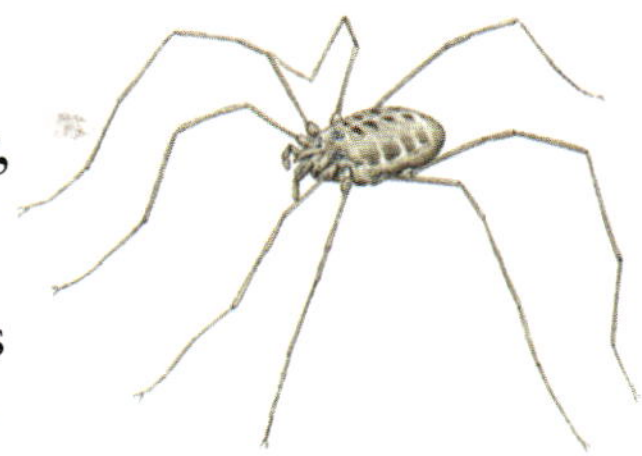

◀ Some kinds of harvestmen can inflict a painful bite or even spray nasty-smelling liquid at an attacker. These arachnids eat tiny animals, bits of plants and moulds.

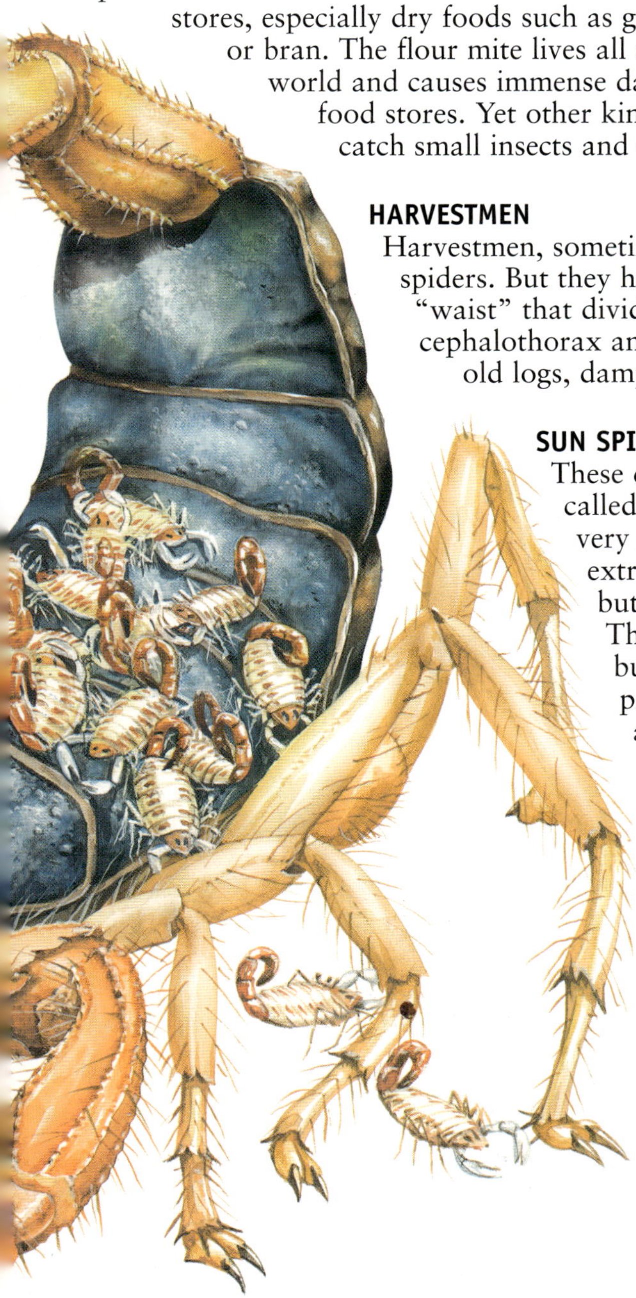

HARVESTMEN

Harvestmen, sometimes called harvest spiders, are like very long-legged spiders. But they have a small, rounded, one-piece body, without the "waist" that divides the body of a true spider into two parts (the front cephalothorax and the rear abdomen). Harvestmen live in rotting leaves, old logs, damp grass and similar places.

SUN SPIDERS

These desert-dwelling arachnids, also called wind spiders or solifuges, look very much like spiders. They have extremely strong fang-like pincers, but lack a poisonous bite. They lurk under stones or in burrows and race after their prey of insects, worms, lizards, and even spiders and scorpions.

▼ Parasitic mites have blade-like mouthparts that they drive into their host, to suck sap or blood.

ARACHNIDS
(continued from page 95):

Scorpions
- 1,200 species
- worldwide, but mainly in warm places
- large pincers
- slim curved tail with poisonous sting
- prey on smaller animals

Ticks and mites
- 32,000 species
- most mites are smaller than ticks
- resemble small, fat spiders
- ticks are parasites of mammals, birds, or reptiles
- some mites are parasites, others are free-living
- some mites are brightly coloured

False scorpions
- 2,000 species
- tiny
- look like miniature scorpions, but without a stinging tail
- live in soil, decaying leaves, old wood

Harvestmen
- 4,500 species
- worldwide
- live in woodland, grassland, gardens
- resemble a spider but with a one-piece body and long, stilt-like legs

Sun spiders *(Solifuges)*
- 900 species
- live mainly in deserts
- huge, non-poisonous pincer jaws
- run extremely fast

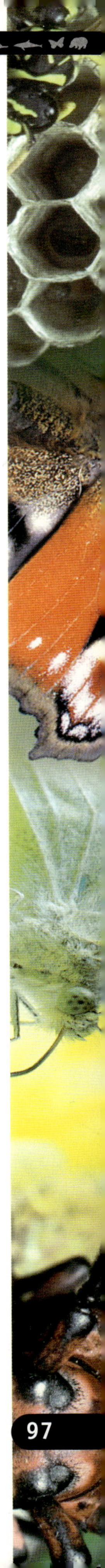

CENTIPEDES AND MILLIPEDES

Various kinds of pill millipedes roll into a ball when in danger. The curved plates, tergites, covering each body segment are jointed so that they overlap to form a smooth, rounded ball.

CENTIPEDES LIVE AND HUNT UNDER LOGS AND STONES, IN SOIL AND AMONG DEAD LEAVES. They locate prey with their long, sensitive feelers on the head, and bite with the sharp, claw-like fangs on the first body segment, injecting a poison that stops the prey struggling. The centipede then tears it apart with its strong jaws. Many centipedes can run very fast on their numerous pairs of legs. The name centipede means "hundred legs", but most species have about 40, although some have more than 340. Millipedes look like centipedes, but have a more rounded, tube-shaped body, shorter feelers and move more slowly. The name millipede means "thousand legs", but the maximum is about 750. Millipedes eat bits of plants, such as roots, buds and flowers, and also mouldy plant parts. Large centipedes can give an extremely painful bite, but millipedes cannot. Instead, they ooze or spray a horrible-tasting fluid from small glands along the sides of the body, to defend themselves against attack.

A millipede such as this one, polydesmus, has short feelers and no tail filaments. Its hard body gives good protection against predators such as birds and spiders.

A giant tropical centipede has two long feelers or antennae on its head, and two long tail filaments. Its poison fangs on the first body segment are held alongside and just under the head.

Most centipedes and millipedes are quite small, measuring less than 10 cm long. But some tropical species grow much larger. The scolopendra centipede of Central and South America can measure up to 33 cm in length. It is strong and fast enough to catch lizards, mice and small birds. Its bite is dangerous, even fatal, to people.

The largest millipedes are found in Africa. Some grow to about 28 cm long. Millipedes have chewing or scraping mouthparts and some damage vegetables, fruits and other crops. However, most millipedes live in woodland and help to recycle dead leaves and rotting wood.

◀ Velvet worms (onychophorans or peripatuses) seem like a combination of centipede and worm. They feed on small animals such as real worms and insects.

▼ The two-headed centipede has only one head, on the right. Its tail is shaped and coloured to look similar and confuse predators.

VELVET WORMS

These caterpillar-like creatures live in warm, damp forests. Their bodies are soft, squishy and velvety, with stumpy clawed legs for walking. Like all arthropods, they grow by moulting.

BLIND CREEPERS

Two smaller groups of arthropods are related to millipedes and centipedes. These are symphylans and pauropods. They are like miniature centipedes, about the same size as ants. They have no eyes and creep about in leaf litter and moist soil. Symphylans eat tiny bits of plants while pauropods scavenge on anything edible.

SEASHORE HUNTERS

Sea spiders are well named because they look like spiders, with four pairs of long legs, and live in the sea. But they have their own arthropod group. Most measure 3 to 5 cm across their outstretched legs. They clamber about on rocks and seaweeds on the lower shore, where they feed on sponges, corals and anemones by piercing them with their sharp mouthparts. Some deep-sea species can grow to 75 cm across.

CENTIPEDE OR MILLIPEDE?

These two types of multi-legged arthropods look quite similar, but there are several differences, as shown here (the millipede is on the left). They also live very differently. Centipedes are fast, active carnivores. They do not mind bright light and sometimes hunt during the day. Millipedes are slow herbivores or detritivores (eating old, decaying bits of plants or moulds). They hide from bright light and usually feed only at night.

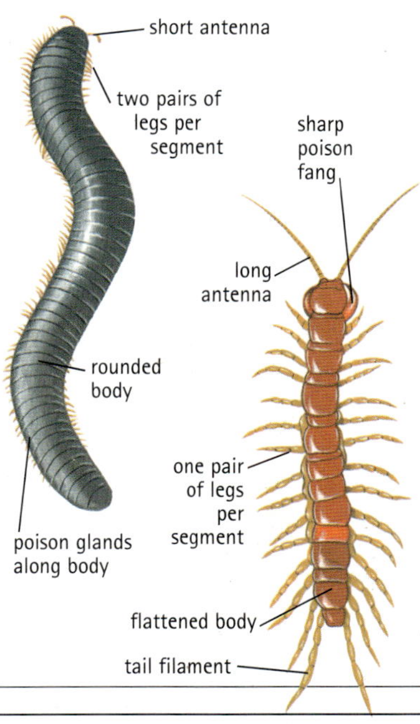

OTHER GROUPS OF ARTHROPODS INCLUDE:

Centipedes
- 3,000 species
- worldwide, mainly in soil, under rocks and leaves, in old wood
- bendy, flattened body
- two legs per body segment
- long feelers
- sharp fangs and strong jaws
- prey on smaller animals

Millipedes
- 8,000 species
- worldwide, mainly in soil, old leaves, rotting wood
- tubular, rounded body
- four legs per body segment
- short feelers
- feed on plants, moulds

Symphylans
- 160 species
- live in soil
- small, ant-sized
- look like small centipedes
- 12 pairs of legs

Pauropods
- 400 species
- live in soil
- tiny
- look like tiny centipedes
- nine pairs of legs

Sea spiders
- 1,000 species
- live in the sea
- resemble true spiders
- four pairs of long walking legs
- prey on other animals

Velvet worms
- 120 species
- live in tropical forests
- resemble large caterpillars
- 17 pairs of stumpy legs

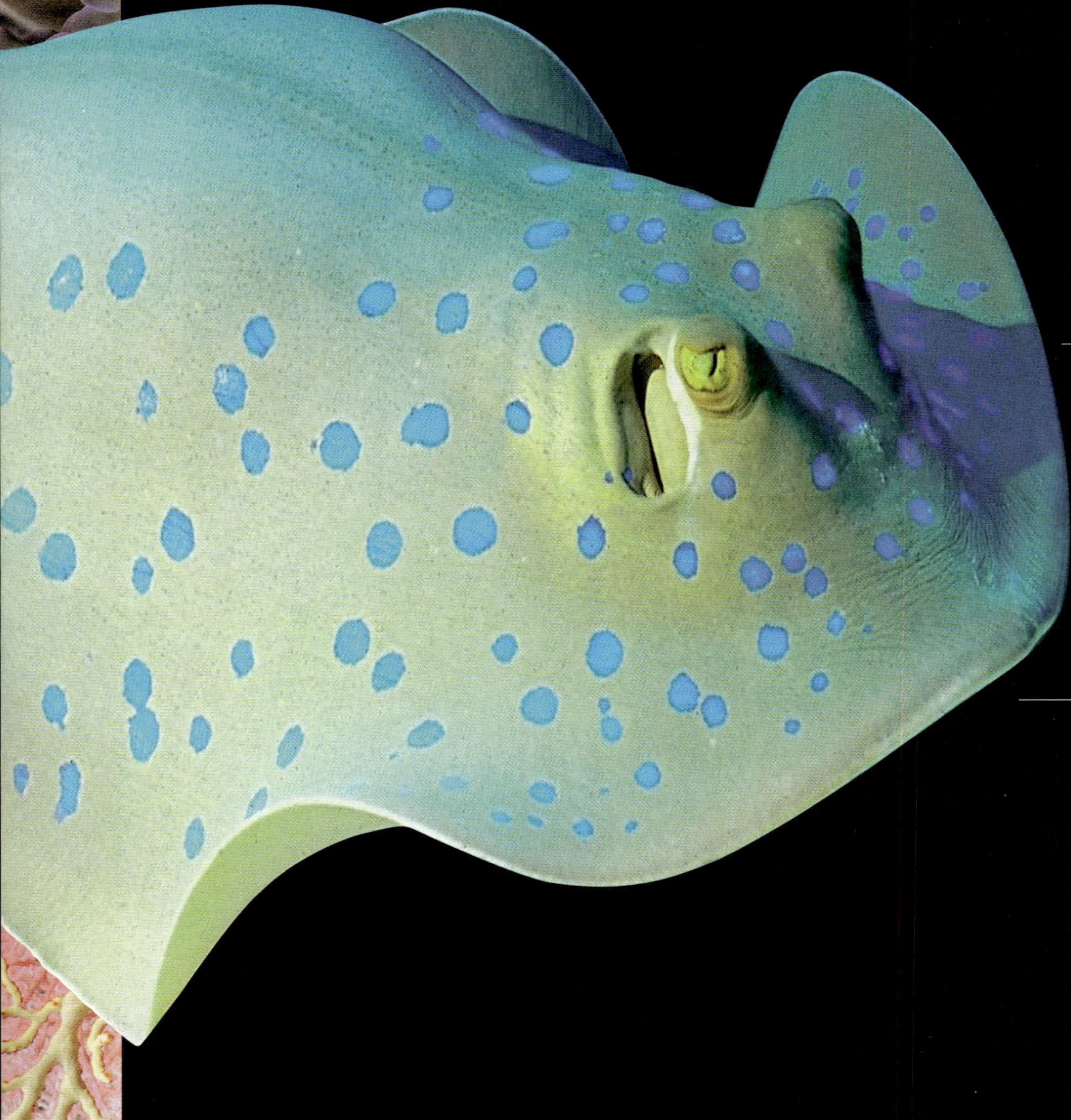

This spotted eagle ray has large eyes and, just behind each one, a flap-covered opening or spiracle. This lets in water which flows over the gills, so that the ray can breathe (take in oxygen from the water). The water then leaves through gill slits on the ray's underside.

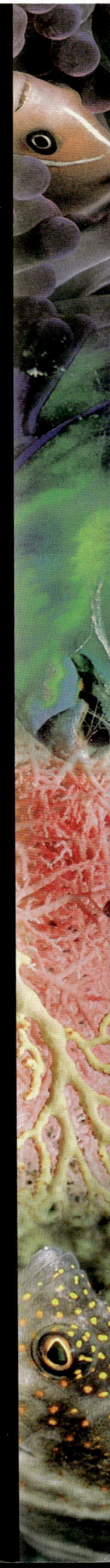

SECTION 4

FISH

FISH ARE EASY TO IDENTIFY. They live in water, breathe through their gills, are covered by shiny scales and swim by swishing their fins and tail. But there are exceptions. Lungfish can live out of water and breathe air. Some eels have no scales. Lampreys and hagfish, and some types of ray, have no fins or tail. But fish, like all other vertebrates, have an inner skeleton with a backbone.

Fish make up a vast and varied group. Their habitats range from the deepest oceans to the clearest mountain streams, from sunlit tropical lagoons to dark, chilly underground lakes. They have a greater size range than almost any other animal group, from dwarf gobies that could fit onto your little fingernail, to massive whale sharks as big as a truck. Fish are almost every shape and colour imaginable, from sharp-nosed, super-streamlined swordfish and marlin, to enormously bulky groupers, snake-like eels, and flatfish that are just that.

Fish obtain food in varied and imaginative ways. Some nibble at seaweed. Others filter tiny bits of food from the water. Sharks are the ultimate razor-toothed predators. Anglerfish use a "rod and line" made from their own bodies to catch their meals – of other fish!

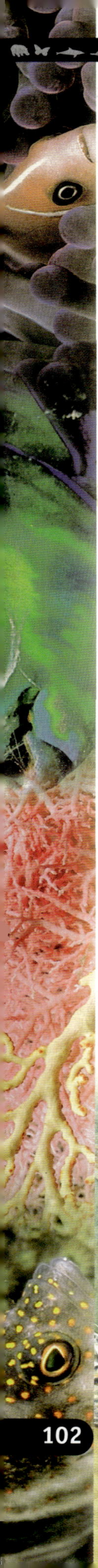

WHAT ARE FISH?

FISH ARE VERTEBRATES (ANIMALS WITH BACKBONES) THAT ARE COLD-BLOODED, LIVE IN WATER, BREATHE BY GILLS, SWIM WITH FINS AND A TAIL, AND HAVE A BODY COVERING OF SCALES. At least, this is true of most fish (page 101). Fish make up by far the largest group of vertebrate animals. There are some 24,000 species, which is more than all other vertebrate animals – amphibians, reptiles, birds and mammals – combined. The first fish to evolve on Earth, some 470 million years ago, were jawless fish. They had sucker-like mouths, rather than biting jaws with teeth. Two small groups, the lampreys and hagfish, survive today. A larger sub-group of fish is the sharks, rays and chimaeras. These are known as cartilaginous fish because they have a "backbone", or vertebral column, made of tough, gristly cartilage rather than true bone. Easily the largest fish sub-group is the bony fish, with skeletons of true bone – as people know if they get the bones stuck when they eat fish. Fish are extremely important as food in many parts of the world.

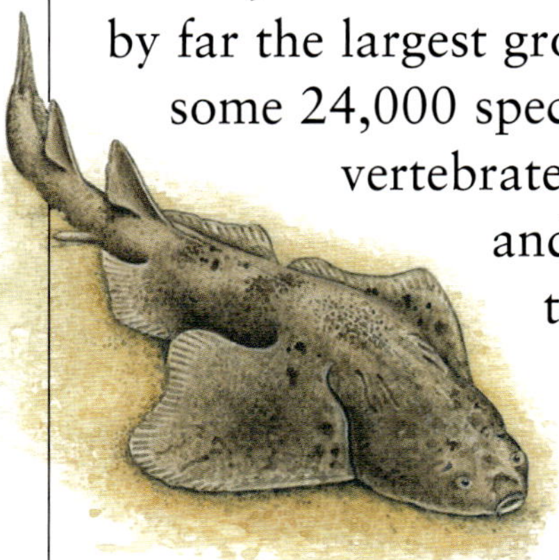

The monkfish, which is an unusual type of shark, has the flattened body shape typical of bottom-living fish.

World Watch

The activities of humans are putting ever more fish species at risk. Some, such as cod, are victims of overfishing – we simply catch too many. Others suffer because we pollute their waters, divert or build dams across their rivers, or take too much water for our own use. We also take fish species to new areas, on purpose or by accident. The large, predatory Nile perch (page 122) was introduced into Africa's Lake Victoria in the early 1960s. It has now eaten many of the lake's own cichlid fish and completely upset the natural balance of life there.

The red-spotted hawkfish is an alert and agile fish of shallow tropical waters around coral reefs.

All animals need oxygen to live. We breathe oxygen gas from the air into our lungs. A fish takes in oxygen dissolved in the water through gills on either side of its head. Most fish have four sets of gills, which are red and feathery. They are made of rows of lamellae, flat, delicate structures, filled with blood. Water flows into the fish's mouth and over the gills, where oxygen passes through the gill coverings into the blood, to be carried around the body. In sharks and other cartilaginous fish, the water then flows to the outside of the body through gill slits. In bony fish, the gills are covered by a bony flap, the operculum or gill cover, with a single slit along its rear edge.

INSIDE A FISH

A typical fish like the salmon has a body that is mainly blocks of muscle, arranged in a zigzag pattern along either side of the backbone. These pull the backbone from side to side to swish the tail and make the fish swim.

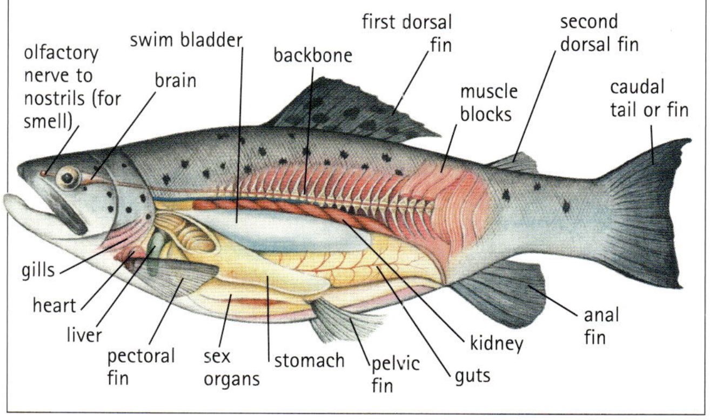

This scene shows members from all the main fish sub-groups. In the centre is a large cartilaginous fish—a wobbegong or carpet shark. It lurks on the sea bed, disguised as a rock. On the lower right is a chimaera, another type of cartilaginous fish. The eel-like creature just above the "wobby" is a lamprey, a jawless fish with a sucker mouth. On the far left three hagfish, also jawless, suck rotting flesh from a carcass. The large silvery fish, upper left, is a tarpon, a type of bony fish.

The common spotted dogfish is one of the smallest sharks.

JAWLESS FISH

Jawless fish have a skeleton made of cartilage, not bone. They also have no side fins, no scales on the long, thin body, round gill openings and a sucking, disc- or funnel-shaped mouth. These creatures are survivors from a very early stage in the evolution of fish. They are mostly scavengers or parasites, sucking the blood of other water creatures.

FISH FINS

Fish have two kinds of fins. These are paired fins, usually somewhere along the sides of the body, and unpaired fins, which are generally the dorsal fins on the top or back, and the anal fins on the underside or belly. The unpaired fins help the fish to swim straight or lean to one side. The tail or caudal fin is also unpaired and provides the main thrust for swimming. The paired fins are the pectoral fins just behind the head and the pelvic fins, usually lower and to the rear. They help the fish turn sideways, slow down and even swim backwards.

Fish *(Pisces)*
- 24,000 species
- most have gills, fins, a tail, and a body covered with scales

Hagfish *(Myxini)*
- about 50 species
- eel-like body
- sucker-like mouth (no jaws)
- live in the sea

Lampreys *(Cephalaspidomorphi)*
- about 38 species
- eel-like body
- sucker-like mouth (no jaws)
- live in the sea and fresh water

Sharks and rays *(Chondrichthyes)*
- about 900 species
- skeleton of cartilage
- no gill flap over gill slits
- most live in the sea
- includes sharks, dogfish, sawfish, rays, skates

Bony fish *(Osteichthyes)*
- over 23,000 species
- skeleton of bone
- gill slits covered by gill flap
- live in the sea and fresh water
- includes vast majority of fish

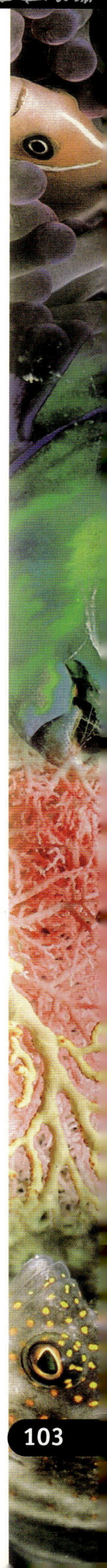

SHARKS AND RAYS

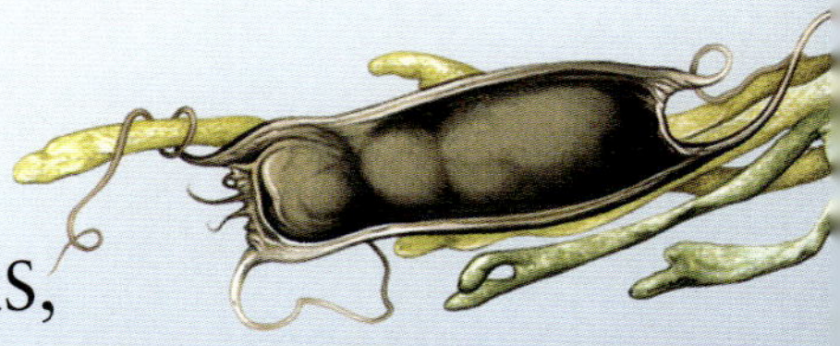

A "mermaid's purse" washed up on a shore is the empty case in which a baby shark or ray developed. It attaches to rocks or weeds by the long, stringy tendrils.

SHARKS AND RAYS, AND THE CREATURES CALLED RATFISH OR CHIMAERAS, MAKE UP THE GROUP CALLED CARTILAGINOUS FISH. Their skeletons are not made of bone, as in other fish, but of cartilage – a gristly substance that is tough, yet light and bendy. The typical shark has a long, streamlined body. It is propelled by a tail with an upper lobe that is usually larger than the lower lobe. The shark's mouth is set back from the snout tip and is full of sharp teeth. The skin is not covered with the usual fish scales, but with tiny pointed structures called dermal denticles. These are much smaller versions of the teeth in the mouth. If you stroke shark skin the wrong way, from tail to head, the dermal denticles make the skin feel so rough that it could cause your hand to bleed.

A typical ratfish has a large head, big eyes, fleshy lips, sharp teeth, a long, tapering body and a "rat's tail" instead of the usual tail fins.

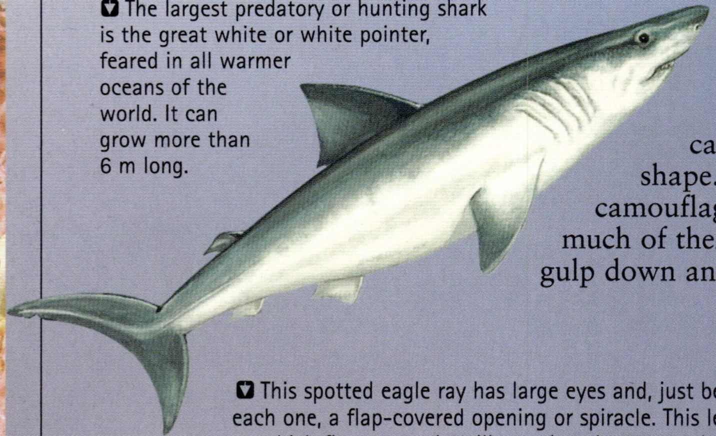

The largest predatory or hunting shark is the great white or white pointer, feared in all warmer oceans of the world. It can grow more than 6 m long.

Most sharks are fast-moving, torpedo-shaped hunters of the open ocean. But others, such as the carpet sharks or wobbegongs, have a flattened body shape. They also have fringes and tassels of skin to camouflage their bodies as seaweed-covered rocks. They spend much of their lives lying on the sea bed, waiting to ambush and gulp down any prey that comes near.

This spotted eagle ray has large eyes and, just behind each one, a flap-covered opening or spiracle. This lets in water which flows over the gills, so that the ray can breathe (take in oxygen from the water). The water then leaves through gill slits on the ray's underside.

World Watch

Every year around the world, 30–50 people are reported as killed by sharks. Also every year, about 100 million sharks are killed by people. They are caught for many reasons – for food, for sport by anglers, because their body parts are thought to have healing powers, and because they might menace tourist areas. Several kinds, including the great white, are now very rare. Some are protected by world wildlife laws.

FLYING THROUGH THE WATER

Most rays also have a body flattened from top to bottom. Their wide, flap-like pectoral fins look and work like a bird's wings. The ray flaps or undulates them to "fly" through the water. The majority of rays have wide, flattened, crunching teeth and feed on shellfish and worms that they uncover on the sea bed.

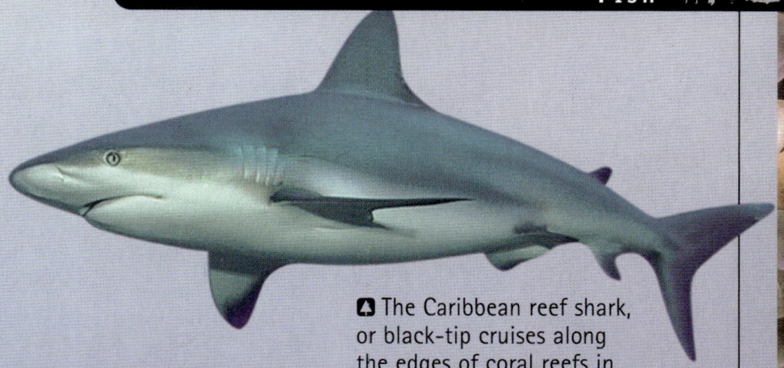

The Caribbean reef shark, or black-tip cruises along the edges of coral reefs in its search for sick or injured fish, seals, seabirds and other likely victims.

POISON FOR DEFENCE

Chimaeras, the fish group also known as ratfish, usually live on or near the sea bed. They can live at great depths of more than 2,000 m. Most chimaeras have long, scale-less bodies. The ratfish (short-nose and long-nose chimaeras) have stringy, rat-like tails. Ploughnose chimaeras have a tail similar to that of a shark. All chimaeras have a long spine at the front of the dorsal (back) fin. This is linked to a venom gland. The poison in the spine can cause a painful wound to an attacker. Most chimaeras eat small sea-bottom creatures such as crabs, clams and shrimps, as well as other fish.

BIGGEST... !

The largest fish in the world is the whale shark, at more than 13 m long. It is not a fierce hunter. It feeds by filtering the tiny plants and animals of the plankton from sea water.

MAKING BABY SHARKS

Different sharks and rays have different ways of producing young. Some, such as the horned or Port Jackson sharks and the dogfish, lay eggs protected by tough, leathery cases. The mother hides these in seaweed or rocks. The youngster develops inside for several weeks, nourished by its large yolk sac, until it is ready to hatch and fend for itself. Others, such as the tiger sharks, produce eggs with thin shells that are kept inside the mother's body. The young feed from their yolk sacs, hatch from the thin shells and are then born. More extraordinary still are the hammerheads, blues, white-tips and bull sharks. The young grow inside the mother, but not inside egg shells. When their yolk is used up, they are nourished directly from the mother's blood. Finally they are born as well-formed young.

Sharks
(Elasmobranchii)
- about 375 species
- all but a couple live in the sea
- includes hammerhead, dogfish, carpet shark, mako, great white

Rays
(Rajiformes)
- about 450 species
- most live in the sea
- includes electric ray, stingray, skate, manta

Chimaeras
(Chimaeriformes)
- about 30 species
- live in the sea
- includes ratfish, chimaera

Most rays, like this southern ray, stay near the sea bed. Like sharks, they have dozens of tiny electricity-sensing pits on the head. These detect weak pulses of electricity from the muscles of buried prey animals, which the ray then digs out. To hide from predators, the ray buries itself in the sand.

STURGEONS AND GARS

There are about 100 species of elephant-nose fish. They live mainly in rivers and swamps in Africa. The fish uses its long, flexible snout to probe in the mud and gravel for small animals to eat.

THE GROUPS OF FISH THAT INCLUDE STURGEONS, PADDLEFISH AND GARS WERE VERY COMMON AND WIDESPREAD MANY MILLIONS OF YEARS AGO WHEN DINOSAURS WALKED THE LAND.

Today there are far fewer species. A typical sturgeon has a long, heavy body with five rows of bony plates. Its mouth has fleshy "whiskers", which are known as barbels. These feel and taste for prey on the bottom of a lake, river or sea. Some types of sturgeon live in rivers and lakes in North America, Europe and Asia. Others grow up in fresh water, then swim out to sea for several years, returning to their rivers to breed. Paddlefish live only in the Mississippi River in North America and the Chang Jiang (Yangtze River) in China. They grow to 1.8 m long and have a flat, spoon-shaped snout. The paddlefish swims along with its mouth wide open, filtering tiny animals from the plankton. The gars or gar pikes of North America are also long, slim fish, with a covering of especially thick, hard scales to protect against attackers. The very long, slender jaws are studded with small teeth. Gars lurk in water weeds, waiting to grab prey.

Most kinds of sturgeon spend part of their lives in the sea, where they feed on bottom-living creatures such as worms, shrimps and flatfish. When they are fully grown, they swim into rivers to breed.

The alligator gar, at 3 m long, is one of the biggest freshwater fish in North America. Like other gars, it is a fierce hunter. It eats smaller fish and shellfish such as crayfish.

ENDANGERED!

Sturgeons are well known for their shiny black eggs, which are called caviar. These are gathered as an expensive food for people to eat. The female sturgeon may be killed in order to take her eggs. Or the eggs can be "milked" from her while she is alive, and then she is put back in the water. Taking eggs for caviar has made most kinds of sturgeon very rare.

The female lays her sticky black eggs among gravel on the riverbed. A large female normally produces more than two million eggs. A female of the largest type of sturgeon, the beluga or white sturgeon, produces up to seven million eggs. After about one week the tiny young hatch out. They stay in the river for up to three years, feeding on small creatures such as water insects, shrimps and worms, which they detect in the mud with their whiskery barbels. Then they swim out to sea, to continue growing.

The plates along a young sturgeon's body are not scales but bony slabs called scutes. These will enlarge and thicken with age.

This sturgeon has the thick bony slabs or scutes of an older fish.

BONYTONGUES

The bonytongue fish group includes the goldeye, mooneye, pirarucu, aruana, butterflyfish and knifefish. They all live in fresh water. The name of the group comes from the structure of the tongue, which has large, stiff bones and teeth.

A GIANT OF FRESH WATER

The pirarucu or arapaima is a huge bonytongue fish that lives in the Amazon region of South America. It grows to more than 3 m long and weighs 200 kg.

Sturgeons *(Acipenseriformes)*
- about 25 species
- most live in fresh water and may travel into the sea
- includes sturgeon, beluga, paddlefish

Bonytongues *(Osteoglossiformes)*
- about 215 species
- live in fresh water
- includes pirarucu, elephant fish

Gars *(Lepisosteiformes)*
- about 7 species
- live in fresh water
- includes longnose gar, alligator gar

Elephant-nose fish *(Mormyriformes)*
- about 100 species
- live in fresh water in Africa
- can make and detect electrical pulses
- some types are caught or farmed for food

Gars have very thick, diamond-shaped scales. They seize prey such as small fish in their long, slim jaws. The common gar pike grows to about 90 cm in length.

This makes it one of the biggest freshwater fish in the world. (Some sturgeons grow larger, but they live partly in the sea.) The pirarucu inhabits stagnant, swampy places where the water has little dissolved oxygen. However, it can gulp air into its swim bladder, which works as a simple lung to absorb the oxygen from the air.

OLDEST... !

Fossils show that coelacanths lived more than 300 million years ago. They were thought to have died out with the dinosaurs, 65 million years ago. Then they were discovered still living in the Indian Ocean near Africa in the 1930s. The fins have fleshy lobes at the base. The legs of the early land animals may have evolved from fins like these.

Unlike most fish, the female pirarucu takes good care of her young. She lays her eggs in a sheltered part of the river, hidden among plants. She guards the eggs against hungry predators, and she also protects the babies or fry when they hatch.

ELECTRIC FISH

Elephant-nose fish are mostly less than 90 cm long. They use the long, flexible snout to dig in the mud for food. These fish are electric! Special muscles at the rear of the body produce weak pulses of electricity, which pass through the water around the fish. The pulses are detected by tiny sensors over the head. The electricity is too weak to stun prey. But another animal nearby disturbs the pattern of pulses and so the elephant-nose fish can detect it. This helps the elephant-nose to avoid enemies and also to find its prey – even in very muddy, murky water and at night.

The beluga of Central Asian lakes and rivers is one of the world's largest fish. The biggest specimens once grew to 8 m long and weighed well over 1.5 tonnes. Few belugas today live long enough to reach 4.5 m. This is due to overfishing and water pollution, and also dams across rivers that interfere with their migration to the sea.

EELS AND HERRINGS

The Atlantic herring is a slender fish with large, silvery, easily damaged scales.

MOST EELS ARE LONG, SLIM, SNAKE-LIKE FISH WITH TINY SCALES OR NONE AT ALL, AND NO PELVIC (REAR SIDE) FINS. Most herrings are small, silvery ocean fish and swim in huge groups or schools. Both these kinds of fish are extremely numerous and are caught by people for food. The largest type of herring is the huge wolf herring, a fierce hunter that can grow more than 3 m long. But most herrings, including sardines or pilchards, sprats and anchovies, are less than 90 cm long. They feed on tiny animals in the plankton. Herrings are, in turn, important food for many larger creatures, including dolphins, and seabirds. Some types of herring live in fresh water in North and South America, parts of Africa and Australia. Most eels live in the sea, but some kinds spend much of their lives in rivers and lakes, and then travel to the sea to lay their eggs. The eggs hatch into thin, see-through young, or larvae. These drift in ocean currents for years before developing into young eels and swimming into rivers.

A spotted moray eel peers from its lair, ready to snap at prey or bite enemies. There are about 100 different species of moray.

The conger, like all eels, has long dorsal and anal fins on the top and underside of the body.

LURKING DANGER

Moray eels live in tropical and subtropical waters, often around coral reefs. Most have scale-less bodies, boldly patterned with bright colours, and strong, sharp teeth. Morays are powerful hunters and tend to hide in crevices in rocks, watching for prey such as fish and squid. The largest morays measure more than 3.5 m long.

The wolf herring has a long body and large, sharp teeth. It lives in the warm, shallow waters of the Indian and West Pacific Oceans.

THE EEL'S JOURNEY

Freshwater eels live in rivers and lakes, but travel to the sea to spawn (lay their eggs and breed). American and European eels migrate to the weed-rich Sargasso Sea, in the western North Atlantic. Here, ocean currents swirl warm water down to great depths. The adult eels dive down many hundreds of metres, breed and then die. The eggs hatch into leaf-shaped larvae as long as a thumbnail. European eel larvae drift across the Atlantic in the Gulf Stream current for three or four years, altering their shape as they go. Near European coasts they change, or metamorphose, into young eels, called elvers. These swim into rivers, where they live for several years until they are 50–100 cm long and ready to breed. American eel larvae drift west and their journey takes only a year or two.

one year after hatching
two years after hatching
three years after hatching
four years after hatching

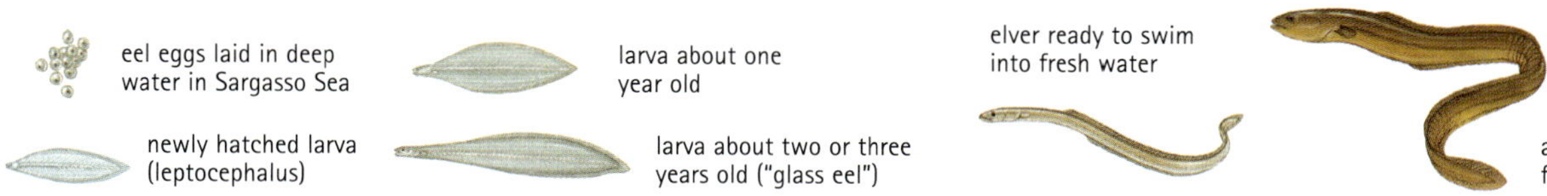

DEEP-SEA EELS

Gulper eels live in the darkness of the deep ocean, where prey is hard to find. They swim with their enormous mouths wide open, ready to engulf any creature that will fit through the jaws. These eels have tiny eyes or none at all, since they live in permanent blackness more than 900 m below the surface. They grow to about 60 cm long.

A GARDEN OF EELS

Garden eels live in colonies on the sea bed, usually in a shallow, sunlit area where water currents bring plenty of plankton. Each eel digs a burrow with its tail and spends much of its time with its rear half anchored inside. Its top half extends upwards so it can feed on the plankton. Lots of these eels close together sway in the current like tall flowers in a garden. If danger comes near, such as a predatory fish, the eels quickly whisk themselves into their burrows and the entire "garden" disappears.

BREEDING HERRINGS

Most types of herring, including the Atlantic herring, lay their eggs close to the sea bed. The eggs stay there until they hatch into tiny larvae 5 mm long. These drift in the plankton until they are able to swim in schools. The herring grows to about 40 cm long, while the sardine is 25 cm. The various kinds of anchovies are about 20 cm long.

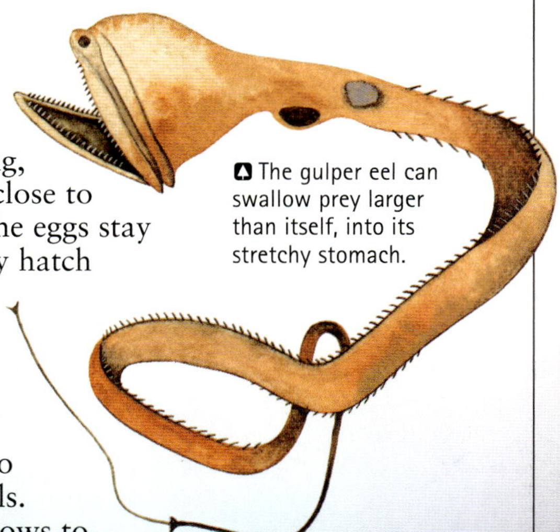

The gulper eel can swallow prey larger than itself, into its stretchy stomach.

Thousands of sardines shoal in the shallow waters near the Galapagos Islands in the Pacific Ocean.

Eels
(Anguilliformes)
- about 690 species
- mostly live in the sea, a few are freshwater
- includes moray, conger, garden, snipe and gulper eels

Herrings
(Clupeiformes)
- about 360 species
- live in the sea, filtering plankton
- includes sardine or pilchard, anchovy, shad, menhaden

SALMON, PIKE AND HATCHETFISH

A viperfish dangles a glowing bait in front of its mouth. Its "fishing rod" is made from the greatly lengthened first or second ray (spine) of its dorsal (back) fin.

SALMON AND THEIR COUSINS – TROUT, CHARR, WHITEFISH, SMELT AND GRAYLING – LIVE MAINLY IN RIVERS AND LAKES IN NORTHERN CONTINENTS. They are mostly sleek fish with slender, tapering bodies and forked tails. Their small, sharp teeth show that they hunt animals for food. The various types of salmon make regular journeys or migrations between salt and fresh water. The young are born in rivers, but after a few years' feeding and growing, they swim into the sea, where they spend the next few years. Then they return to the rivers where they grew up, to spawn. Pike and pickerels spend all their lives in fresh water. Hatchetfish and viperfish live in deep oceans. Many have special light-producing parts on their bodies. The eerie glow from these lights helps to lure prey, attract a mate and confuse an enemy.

A close-up of the viperfish's mouth shows its long, needle-shaped teeth, at the front of the lower jaw. Viperfish grow to about 30 cm in length.

The rainbow trout has pink-tinged sides and spots on its tail. It has escaped from fish farms into rivers around the world.

How Atlantic and Pacific salmon return from the middle of the ocean to the exact stream where they hatched from eggs is one of the marvels of the animal world. It is known that they can detect the "smell" of their home river, from dissolved minerals and other substances, but how they navigate from far out at sea is not fully understood. The journey upstream is dangerous and tiring. Pacific salmon, in particular, must leap many waterfalls on the way. The males change in colour and the lower jaw grows a hooked tip as they reach home.

POP-EYED!

The baby black dragonfish looks pop-eyed. Its eyes are on long stalks, almost like a garden snail. As the dragonfish grows, the stalks shrink back into the head. The eyes finally settle and slot into the normal sockets in the skull.

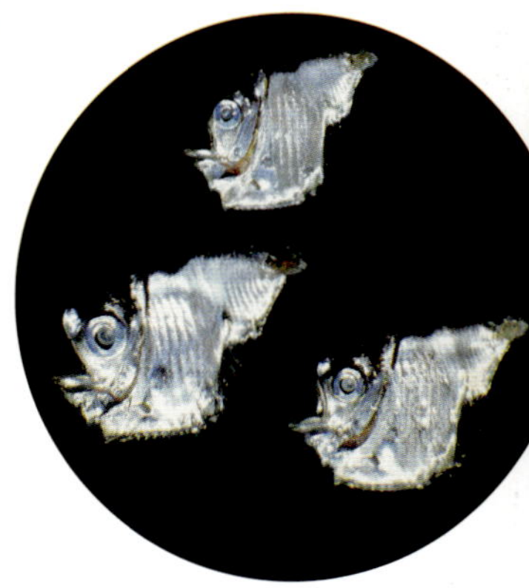

Deep-sea hatchetfish are named from their silvery, narrow, deep-chested body shape, which resembles an axe or hatchet.

Salmon gather below a waterfall, ready to surge upwards and leap the obstacle.

Salmon leap up rapids and waterfalls with powerful thrusts of the tail. They can swim 100 km upstream each day.

In the spawning stream, male and female court briefly. Then she sheds her eggs (spawn) on the gravel bed and he fertilizes them with his sperm (milt). By this time many of the salmon are so exhausted that they are easy prey for eagles, bears or wolves. Most Pacific salmon die after they have spawned. Atlantic salmon may survive, return to the sea, and make the journey again two or three times. Large salmon grow to 1.2 m in length and weigh 27 kg.

THE VARIABLE TROUT

There are two forms of the common trout. These are the silvery sea trout, which migrates between river and sea, and the smaller, darker-spotted brown trout, which stays in fresh water.

Copper sweepers are reddish-gold members of the hatchetfish group, the bristlemouths. This shoal is sheltering from danger below a deep rock overhang.

Salmon *(Salmoniformes)*
- about 140 species
- freshwater and sea-dwelling
- includes salmon, trout, smelt, charr, grayling

Pike *(Esociformes)*
- about 12 species
- freshwater
- includes pike, pickerel, muskellunge *(muskie)*

Bristlemouths *(Stomiiformes)*
- about 250 species
- live only in the sea
- includes hatchetfish, dragonfish, viperfish, snaggletooth, loosejaw

Most trout eat baby fish, worms and other small prey. Some types are farmed as food for people.

HIDDEN DANGER

The largest member of the pike group is the muskellunge or muskie of North America, which grows up to 1.5 m long and can weigh as much as 30 kg. The northern pike looks similar, but shorter. It lives in rivers and lakes in northern regions around the world. This huge-mouthed predator lies hidden among water plants, watching for prey. When it spots a victim, the pike lunges like lightning from the weed and seizes the prey with its sharp teeth.

SWIMMING HATCHETS

Common hatchetfish are numerous in warm seas, at depths of about 180–750 m. They measure only 8 cm long and are preyed on by many larger sea hunters. The common hatchetfish has a deep, flattened body, a large mouth, bulging eyes and rows of light-producing organs along the belly. The pattern of lights along the body helps each type of hatchetfish to recognize its own species at mating time in the darkness.

Fierce-looking deep-sea viperfish have long, backwards-pointing teeth. They grab prey, which are lured by the long fin spine tipped with a light-producing organ.

The female salmon hides her eggs in the gravel on the riverbed. The eggs contain reddish-yellow yolk, which nourishes the baby fish.

CHARACINS, CARP AND CATFISH

The many colours and shapes of goldfish have been bred over centuries from wild carp.

THESE THREE GROUPS INCLUDE NEARLY A THIRD OF ALL FISH – MORE THAN 6,000 SPECIES. They vary widely in appearance, but most live in fresh water. The majority can detect sounds in water, by picking up sound waves in the swim bladder, which other fish cannot do so well. In addition, these fish have special alarm substances in the skin that are released into the water if the skin is damaged. When a fish is seized by a predator, the substance passes into the water, alerting other members of the species to escape.

Various kinds of characin tigerfish are named after their tiger-like stripes and the way they stalk and eat other fish.

Members of the carp group live across North America, Europe, northern Asia and Africa. They lack teeth in their jaws. Instead, they have a pair of toothed bones in the lower throat that they use to crush and grind food against a hardened pad at the base of the skull. Most carp eat a wide range of foods, including plants, fish and shellfish.

Some types of carp, including the roach, bream, common and crucian carp, have been introduced to lakes and slow rivers around the world. They are caught by anglers and are popular as food. These types of carp are bottom feeders. They grub in the mud, using their sensitive whisker-like barbels to find worms, snails and shrimps.

AN UNUSUAL NURSERY

Most members of the carp group simply scatter their eggs in water and leave the young to hatch and fend for themselves. But the small carp, known as the bitterling, has a more unusual method. At the start of the breeding season the female develops a long egg-laying tube, the ovipositor.

The European catfish, or wels, is one of several kinds of catfish that grow to a massive size, reaching more than 1.8 m long.

Blue piranha

She uses this to place her eggs inside the shell of a freshwater mussel. The male bitterling releases his sperm near the mussel. As the mussel filter-feeds, the sperm are sucked in to fertilize the eggs.

Bream

The neon tetra's colours are so bright, they seem to glow like electric neon lights.

Glassfish, types of small carp, form large schools. Like most carp, they feed at night.

CHARACINS

The characins live in rivers and lakes in Central and South America and Africa. They include the piranhas of South America, and the tetras that have been bred in many colours as popular aquarium fish. Some characins eat plants, others eat small creatures such as insects and worms, and still others are hunters of larger animals such as fish and frogs. One group, the toothless characins, survive by sucking up the slime that covers leaves, stones and other underwater objects.

NOT ALL SO FIERCE

The piranhas of South America have a fearsome reputation as bloodthirsty hunters. But some types of piranha, such as the pacu, feed on plants. The flesh-eating types include the red piranha. They are only about 30 cm long, but they have strong jaws and razor-sharp teeth for slicing chunks of flesh out of their victims.

One piranha cannot do much harm. But a large school of them can strip the flesh from a large animal like a horse in minutes. Piranhas are attracted by blood in the water. So a wounded animal that comes to drink at the river is in real danger.

The electric eel is shaped like an eel, but it is really a type of knifefish. It grows more than 2 m long and can give a 550-volt electric shock.

CAT'S WHISKERS

Catfish are named for the very long, whisker-like barbels around the mouth. The fleshy barbels taste the water to find food. Most catfish also have stiff spines at the front of the dorsal and pectoral fins. These can be "locked" in position, sticking outwards, so the fish is hard to swallow.

Carp *(Cypriniformes)*
- about 2,050 species
- almost all live in fresh water
- includes goldfish, loach, minnow, tench, barbel, mahseer

Characins *(Charciformes)*
- about 1,400 species
- live in fresh water
- includes pike characin, tetra, piranha, pacu, giant tigerfish

Catfish and knifefish *(Siluriformes)*
- about 2,415 species
- most live in fresh water
- includes wels, walking catfish, knifefish, butterfish, electric eel

SHOCKING FISH

Knifefish are close relatives of catfish. They have special muscles that can produce pulses of electricity in the surrounding water. These pulses help them to find their way in muddy, dark lakes and rivers. The knifefish that produces the most powerful electrical pulses is the electric eel of northern South America. The electricity is so strong, it can stun prey fish.

Another amazing catfish is the walking catfish. It can crawl on land, using its strong pectoral fins, and breathe air while it does so.

The mirror carp has shiny, extra-large scales.

A female bitterling lays her eggs into a mussel, and the male waits to fertilize them. The baby fish emerge about 2–3 weeks later.

COD, ANGLERFISH AND TOADFISH

Atlantic cod can be recognized by their three dorsal fins.

THE VARIOUS TYPES OF COD INCLUDE HAKE, HADDOCK AND WHITING. They are mostly long, fast-swimming fish with large fins, and live in cool seas around the world, some at great depths. They are extremely valuable as food and in the past millions of tonnes were caught every year. But overfishing has greatly reduced their numbers in some areas. Anglerfish, batfish and frogfish live in warmer seas and are much more squat in shape, with a short body, large head, and gaping mouth. They are not built for speed and prefer to lie in wait for prey. The front spine of the anglerfish's dorsal (back) fin is separate from the rest of the fin. It forms a long "fishing rod" with its fleshy tip as a bait to attract other fish. Once a victim is near enough, the angler opens its huge mouth and the rush of water sucks in the prey. Toadfish live in warm coastal waters. They have excellent camouflage with lots of fleshy fringes, flaps and whiskery barbels around the big head and wide mouth, so they look like seaweed.

The football-fish is a type of anglerfish. It is about 60 cm long and has stud-like bony plates on its body. Like all anglerfish, it lures its prey.

The Atlantic cod grows to about 1.2 m long and is the best-known fish of the cod group. This group includes many other fish eaten as food, such as ling, pollock, rockling and pout. Like many of these fish, the haddock has a fleshy, sensitive barbel on its chin to help it find food such as worms and shellfish on the sea bed.

The rosy-lipped batfish crawls well on its strong, leg-like fins. It spends more time walking than swimming.

Haddock usually spawn in spring, shedding large numbers of eggs into the water, where they float near the surface. When the young fish hatch, they stay in the surface waters until they are about 5 cm long. At this stage they move closer to the ocean floor.

RAT-TAILS

The cod group also includes the grenadiers or rat-tails, which live between 150 m and 1,800 m below the surface of the sea. With a large head, short body and long, rat-like tail, the grenadier resembles the ratfish (page 104). The male makes loud sounds using muscles linked to his swim-bladder, probably to attract a mate.

Toadfish look like toads, and make toad-like croaks. The male makes a nest hole in weed and mud, and croaks by vibrating his swim-bladder to encourage a female to lay eggs in the nest.

A toadfish's face, with its broad mouth and big eyes, looks like the face of a toad.

A flagtail rock cod shows off its small, sharp teeth and its gills in the cheek region.

This deep-sea anglerfish has a glowing lure above its head. Its long, frilly chin barbel resembles a frond of seaweed.

The female glues each egg into the nest by a sticky disc on its underside. The male guards the nest until the baby fish hatch. They remain glued to the nest for a few days. Even when they break free, he continues to guard them.

ANGLERS AND FROGFISH

Anglerfish are so-named because they do what human anglers do – use a "rod and bait" to catch other fish. There are coastal and deep-sea kinds. The lure or bait of the female deep-sea anglerfish glows in the darkness, to attract curious fish. The male deep-sea angler is one tenth the size of the female. He has no lure, and no teeth either, so he cannot feed. But he does have an excellent sense of smell, to find the female.

Once he locates a mate, he attaches himself to her and fertilizes her eggs. He may then merge partly into her body and live as a parasite on her. This saves both partners a long search, since mates are difficult to find in the vast, deep ocean!

The frogfish lies on the sea bed, watching for prey. Its lumpy, frilly body gives amazing camouflage among seaweeds, corals and sponges. It can even change colour to match the surroundings. Frogfish grow up to 20 cm long and eat small fish, shellfish and worms.

Among the sponges and corals of the Caribbean lurks a dark grey, long-lure frogfish (its mouth is to the left of the picture). Behind it, a smaller, pale frogfish looks at the camera.

Cod
(Gadiformes)
- about 500 species
- nearly all live in the sea
- includes cod, grenadier, hake, ling

Anglerfish
(Lophiiformes)
- about 300 species
- all live in the sea, often at great depths
- includes frogfish, batfish, football-fish, sargassumfish

Toadfish
(Batrachoidiformes)
- about 70 species
- most live on the sea bed
- includes midshipman

SCORPIONFISH AND SEAHORSES

SCORPIONFISH RANGE IN SHAPE FROM LONG AND SLENDER TO ALMOST AS ROUND AS BALLOONS. Most have spines, especially on the head and fins. Some, including the lionfish and stonefish, are extremely dangerous because the venom from their spines can kill people. Scorpionfish are all predators, catching other fish and shellfish. The pipefish and seahorse group is also extremely varied in shape, but most of the members have long, tube-shaped snouts. They live in warm, shallow waters near the coast. This group includes seadragons, shrimpfish, sea moths and trumpetfish. There is also a fish called the tubesnout, with a tubular snout, but it is in yet another fish group – the sticklebacks. They are found in rivers and lakes in northern continents and in the Atlantic and Pacific Oceans. Sticklebacks get their name from the strong, prickle-like spines on their backs.

▲ The lionfish has lacy, fan-shaped fins. These look delicate, but their spines jab deadly poison.

World Watch

Every year, millions of seahorses are killed. Their bodies are dried and ground up to make powders which are supposed to have medical uses, such as relieving asthma. Other seahorses are dried and used to make souvenirs such as fobs for key rings. In some years an estimated 8 million seahorses are killed in Southeast Asia. These little fish have become extremely rare in some places. One idea is that seahorses should be caught only in certain areas, and left to breed and keep up their numbers in nearby areas.

The scorpionfish's lumpy, mottled body is difficult to see as it lies among stones on the sea bed, watching for prey. Sharp spines in its dorsal and pelvic fins are linked to venom glands and can cause serious wounds. Its close relative, the lionfish, is far easier to see, with its bright colours, fan-like fins and lazy swimming. These features warn other creatures that the lionfish has deadly poison in its fin spines.

SUCKERED TO THE ROCKS

The lumpsucker, a relative of the scorpionfish, has a sucking disc on its throat formed from its pelvic fins. With this disc, the fish clings onto rocks in the shallows, to avoid being battered by waves. The small, dark eggs of lumpsuckers are sold as a type of caviar.

FATHER GIVES BIRTH

The seahorse does not lay eggs, but seems to give birth to its baby fish – and it is not the female that does this, but the male! The female seahorse lays her eggs into a special pouch on the male's front. He keeps the eggs safe here while they hatch and grow.

◀ The stonefish lies in shallow water, among weed and rocks, or part-buried in sand. People sometimes accidentally step on it when wading along a beach. The small spines on its back contain one of the most powerful venoms in the animal kingdom.

The flying gurnard of the Atlantic Ocean has enormous pectoral fins, like wide wings. But this fish cannot fly, or even glide like the flyingfish.

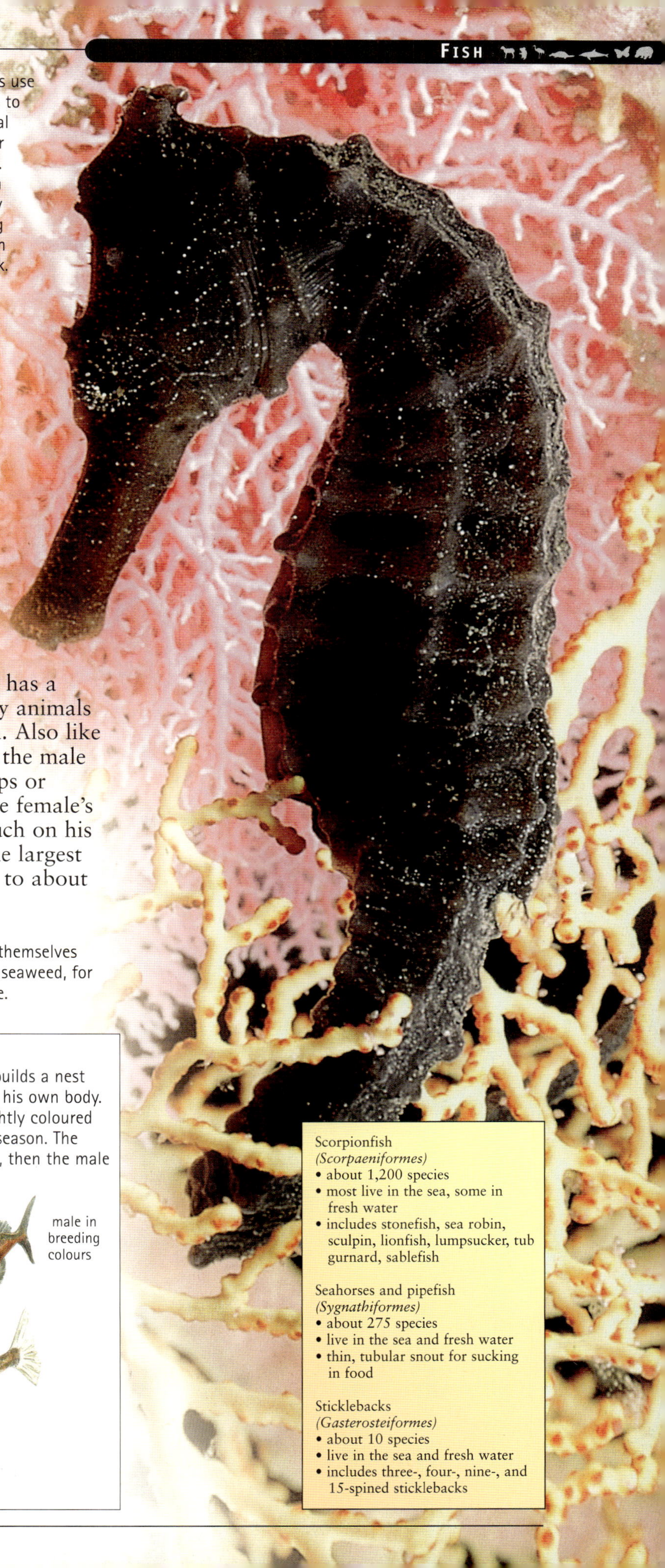

Seahorses use their curly tails to hang onto coral branches or seaweed fronds. They swim slowly by rapidly flapping the dorsal fin on the back.

The male seahorse even nourishes the tiny babies with a special substance from his own body. When the young are ready for the outside world, they shoot out through the opening of the pouch. They quickly attach themselves to floating weed or other objects and, like their parents, feed on tiny animal plankton.

PIPEFISH

The pipefish has a pencil-sized body encased in bony armour plates. Like its cousin, the seahorse, it has a long snout but no teeth, and feeds by sucking in tiny animals from the plankton. Also like the seahorse, the male pipefish keeps or incubates the female's eggs in a pouch on his own body. The largest pipefish grow to about 50 cm long.

Pipefish curve themselves into the shape of seaweed, for better camouflage.

CARING PARENT

The male three-spined stickleback takes good care of his young. He builds a nest from bits of water plants stuck together with sticky substances from his own body. He then "dances" to attract a female, swimming to show off his brightly coloured throat and underside. These have turned bright red for the breeding season. The female comes to the nest and lays her eggs, then the male fertilizes them. He stays at the nest and chases off intruders. When the fry (baby fish) hatch, he guards them for a few weeks, until they can fend for themselves.

Scorpionfish
(Scorpaeniformes)
- about 1,200 species
- most live in the sea, some in fresh water
- includes stonefish, sea robin, sculpin, lionfish, lumpsucker, tub gurnard, sablefish

Seahorses and pipefish
(Sygnathiformes)
- about 275 species
- live in the sea and fresh water
- thin, tubular snout for sucking in food

Sticklebacks
(Gasterosteiformes)
- about 10 species
- live in the sea and fresh water
- includes three-, four-, nine-, and 15-spined sticklebacks

FLYINGFISH, SILVERSIDES AND KILLIFISH

Mosquitofish have been put into streams around the world, to control mosquito pests.

THE FLYINGFISH GROUP INCLUDES NEEDLEFISH, LONGTOMS AND HALFBEAKS. They are mostly very silvery, slim and streamlined, with spear-like pointed snouts, and dorsal and anal fins near the tail. Flyingfish themselves should really be called glidingfish. They swoop above the surface for a few seconds using their wing-like pectoral fins. Silversides are small, shoal-dwelling fish of tropical and temperate seas and fresh water. Most have large eyes, extremely shiny and silvery scales and two dorsal fins. Some, such as the rainbowfish, are popular in aquaria. Killifish are mostly small and hardy, and live in fresh water – even in the stagnant or brackish (slightly salty) water of ditches, canals, salt marshes and estuaries. Most types live near the surface, feeding on insects and bits of plants. One of the most common is the mosquitofish, named because it feeds on mosquito larvae. It has been introduced to most parts of the world. Without it, there would be many more mosquitoes!

The Atlantic flyingfish is about 40 cm long, and is "four-winged". Its large pelvic fins lie behind and below the main pectoral fins.

All flyingfish have large, wing-like pectoral fins just behind the head. Some "four-winged" types also have large pelvic fins, to help them glide. If danger threatens the flyingfish builds up speed just under the water's surface, thrashing its tail powerfully and holding its fins against its body. Then it leaps into the air and stretches its fins out sideways to soar along. A long glide may last 20–30 seconds and cover 180 m at 90–180 cm high. Flyingfish feed on plankton and small animals. They, in turn, are eaten by many larger fast-swimming fish, such as tuna and marlin.

The four-eyed fish has only two eyes, but each is divided into two by a dark band. The lower part is curved to see clearly in water, while the curvature of the upper part is suited to air. Floating at the surface, this fish can look out for prey and enemies, both above and below the water.

World Watch

Among the rarest fish in the world are Devil's Hole pupfish, small killifish less than 2.5 cm long. They live in an underground pool in the flooded cave system under Death Valley, California, USA – and nowhere else. Water was pumped out of the cave network for use by people and farms. But the water level in the pupfish pool fell so much that the species was in danger of extinction. The US Supreme Court ordered that enough water must remain in the pool for the pupfish to survive.

HALF A BEAK

The slender-bodied halfbeak is named for its half-a-beak – its long, sharp snout is made of its lower jaw only. The upper jaw is much shorter. Many halfbeaks feed on the seaweed called sea grass, which they gather with the lower jaw. Others feed on smaller fish or floating insects.

The silver needlefish is typical of the 25 or so kinds of needlefish and garfish. Some needlefish in the Amazon region grow to only 5 cm long.

GRUNIONS

The grunion is a silverside about 20 cm long that lives along North American Pacific coasts. Its breeding times are linked to the cycle of the moon and tides. At a full moon and spring (extra-high) tide, huge numbers of grunions "surf" ashore on the incoming breakers. They mate on the beach, lay their eggs in the sand and return to the sea on receding waves. Two weeks later, at the new moon and next spring tide, the eggs hatch and the young grunions are swept out to sea.

GUPPIES GALORE

Guppies come from tropical South America, but have now been introduced to most other parts of the world. Like mosquitofish, they eat the water-dwelling larvae and pupae of mosquitoes. The babies develop inside the female. So she gives birth to tiny young, rather than laying eggs. The babies are ready to breed at 10 weeks old.

Guppies belong to the killifish group. They are bred in many colours for aquaria.

The small, pointed teeth of longtoms grab small, wriggling prey.

Flyingfish *(Beloniiformes)*
- about 160 species
- live in the sea and fresh water
- includes two- and four-winged flyingfish, halfbeak, garfish, saury, houndfish, ricefish, needlefish

Silversides *(Atheriniformes)*
- about 250 species
- live in the sea and fresh water
- includes grunion, silversides, rainbowfish, swordtail

Killifish *(Cyprinodontiformes)*
- about 600 species
- live mainly in fresh water
- includes guppy, mosquito fish, four-eyed fish, mummichog or common killifish, toothcarps

FLATFISH AND TRIGGERFIS

Different types of pufferfish have vivid colours and patterns. They "puff" up by swallowing water, so becoming too big to be swallowed.

FLATFISH LIVE IN ALL THE WORLD'S OCEANS, EXCEPT IN POLAR REGIONS. There are a few species in fresh water. The body of a flatfish is extremely flattened from one side to the other. (Rays look similar, but their bodies are flattened from top to bottom.) The flatfish spends much of its life swimming or lying on one side on the sea bed. Both its eyes are on the other side, facing upwards, so it can watch for prey and predators. Some flatfish have both eyes on the right side; others have them on the left. Many flatfish are also masters of camouflage. They change their coloration and pattern to match the surroundings, making them very hard to see. All flatfish are predators and feed on shellfish, worms and similar sea bed animals. The triggerfish group includes poisonous pufferfish, spiny porcupinefish that can puff up their bodies like balloons, and the giant ocean sunfish. In most of these fish the mouth and a few teeth form a structure like a bird's beak. Most live along tropical coasts near the sea bed.

The peacock flounder has both eyes on the left body side. It also has a large, spiny dorsal fin that begins just below its mouth.

Ocean sunfish

When a baby flatfish first hatches from its egg, it has a normal fish-like body shape, with an eye on each side of its head. Over the next few weeks, one eye moves across the top of its head, so it is close to the other eye. At the same time the body becomes thin or flat and the mouth twists so that it lies on the same side as the two eyes. Turbots, some flounders, topknots, brill and the windowpane (an exceptionally flat flatfish) usually have both eyes on the left side, and so lie on the right or blind underside. Halibut, plaice, dab, other flounders and most soles are right-eyed. A resting flatfish usually flicks a little sand or gravel over its body, to conceal its fins and blur its outline for even better camouflage.

TASTY?!

Some pufferfish have extremely poisonous flesh, yet they are eaten as a delicacy, fugu, by people in some Asian countries. The fish are prepared by specially trained chefs, who know which body parts contain the poison.

The common flounder grows to about 50 cm long. It lies on its left side, unlike the summer, starry and peacock flounders.

BIGGEST FLATFISH

The Atlantic halibut is one of the biggest of all the flatfish, at 2.5 m long and 295 kg in weight. However, due to overfishing, halibut of this size are now rare. They are more active than most flatfish, and chase prey rather than just lying in wait on the sea floor. Halibut feed on other fish, as well as on squid and crustaceans such as shrimps.

The cowfish is a type of triggerfish named for the two spines above its eyes, which look like a cow's horns.

TRIGGERFISH

Most triggerfish are brightly coloured and live around coral reefs. They are named for the special tilting spines of the first dorsal fin. The front, larger spine can be "locked" upright by the second spine just behind it, like cocking the trigger of a gun. When in danger, the triggerfish takes shelter in a crevice among the rocks and locks its strong spine in the upright position. It is then very difficult for a predator to attack and remove the triggerfish.

Plaice, like most flatfish, have a pale or white underside. This is because it is rarely seen.

PUFFERS AND PORCUPINE SPINES

The slow-swimming porcupinefish grows to about 90 cm long and lives in warm coastal waters, where it feeds on prey such as sea urchins, starfish and shellfish. For protection, it is covered with large, sharp spines. Normally these lie flat against the body. But if threatened, the porcupinefish gulps in water to make its body swell in size, until it is almost round. This forces the spines to stand out, making the fish like a huge prickly beach ball.

SUNBATHING FISH

The amazing ocean sunfish is shaped like a huge pancake. It has tall, thin dorsal and anal fins, and a fleshy frill for a tail. This massive fish grows to 4 m long and weighs up to 2 tonnes. Ocean sunfish are rare and live far out at sea, eating jellyfish, comb-jellies and other soft-bodied creatures. The name comes from this fish's habit of lying on the sea's surface, as though it is sunbathing.

The porcupinefish can puff itself up and has the added deterrent of sharp spines. Its hard, beak-like mouth crushes shellfish, urchins and crabs.

Flatfish
(Pleuronectiformes)
- about 540 species
- nearly all live in the sea
- includes sole, plaice, turbot, brill, tonguefish, adalah

Triggerfish
(Tetraodontiformes)
- about 350 species
- mostly sea-dwelling, some freshwater species
- includes boxfish, pufferfish, burrfish, cowfish, filefish

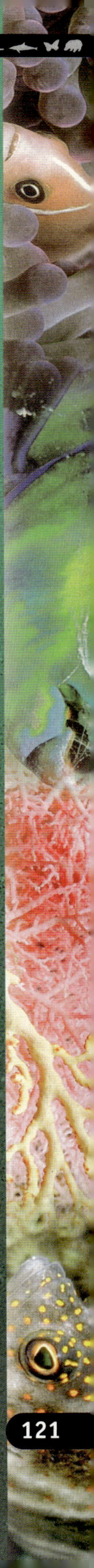

PERCH, GROUPERS AND DRUMS

THE HUGE GROUP OF PERCH-LIKE FISH, THE PERCIFORMS, CONTAINS MORE THAN 9,000 SPECIES – ALMOST HALF OF ALL KINDS OF FISH. They range from tiny gobies smaller than the word 'goby', to huge, strong, superfast, open-ocean predators such as marlin and barracudas, to ponderous, massive, vast-mouthed, heavy-bodied groupers. Perch-like fish live in all aquatic (watery) habitats, from rushing mountain streams to tropical coral reefs, icy polar seas and the ocean depths. Most have a front dorsal fin with spiny fin rays (the "rods" that hold up the soft fin parts). Some have a second dorsal fin too, but this has soft, bendy fin rays. There is also a spine at the front of each pelvic fin, and the pelvic fins are quite far forward on the body, below the pectoral fins.

Archerfish are small, perch-like fish of tropical rivers, swamps, bays and estuaries. The archer gulps in a mouthful of water and squirts it hard from just under the surface at a small insect or similar target on a plant above. The victim is knocked into the water and gobbled up.

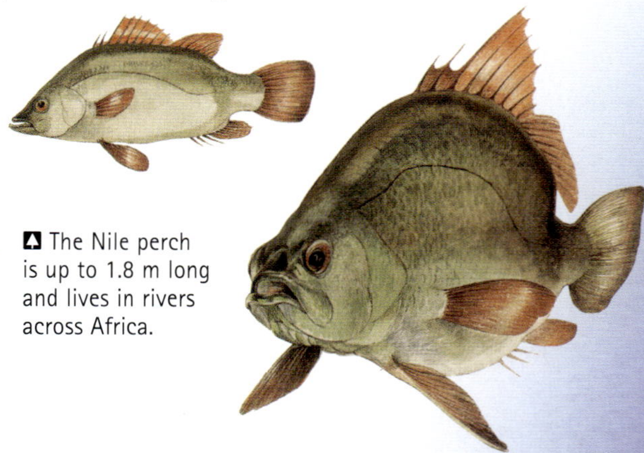

The Nile perch is up to 1.8 m long and lives in rivers across Africa.

Groupers and seabass make up one of the biggest sea-dwelling families of perch-like fish. Most have robust, powerful bodies and two or three spines on the gill flap. Some seabasses and groupers, such as the striped bass and Nassau grouper, are important food fish and are caught in large numbers. The giant seabass of the Pacific North American coast grows to 1.8 m long. The jewfish is the largest member of the family. It can grow to more than 2.4 m long and weigh as much as 295 kg. It usually lives in shallow water close to the shore, where it preys on a range of creatures including fish, squid, crabs and shellfish.

AGGRESSIVE GROUPERS

Groupers are fierce hunters and usually ambush their prey. They hide among rocks and seize anything that comes near in their huge mouths. Dusk is the favourite hunting time. Groupers have been known to follow human divers, but attacks are rare.

A coney grouper, 30 cm long, watches from near its lair, a cave in a coral reef.

NOISY FISH

Another large group of perch-like fish is the drum and croaker family. Most live in shallow tropical seas. As their names suggest, these fish make a variety of sounds using special muscles to vibrate the swim bladder. The black drum of the western Atlantic Ocean grows to 1.8 m long and can weigh as much as 65 kg. The white seabass is also a type of drum, and about the same size.

World Watch

Many darter species live only in one small area and so easily become endangered. One species, the snail darter, was threatened by a new dam in the Little Tennessee River, USA. This river was thought to be its only home. Despite the efforts of conservationists, plans for the dam went ahead. However, to save the fish, plans were also made to move some of the snail darters to the nearby Tennessee River and its branches. These rivers were studied to see if they were suitable. Amazingly, small and previously unknown populations of snail darters were discovered in them. Luckily the fish species was saved from extinction.

The Murray cod is a type of seabass, but it lives in lakes and rivers in eastern Australia. It may reach a length of 1.8 m.

Jack-knife drum fish

FAST DARTERS

The largest freshwater group of perch-like fish is the perch family itself, with more than 160 species living in North America, Europe and Asia. The perch, with its spiny dorsal fin and greenish dark-barred body, has been introduced to lakes and slow-flowing rivers in many parts of the world. Some members of this family are small, colourful fish called darters, which live along the beds of fast-moving streams in North America. Most are less than 10 cm long. The males are especially brightly coloured during the breeding season, when they swim and dart to attract female darters.

The male finds a nesting area among gravel on the stream bed, where the female lays her eggs. He fertilizes the eggs and guards them until they hatch.

The walleye is one of the largest in the perch family, at 90 cm long. It lives deep in large rivers and lakes, eating fish, frogs and insects. Newly hatched fry drift for a few days near the surface, nourished by their yolk sacs. Then they feed on plankton until they are big enough to catch fish.

SOME PERCH-LIKE GROUPS:

Perches *(Percidae)*
- about 160 species
- live in fresh water
- includes darters, ruffe, zander

Groupers and seabass *(Serranidae)*
- about 400 species
- most live in the sea
- includes jewfish, coney

Drums and croakers *(Sciaenidae)*
- about 270 species
- most live in the sea
- includes Atlantic croaker, jack-knife fish, red drum, black drum, red mullet, spotted seatrout

The brown marbled grouper is one of several groupers that grows larger than an adult human. It can easily swallow prey up to 90 cm long, into its cavernous mouth.

TUNAS AND MARLINS

FEW FISH ARE SLEEKER AND FASTER THAN THESE SUPER-STREAMLINED MEMBERS OF THE PERCH-LIKE GROUP (PAGE 122). Tunas and their smaller cousins, bonitos and mackerels, are known as scombrids and have torpedo-shaped bodies. The crescent tail gives maximum power as it thrashes from side to side, to thrust the fish through the water. These types of fish live around the world, especially in warm waters, and are caught in huge numbers as food for people. The marlins and sailfish, called billfish, are also high-speed swimmers. They cruise long distances across oceans in their hunt for prey. Barracudas are another type of fierce fish predator. They usually prefer tropical waters, especially around coral reefs. Smaller barracudas tend to hunt in schools (groups). Larger barracudas travel alone and may threaten human divers.

▲ The swordfish has the crescent-shaped tail of a very fast swimmer. Unlike marlins and sailfish, it has a flattened snout and lacks pelvic fins.

▲ Small barracuda, each about 90 cm long, form a hunting group. They may circle prey fish, to round them into a school that is easier to attack.

FASTEST... !
The sailfish is probably the fastest fish. It has been timed swimming at more than 110 km/h over short distances. Another speedy fish is its close relative, the wahoo.

Most kinds of tuna, such as the bluefin and yellowfin, are large, powerful fish. They prey on smaller fish and squid, and in turn are eaten by large sharks and toothed whales such as the killer whale. The skipjack tuna is smaller, only 90 cm long. It swims in vast shoals of tens of thousands of fish, and is caught as a food by people.

MACKEREL
Large schools of mackerel are common in the Atlantic Ocean. In spring, summer and autumn, they usually stay near the surface and the shore, where they feed on small fish and crustaceans.

◄ The bluefin tuna is the biggest of the tuna family. It can grow up to 3 m long and weigh more than 635 kg.

SHARP!

A swordfish's "sword" is so strong that it has been known to pierce the sides of wooden boats to a depth of 30 cm. It is slightly flattened from top to bottom and covered in sharp scales. Exactly what the fish uses it for is not clear. It may be for extra streamlining. It could be to attack enemies. It might be a hunting weapon to lash out at prey, to slice or impale them.

The blue marlin has a long, pointed nose like a bird's beak or bill, hence the name "billfish".

In winter, mackerel move into deeper water and appear to eat little. They usually breed in late spring or early summer, when females shed as many as half a million eggs into the water. The pinhead-sized eggs float until they hatch about five days later, although most are eaten by small plankton-feeders. The tiny young mackerel grow fast and reach a length of 35 cm by the time they are only two years old. When fully grown, they may be as much as 65 cm long.

The sailfish is named for its dorsal fin, which sticks up like the sail of a boat. It lives in cooler seas in summer, but migrates back to tropical areas for winter.

TIGER OF THE SEA

There are some 18 species of barracuda living in warm oceans around the world. The largest is the great barracuda, a slender fish found worldwide, especially well known in the Caribbean Sea. It grows up to 1.8 m long and can weigh as much as 41 kg. It is an aggressive hunter, and is known as the "tiger of the sea" because it charges at its prey and bites off mouthfuls of flesh with its sharp teeth. Some barracudas are believed to cooperate in groups, herding their fish prey into a shoal before racing in for the attack.

SWORDS AND SPEARS

The mighty swordfish may weigh more than 500 kg and grow to an incredible 4 m or more in length. Almost one third of this length is the "sword".

A young swordfish has jaws of equal length. The upper jaw lengthens into the sword as the animal grows. The spearfish is very similar to the swordfish, but slightly smaller. The sailfish is another large, fast predator. It grows to more than 3.5 m long and stays closer to coasts than the swordfish and spearfish. It has a huge sail-like fin on its back and long pelvic fins. The upper jaw comes to a point at the front, but is rounded like a long rod, rather than flattened as in the swordfish.

Tuna and mackerel *(Scombridae)*
- about 160 species
- all live in the sea
- includes bonito, wahoo

Swordfish *(Xiphiidae)*
- 1 species
- lives in the sea
- long, flattened snout

Sailfish and marlin *(Istiophoridae)*
- about 11 species known as billfish
- all live in the sea
- long, rounded snout
- includes sailfish, blue marlin, black marlin, striped marlin, spearfish

Barracuda *(Sphyraenidae)*
- about 20 species
- all live in the sea
- includes sennet

A hooked black marlin leaps in a fight for its life. "Sport" fishing has reduced the numbers of these and similar billfish.

CICHLIDS, DAMSELS AND PARROTFISH

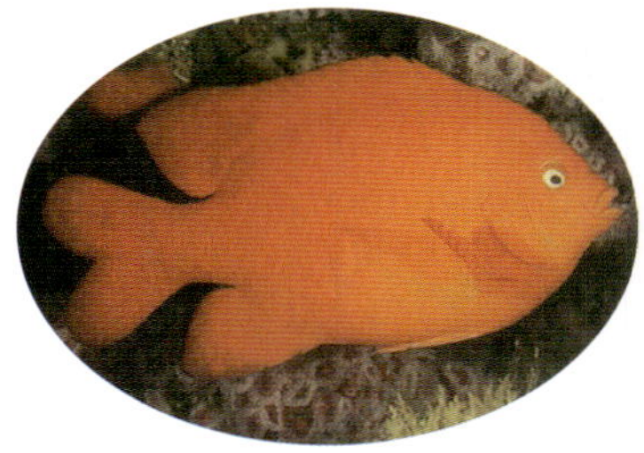

The male garibaldi, a type of damselfish, collects only red seaweeds to make his nest. Here, he guards his mate's eggs.

THE CICHLIDS, DAMSELFISH AND PARROTFISH ARE YET MORE TYPES OF PERCH-LIKE FISH (PAGE 122). Cichlids are one of the largest groups of fish that live entirely in fresh water. Most dwell in tropical and subtropical lakes and rivers, mainly in Africa and also in South America. Most are less than 50 cm long, and they are generally silver in colour. They all share the feature of a set of teeth in the throat, called pharyngeal teeth, as well as the normal teeth in the jaws. The throat teeth are used to slice and grind up the food grabbed by the jaw teeth. Their shape varies according to the type of food they eat. Shellfish-eaters have large, flat throat teeth, and in fish-eaters they are sharp for cutting through flesh. Damselfish are brightly coloured and common around coral reefs. Some species eat little coral polyps, some rasp at seaweeds and others feed on tiny plankton. Parrotfish also live on coral reefs and, like cichlids, have throat teeth as well as jaw teeth. The jaw teeth are fused or joined into a sharp parrot-like beak for scraping and chopping food.

Sea-living angelfish like the emperor angelfish are mostly tall, thin and colourful. They are related to the butterflyfish group and popular as aquarium fish.

A clown fish peeps from its safe home among the stinging, paralysing tentacles of a sea anemone.

SANDY!

Sand grains on a beach are usually worn-down chips cracked off larger boulders. But around a coral reef many of the fine, white grains have been made by parrotfish. These fish scrape food off the rocks with their very strong "beaks". Some stony fragments fall away as they feed. Others are swallowed, to emerge from the fish's other end as a shower of silvery sand.

Male cichlids are usually more brightly coloured than females. They perform courtship displays, swimming to and fro and waving their fins to show off their patterns and attract a mate. The firemouth cichlid has a red patch on its chin that becomes even brighter and more glowing during the breeding season. Some male cichlids even build a special structure to attract a female and serve as a nest for the eggs. This may be a deep pit in the mud on the bottom of the river or lake, or a mound of sand up to 90 cm high.

▲ At night, a parrotfish makes a bag-like cocoon of mucus (slime) around its body, to protect it from predators while it sleeps. The mucus "sleeping bag" may make it harder for predators to detect its smell.

World Watch

The great lakes of Africa include Victoria, Malawi and Tanganyika. They contain more different species of fish than any other lakes in the world. And most of these fish are cichlids. For the great majority, each species is found in one lake – and nowhere else. Sadly, many of these cichlid species are in grave danger of extinction. This is due to overfishing, pollution, and especially the introduction of predatory fish such as the Nile perch (page 103).

▲ Various types of damselfish have become popular as aquarium fish. However, they can be aggressive to other fish in the tank. This is because, in their natural home, they have to battle for their patch of territory on the crowded coral reef.

All members of the cichlid group look after their eggs or babies in some way. Some simply guard the eggs in their nest on the river or lake bed, until the baby fish hatch. Others take the eggs into their mouths and carefully hold them until they hatch. Some cichlids even care for the baby fish in the same way. This is called mouthbrooding. It looks as if the adult has sucked them in and swallowed them! But after a few minutes, the babies emerge.

HELPFUL PARTNERS

Damselfish are mostly less than 20 cm long. Several types, known as clown fish, have partnerships with sea anemones. The clown fish lives among the anemone's stinging tentacles, where it is protected from attack by predators. It survives mainly because it has a special coating of slime that resists the anemone's stings or prevents them being fired (pages 34–35). In return, the clown fish cleans any dirt or scraps of food from the anemone. Its presence may even lure predators to the anemone, which can then sting and eat them. Such a relationship, in which both partners gain, is called symbiosis.

SEX CHANGE

Parrotfish, like wrasses (page 128), are able to change sex. Most parrotfish start life as females. As they grow older they become males. Some species also change colour when they change sex. For example, the female stoplight parrotfish of Caribbean coral reefs are brownish-red. Males are blue and green. Old males of the blue parrotfish even change shape too. They develop a large bump on the upper snout that looks like the beginning of a nose-horn! The feeding activities of parrotfish keep the life of the reef turning over, since they clear areas of rock for new growths of sponges, corals, sea mats, barnacles and similar animals, as well as seaweeds.

▲ Mouthbrooders are named because they care for, or brood, their eggs and young in the mouth. There are many mouthbrooders in the cichlid group, such as this Nigerian mouthbrooder.

Cichlids *(Cichlidae)*
- at least 1,200 species (may be many more to discover)
- live in fresh water
- includes zebra cichlid, discus fish, freshwater angelfish

Damselfish *(Pomacentridae)*
- about 300 species
- live in warm seas
- includes clown fish *(anemone fish)*, sergeant major, garibaldi, beau-gregory

Parrotfish *(Scaridae)*
- about 70 species
- live in warm seas
- includes blue parrotfish, stoplight parrotfish, rainbow parrotfish

BLENNIES, GOBIES AND WRASSES

A cleaner wrasse picks dirt and pests from the huge mouth of a coral hind, which does not try to eat the cleaner.

The sailfin goby erects its flag-like dorsal fin. To rivals of the same species, this means: "Stay off my patch of shore!"

MOSTLY SMALL AND FOUND IN SHALLOW WATER, THE BLENNIES, GOBIES AND WRASSES ARE THREE LARGE FAMILIES OF FISH, EACH WITH HUNDREDS OF SPECIES. They belong to the main perch group (page 122). Most blennies have a tall dorsal fin, and small pelvic fins that are in front of the pectoral fins (rather than behind them as in other fish). They also have a hair-like covering, cirri, on the nostrils or eyes – which are on stalks in some species. Gobies are found all over the world, except in polar waters. Most are less than 10 cm long and have two dorsal fins. The two pelvic fins are joined to make a sucker on the underside. This enables the fish to cling to rocks or seaweed. Wrasses are mostly less than 15 cm long and are very brightly coloured. They live singly, not in schools, along coral reefs and rocky shores in all warmer seas.

Snappers, like this school of blue-striped snappers, are yet another group of perch-like fish. There are about 230 species. Most are brightly coloured fish of warm seas.

Mudskippers live among the tangled roots of mangrove, especially on the shores of the Indian and Pacific Oceans. Their pectoral fins are almost like walking legs.

SMALLEST...!
The smallest fish are dwarf gobies in the Philippine Islands. They are 8 mm long.

Like most shore fish, the mudskipper has a tough, rubbery body, as protection against crashing waves and rolling pebbles on the shore.

The largest blenny is the giant kelpfish, at 60 cm long. Like all the kelp blennies, it lives among seaweed. Its colouring varies from red to yellowish-green or brown, to match the type of kelp or other weed in its surroundings.

Stargazer blennies, like many other blennies, have eyes on stalks. The stargazer buries itself in the sand or mud of the sea bed, but its eyes stick out above the surface, like periscopes, so it can still watch for danger or food.

USEFUL SERVICE

Many kinds of wrasse carry out a useful service for other creatures on the reef. They are called cleaner fish. A large "customer" fish, such as a grouper, swims to a certain place, the cleaning station, and stays still, with mouth and gill covers open. The cleaner wrasse approaches. The customer recognizes its bright colours and zigzag way of swimming, and allows the cleaner wrasse to use its sharp front teeth to nip off fish lice and other pests and parasites from around its head, gills, mouth and scales. The wrasse eats the parasites as food and the customer is cleaned of its pests.

A NASTY TRICK

This helpful partnership between different kinds of animals is known as symbiosis. But it is open to trickery. The sabre-toothed blenny looks so like a particular cleaner wrasse that it is very hard to tell one from the other. This resemblance is known as mimicry. A customer fish allows the sabre-tooth blenny to swim near. But the blenny does not clean it. Instead it takes a bite out of the customer with its sharp teeth. If the customer tries to eat the blenny, the sabre-tooth bites the inside of its mouth and is quickly spat out.

FISH OUT OF WATER

Mudskippers are small types of goby that can live out of water for minutes, even hours. They take in oxygen from small pools of water trapped in their large, cheek-like gill chambers. Every few minutes the mudskipper dips its head into a puddle to refresh this water. Mudskippers live in coastal mangrove swamps in tropical areas. At low tide they come out of their burrows to feed on insects and other small animals. They skitter across the mud on their strong pectoral fins, and watch for danger with their "pop-eyes" on stalks.

Montagu's blenny is typical of its group. It is a hardy fish of rock pools that grows to 8 cm long and eats a wide variety of food.

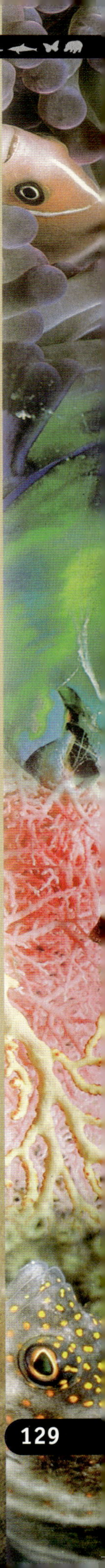

Blennies *(Blenniidae)*
- about 275 species
- nearly all sea-living
- includes shanny, redlip, rock, and boss and butterfly blennies

Gobies *(Gobiidae)*
- about 2,120 species
- most live in the sea
- a few are cave fish
- includes mudskippers, guavina, bunaka

Wrasses *(Labridae)*
- about 600 species
- live in the sea
- includes bluehead, ballan and cuckoo wrasse, corkwing, hogfish, razorfish

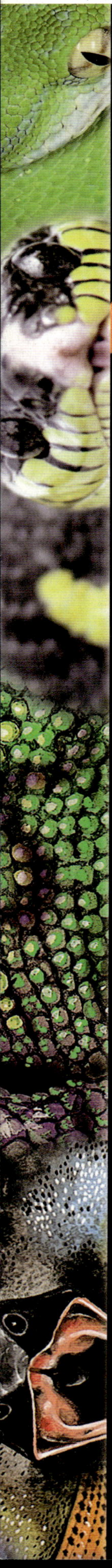

The red salamander of North America.

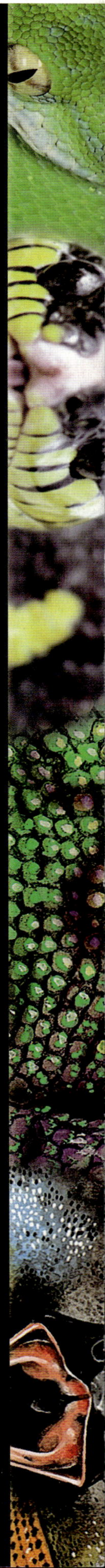

SECTION 5

AMPHIBIANS & REPTILES

AMPHIBIANS LIVE A STRANGE DOUBLE LIFE. Most begin as tiny black dots in little balls of jelly floating in water. These eggs, or spawn, hatch into tadpoles that breathe by gills and swim with their tails. But as they grow, tadpoles undergo an amazing change called metamorphosis. They lose their gills and tails, and develop lungs for breathing air and legs for hopping on land. They develop into adult frogs, toads, salamanders and newts.

Most amphibians have soft, moist skin. Reptiles do not. They can be recognized by their tough, scaly skin. The reptile group includes some of the most dangerous animals. There are poisonous snakes with deadly venom, such as cobras, rattlers and vipers. Constrictor snakes, like pythons and boas, squeeze the life from their victims. Crocodiles and alligators threaten enemies with their large, gaping mouths, equipped with rows of pointed teeth.

Turtles, tortoises and terrapins live a slow-paced life, safe in their domed protective shells. Much speedier are the lizards, another reptile sub-group. Some dart about so fast that we can hardly follow their movements. Lizards range in size from little geckos that make a big meal of a fly, to monitors, such as the Komodo dragon, that can devour a small goat.

WHAT ARE AMPHIBIANS?

AMPHIBIANS ARE COLD-BLOODED ANIMALS THAT HAVE A "DOUBLE LIFE". They begin in water, as jelly-covered eggs which hatch into tadpoles that breathe by gills and swim with their tails. The tadpoles change shape or metamorphose as they grow, into adults that breathe by lungs and walk on land on four legs. The 4,000 or so species live in all regions except Antarctica and the far north.

The spring peeper frog is named for its "peep-peep" call.

Some newts have frilly crests of skin along the back. At breeding time, the male's crest becomes larger and his body develops brighter colours.

Like fish and reptiles, amphibians are cold-blooded. Unlike birds and mammals, they cannot make body heat to keep themselves at a constant warm temperature. Their bodies are usually at about the same temperature as the air or water around them. When they are warm, they can move actively. But in cold conditions, they cannot. They become still and their body processes slow down. This is called torpor. In temperate regions, many amphibians are torpid or "asleep" in winter.

BIGGEST... !

The biggest amphibians are the giant salamanders of eastern Asia, especially China and Japan. They grow up to 1.5 m in total length.

AMPHIBIAN EGGS

An amphibian begins life as a small, dark, dot-like egg. This contains yolk for nourishment and is surrounded by several layers of jelly. It does not have a protective outer shell like a reptile egg, so it must be laid in water or moist surroundings, to prevent it drying out. Lots of jelly-covered eggs clustered together are known as spawn.

BREATHING IN WATER

The eggs grow and become comma-shaped, then hatch into larval amphibians – tadpoles. These have feathery gills on the sides of the head (external gills) for absorbing oxygen from the water. Most amphibians lose their gills when they become adults, and take in oxygen through their lungs and moist skin. But some, such as the mudpuppy, keep their gills.

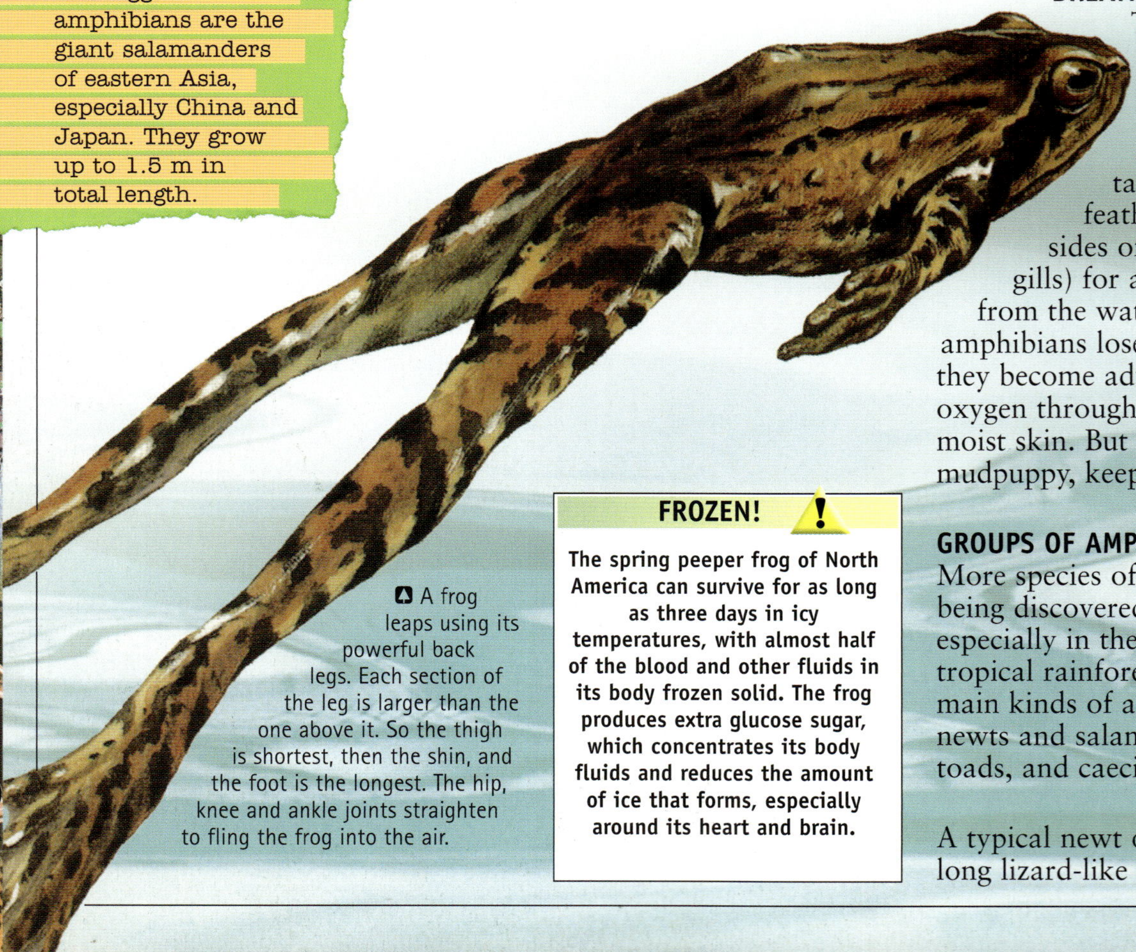

A frog leaps using its powerful back legs. Each section of the leg is larger than the one above it. So the thigh is shortest, then the shin, and the foot is the longest. The hip, knee and ankle joints straighten to fling the frog into the air.

FROZEN!

The spring peeper frog of North America can survive for as long as three days in icy temperatures, with almost half of the blood and other fluids in its body frozen solid. The frog produces extra glucose sugar, which concentrates its body fluids and reduces the amount of ice that forms, especially around its heart and brain.

GROUPS OF AMPHIBIANS

More species of amphibians are being discovered every year, especially in their main habitats, the tropical rainforests. There are three main kinds of amphibians. They are newts and salamanders, frogs and toads, and caecilians.

A typical newt or salamander has a long lizard-like body and tail.

Many frogs have brightly coloured skin, like the tomato frog. Usually, the brighter they are, the more horrible-tasting the frog's flesh. The colours warn predators to leave the frog alone.

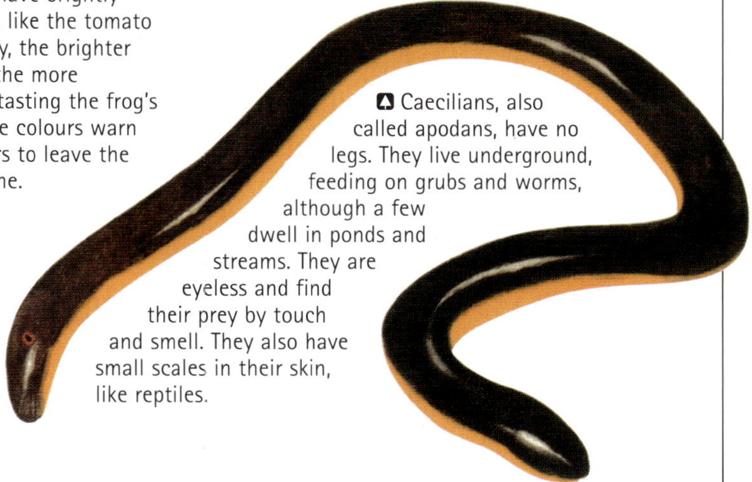

Caecilians, also called apodans, have no legs. They live underground, feeding on grubs and worms, although a few dwell in ponds and streams. They are eyeless and find their prey by touch and smell. They also have small scales in their skin, like reptiles.

It has four usually small, sprawling legs at its sides, and smooth, scale-less skin. Most are active in the evening or at night, when they hunt for small creatures such as insects, spiders and worms. In fact, all amphibians are predators. They cannot chew so they gulp down their victims whole, often still alive and struggling.

The axolotl is a strange salamander that keeps its feathery gills even when adult (page 135).

A typical frog or toad is in many ways the opposite of a salamander. It has a short, compact body, very long back legs for jumping, and no tail. The third amphibian group is the caecilians. These have no limbs at all and resemble overgrown earthworms. They burrow in the earth and dead leaves of tropical forests, searching for and devouring small soil creatures.

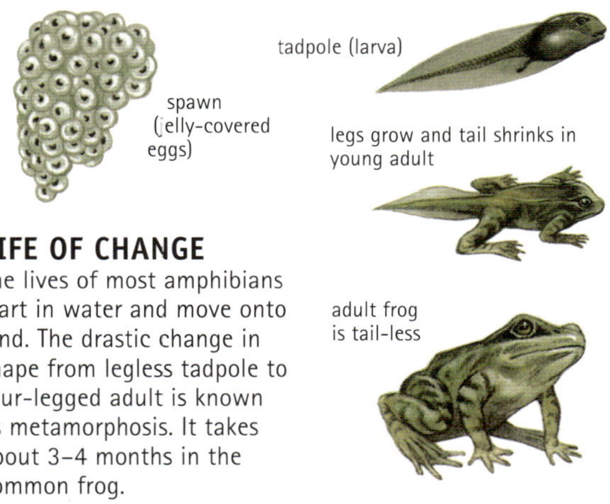

LIFE OF CHANGE

The lives of most amphibians start in water and move onto land. The drastic change in shape from legless tadpole to four-legged adult is known as metamorphosis. It takes about 3–4 months in the common frog.

Bullfrogs are large, powerful frogs that eat a range of fish, insects, lizards, snakes, small mammals such as mice and other prey—including smaller frogs. There are bullfrog species in North America, South America and Africa.

AMPHIBIANS

- about 4,000 species
- vertebrates (animals with backbones)
- larvae or tadpoles live in water
- adults mostly live on land
- worldwide except coldest regions

Newts and salamanders *(Caudata)*
- about 360 species
- long body and tail, most four-legged

Frogs and toads *(Anura)*
- about 3,400 species
- no tail in adult
- long back legs for leaping

Caecilians *(Apoda)*
- about 160 species
- long worm-like body, no legs
- tropical and warm forests

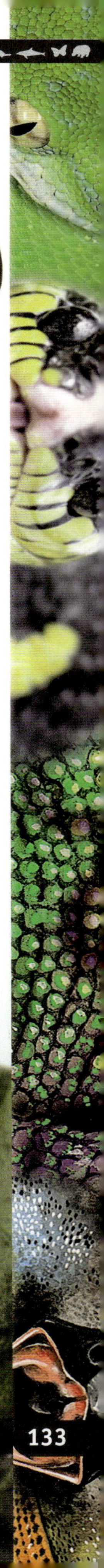

NEWTS AND SALAMANDERS

NEWTS AND SALAMANDERS ARE SHY, RARELY SEEN CREATURES. Most live in the northern half of the world, although there are some species of salamanders in South America. They usually stay hidden in cool, damp places during the day and come out at night to catch small creatures such as insects, snails and worms. Some are typical amphibians in that they spend time both on land and in water. Others live entirely on land, or wholly in the water. The name "newt" is usually given to the types that are mainly aquatic (water-dwelling). Some salamanders have bright warning colours on their bodies. These signal to predators that their flesh is foul-tasting. Some can also ooze poisonous or horrible-tasting fluids from their skin.

The fire salamander has distinctive black and yellow markings. These warning colours are shared by other animals, such as wasps, bees and poisonous beetles.

Salamanders and newts are hunted by many other creatures, including birds and snakes. So apart from their nasty-tasting flesh, they have various ways of defending themselves. If the Chinese spiny newt is seized by a predator, it pushes its sharp-tipped ribs through its skin. The ribs pass through its skin glands on the way and release an extremely unpleasant poison.

Many newts have long flaps of fin-like skin along the upper and lower surfaces of the tail, which they keep from their tadpole stage. The fish-like tail is swished from side to side and helps the newt to swim faster.

HOT!

Legend says that the fire salamander walks through flames. Of course, it does not. But it does tend to hide away during winter in an old fallen log—which may be collected as firewood. When the log is thrown on the flames, the heat wakes the salamander, which quickly tries to escape!

BREEDING TIME

In most salamander species, male and female do not have to link in a mating position. Instead the male leaves a "packet" of sperm on the ground, which the female then takes into her body. The sperm may join with or fertilize her eggs straight away, or they may be stored until she finds a more suitable time or place for her eggs.

FEW EGGS OR MANY?

Some salamanders lay their eggs in damp places on land, such as under stones or old logs, or in moss. Others attach them to rocks or logs under the water.

The yellow-eyed salamander is one of many species that lives on the damp forest floor. Its large eyes show that it is nocturnal, or active at night.

The red salamander of North America is also called the eastern newt. It has an extra stage in its life known as the eft. This is a sub-adult, a halfway form between the tadpole and the full adult. After the tadpole stage, the eft develops and lives on land for up to three years before growing into a mature adult.

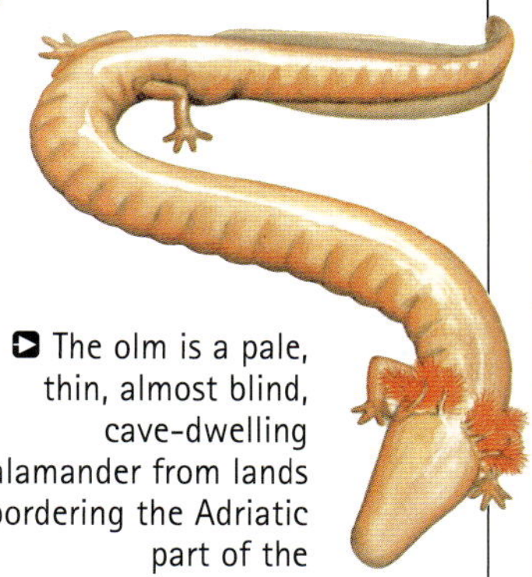

The olm is a pale, thin, almost blind, cave-dwelling salamander from lands bordering the Adriatic part of the Mediterranean Sea.

The number of eggs a salamander lays varies from only four or five to more than 5,000, depending on the species. If eggs are laid in water, they hatch out into tadpoles (larvae) with feathery gills. These gradually change to the adult form, developing legs and lungs. However, eggs laid on land usually miss out the tadpole stage and hatch into fully formed miniature salamanders. Some species, such as the fire salamander, do not lay eggs at all. The eggs develop inside the female's body and she gives birth to tiny offspring.

Mudpuppies never lose the feather gills that they have as tadpoles. These salamanders grow to about 40 cm long and inhabit creeks and rivers in North America. They hunt small fish, water worms and young crayfish.

WARNING COLOURS

The gaudy markings of many amphibians warn enemies that they are very nasty-tasting indeed. The skin glands of the fire salamander ooze a poisonous fluid that causes severe redness and swelling if another animal bites it. The effects are so severe that they can even kill small mammals, including pet dogs, if they pick up a salamander. Potential predators learn to recognize these types of warning colours and avoid the salamanders.

SOME GROUPS OF SALAMANDERS (continued from page 133):

Lungless salamanders *(Plethodontidae)*
- about 200 species
- long, slender body and tail
- live in water or caves
- includes red salamander, dusky salamander

Mole salamanders *(Ambystomatidae)*
- 32 species
- broad head, thick body
- adults usually live on land
- includes axolotl, tiger salamander

Newts *(Salamandridae)*
- about 60 species
- slender body and long tail
- strong legs
- includes fire salamander, warty newt, striped newt

Sirens *(Sirenidae)*
- 3 species
- eel-like body and feathery gills
- live in water
- includes dwarf siren, greater siren

Olm and mudpuppies *(Proteidae)*
- 5 species
- feathery gills
- long body and short tail
- live in water

Giant salamanders *(Cryptobranchidae)*
- 3 species
- large, heavy body
- short tail
- live in water
- includes hellbender

THE SALAMANDERS THAT NEVER GROW UP

The axolotl (page 133) is a kind of mole salamander from Mexico. Some axolotls develop into full adults and live on land, like other salamanders. But others stay in water throughout their lives and keep their larval features, such as feathery gills. They become mature and breed, even though most of the body is still in the immature larval stage. This condition is called neotony.

Lungless salamanders have no lungs. They must absorb oxygen through the skin and the lining of the mouth. This means the skin must always stay moist. If it dries, oxygen cannot pass through. Most lungless salamanders are found in North and South America.

Spiny salamanders like the Chinese spiny newt have sharp ribs that almost poke out of the skin. They are too prickly for most predators to eat.

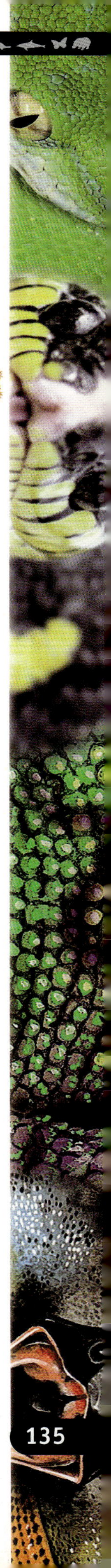

FROGS AND TOADS

Surinam toad

Tree frogs have sucker-like disks at the ends of their toes.

FROGS AND TOADS ARE BY FAR THE BIGGEST GROUP OF AMPHIBIANS, WITH MORE THAN 3,400 SPECIES. They live on all continents except Antarctica, and in habitats ranging from deserts to cold mountain streams. But they are most common in tropical and subtropical swamps and rainforests. The name "frog" was once used for the slender, smooth-skinned types that could leap well, and "toad" for the plump, rough-skinned species that prefer to waddle. Now both names are used for similar species and there is no clear difference between a frog and a toad.

All frogs and toads are tail-less and have strong back legs for jumping. The front legs are smaller and cushion the landing. A frog's body is short, with a strong backbone to cope with the physical stresses of jumping, and there is no narrow neck between the head and body. The large eyes are usually on the top of the very wide-mouthed head, so the frog can still see when it is almost submerged in water.

SMALLEST... !
One of the smallest frogs in the world was discovered on the island of Cuba in 1997. It measures only 1 cm long. Its scientific name is Eleutherodactylus iberia.

The water-holding frog of Australia lives in the desert. During a drought, it stays in a burrow underground. Its outer layer of slime detaches to form a cocoon that fills with the frog's urine and other body fluids, like a water-filled sleeping bag.

A FROG'S LIFE CYCLE

A typical frog or toad lays its eggs in water. These hatch into tiny tadpoles with tails for swimming and fluffy gills for breathing in water. The young tadpole feeds on plants. As it grows, it loses its external gills and develops lungs in its chest for breathing air. It gradually loses its tail too, and develops legs. The head broadens, the body become short and thick, and the tadpole has metamorphosed into a froglet, ready to venture onto land.

A frog pushes off with its toes, launching its small, streamlined body into a leap at least 10 times its own length.

In Central American rainforests, it is so damp that the strawberry poison-arrow frog can carry her tadpole on her back, without it drying out.

The cane toad is also called the marine or giant toad. It was taken from South America to Australia, to eat beetle pests in sugar cane fields. But it prefers small creatures that are natural inhabitants in the area, making some of them very rare animals.

FROG CALLS

Male frogs and toads make loud calls to attract females. Each species has its own particular call, and the green frog can be heard hundreds of metres away. The calls of frogs are made louder in a vocal sac below the chin, as air from the lungs is forced over the vocal cords in the neck. Females do not usually make any sounds.

CARING FOR YOUNG

Some frogs do not leave their eggs in water to hatch, but carry them around to make sure they do not get eaten. As the female marsupial frog lays her eggs, the male fertilizes them and helps her pack them into a backpack-like skin pouch on her back, where they hatch and start to develop. After a few weeks the young hop into the water to complete their growth. The female Surinam toad carries her young in separate skin pouches on her back, until they are fully formed mini-toads.

Many frogs and toads make their calls louder by blowing up the chin skin like a balloon. The stretched skin vibrates or resonates to increase the volume of the sound.

POISONOUS FROGS

The bright colours of the poison-arrow (or arrow-poison) frogs warn other animals to stay away. Glands in the body release a strong venom into the frog's skin. Even a few drops of this can be lethal to a predator. Traditionally, local people in Central and South America tip their hunting arrows with this substance.

The flying frog of Southeast Asia does not really fly, but spreads its huge webbed feet to glide 12 m from tree to tree.

USEFUL!

The poison fluid or secretion from poison-arrow frog skin may have medical uses. The secretions of the phantasmal poison-arrow frog are far more effective at stopping pain than the usual pain-killing drugs. Those of the golden poison-arrow frog may help patients who have had heart attacks.

SOME GROUPS OF FROGS AND TOADS (continued from page 133):

Ranid or "true" frogs *(Ranidae)*
- about 650 species
- slim, smooth-skinned body
- pointed head
- mostly live in water but some dwell in trees
- includes common frog, bullfrog

Bufid or "true" toads *(Bufonidae)*
- about 400 species
- stout body
- often rough, warty skin
- most live mainly on land
- includes cane toad, natterjack

Tree frogs *(Hylidae)*
- more than 770 species
- slender body
- long legs
- most live in trees
- webbed feet with sticky pads on disc-like toe-tips

Leptodactylid frogs *(Leptodactylidae)*
- more than 900 species
- varied body form
- land-living and water-living species
- includes horned frog, chirping frog

Narrow-mouthed frogs *(Microhylidae)*
- more than 320 species
- stout body
- small mouth
- live in burrows or trees
- includes rain frog

Poison-arrow (arrow-poison) frogs *(Dendrobatidae)*
- over 170 species
- mainly tropical rainforests
- slim, small body
- sticky discs on toes
- brightly coloured
- live on ground or in trees

Green tree frogs are camouflaged among the leaves as they wait for their small insect prey. They can cling to twigs, wet glossy leaves and even window glass using the sucker-like discs on their toes.

WHAT ARE REPTILES?

REPTILES ARE ANIMALS WITH BACKBONES (VERTEBRATES) THAT ARE COLD-BLOODED, HAVE SCALES ON THEIR SKIN AND LAY EGGS (PAGE 131). Most reptiles have four legs with five toes on each foot, but snakes have no limbs at all. Most reptiles live on land, but marine turtles and sea snakes stay in the sea, except to come ashore briefly and lay their eggs. Most reptile eggs have shells that are tough yet leathery and flexible, unlike the hard, brittle shells of birds' eggs. However, some snakes do not lay eggs, but give birth to babies.

The pond slider is a common turtle in North, Central and South America. It rarely leaves the water.

The main groups of reptiles are the turtles and tortoises, the crocodiles and alligators, the lizards and the snakes. Most live on land, but many turtles and terrapins, also most crocodiles and alligators, and even some snakes, spend time in ponds, swamps and rivers. A few, including the saltwater crocodile, venture into the sea.

Reptiles may not seem to be social animals, in the way that birds form flocks or monkeys live in troops. Yet they have many ways of communicating, especially with others of their own species at mating time. Lizards bob their heads and show off their skin crests and brightly coloured patterns. Snakes leave chemical messages for their partners, which consist of scent-like substances called pheromones, produced in their bodies. Some reptiles, including crocodiles and geckos, make hisses, grunts and calls to attract mates.

THE REPTILE'S EGG

The leathery shell of a reptile egg gives protection and prevents it from drying out, even in the desert heat. Inside are layers of fluid to protect the developing embryo (unhatched baby), and yolk to provide it with nourishment.

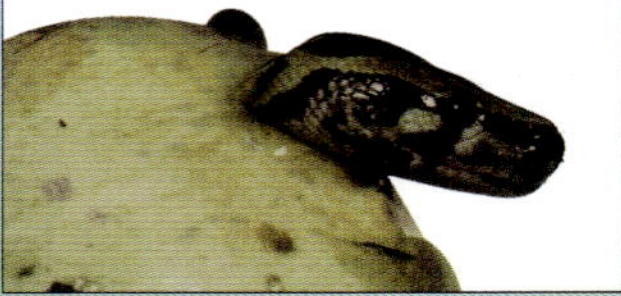

Worm lizards are not worms or lizards, but reptiles that resemble large earthworms. They burrow in the soil of tropical forests.

Hingeback tortoises can tilt down the rear of the shell to give extra protection to the back legs and tail.

SCALY!

The skin of a reptile is covered with hard scales. These are made of keratin, the same substance that forms our nails and hair. In some reptiles, such as crocodiles, the scales are strengthened by plates of bones, making a tough armour.

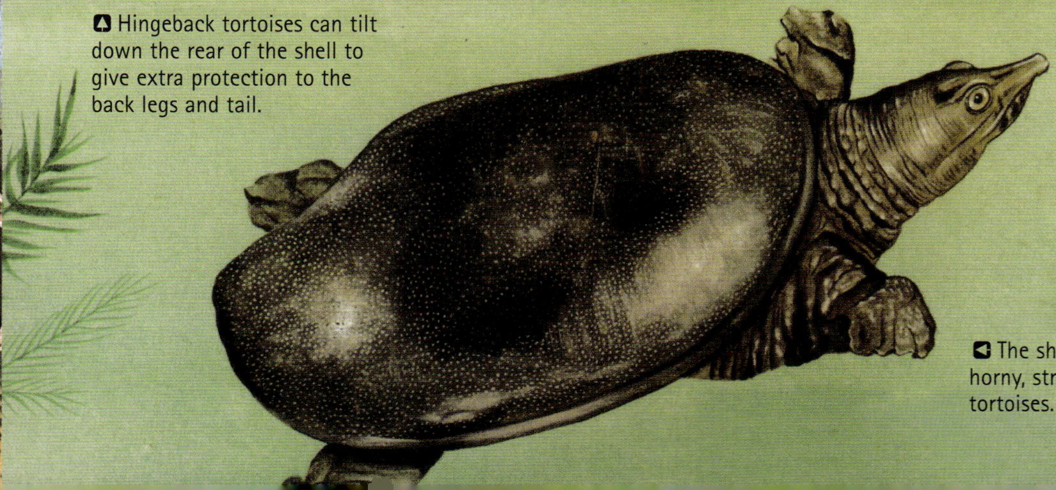

The shell of a softshell turtle does not have ha horny, strengthening plates, as in other turtles ar tortoises. So it feels slightly soft and rubbery.

Marine iguanas are some of the few reptiles that spend time in the sea. These large lizards dive to munch on seaweeds.

When breeding, most female reptiles lay eggs and then leave these to develop and hatch on their own. But a few species, such as some skinks, pythons and crocodiles, guard their eggs and even the babies too, protecting them from enemies. Some snakes and lizards keep their developing eggs inside their bodies, where they hatch and the mother gives birth to the young.

COLD BODIES

Reptiles are cold-blooded creatures. This means they cannot control their body temperatures themselves. They depend on the heat of the sun to become warm, so that they can be active and move about. In cold conditions, reptiles move slowly or not at all. This cold, immobile condition is known as torpor. One advantage of being cold-blooded is that reptiles do not need to use so much energy as warm-blooded animals, who must "burn" energy from their food to produce body heat. So reptiles need to eat far less food than warm-blooded birds and mammals of the same body size – perhaps only one-tenth of the amount.

REPTILES

- about 6,560 species
- cold-blooded vertebrates
- scaly skin
- lay eggs
- most have four legs
- worldwide except polar regions

Lizards *(Sauria)*
- about 3,750 species
- long, slim body, long tail
- includes skinks, geckos, chameleons, iguanas, monitors

Crocodiles *(Crocodilia)*
- 22 species
- long body armoured with thick scales, long tail
- includes crocodiles, caimans, alligators, gharial

Tuatara *(Rhynchocephalia)*
- 1 species
- lizard-like, with head and back crest
- only in New Zealand

Worm lizards *(Amphisbaenia)*
- about 140 species
- long slender body, no limbs
- includes worm lizards, shield snouts

Snakes *(Serpentes)*
- about 2,400 species
- long worm-like body, no limbs
- includes pythons, boas, vipers

Turtles and tortoises *(Chelonia)*
- about 250 species
- body protected by a hard, domed shell
- includes tortoises, terrapins, turtles

Water dragons (below) are mostly large tropical lizards that swim well by lashing their tails from side to side. Caimans (right) are smaller members of the crocodile group from Central and South America. They grow to about 1.8 m long.

The spotted water snake lives in swamps and creeks in northern parts of Australia. Its nostrils are set high on its head, so it can take a breath without poking its whole head out of the water.

Most terrapins have wide feet with partly webbed toes, for efficient swimming.

TORTOISES, TURTLES AND TERRAPINS

THERE ARE ABOUT 250 SPECIES OF TURTLES, TORTOISES AND TERRAPINS, FOUND IN MOST WARM PARTS OF THE WORLD. They are easily recognized by the hard, rounded shell that protects the main part of the body. The mostly land-dwelling tortoises thrive in all kinds of habitats, including desert, woodland and mountains. Turtles and terrapins live chiefly in rivers and ponds. They are slow and ungainly on land, but swift in the water. (Marine turtles are a separate group, page 142.)

▲ The matamata is an extraordinary-looking turtle about 40 cm long from the Amazon region of South America. It has an arrow-shaped head and a very wide mouth, to gulp in fish and other water animals. Its tiny eyes are about halfway along the sides of the "arrow".

▼ Snapping turtles lurk in ponds and lakes from Canada, south through North to Central America. They grab any small animal as prey.

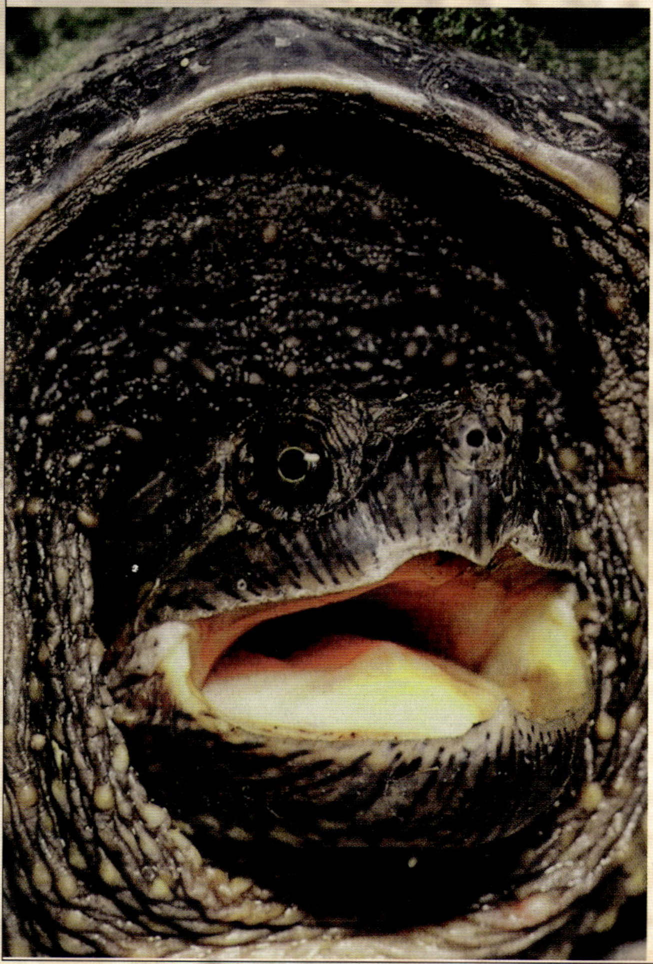

OLD!

Turtles are among the longest-lived of all animals. Box turtles of North America and spur-thighed tortoises in Europe survive to over 100 years old. A Marion's tortoise, taken from the Seychelles to Mauritius in 1766, lived until 1918. It died due to an accident – at least 152 years old.

Turtles, terrapins and tortoises are known as chelonians. They do not have teeth. Instead, a turtle or tortoise has a strong, beak-like mouth with hard ridges along the jaw edges for biting food. Many chelonians are predators, catching other animals to eat. Others, including many tortoises, are plant-eaters. They swallow each piece they bite since they cannot chew.

Turtles reproduce by laying eggs, usually in a hole in the ground. The female lays her eggs in a warm place and leaves them to incubate and hatch alone. The young receive no parental care.

THE TURTLE'S SHELL

The shell of a turtle or tortoise has two parts—the upper carapace and the lower plastron. Each part has two layers of plates like jigsaw puzzle pieces. These are made of bone on the inside, and horn on the outside like normal reptile scales. The outer plates are called scutes. The two parts meet at the sides, with openings for the turtle's head, legs and tail. The ribs and backbone are fixed to the upper inside of the carapace.

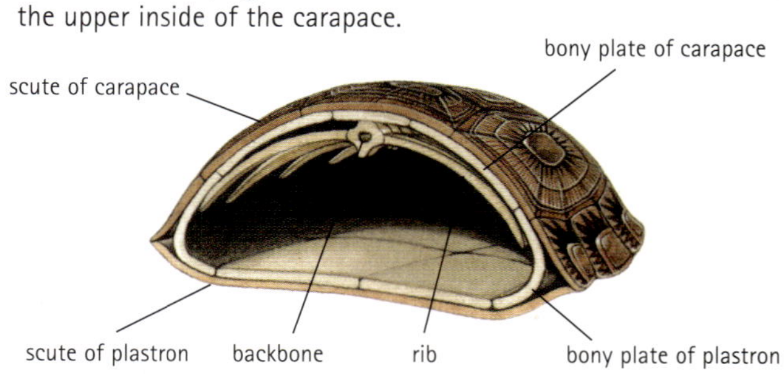

Wood turtles catch worms, insects and grubs, and can climb into bushes. They were once caught and kept as pets, but this has made them rare.

CAMOUFLAGED MATAMATA

Many turtles and tortoises are brownish or green, to blend with their surroundings of mud, leaves and waterweeds. This helps them to hide as they wait for prey to come near or stay unnoticed by predators. The matamata is a member of the snake-necked turtle family, and has most unusual camouflage. With its ridged shell and flattened head, fringed with flaps of skin, it looks like a clump of bark and leaves in the water. When a victim passes by, the matamata simply opens its large mouth. Water – and the prey – rush in. The turtle then closes its mouth, squeezes the water out at the sides and swallows its meal.

GALAPAGOS GIANT TORTOISE

The largest tortoises are found on the Galapagos Islands, off the coast of Ecuador in the Pacific Ocean. These lumbering giants are strong enough to carry a person. Each island in the Galapagos group has a variety or subspecies of giant tortoise that is recognizable by the shape of its shell or the size and length of its legs. These slight variations were noticed by English naturalist Charles Darwin when he visited the islands in the 1830s. The tortoises, finches and other animals of the Galapagos set Darwin thinking about the idea of evolution by natural selection. He described this idea in his book *On the Origin of Species* (1859), which is now central to the study of the natural world.

Several kinds of giant tortoises live on Pacific and Indian Ocean islands, such as the Galapagos.

CIRCULAR SHELL

The spiny softshell turtle has an almost circular shell, covered with leathery skin and small, spiny projections on the front. This turtle is a good swimmer and spends most of its life in water, catching insects, crustaceans and fish.

BIGGEST... !

The largest land tortoise is the Galapagos giant tortoise. It weighs a staggering 230 kg or more and its shell can be 1.2 m long.

The largest freshwater turtle in North America is the alligator snapping turtle. It has a large head and a rough, lumpy shell. Inside its gaping mouth is a small, pink, fleshy flap that resembles a worm. When a fish comes to eat the "worm", it is quickly snapped up in the turtle's jaws.

The leopard tortoise of Africa has a high-domed shell with bold markings. It lives in woods and grassland.

MAIN GROUPS OF TURTLES (continued from page 139):

Snake-necked turtles *(Chelidae)*
- about 30 species
- live mainly in water
- most have long necks
- includes giant snake-neck turtle, matamata

Helmeted side-necked turtles *(Pelomedusidae)*
- about 20 species
- live mainly in water
- includes Arrau river turtle, West African mud turtle

Alligator turtles *(Chelydridae)*
- 3 species
- large head and long tail
- live in water
- includes snapping turtle, big-headed turtle

Softshell turtles *(Trionychidae)*
- about 22 species
- shell covered with leathery skin
- live mainly in water
- includes spiny softshell, Indian flapshell

American mud and musk turtles *(Kinosternidae)*
- about 20 species
- musk glands below carapace give off strong-smelling scent
- live mainly in water
- includes striped mud turtle, common musk turtle

Pond turtles *(Emydidae)*
- about 85 species
- well-developed shell, strong limbs and webbed feet
- live mainly in water, some stay on land
- includes box turtle, river terrapin, wood turtle

Tortoises *(Testudinae)*
- about 41 species
- domed shell, strong back legs
- land-living
- includes gopher tortoise, pancake tortoise, spur-thighed tortoise, Galapagos giant tortoise

SEA TURTLES

The hawksbill is the most tropical of sea turtles, usually found in shallow coastal waters around reefs and bays. It is one of the few large animals to feed mainly on sponges.

SEA OR MARINE TURTLES ARE THE LARGEST MEMBERS OF THE CHELONIAN GROUP. There are only seven species, found mostly in tropical and subtropical seas and oceans. Apart from a few sea snakes, they are the only reptiles that spend virtually their whole lives at sea. Only females come ashore, and then for only a few hours each year, to lay their eggs. Sea turtles have flatter or less domed shells than freshwater turtles, and swim with their front limbs, which are larger than the back limbs. Awkward on land, they flap their flipper-like front legs to "fly" through the sea with amazing grace. When on the move, they must surface every few minutes to breathe air. But when resting or sleeping, they may remain underwater for several hours. They have good senses of sight and smell, used to find food, detect danger and locate a mate.

Turtle front flippers, like this loggerhead's, are wide and flattened. The turtle does not so much row with them, but rather flaps them up and down, like a bird flapping its wings.

SMALLEST... !
The Pacific ridley, found in open ocean and coastal waters, is the smallest sea turtle. It measures about 70 cm long and weighs less than 41 kg.

Like freshwater turtles and land tortoises, sea turtles do not have teeth. They bite and crush their food with the strong, hard edges to their beak-like jaws. Young turtles feed on plankton, and later, slightly larger creatures. Adult green sea turtles feed mostly on sea grass. But the other species eat creatures such as jellyfish, squid, shrimps and fish.

Loggerhead turtle

THE BREEDING BEACH

After mating at sea, female turtles tend to return to the same place year after year, to lay their eggs. At the nesting beach, the female drags herself slowly up the sand to beyond the high tide mark. She digs a pit with her flippers, then begins to lay her eggs, 2–3 at a time. She may lay from 50 to more than 150 eggs in the clutch. She then covers the nest with sand and rakes over the site with her flippers. Finally she returns to the sea, leaving her eggs to incubate in the sun-baked sand. She does this several times, laying clutches in different places at intervals of about ten days.

A DANGEROUS JOURNEY

Sea turtle eggs take about eight weeks to hatch, depending on the temperature of the sand. The babies break out of their shells and then have to struggle out of their sandpit nest by themselves.

World Watch

Turtles have long suffered from human activities. People hunted them and dug up their eggs. "Turtleshell", obtained mainly from hawksbills, was prized for making decorative items such as combs. Now turtles are losing their breeding grounds. Tourist centres are built on the beaches where they nest. Conservationists help by rearing baby turtles in protected hatchery areas and releasing them in the sea, hopefully to return and breed in safety.

It is a group effort and it may take several days to reach the surface. Once out on the beach, the tiny turtles make a dash for the sea. Many fall victim to predators such as seabirds, crabs, otters, foxes and lizards, who soon gather for the feast. Those that reach the sea begin to swim at once into deeper water. But here they face new hazards such as predatory fish.

LEATHERY BACK

The huge leatherback sea turtle is named for its unusual shell, which is made of a thick, leathery substance strengthened by tiny bones. Leatherbacks feed mostly on jellyfish, which they catch and cut up with their scissor-like jaws. They are known to dive to depths of more than 900 m in their search for food.

The loggerhead sea turtle has a large head in proportion to the rest of its body. The sides of the head house powerful jaw muscles that enable this turtle species to crush hard-shelled prey such as clams, scallops, sea snails, crabs and lobsters.

MIGRATION

Some sea turtles spend their lives within a small area. Others make long journeys between the areas where they usually feed, and the beaches where they breed. Most green turtles are in the second group. Some feed off the Atlantic coast of South America and then migrate to tiny Ascension Island some 1,500 km away.

The green turtle was hunted in great numbers for its meat, shell, eggs and skin. It has become very rare and, like other sea turtles, it is now on the official list of threatened animals. Trade in its products is strictly controlled.

TURTLES (continued from page 141):

Sea turtles *(Chelonidae)*
- 6 species
- flat, bony shell covered with horny plates
- flipper-like limbs
- includes green turtle, ridley sea turtles, hawksbill, loggerhead

Leatherback sea turtle *(Dermochelyidae)*
- 1 species
- shell covered with leathery skin

A female leatherback digs a hole on a sandy beach, where she will lay 50–150 eggs. The leatherback is the largest of all turtles and tortoises. It can weigh more than 500 kg, although most of this great bulk is buoyed up by the water.

CROCODILES AND ALLIGATORS

The Nile crocodile has become very rare. Its natural river and swamp habitats have been drained and changed to farmland, industrial sites and tourist areas.

CROCODILES HAVE CHANGED LITTLE SINCE THEY SHARED THE PREHISTORIC WORLD WITH THEIR CLOSE REPTILE RELATIVES, THE DINOSAURS, MORE THAN 100 MILLION YEARS AGO. There are three sub-groups in the crocodile group, known as crocodilians. These are the crocodiles themselves, the alligators and caimans, and the single species of gharial (gavial) from northern India. Crocodilians are found in all tropical and subtropical regions of the world. They are powerful predators, equally at home on land and in water.

The massive saltwater or estuarine crocodile is regularly seen swimming offshore.

A typical crocodile or alligator has a long body covered with thick scales. Bony plates that are embedded in the skin along the back give further protection. The snout is long too, with nostrils and eyes set high on the head. The tail is also long and tall, and very muscular, for swimming. The two pairs of legs are short but strong, with five toes on the front feet and four on the back feet. All of these toes are partly webbed.

LAZY DAYS, BUSY NIGHTS

Crocodiles spend much of the day basking in the sun on sandy riverbanks and mudflats. They become active in the evening and usually hunt for prey at night. They are among the most patient, silent, and stealthy of all large predators. Often the croc lurks in water near the shore, almost totally submerged like an old floating log. It waits for an animal to come and drink. When the prey is almost within reach, the crocodile makes a sudden dash from the water, drags the victim below the surface, and holds it there, usually with the croc's jaws clamped onto its throat, until it dies.

A crocodile is almost entirely covered in thick, horny scales, with extra plates of bone along the back.

CROC OR ALLIGATOR?

The main difference between a crocodile and an alligator is that, in an alligator, the fourth tooth on each side of the lower jaw fits into a pit in the upper jaw.

The gharial's very long, narrow jaws, armed with about 100 teeth, can be swished sideways through the water at speed to grab prey. The lump or "pot" at the upper end of the snout is a feature of old males.

The tooth cannot be seen when the mouth is closed. In a crocodile, these fourth lower teeth are visible when the mouth is shut, on the outsides of the upper jaw. Crocodiles live in tropical and subtropical areas of Central and South America, Africa, Asia and Australia. Most alligators and caimans live in North, Central and South America, with one species, the Chinese alligator, in East Asia. The gharial lives in northern India and neighbouring countries, and is recognized by its very long, narrow snout.

CROCODILE DIET

The food of a crocodile or alligator tends to change as the animal grows. A young Nile crocodile less than 50 cm long feeds mostly on small creatures such as frogs, insects and spiders. As it nears 100 cm in length, it starts to catch larger prey such as birds, lizards, small mammals and fish. The full-grown Nile crocodile preys mainly on mammals up to the size of zebras.

NEW TEETH

A crocodile has teeth which are strong and pointed, but not especially large. Each tooth is set in its own deep socket in the jawbone. As teeth become worn, they are replaced by new teeth which grow at the bases of the old ones.

LARGEST... !

The biggest reptile is the saltwater or estuarine crocodile of the Indian and Pacific Oceans. It grows to 7 m long and weighs about a ton.

ON THE MOVE

On land, crocodiles walk slowly with the legs splayed out to the sides, swinging the body with a snake-like wriggling motion. But a crocodile in a hurry holds its legs straighter, stiffer and more upright under its body. This "high walk" allows a speed of about 5 km/h. A few species, such as Johnston's crocodile, can even break into a gallop and sprint almost as fast as a person, at a speed of about 20 km/h.

In water, the crocodile is an excellent swimmer. It pushes itself along with side-to-side sweeps of its powerful tail. It can also use its tail to drive itself suddenly and powerfully out of the water, in a sudden upward lunge to snatch prey. The legs are held close against the body to reduce resistance as the reptile swishes along.

The black caiman is not always black. It may be brown and have creamy patches on its chin and underside.

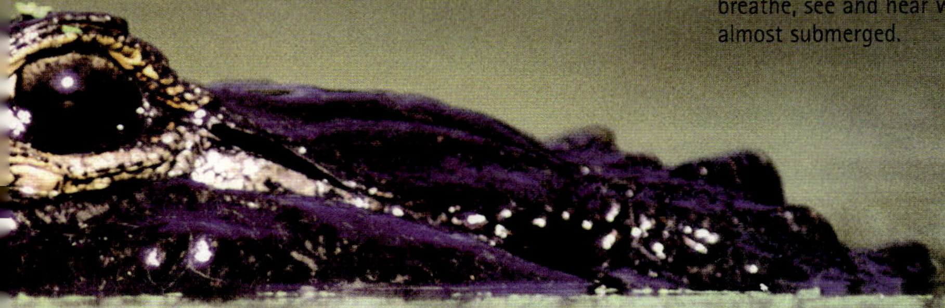

All crocodilians have their nostrils, eyes and ears on the top of the head. They can breathe, see and hear while almost submerged.

MAIN GROUPS OF CROCODILIANS (continued from page 139):

Alligators and caimans *(Alligatorinae)*
- 7 species
- teeth not visible when mouth is closed

Crocodiles *(Crocodylinae)*
- 14 species
- fourth tooth in lower jaw visible when mouth is closed
- includes mugger, false gharial

Gharial *(Gavialinae)*
- 1 species
- long, slender jaws

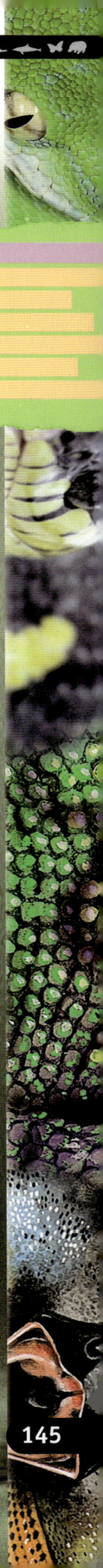

HOW CROCODILES BREED

Young crocodilians have longer legs, larger eyes, and shorter snouts relative to their body size, compared to the adults. But they are still fearsome hunters.

CROCODILES MAY SEEM LIKE ROBOTIC, UNTHINKING KILLERS. We notice few facial expressions or sound signals to show their moods and intentions. But among themselves, crocodiles have surprisingly complicated behaviour, social lives and breeding methods. They communicate using a wide variety of sounds, smells and movements. And, unlike nearly all other reptiles, the female guards her nest and takes care of her young.

World Watch

Like many large predators, crocodiles and alligators are killed because they occasionally harm people. Their strong, hard-wearing skins have been used for centuries, mainly by native peoples. However, the mass production of crocodile-skin clothing, belts, shoes and bags led to a surge in the numbers killed for the trade. Some species are now farmed. But others, like the gharial, have become very rare.

In the backwater swamps of the Everglades National Park, in Florida, USA, a female American alligator lurks half submerged. Her back provides a safe resting place for her babies.

A female crocodile deposits her eggs in the nest hole. Breeding time is usually in the warmest, dampest part of the year. It may be delayed if the rains do not come to soften the soil.

Crocodiles are polygamous animals. This means a member of one sex, in this case the male, mates with several partners. But the male crocodile must first establish a territory, by pushing out rival males. Then he must attract the attention of possible mates. He swims high in the water with his body exposed, occasionally slapping the surface with his chin to make loud sounds. His antics may also attract rival males, who try to take over by having head-butt contests. Females watch the males and, before mating, rub the male's head or blow bubbles underwater.

THE CROCODILE'S NEST

Soon after mating, the female prepares to dig her nest. The details vary slightly among the species, but the Nile crocodile is fairly typical. She finds a suitable site, in sunny soft ground up to 50 m away from water. She may have to threaten rival females, since the best sites are in short supply and used year after year.

She digs her nest with her strong back feet and positions herself over the hole, to start laying eggs. Young females may lay only about 20 eggs, but older ones can spend up to an hour laying about 80 eggs. She then covers the eggs and watches over the nest. She does not feed during this time, and only moves away from the nest to drink. Even so, rapid predators such as mongooses, foxes or monitor lizards may dart in and steal an egg or two.

INSIDE A REPTILE

A crocodile has most of the main body parts of other vertebrates, including birds (page 185) and mammals (page 192). However, its digestive wastes (faeces), liquid wastes (urine) and reproductive system all open into a common chamber, the cloaca, which leads to the outside. This is similar to birds, but different from mammals.

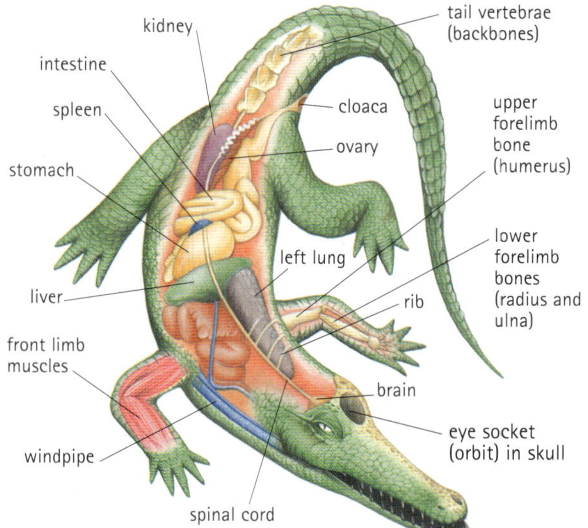

CALLS FOR HELP

Crocodile eggs usually incubate for 60–100 days, depending on temperature. When the babies are ready and hear footsteps above, they call from inside their eggs with loud squeals. The mother digs down to the eggs, and the hatchlings start to break out of their shells. As they emerge, the mother reaches down and gently picks them up, one at a time, in her sharp-toothed jaws.

When she has collected several, she carries them in her mouth to a safe, quiet "nursery pool", where she releases them into the water. She then quickly returns to the nest to collect the next batch. Finally all the young and the mother are safe in their nursery pool.

CLOSE TO MOTHER

For the first few weeks, baby crocodiles stay close to their mother. At any sign of danger, the mother vibrates her body muscles. The vibrations pass through the ground and water, and are a signal for her young to dive beneath the surface. In some species, the male may help to defend the offspring. But if food is very scarce, he may eat one of them!

ALLIGATOR NESTS

Alligators and caimans lay their eggs in mounds, which they scrape together from plants, soil and dead leaves. The mounds are usually up to 1.8 m across and 90 cm high, and the mother guards the eggs and the babies.

The sex of a crocodile is determined by the temperature of the egg during incubation. American alligator eggs at 32–34°C produce males, while below 30°C the babies are females. Both males and females result at 30–32°C. In crocodiles, high and low temperatures produce females, while in-between temperatures result in males.

GRUNT!

All crocodiles make some sounds, from simple hisses to husky roars. But alligators are particularly vocal. Baby alligators keep in touch with each other using high-pitched grunting calls, as they search for food in their "nursery" pool. If danger threatens, the youngster who detects it first makes a special distress call. This alerts all the others, and it also attracts the mother's attention so she returns.

A mother crocodile scoops up one of her newly hatched young to carry it to the nursery pool.

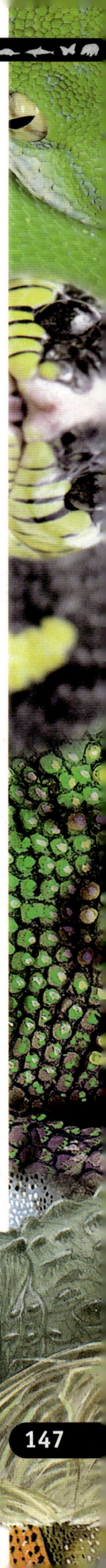

IGUANAS, AGAMIDS AND CHAMELEONS

Galapagos marine iguanas grow to 1.5 m in length (including the tail). They vary in colour from green-brown to pink.

A frilled lizard in defensive posture.

LIZARDS ARE THE LARGEST GROUP OF REPTILES. There are more than 3,700 species. They are most common in tropical areas, but there are species in nearly all regions except the far north and Antarctica. The iguanas are one of the largest lizard sub-groups. Most live in North and South America, but there are some in Madagascar and Fiji. The agamids, or chisel-teeth lizards, are similar in appearance and habits to the iguanas, but live in the Old World – Africa (except Madagascar), Asia and Australia, with one species in Europe. Most chameleons come from tropical Africa and India, and are well adapted for life in the trees.

Some iguanas and agamids are quite large for lizards, growing to more than 50 cm in length (including the tail). Many are adorned with crests and frills, and the males especially are brightly coloured. They live on land and in trees, and are active during the day.

Most prey on insects and other small creatures, but a few species, such as the chuckwalla and desert iguana of North America, feed on plant material.

RUNNING AT SPEED

The basilisk lizard is a type of iguana from South America. It has very muscular back legs and long, thin toes. It is one of the fastest runners of all lizards, reaching more than 10 km/h.

Striped agama

LITTLE AND LARGE... !

Chameleons range in size from the tiny brown brookesia, about as long as a little finger, to the huge oustaleti chameleon at 55 cm long.

The basilisk lizard runs so fast that it can even move for short distances over water, its long toes supported by the skin-like film on the surface.

It runs with its long tail held out behind for balance. Male basilisks have a large, bony "helmet" on the head and crests of skin along the back and tail. In females the helmets are smaller.

DIVING BELOW

Unlike other iguanas, the marine iguana (page 139) spends much of its life in the seas around the Galapagos Islands. An expert swimmer and diver, it uses its strong tail to propel itself through water, diving to eat seaweeds. Although the iguana must come to the surface to breathe, it can eat while submerged. Its heart rate slows as it dives, to reduce its need for oxygen, so it can stay under water for longer.

FRILLED LIZARD

The frilled lizard is an agamid from Australia and New Guinea. It has a very long tail and an unusual, brightly coloured collar of skin, like a ruff, around its neck. Normally this neck frill lies folded flat against the shoulders. If the lizard is alarmed, it opens its mouth wide and spreads out the frill around its head. This makes it appear much larger, to deter possible enemies.

FLYING LIZARDS

The flying dragon is another type of agamid lizard, found in Southeast Asia. It lives in thick rainforest and has also taken to rubber tree plantations. It does not really fly, but can glide long distances between trees without having to come down to the ground. It has wing-like flaps of skin at each side of its body, which viewed from above, make a circular shape. The flaps are held against the body, and extended as the lizard launches itself into the air.

LIFE IN THE TREES

The chameleon is adapted for hunting insects in trees. Its feet are specially arranged to provide a strong grip on branches, with three toes wrapped around one side and two on the other. The chameleon also has a strong prehensile tail, which can be curled around the branch and used like an extra leg. With these gripping aids, the chameleon can remain still for long periods. It also changes its colour to match the background. When prey comes near, the chameleon takes aim with the help of its excellent eyesight, and shoots out its long, sticky-tipped tongue at the victim.

Chameleons change colour to blend in with their surroundings.

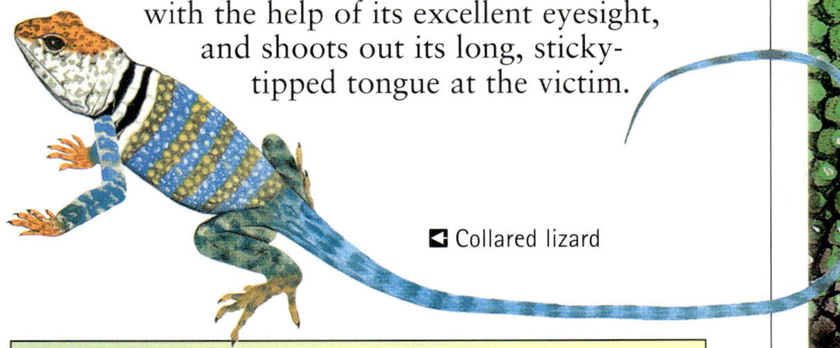

Collared lizard

SOME GROUPS OF LIZARDS:

Iguanas *(Iguanidae)*
- more than 850 species
- limbs usually well developed
- includes marine iguana, basilisk lizard, anole

Agamid lizards *(Agamidae)*
- about 350 species
- large head and long tail
- includes frilled lizard, flying dragon

Chameleons *(Chamaeleontidae)*
- 135 species
- flattened body, prehensile tail
- large eyes can move separately
- changes colour to match scenery

The chameleon's tongue darts out so fast that it can reach its prey in less than one-hundredth of a second.

GECKOS, LACERTIDS AND TEIID LIZARDS

The viviparous lizard grows to about 18 cm in total length. It is usually grey, brown or yellow, but like many lizards, the colour varies in different parts of its range.

GECKOS ARE AMONG THE MOST SUCCESSFUL LIZARDS. They live in all warmer areas of the world, and are particularly common and varied in the tropics. Typically, a gecko is active at night. It has large eyes to help it see in dim light. Most geckos do not have eyelids. A special transparent version of the normal reptile scale permanently covers each eye. Most wall and sand lizards, or lacertids, live in warm parts of Europe, Africa and Asia. But one species, the viviparous lizard, survives in Scandinavia, inside the Arctic Circle – farther north than any other lizard. Most teiid lizards live in South America. In many ways they are New World versions of Old World lacertids.

Leaf-tailed gecko

Geckos are known for their ability to climb smooth surfaces, even glass, with ease. The underside of each toe is covered with many tiny bristles, like a miniature brush. Each bristle ends in a disc-like sucker. These discs help the gecko cling to smooth surfaces. The night lizards of the southern USA and Central America look similar to geckos, and are also active at night.

LEAFY TAIL

The leaf-tailed gecko has a spotted body and flattened tail, which gives amazing camouflage as the lizard lies flattened against bark or lichen on a tree trunk. Like other geckos, it often licks its eyes with its long tongue, to keep them clear of dust and dirt.

Day geckos are only about 15 cm long, active by day, and live mainly in forests. Their green colour is good daytime camouflage.

SOFT!

The web-footed gecko lives in the Namib Desert in southwest Africa. It does indeed have webbed feet. These work like sandshoes, to help the lizard run over soft sand without sinking in.

The tokay gecko, like several other geckos, is a welcome visitor in homes across Asia. It feeds on troublesome insects, from mosquitoes to cockroaches. Like most geckos, the female tokay gecko lays only a couple of eggs at a time. They are slightly sticky and the female attaches them to a rock or tree. Several females may lay eggs in the same place.

▲ The caiman lizard, a type of teiid, spends much of its life in water, being an excellent swimmer and diver. It feeds mainly by crushing water-living snails with its strong jaws and flattened teeth. Caiman lizards grow to 90 cm long and have large, rough scales along the back, similar to those of a crocodile.

LACERTIDS

Lacertid lizards include the green and wall lizards, sandracer and racerunner. A typical lacertid has a long, slim body and tail. Males usually have larger heads than females and are often brightly coloured, particularly in the breeding season. Like most lizards, lacertids lay eggs hidden under stones or in holes. The exception is the viviparous lizard. It gives birth to babies rather than laying eggs, as described below. This species lives over much of Europe, including the far north, and Central Asia. In the summer months it is lively and active, feeding on insects, worms and other small creatures. When the weather gets cold in the north of its range, it becomes inactive or torpid, and stays in its burrow for up to six months.

▲ The tokay gecko is named for its barking "to-keh!" call.

LIZARD EATER

Like lacertids, teiid lizards have long bodies and tails, are active by day and hunt insects and other small creatures. The jungle runner is a teiid from Central and South America. It is an extremely busy predator, catching small birds and mammals, and even smaller lizards.

EGGS OR BABIES?

Most lizards, like most reptiles, reproduce by laying leathery-shelled eggs. But geckos produce hard-shelled eggs, like those of birds. In most cases, the eggs are left to incubate and hatch by themselves. In a few species, the female may curl around her eggs to protect them, but this is rare among lizards. However, some lizards, including types of geckos, night lizards, anguids, lacertids and skinks, do not lay eggs. The female keeps the developing babies inside her body, in their thin-walled shells. The young are nourished by their egg yolks, and also by substances from the female's body, in a similar way to a mammal mother. The babies hatch from their eggs inside the mother, and then she gives birth. The viviparous lizard produces about 6–8 young in this way. But after the mother has given birth to her babies, she takes no interest in them. They must manage for themselves straight away.

THE TUATARA

The tuatara (or sphenodon) may look like a lizard. In fact, it is a rhynchocephalian – a type of reptile common many millions of years ago, at the time of the dinosaurs. There is only one species alive today, and it is found only on a few offshore islands of New Zealand, in sanctuaries. They are extinct on the New Zealand mainland, largely due to human-introduced predators such as cats and rats, which eat their eggs. Tuataras shelter in burrows during the day and come out at night to hunt insects, snails and spiders. These "living fossils" are 45–60 cm long. Their eggs take 15 months to hatch – longer than any other reptile.

▶ Whiptail lizards are among the few reptiles whose females lay eggs without first mating with a male. This is called parthenogenesis.

MORE GROUPS OF LIZARDS:

Geckos *(Gekkonidae)*
- more than 900 species
- large eyes with transparent covering
- climb on smooth surfaces
- includes banded and tokay geckos

Wall and sand lizards *(Lacertidae)*
- about 215 species
- long body and tail, well-developed limbs
- includes wall lizard, green lizard, racerunner

Teiid lizards *(Teiidae)*
- about 105 species
- varied body shape, long tail
- includes caiman lizard, jungle runner, whiptail

SKINKS, MONITORS AND SLOW-WORMS

Gila monsters feed mainly on other lizards and snakes, small mammals, birds and the eggs of reptiles and birds.

SKINKS ARE THE LARGEST GROUP OF LIZARDS, WITH MORE THAN 1,300 SPECIES. They live in tropical and temperate areas all over the world, particularly in Southeast Asia and Australia. Skinks are very varied in body shape and are found in almost every habitat, from rainforest and stream bank to desert and mountaintop. They have tiny legs, or none at all. Slow-worms are limbless lizards. Monitors are large, powerful lizards with strong legs, a long neck and tail, and a snake-like forked tongue.

The slow-worm eats worms, slugs, grubs and spiders. It is about 50 cm long and lives in Europe, Asia and North Africa.

The monitor lizard family includes the largest of all lizards, the Komodo dragon of Southeast Asia. It lives on Komodo and neighbouring Indonesian islands, where it hunts wild pigs, deer and monkeys. It also scavenges on carrion. Young Komodo dragons catch insects and small mammals. These mighty creatures, once very rare, now benefit from being a tourist attraction. People pay to throw them dead animals to eat, while taking photographs and videos.

RACY MONITORS

Monitor lizards live in Africa and Southeast Asia, and also in Australia, where most species are found. Some are known as goannas. The sand monitor is also called the racehorse goanna because it runs so fast. The shy Australian perentie of desert and rocky scrub is the world's second-biggest lizard, at 2.5 m long.

LEGLESS SKINK

Many skinks are slim and fast-moving. They wriggle on their bellies, rather than walking on their legs.

The gila monster is one of only two kinds of lizard with a poisonous bite. The other is the Mexican beaded lizard.

WORM LIZARDS

The snake-like worm lizards are neither worms, nor lizards, nor snakes. They make up a separate reptile group, amphisbaenids. A typical worm lizard has a scaly, loose-skinned body from 10–70 cm long, and no legs (although a few have tiny front limbs). It lives in burrows, which it digs by forcing its blunt head through the soil. Most live in Africa, South America and the West Indies.

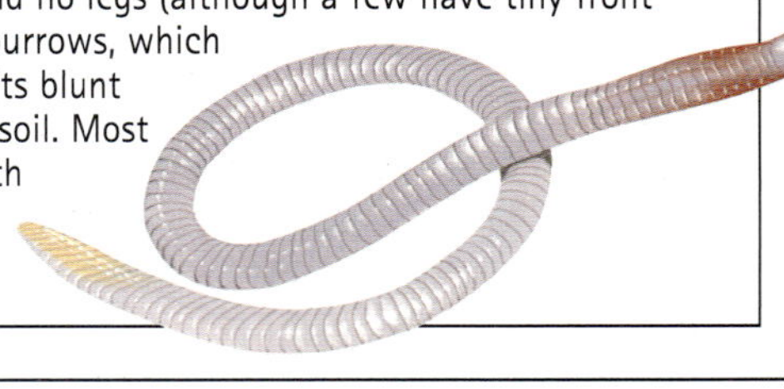

GONE!

Many lizards, including most skinks, can break off part of the tail if this is seized by a predator. The break happens at a particular place, the "weak point", causing little harm. The detached piece may wriggle, perhaps confusing the predator. The stump usually grows into a new tail after a few months.

The blue-tongued skink of Australia grows to about 45 cm long. It lives in dry scrub and eats small animals, fruits and berries.

Indeed, some skinks have no limbs. The legless skink has a snake-like body and lives in burrows in South Africa and Madagascar. It moves surprisingly quickly with curving body movements.

LEG FLAPS

Scaly-foot lizards, also known as snake lizards, have long snake-like bodies. They have no front legs. The tiny back legs are little more than flaps held close against the body.

POISONOUS LIZARDS

The gila monster and the beaded lizard are in a group of their own, related to monitors. They live in southwestern North America and parts of Central America, and are the only venomous lizards. They feed mainly on small animals and eggs, so their poison is probably more for defence than for killing prey. Both of these lizards have thick tails, used to store body fat in times of food shortage.

WEDGED IN A CRACK

Plated lizards live in Africa, usually in rocky, dry areas. The imperial flat lizard, as its name suggests, has a flattened head and body so it can slide into narrow crevices among the rocks. Once in the crack, the lizard puffs itself up with air, wedging its body and making it almost impossible to remove.

Plated lizards include the armadillo lizard from Southern Africa. It is named for its defence of rolling into a ball like an armadillo, its spiny scales sticking out. It is fairly small, only 20 cm long including its tail, and hunts by day for a wide range of small creatures, including spiders.

The Komodo dragon of Indonesia grows up to 3 m long and weighs more than 150 kg.

SLOW LIZARDS

The anguid lizards include some legless types, such as the slow-worms, and also species with large and strong legs, such as the alligator lizard. The galliwasp is an anguid lizard from Central and South America with an orange head, a red underside and a dark blue back with black crossways stripes. It has smooth, shiny skin and looks more like a brightly coloured salamander than a lizard.

MORE GROUPS OF LIZARDS:

Skinks *(Scincidae)*
- more than 1,300 species
- body typically long with a small head and short legs
- some limbless species
- includes Great Plains skink, sandfish, blue-tongued skink

Monitor lizards *(Varanidae)*
- 48 species
- large body, long neck, strong legs and tail
- includes Komodo dragon, Gould's monitor, Nile monitor

Anguid Lizards *(Anguidae)*
- about 100 species
- long, smooth body and tail
- some limbless species
- includes slow-worm, alligator lizard, legless lizard, glass snake, galliwasp

Scaly-foot lizards *(Pygopodidae)*
- about 35 species
- very long slim body, tiny back legs, no front legs
- includes western scaly-foot, Burton's snake-lizard

Girdle-tailed lizards *(Cordylidae)*
- 50 species
- heavily armoured body covered with bony plates
- includes imperial flat lizard, plated lizard, armadillo lizard

Blind lizards *(Dibamidae)*
- 11 species
- small, long-bodied with tiny limbs
- includes Asian blind lizard

Beaded lizards *(Helodermatidae)*
- 2 species
- bulky body, large head, short thick tail
- venomous
- includes gila monster, beaded lizard

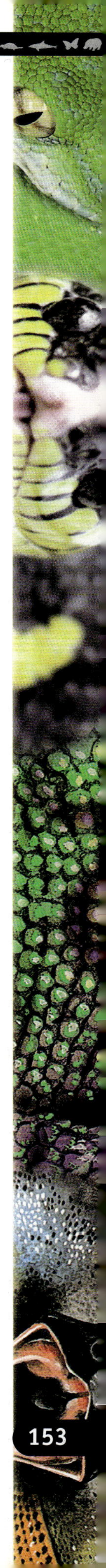

PYTHONS, BOAS AND THREAD SNAKES

SNAKES HAVE NO LEGS. Yet they can wriggle at speed along the ground, climb trees easily, swim well – and a few can even "fly"! Snakes are a hugely successful group of reptiles with almost 2,400 species. They live on all continents except Antarctica. They are also absent from Ireland, Iceland and New Zealand. They are all predators. Most can open their mouths wide to swallow prey whole. Some have suffocating coils and others strike with deadly poison fangs.

The sunbeam snake of Southeast Asia burrows and swims well, and eats fish, frogs, mice and small birds. Its body has a mixture of primitive (ancient) and advanced (modern) features.

Snakes evolved millions of years ago, from reptiles similar to lizards which had four limbs. Gradually the limbs became smaller, and in most snakes today, they have completely disappeared. But some snakes have tiny, useless remnants of limbs, such as hip and rear leg bones. These include thread snakes, blind snakes and pipe snakes. They are called primitive snakes because they most resemble their distant ancestors. Like the first snakes, most of them burrow into soil and spend much of their lives underground.

Blind and thread snakes have tiny eyes hidden beneath scales. Most thread snakes are blunt-headed, while blind snakes have narrow heads. Both designs help them to tunnel through soil. They eat small worms, grubs, ants, termites and similar soil creatures.

PIPE SNAKES

Pipe snakes also spend much time burrowing underground. Unlike most other snakes, a pipe snake cannot open its mouth very wide. So it feeds mainly on slender-bodied animals such as worm lizards and other snakes, which it sucks in like spaghetti.

The green python coils around itself to rest, almost as it would squeeze or constrict its prey.

Boas often rest in trees. Like pythons, they can tilt forward the large scales on the underside of the body. This raises the rear edges of the scales for extra grip as the snake moves forwards.

Pythons are mainly large snakes of the tropics in Africa, Asia and Australia. They like to stay near water and climb trees well. Boas are similar snakes of the Americas, although they stay more on the ground. Both pythons and boas are primitive snakes, with tiny hip and back leg bones embedded in their bodies. They all have two lungs as well. Most other snakes have lost one lung during evolution, to help achieve their narrow, streamlined shape.

The false coral snake is a type of pipe snake. It grows to about 80 cm long.

Both pythons and boas are fierce predators. They kill their prey by coiling their bodies around it and crushing it until the victim suffocates. They prey mainly on mammals and birds. The reticulated python is the longest snake, reaching 10 m. Boas have slightly different bones in the head and the teeth compared to pythons. They include the second-longest but heaviest snake, the anaconda. The anaconda spends much of its life in swamps and slow-moving streams, in its rainforest habitat. Half-hidden in the shallows, it lies in wait for animals to come and drink. When a victim is near enough, the anaconda bites and envelops it in crushing coils.

HEAVIEST... !

The bulkiest snake is the anaconda, a type of boa. It weighs up to 250 kg, which is more than three adult humans.

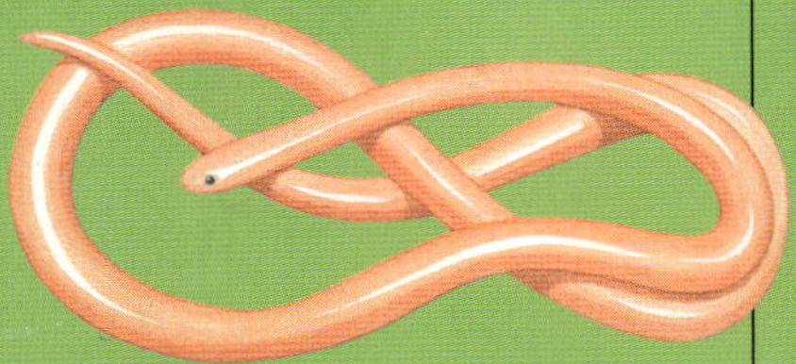

The western blind snake is a type of thread snake. It has very small, simple eyes hidden beneath its skin. It can slide into ants' nests to eat the larvae.

This emerald tree boa is just beginning to swallow a woolly opossum. It may take an hour or more, and the boa may not eat again for a month. The snake's bright green body gives excellent camouflage among the leaves of its forest home in northern South America.

World Watch

Large snakes such as pythons and boas were once hunted for their leathery, beautifully patterned skin. This was used to make shoes, bags, belts, trousers and similar hard-wearing items. However, the hunting made some species extremely rare. It is more difficult to farm snakes for the skin trade compared to, for example, crocodiles. Most snakes will only eat a victim if it has only just died and is still warm.

The anaconda is a massive-bodied swamp snake from South America. It grows to 9 m in length and can eat animals the size of goats, tapirs and peccaries. Females give birth to about 30 babies, each 60 cm long.

CARING MOTHER

Most snakes lay their eggs in holes and leave them to hatch. The Indian python is one of the few snake species that incubate their eggs with their own bodies. The female lays up to 100 eggs and curls around them to keep them warm and protected. She also adjusts her body to cover them more or less, according to the weather.

SOME GROUPS OF SNAKES
(continued from page 139):

Thread snakes *(Leptotyphlopidae)*
- about 64 species
- small, slender body, blunt head and tail

Blind snakes *(Typhlopidae)*
- about 150 species
- smooth, cylindrical body
- teeth only in upper jaw

Pipe snakes *(Aniliidae)*
- 11 species
- blunt head
- body often boldly marked
- includes coral pipe snake, false coral snake

Pythons and boas *(Boidae)*
- about 60 species
- flexible jaws
- tiny remnants of rear limbs
- squeeze or constrict prey

COLUBRID SNAKES

The brown water snake lurks in muddy creeks and ponds, ready to strike. There are about 30 kinds of water snakes. They all have their nostrils on the top of the snout for breathing while almost submerged.

THE COLUBRIDS ARE THE LARGEST GROUP OF SNAKES. Found on all continents except Antarctica, they are the most common snakes everywhere except Australia, where they are outnumbered by the various types of cobras.

Most colubrids are medium-sized snakes, about 50–150 cm long. Unlike pythons, they have no remnants of any limbs, and the left lung is either very small or absent, in order to streamline the body. Colubrids live on land, in burrows under the ground, in trees and even in water. They eat a wide range of foods, from eggs to mice and small birds. Most species are harmless to humans. But a few, such as the boomslang, have poisonous bites. They are called back-fanged venomous snakes because their poison fangs are near the rear of the jaws, not at the front.

The grass snake is extremely varied in colour and pattern. Its bite is poisonous, but only to small animals such as frogs, fish and voles. It grows to about 1.2 m in length.

This egg-eating snake is ready to crack an egg with its spiny neck bones.

The poisonous types of colubrid snakes are few in number, and they do not have hollow fangs at the front of the mouth like other venomous species. Instead they have grooved teeth at the back of the upper jaw, which are linked to a poison gland. As the snake bites, the poison flows down the groove into the prey. This means the snake must get its mouth well over the victim, to deliver its venom.

THUMB-THIN SNAKE

The venom of the African boomslang is strong enough to kill a human. But this dark or olive green snake usually prefers to slide away if threatened, rather than strike. It needs to conserve its poison to kill its prey, which is mostly birds and lizards such as chameleons. The boomslang is up to 1.8 m long, but its body is very slender, hardly thicker than a thumb. This means it is also very light and a good climber, spending much of its life among the branches.

The vine snake may be more than 1.8 m long. Yet its body is as thin as a little finger. This amazing camouflage hides it among the creepers and vines in trees. If the wind increases, the snake sways with the stems around it. Vine snakes eat small tree-dwelling lizards and baby birds.

EGGS AND SNAILS

Many snakes eat eggs as part of a varied diet. But the egg-eating snake of Africa eats only the hard-shelled eggs of birds. It can open its jaws very wide to take the egg into its mouth. As the egg passes into its throat, spiky projections on the snake's neck bones jab and saw the shell open, allowing the contents to ooze out and be swallowed. The snake then brings up or regurgitates the bits of shell and settles to digest its meal.

The snail-eating snake is another specialist. Its lower jaw is equipped with strong, curved teeth. The snake hooks these teeth into the fleshy body of a snail, drags the snail out of its shell and swallows its meal.

BABIES!

Garter snakes are among the most numerous and widespread snakes in North America. In autumn, in the north of their range, they gather in holes and caves to spend the winter. However, they may mate first, each large female being almost completely buried under a writhing mass of smaller males. She does not lay eggs. Instead, up to 80 babies develop inside her body. The babies are born as the warmth returns in late spring.

FLYING SNAKE?

The tree-living paradise snake from Southeast Asia is sometimes known as the flying snake, because it can glide through the air between trees. As it hurls itself from a high branch, it spreads its ribs out sideways and draws its belly up and in, to make a long, ribbon-like shape with a curved underside. This works almost like a bird's wing to provide an upwards force. As the paradise snake "flies", it wriggles its body as it would on the ground, gliding perhaps 18 m to the ground or to a lower branch. It is not a very well controlled glide, however, and a gust of wind can blow the snake into the trunk of a tree. The flying snake is about 1.3 m long and feeds on birds and lizards.

WATER SNAKE

Although water snakes bask on land, they spend most of their time in swamps, streams and rivers. They are excellent swimmers and pursue fish and other water-living creatures, such as frogs and crayfish.

THE LARGEST SNAKE GROUP
(continued from page 155):

Colubrid snakes
(Colubridae)
- about 1,600 species
- no remnants of limbs
- flexible lower jaw to allow mouth to open very wide, for biting and swallowing
- most lack venom, or the venom is not strong enough to harm humans
- includes grass snake, garter snake, rat snake, cat-eyed snake, milk snake, mud snake, slug snake, spotted water snake, gopher snake

Mangrove snakes hunt crabs, fish and frogs among the mangrove swamps of Southeast Asia and Australia.

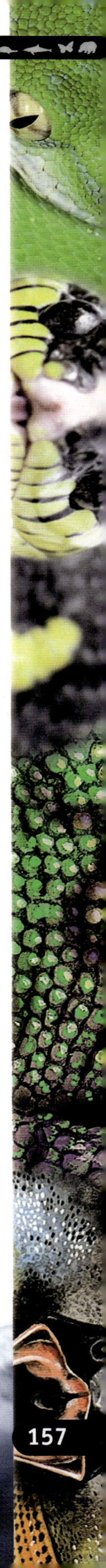

COBRAS, VIPERS AND RATTLERS

An Indian cobra spreads its "eyed" hood when ready for action, to look more menacing.

THERE ARE TWO MAIN GROUPS OF VENOMOUS SNAKES. These are the cobras and the vipers. The cobras have short fangs, fixed in position at the front of the upper jaw. When the snake bites, venom passes from the poison glands through the fangs and into the victim. The fangs must be relatively short or the snake would not be able to close its mouth. Vipers have longer fangs that fold up and back when not in use, to keep them safe and sharp.

The Gaboon viper has a very noticeable neck for its size. It is one of the largest vipers, at up to 1.8 m long. Its brown pattern makes it blend in among old leaves on the rainforest floor.

The cobra group includes many kinds of poisonous snakes besides the hooded species named cobras, which live in Africa, the Middle East and Asia. Other group members are the brightly coloured coral snakes of North and South America, the highly venomous mambas of Africa, and the fish-eating sea snakes which live all their lives in the oceans. The cobra group is common in Australia, with far more members there than any other type of snake. They include the eastern brown snake of forests and swamps.

THE COBRA'S HOOD

To warn off enemies, hooded cobras raise the front of the body off the ground, spread the ribs and loose skin at the sides of the head to make the cloak-like hood and sway gently. This makes the snake look bigger than it really is, and warns the enemy that it may strike. In the Indian cobra, the hood has eye-like markings to further alarm the attacker.

SNAKES AT SEA

About 50 species of sea snakes, such as the banded sea snake, spend all their lives at sea. The female carries the developing babies inside her body and gives birth to the young, so does not need to go onto land to lay eggs. Sea snakes have other adaptations to a watery life, including a flattened tail that works as a paddle, and nostrils on top of the head so the snake can breathe even when most of its body is under water. Flaps close the nostrils when the snake dives. Sea snakes feed mostly on fish and have extremely powerful venom. On land, without the water to buoy them up, they are floppy and can hardly move.

The bandy-bandy is a distinctive black and white snake from Australia. It eats mainly smaller snakes, especially blind snakes, and lives in a wide variety of habitats.

The sidewinder, a type of viper, pushes up and forwards mainly with its head and tail, leaving J-shaped indents in the desert sand.

Wagler's viper

VIPER FANGS

Vipers have the most complicated killing equipment of any snake. A viper's large, thin teeth, or fangs, are much longer than the fangs of a cobra. Also they are hinged so that they can be folded back against the upper jaw when not needed. When the viper attacks, it opens its mouth wide and the fangs swing forward. Venom is pumped into them from the poison glands behind the eyes. Members of the viper family include pit vipers and rattlesnakes. While cobras tend to chase after their prey, vipers usually lie in wait and ambush their victims.

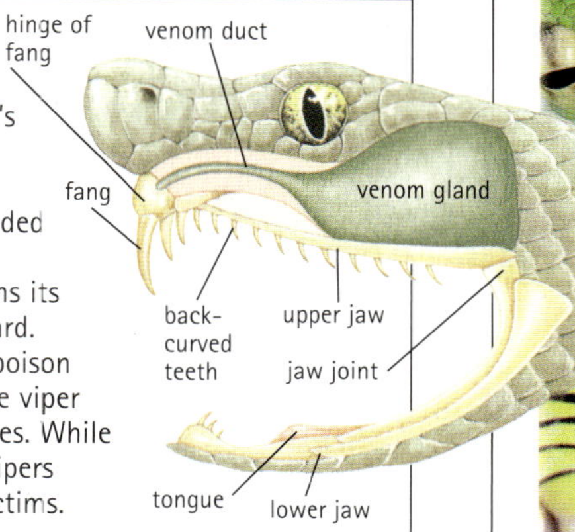

MAMBAS

The African mambas are feared for their surprising speed, their readiness to strike, and their venom. Mamba bites are fatal more often than the bites of almost any other snake. Mambas chase birds and small mammals to eat. They can crawl with a large part of the front body held upright, so the head is more than 1 m off the ground.

The black mamba of Africa is 4.2 m long. It is one of the deadliest of all snakes, and can slither along at more than 11 km/h.

PIT VIPERS

The types of vipers called pit vipers can hunt even on the darkest night. They are named for the small, sensory holes or pits on each side of the head. These detect heat (infra-red rays) coming from warm-blooded prey. Like infra-red "night binoculars", the two pit organs provide a "heat picture" of the surroundings. By moving its head from side to side, the snake can pinpoint the exact position of a mouse or small bird.

THE WARNING BUZZ

North American rattlesnakes belong to the pit viper group. At the end of the tail is a rattle made of hard rings of skin. When the snake shakes this, the rings make a buzzing, rattling sound to warn enemies. New rings are added to the rattle as the snake grows.

Having made its warning noise, this rattlesnake is in mid-strike, mouth wide open and fangs about to stab poison. The largest rattlers grow more than 2.1 m long and are the most dangerous snakes in North America.

LARGEST... !

The largest venomous snake in the world is the king cobra, which grows to more than 5 m in length

MAIN GROUPS OF POISONOUS SNAKES:

Cobras *(Elapidae)*	Vipers *(Viperidae)*
• about 250 species	• about 200 species
• fixed fangs at front of upper jaw	• tilting hollow fangs in upper jaw
• usually slender-bodied	• heavy-bodied
• includes black mamba, king cobra, banded sea snake	• includes common viper, puff adder, rattlesnakes

The white pelican is one of the biggest waterbirds, with a wingspan of 2.7 m. It is known for its big beak with a stretchy pouch.

SECTION 6
BIRDS

BIRDS ARE PROBABLY THE MOST EASILY RECOGNIZED OF ALL ANIMALS. Any creature with wings, feathers and a beak must be a bird. But not all birds use their wings for flying. The ostrich uses its wings as a sunshade to keep its eggs cool in the desert heat. Puffins, razorbills and guillemots flap their wings to swim underwater, with the help of their webbed feet.

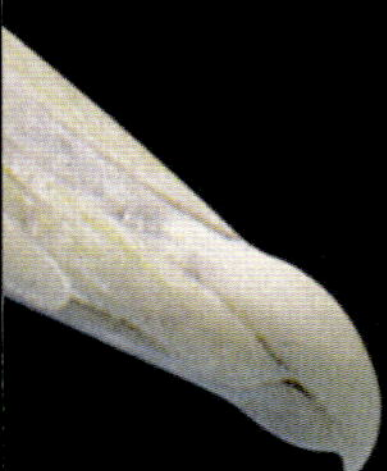

Feathers and beaks vary enormously, too. The kiwi is flightless, like the ostrich, and its feathers look like hairs. The peacock's colourful tail feathers are longer than your arm. The shape of a bird's beak usually shows the type of food it eats. An eagle's beak is sharp and hooked, for tearing flesh. A parrot's beak is thick and massive, for cracking nuts. A pelican's beak has a stretchy throat pouch which it uses as a fishing bag. A curlew's beak is like long, slim tweezers for probing into mud.

Birds are one of only two groups of animals that are warm-blooded. (The other group is mammals.) Being warm-blooded means being able to stay active even in cold conditions. Penguins survive some of the lowest temperatures on Earth, in the bitter cold and driving snow of Antarctica. Other birds experience intense cold at great heights, on mountains and during long-distance journeys. Some migrating geese fly as high as jet planes.

FLIGHTLESS BIRDS

The dodo was a huge-beaked, turkey-sized flightless bird from the Indian Ocean island of Mauritius. In this remote place it had no natural predators and so no need to fly. But when European people came to the island in the 1500s, they brought rats, pigs and monkeys, which ate the dodos' eggs. By 1680, they were extinct – "dead as a dodo".

ALL BIRDS HAVE WINGS, BUT NOT ALL OF THEM CAN FLY. Penguins are so well adapted to life in the sea that they use their short, stubby wings for swimming, not flying. The rare kakapo parrot of New Zealand has lost the power of flight because it has no natural predators where it lives, and so does not need to escape by flying. The most distinctive flightless birds are the ratites. These are mostly big – ostriches, emus, cassowaries, rheas and kiwis. They are part of a group of birds that, like penguins, never evolved the ability to fly. Ratites have always walked or run everywhere.

The emu of Australia grows up to 170 cm tall and weighs almost 45 kg. In some areas they have become pests because they eat crops and break fences.

OUCH!

The kiwi's huge white eggs are the biggest eggs of any bird, compared to the size of the adult. Each egg weighs about 454 g, which is almost a quarter of the mother's normal body weight – and she may lay two of them!

FLYING IN WATER

Penguins are so well adapted to life in the water that their wings are more like flippers. Their coats are so thick and well waterproofed with oil that they can survive even in the icy waters of the Antarctic. They are superb swimmers, and dash through the water by flapping their wings with the same motion that other birds use to fly through the air. On snow and ice, penguins often slide head-first down slopes, as if tobogganing. In the water they are swift and agile, pursuing their prey with ease. They eat mainly krill, squid and fish. Emperor penguins are the largest species. They can dive as deep as 250 m in search of food.

BIGGEST BIRDS

Millions of years ago there were many species of ratites all over the world. Now there are just ten species left, scattered as far apart as Africa and New Zealand. They are different to other birds in various ways, besides being flightless. For example, their feathers lack the smooth, flat, airproof surfaces which other birds have for flying. Instead, ratites have downy, "hairy" feathers. The leg bones of ratites are sturdy, more like a mammal's legs than a bird's. This is why some ratites can grow so large. The ostrich is the biggest living bird, towering up to 2.75 m tall.

Penguins dive into the water in a large group to hunt for their food. The mass dive helps to confuse any predators such as leopard seals and killer whales that may be lurking nearby.

The world's biggest bird, the ostrich, is also the only bird with just two toes on each foot. The toes have sharp claws, and a kick from an ostrich can be deadly.

Even bigger than an ostrich was the giant moa of New Zealand. Some moas were 3 m tall and weighed as much as a pony. They became extinct after people arrived.

The cassowary uses its helmet-like head crest for pushing through thick scrub.

OSTRICHES AND RHEAS

With their soft, downy plumage and bare necks, ostriches look rather comical and vulnerable as they strut across the grasslands of Africa. But they can sprint at up to 60 km/h, and can kick like a mule – which is why they rarely fall prey to lions. The idea that they bury their heads in the sand when afraid is a myth. It comes from the way the bird moves its eggs in the nest so that they stay evenly warm.

The rhea lives on the plains of southern Brazil and Argentina. It looks like a small ostrich, but has more feathers on its neck, and larger wings. On rare occasions it can struggle a very short distance through the air. Unusually for birds, male rheas and ostriches do most of the work at breeding time. The male scoops out a hole in the ground for a nest. Then, when several females have laid their eggs in it, he keeps them safe and at the correct temperature until they hatch, and he cares for the young chicks too.

The flightless kakapo of New Zealand is the world's largest parrot. It was once thought to have been wiped out by cats, rats and dogs. But recently, a few survivors were found and taken to a protected area on Little Barrier Island near Auckland, where there are no such predators. There the kakapos can breed and the species might be saved.

AUSTRALIAN RATITES

In the thick forests of tropical Australia and nearby islands, such as New Guinea, live three species of shy ratites called cassowaries. They are the same size as rheas, about 1.5 m tall. But they look more like long-legged turkeys, with a brightly coloured neck and a bony crest. They eat fruits, seeds and other plant parts. Another Australian ratite is the emu. It is second only to the ostrich in size, and can run almost as fast. It eats an extremely varied diet in grasslands and woodlands.

LARGEST... !

The biggest bird of historic times was the elephant bird of Madagascar. This gigantic ratite almost lived up to its name. It grew up to 4.5 m tall and weighed as much as an ox. Its eggs had a volume of 7 litres, the size of a soccer ball.

New Zealand's ratites are chicken-sized kiwis. Their wings are tiny, hidden beneath fur-like feathers. Kiwis are secretive birds, active only at night in bushy scrub or forests. They are rarely seen as they search for grubs, insects, berries and fruit.

Kiwis are tubby birds, covered in shaggy feathers like a furball. They have the best sense of smell of almost any bird, using the nostrils on the end of the beak to sniff out food in the leaves and soil.

BIRDS (*AVES*)

- about 8,800 species
- warm-blooded
- feathers
- beak or bill

Some flightless birds:

Ostrich
- 1 species
- Africa
- savanna
- male black and white; female brown

Rheas
- 2 species
- South America
- scrub, grassland
- brown or grey

Emu
- 1 species
- Australia
- woodland, scrub, and grassland
- dark brown

Cassowaries
- 3 species
- Australia, New Guinea
- rainforest
- mainly black

Penguins
- 16 species
- Antarctic region and southern parts of main oceans
- rocky islands and icebergs
- mainly black and white
- expert swimmers

Kiwis
- 3 species
- New Zealand
- forest and scrub
- brown or grey

Tinamous
- 49 species
- Central and South America
- resemble guinea fowl or pheasants
- some can fly but do so rarely

SEABIRDS

Shearwater

HUGE NUMBERS OF BIRDS LIVE BY, OR ON, THE SEA. Some feed mainly along the shore or dive for fish in coastal waters, such as various gulls, cormorants and gannets. Others, like auks, terns, skuas and frigate birds, live for weeks far out in the ocean. They come to the surface occasionally in calm weather, to float and rest. Still others, such as albatrosses, shearwaters and petrels, spend weeks at a time in the air. They land only rarely, usually to breed. They are superb flyers, soaring across the oceans for thousands of kilometres.

Albatrosses may be at sea for 2–3 weeks at a time. The wandering albatross has the longest wingspan of any bird, at up to 3.5 m. The waved albatross shown here is slightly smaller.

The male frigatebird has a bright red, balloon-like skin pouch on his throat. He blows this up to attract a female.

There are about 90 species of gulls, skuas and terns. They usually wheel and call along the coast, but gulls especially have adapted to new sources of food far inland. They hunt for worms and grubs in freshly ploughed fields, and squabble over leftovers on rubbish tips, especially in winter. The herring gull, in particular, is aggressive and threatens other birds. Gulls eat almost anything, including fish, crabs, insects, rotten meat and the eggs of other birds.

Boobies were named from the Spanish word *bobo*, meaning "stupid", because these birds were easily caught by sailors for food.

Most gulls have white and grey plumage, matching the reflections of sunlight on the sea. Some species have black markings on the back, wings and head. The larger gulls, like the great black-backed gull, have heavy, hooked beaks. They can easily kill smaller birds, baby rabbits and similar prey.

Guillemot

PIRATES AMONG BIRDS

Skuas resemble the larger gulls and have fearsome hooked beaks. In North America they are known by the German name of jaeger, meaning "hunter", due to their habit of chasing other birds who are carrying food. They harass the other bird, force it to drop its meal, then swoop to steal it. Big skuas like the great skua may catch and kill birds even larger than themselves.

Terns are like slim, graceful gulls. Many have forked tails, earning them the nickname of "sea-swallows". Many terns catch their fish prey by plunge-diving straight down into the water.

Royal terns

Common gulls use the wind to stay aloft without flapping.

LIGHT!

Arctic terns fly 40,000 km each year! They spend the northern summer in the Arctic where they breed. At the end of the summer, they migrate all the way to Antarctica, in time for the southern summer. So they live in almost endless daylight.

They are mainly summer visitors to temperate regions, migrating to warmer areas to avoid the cold winter months.

SKIMMING ALONG

Skimmers are tern-like birds, but with an unusual feature. The lower mandible (part of the beak) is longer than the upper part. The skimmer flies low and dips this lower mandible in the water, to snatch any fish.

MASTERS OF THE OCEAN WINDS

Albatrosses and petrels are master flyers, feeding far out at sea. Albatrosses are so big and heavy that they usually need a cliff to leap from, or a headwind to launch themselves into the air. Once aloft, they glide for hours in winds and air currents, without flapping. Shearwaters are smaller but have similar bodies, with long, narrow wings. Storm petrels are smaller and darker.

PLUMP DIVERS

Auks are plump seabirds resembling penguins. Their tight feathering keeps body warmth in and water out. They spend much time diving for food. Guillemots and razorbills breed in colonies on rocky ledges and cliffs, where most predators cannot reach.

The puffin is a strange-looking seabird that nests in clifftop burrows. Its brightly patterned beak is large enough to hold a dozen small fish such as sand-eels.

Cormorants are related to pelicans and have a similar but smaller throat pouch. Their feet are webbed across all four toes. They are black or dark birds, expert at diving and swimming after fish. They prefer rocky coasts and, unusually for seabirds, the oily waterproofing on their feathers is not very effective. So they spend long periods sitting with their wings spread out to dry in the sun.

FRIGATEBIRDS

Frigatebirds live along tropical coasts and are among the most graceful seabirds. The magnificent frigatebird has long wings and a long tail, which it uses as an aerial rudder and air-brake. It can swoop to catch fish leaping above the surface or snatch baby turtles hatching from their eggs on the beach.

SOME GROUPS OF SEABIRDS:

Gulls and terns
- 95 species
- mostly white or grey
- narrow wings
- black and white plumage

Skuas *(jaegers)*
- 6 species
- brown and white
- hooked beak

Skimmers
- 3 species
- black or dark brown and white
- long lower bill

Albatrosses, shearwaters, and petrels
- 93 species
- oceanic
- long, narrow wings

Auks
- 22 species
- compact and dumpy
- dive well

Cormorants
- 29 species
- black or dark plumage
- swim low in water

Gannets and boobies
- 9 species
- white, with black or dark markings

Frigatebirds
- 5 species
- large and long-winged
- black or dark and white

Tropicbirds
- 3 species
- white with black markings
- graceful flyers
- tail streamers

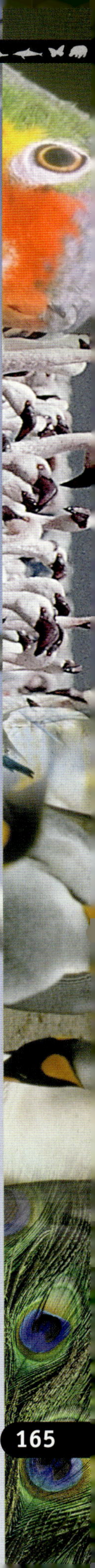

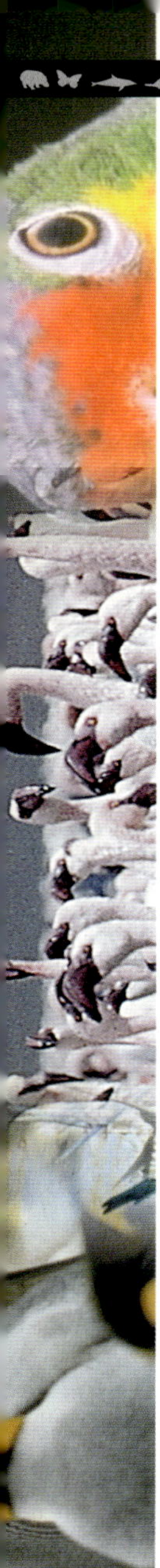

SHOREBIRDS AND WATERBIRDS

Many wading birds have clear, sad-sounding cries, like lonely wails. The curlew's "koor-lee" call can be heard far across the marshes, moors and mudflats of northern Europe.

THE WATER'S EDGE IS ONE OF THE RICHEST OF ALL BIRD HABITATS. The shallows of marshes, and the shores of lakes, estuaries and seas, are home to hundreds of small wading birds, such as oystercatchers, plovers, avocets, stilts, sandpipers and curlews. They stride through the water on spindly legs, dipping their long beaks into the water to grab worms and other food in the mud. There are bigger wading birds, too, such as flamingoes (page 168), herons and storks, which feed mainly on fish. Many other birds live in these water-edge and shallow-water habitats, but they dive or swim after food, rather than wading. The largest diving birds are pelicans. Expert underwater swimmers include grebes, darters and (despite their name) divers.

ZOOM!

Courting western grebes rear up and run at amazing speed across the surface. They zoom along like powerboats, driven by their splashing feet. This shows that they are fit and healthy, and so suitable as breeding partners.

The water's edge is home to many of the 300 bird species in the huge group called the Charadriiformes. They include most types of waders, as well as seabirds which fly rather than wade, such as skuas, gulls and auks.

Jacanas, or lily-trotters, are waders that spend much time walking across water lily leaves. They have the longest toes, for their body size, of any bird.

Waders have long, spindly legs for walking through water, and widely spread toes for standing on soft mud. The black-winged stilt has the longest legs of any bird compared to its body size – they are over half the stilt's total height of 40 cm.

The white pelican is one of the biggest waterbirds, with a wingspan of 2.7 m. It is known for its big beak with a stretchy pouch.

Waders' beaks are mostly also long and thin, for probing in water and mud. The precise shape of the beak varies according to how the bird feeds, and on what. Most waders poke about in mud and sand for small insects, worms and shellfish. Sandpipers have long beaks for digging softer sand and mud. Curlews have longer bills and gouge farther down for deeper-dwelling worms. The oystercatcher uses its strong, chisel-like bill to prise apart shellfish such as mussels.

THE PELICAN'S FISHING BAG

Pelicans are among the largest and heaviest waterbirds. They live on shallow coastal lagoons and inland lakes throughout the warmer parts of the world. They waddle awkwardly on land, but they swim and dive well, and soar gracefully.

TRAPPED!

White pelicans sometimes work together as a team. Up to 40 of them surround a spread-out shoal of fish, then they beat their wings on the water and kick their feet. This drives the fish into a smaller, denser shoal, in shallow water where they cannot escape by swimming deeper. Every 20 seconds or so, all the pelicans plunge their beaks into the middle of the shoal and scoop up their prey.

The stilt sandpiper has long, thin legs, as its name implies, to wade in deeper water. The sandpiper family includes about 80 species of waders, found across the world.

Pelicans are fish-eaters. They feed by dipping their heads under the surface and scooping up a huge mouthful of water and fish, in their big beaks. The chin and throat have loose skin that stretches like a balloon. The pelican tips out the water and swallows the fish. The Australian pelican has the longest bill of any bird. It can measure up to 47 cm.

The pelican's chin-and-throat bag, or gular pouch, expands to hold more than twice as much as the stomach. But not all pelicans scoop for fish. The American brown pelican dives from heights of 9 m into the sea, to dive-bomb and catch unsuspecting fish.

The avocet is a graceful wader that sifts tiny worms, shrimps and similar animals from the water with its slender, distinctive, up-curved beak. It skims its beak from side to side across the surface to gather food.

GREBES

Grebes, unlike pelicans and divers, have lobed rather than webbed feet. They are found in most parts of the world, mainly in freshwater lakes, rivers and marshes. In the winter, many grebes move toward the coasts, to feed along estuaries, mudflats and saltmarshes. Grebes are known for their elaborate courtship "dances". At breeding time, the female and male often swim and dive together. They surface holding weeds in their beaks, which they exchange as though swapping presents. Then they circle round, approach front-to-front, touch breasts, and stretch upwards, with beaks pointing up in the air.

African darter

SUPREME SWIMMERS

Divers or loons are streamlined waterbirds of northern regions. In the breeding season they make ghostly, wailing cries to attract a mate. They spend most of their time on lakes or out at sea, swimming with ease because their legs are set far back on their bodies. But this makes them unbalanced and clumsy when walking on land. When a diver swims, it almost lies on the water, so that it can slip easily beneath the surface. It may stay submerged for many minutes.

DARTERS

The darter is one of the most streamlined of swimming birds. It has a slender body, snake-like neck and dagger-shaped beak. It is very agile on and under the water, but swims slowly, creeping up on its prey to deliver a stabbing peck. Darters are found mainly in the tropics and prefer large, quiet lakes with plenty of insect and fish life.

SOME WATERBIRD GROUPS:

Waders
- 200 species
- most are wetland birds
- long legs, many have long bills
- medium-sized or small

Pelicans
- 7 species
- gliding and soaring flight
- feet completely webbed (all four toes)
- balloon-like throat pouch

Divers or loons
- 4 species
- waterbirds, excellent swimmers and divers

Grebes
- 20 species
- waterbirds, very good swimmers and divers
- 3 species are flightless

Darters
- 4 species
- thin, snake-like, darting neck

A red-necked grebe sits on its floating nest. Most grebes build nests of water-plant stems and leaves, piled up so that they float.

Herons, ducks and geese

At more than 3 m, the marabou stork of Africa has the largest wingspan of any land bird.

THE FRESH WATERS OF LAKES, RIVERS AND MARSHES ARE HOME TO A WEALTH OF BIRDS. There are long-legged waders like herons, storks and flamingoes, smaller cranes and rails, and hundreds of species of waterfowl – ducks, geese and swans. Many are excellent swimmers and can cope with fast-flowing rivers, but they prefer the calmer waters of lakes and swamps, where there is no energy-sapping current. Some species nest on the water among reeds, but most nest on the shore and feed in the water. The taller waders are mostly predators, using their long, sharp beaks to spear fish, frogs, shellfish and other water creatures. Waterfowl are mainly vegetarians, feeding on grass, waterweeds and other plants, although some ducks take insects and shellfish.

The mute swan weighs 18 kg. It needs a long stretch of water for take-off and landing.

Flamingoes live and nest in huge colonies in the tropics. To feed, a flamingo bends its neck and tips its head over, to hold its strange, kinked beak upside-down and sweep it from side to side. Inside the beak, the tongue works like a piston to suck water in and squirt it out. Hair-like fringes on the beak filter out small shrimps and similar food.

Most wading birds have long, featherless legs for striding through the water, a long neck to reach down and feed, and a long beak to grab or stab prey. The biggest group of large freshwater waders includes herons, egrets and bitterns, with 60 species throughout temperate and tropical regions. Most are grey or brown. When hunting fish and frogs, a heron stands motionless on one leg in the shallows, apparently asleep, until it suddenly spears down into the water with its long beak. The prey is caught and then flipped around so the bird can swallow it head-first.

Herons fly slowly with extravagant, steady wingbeats. They keep their long necks tucked into their shoulders – unlike cranes, storks and ibises, which fly, with the head and neck extended. Herons usually nest in colonies called heronries, building their untidy pile-of-sticks nests high in trees.

SOARING STORKS

Storks are even bigger than herons, some standing 1.2 m tall. They fly through the air with slow, strong wingbeats, neck stretched out in front and legs trailing behind. On their long annual journeys, or migrations, they find an up-current of warm air to gain height, then flap on their way.

BOOM BOOM!

The male bittern has one of the loudest bird calls. It is an extraordinary boom, made to warn others off its territory. The bittern makes this deep booming in its throat, and it can sound almost like a bull roaring as it echoes across the marsh at night. The bittern's scientific name is Botaurus, which comes from an ancient Latin term meaning "bellow of the bull".

In Europe and Asia, white storks often build their great twig nests on the roofs of houses. Many people see the return of the same pair year after year from Africa, to build their nest in the same place, as a sign of continuing good luck. Storks raise their young with great care.

The heron is a patient hunter, standing still and silent on one leg for hours. Then it makes a lightning dart with its long beak, to spear a fish which mistook the heron's single leg for a reed stem.

SPOON-FED

Spoonbills are medium-sized waders named after their flattened, spoon-shaped beaks. The spoonbill swishes its beak from side to side through the water, to catch prey such as fish and small crabs.

Spoonbills are close relatives of ibises. An ibis has a long, thin, down-curved beak. Like spoonbills, ibises have webbed toes to help them swim and walk on soft mud. Both ibises and spoonbills feed in muddy water, detecting prey with their sensitive beaks. The brilliant pink plumage of the scarlet ibis makes it one of the most striking of all tropical birds.

Scarlet ibis

WATERFOWL

The body of a duck or goose is so buoyant, it can float for hours, paddling with its big webbed feet. But on land, waterfowl – especially ducks – waddle awkwardly. The pochard and tufted duck are diving ducks, descending to the bottom to find roots, shoots, shellfish and insects. Dabbling ducks such as the mallard lap at the water's surface, or up-end to sift waterweeds and snails from the muddy bed.

Swans are the largest waterfowl. A swan uses its long, elegant neck to reach down and grab plant bits and small creatures. Most swans have pure white plumage, apart from the black swan of Australia and the black-neck swan of South America. Geese are slightly smaller, and come onto land to graze on grass. Geese and ducks are powerful long-distance flyers. Bar-headed geese have been seen from planes at altitudes of 9,000 m crossing the Himalayas. Many geese breed in the Arctic and migrate south in the autumn to warmer places.

The roseate spoonbill is one of the most colourful of waders. It dwells in the warmer areas of the Americas.

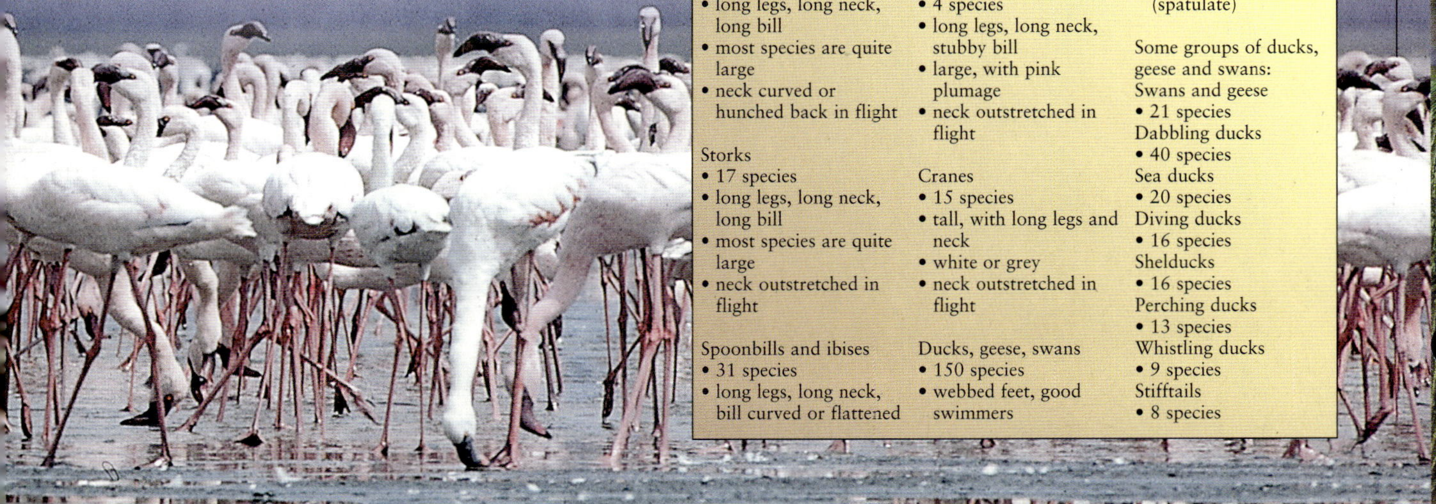

HERONS, EGRETS AND BITTERNS
- 60 species
- long legs, long neck, long bill
- most species are quite large
- neck curved or hunched back in flight

Storks
- 17 species
- long legs, long neck, long bill
- most species are quite large
- neck outstretched in flight

Spoonbills and ibises
- 31 species
- long legs, long neck, bill curved or flattened
- neck outstretched in flight

Flamingoes
- 4 species
- long legs, long neck, stubby bill
- large, with pink plumage
- neck outstretched in flight

Cranes
- 15 species
- tall, with long legs and neck
- white or grey
- neck outstretched in flight

Ducks, geese, swans
- 150 species
- webbed feet, good swimmers
- most species are long-necked
- bill usually flattened, quite short and wide (spatulate)

Some groups of ducks, geese and swans:

Swans and geese
- 21 species

Dabbling ducks
- 40 species

Sea ducks
- 20 species

Diving ducks
- 16 species

Shelducks
- 16 species

Perching ducks
- 13 species

Whistling ducks
- 9 species

Stifftails
- 8 species

BIRDS OF PREY

Despite wildlife protection laws, golden eagles are still shot and poisoned by farmers and gamekeepers.

A SHARP, HOOKED BEAK AND CURVED CLAWS CALLED TALONS MARK OUT THE RAPTORS – BIRDS OF PREY – AS THE DEADLY HUNTERS OF THE BIRD WORLD. Most are masterful flyers, able to stay aloft for hours while searching for prey with their incredibly keen eyes. Then they dive like a bullet onto the chosen victim. Smaller raptors like the sharp-shinned hawk are no bigger than a robin. They eat mainly insects, frogs and similar small creatures. Hawks and eagles take rats and rabbits, snakes and lizards, and other birds. The huge harpy eagle of the Amazon jungle snatches monkeys and sloths from the treetops. The osprey and fish eagles grab fish. Vultures and condors feed mostly on carrion (dead animals).

The hobby is one of the most brightly coloured of hawks. It is so speedy and agile that it can catch dragonflies, swallows and swifts.

There are some 295 species of raptors. They hunt across a huge range of habitats, from mountains to rainforests. The condors are among the largest flying birds, with wingspans of 3 m. Falcons such as the peregrine are the greatest winged acrobats, able to catch other birds in mid-flight with amazing agility.

All kinds of large predators, such as sharks and tigers, are scarce because of the balance of nature. This also applies to large birds of prey, especially eagles. Sadly, people try to kill them in case they attack farm animals or gamebirds. And they are shot as trophies, or their eggs are stolen for collectors.

The gyrfalcon is a powerful flyer. It plunges, or stoops, from above at tremendous speed, to grip its victim in its sharp-taloned feet. Hawks do this too, but they kill their prey with their claws, whereas a falcon's fatal blow is a sharp bite to the neck.

DIVE!

The peregrine falcon is the fastest-moving of all animals. It can streak down onto prey, or charge at an intruder in its territory, in a powered dive called a stoop. Some stoops have been timed at more than 350 km/h.

A buzzard glides on a warm air current, waiting to spot its prey.

Many large raptors survive today only in remote, often mountainous terrain. However others, like certain kestrels and kites, have adapted to living near people. They wheel over high-rise city buildings and motorways, just as they would soar along cliffs or shores.

SYMBOL OF POWER

Eagles, with their graceful soaring that can turn into a deadly swoop, have long been symbols of power. The bald eagle is the national bird of the USA. The golden eagle was the figurehead of the armies of Ancient Rome. The golden eagle is often called the "king of birds". It hunts rabbits, marmots, ground squirrels and birds. Its nest, or "eyrie", is a bed of twigs perched high on a cliff, to which pairs return year after year.

The osprey has rough-skinned toes which help the sharp, curved claws to grip slippery fish.

The American bald eagle has been the victim of hunting, water pollution and loss of natural habitat. By the mid-1970s there were just 2,000 left in the USA. Conservation laws were introduced and now there are more than 20,000.

SMALLER RAPTORS

Hawks, sparrowhawks, goshawks, falcons, kestrels and hobbies are smaller than eagles. They often take other birds as well as ground-living animals.

There are two main kinds of hawks: accipiters and buteos. Accipiters, such as the goshawk, tend to wait on a branch and then dash out to ambush smaller birds under the cover of the foliage. They have short, rounded wings and a long, narrow tail, for great manoeuvrability. Buteos, such as the kestrel, have longer wings and fan-shaped tails.

They soar high and scan the scene below, ready to swoop. The kestrel is often known as the windhover, because it hovers in mid-air, wings and tail moving but head held still, focusing on the ground. When it sees a victim, it drops suddenly and pounces on its prey.

The bald eagle is not bald, but its white head looks featherless from a distance. It is a fish-eater, like the osprey.

WINGED SCAVENGERS

The biggest birds of prey are not predators, but carrion feeders. Vultures and condors have weak bills and the flesh they eat must be soft and rotten before they can rip off mouthfuls. The bearded vulture or lammergeier takes bones from the carcass and flies high to drop them onto rocks. The bones smash to reveal the soft, juicy marrow inside. All of the vultures have vast wings and spend hours soaring high, peering across the landscape for corpses. Condors have such keen smell that they can even locate dead meat under a canopy of trees by scent alone.

Condors are among the biggest flying birds. The wingspan of the Andean condor of South America can exceed 3 m. Sadly, as a result of human persecution, the Californian condor is now one of the world's rarest birds. It also tends to crash into power cables. Conservationists in the 1980s captured the few remaining wild birds in a desperate bid to breed them in captivity. Some of the young have been released into the wild, but this species remains on the very edge of extinction.

The rare Everglades kite feeds only on one type of water snail, the apple snail.

MAIN BIRDS OF PREY:

Eagles, hawks, buzzards and vultures
- 224 species
- worldwide
- medium to large
- sharp hooked beak
- sharp curved talons

American vultures
- 7 species
- large
- naked head and neck
- soaring flight

Osprey *(fish eagle)*
- 1 species
- worldwide
- hunts fish
- brown and white

Falcons, falconets and caracaras
- 62 species
- worldwide
- small to medium
- long tail

Secretary bird
- 1 species
- African grassland
- long legs and feathered head crest
- eats reptiles

GAMEBIRDS AND RAILS

A peacock is a male peafowl. He is the most spectacular pheasant, with a metallic turquoise neck, shimmering indigo breast feathers and a long train of brilliant green tail feathers. A courting peacock throws up his tail feathers into a gigantic fan, revealing dozens of beautiful eye-like spots.

MANY LARGE BIRDS THAT LIVE MAINLY ON THE GROUND HAVE SUCH TASTY FLESH THAT THEY HAVE LONG BEEN HUNTED FOR MEAT, AND SO ARE CALLED GAMEBIRDS. They include pheasants, grouse, partridges, capercaillies, quails, wild turkeys, guinea fowl, curassows and the guans of South America. Most of the females have dull, mottled brown plumage that blends in well with their woodland, scrub or moor home. Their chicks also have this camouflage plumage. Yet some of the males, especially pheasants and their relatives the tragopans, have extremely striking coloration. Their huge and brilliantly patterned feathers shimmer in all the hues of the rainbow.

The gamebird group Galliformes includes more than 240 species. The world's most numerous bird, the domestic chicken, is among them. Gamebirds are mostly quite large, stout-bodied, heavily built birds that spend their time on the ground, pecking for seeds, buds, shoots and fruits. They can fly, but prefer to run, and only take to the air in emergencies.

The word "grouse" covers a wide range of birds, including quails and partridges. Also, grouse are often called partridges! The spruce grouse (above) of conifer forests is also known as the swamp partridge and spruce partridge.

PHEASANTS

Many of the 165 species of pheasants lived originally in China and central Asia. But they have been taken to many other parts of the world, mainly to be hunted. They range in size from the sparrow-sized painted quail to the turkey-sized argus pheasant. The smaller species, including quails and some partridges, are usually drab browns and greys. So too are the females or hens of the larger species, to escape the notice of predators while sitting on their eggs. But in the breeding season the larger male or cock pheasants are extremely noticeable, with flowing tails and beautiful blue, red and gold feathers.
The peacock's amazing "eyed" tail is well known. The Himalayan monal pheasant also has brilliant iridescent plumage in shiny shades of blue, green, purple and orange. The male argus pheasant has long wing feathers with eye spots.

Cock common pheasant

WHY ARE THESE BIRDS SO COLOURFUL?

To attract a mate. The cocks strut and fluff out their plumage to show how fit and fine they are, using cackles, whistles and screams to increase the effect. The Reeves cock pheasant shakes its feathers and jumps up high in the air, again and again, to make sure the females notice.

A male monal pheasant displays his breeding plumage.

Rival cocks may threaten or even battle with each other to gain a mate.

The habitat of the ptarmigan (pronounced "tar-mig-un") is the cold mountains and treeless tundra of the north. This bird changes with the seasons. In summer (far left) it has dull brown feathers, like most other grouse. In winter (near left) its plumage turns mostly white, to blend in with the snow and ice. Its diet changes too, from buds and insects in summer to seeds and shoots in winter.

World Watch

Several types of flightless rails are at risk from dogs, rats and other animals brought to their region by people (page 162). The takahe of New Zealand is a flightless rail that looks more like a parrot. It was thought to be extinct until its rediscovery in 1948. Only a few hundred takahes survive in the Murchison Mountains of New Zealand's South Island. Introduced deer compete for their food.

BATTLE AT THE LEK

Grouse, partridges and ptarmigan are hunted by many birds of prey and by mammals such as foxes and cats. So they are usually well camouflaged, to blend in with the undergrowth. They may be dull in colour, but grouse mating displays are just as dramatic as those of pheasants. Male capercaillies, the largest of the grouse, gather at a traditional breeding place called a lek. They strut aggressively to and fro and make extraordinary hissing, popping and gurgling sounds, while the females watch from nearby. Each male tries to gain a site near the centre of the lek area, which will guarantee a mate.

Bustards are strong, turkey-sized birds of open habitats. Most species live in Africa, with a few in Asia and one in Australia. They are heavily built and stride along on their powerful legs, reluctant to fly. When they do take to the air, it is a struggle since they are the heaviest of all flying birds. A bustard's varied diet includes seeds, fruits, insects and other small animals. Like most gamebirds, the female nests on the ground or on a low branch, usually in dense undergrowth.

Sandgrouse are pigeon-like birds of dry, desert habitats. The males fly tens of kilometres to a water hole, soak their breast feathers, and then fly back to the nest so the chicks can sip the water.

SKULKING RAILS

Rails are related to cranes. They are found mainly in wetland habitats. All rails swim well, and walk in a slow, deliberate fashion. They are shy birds and skulk in the undergrowth, camouflaged by their drab plumage. The rail group includes moorhens, coots and the endangered flightless takahe of New Zealand.

The great bustard (left) and the kori bustard are the world's heaviest flying birds, weighing about 20 kg.

GAMEBIRDS
- about 250 species
- mainly ground-living
- includes pheasants and grouse
- males often have elaborate plumage at breeding time

Rails
- 124 species
- mostly small, drab grey or brown
- a few are brightly coloured
- make calls that sound like engines or machines
- some are flightless
- rivers, lakes and marshes

Bustards
- 21 species
- large, heavy
- open plains and grassland

Sandgrouse
- 16 species
- resemble pigeons
- deserts and other dry habitats

PIGEONS, DOVES AND PARROTS

Crowned pigeon

Parrots have strong hooked beaks to crack open nuts and scoop out soft fruits.

CITY PIGEONS MAY NOT BE THE MOST APPEALING BIRDS, DRAB AND GREY, LEAVING A MESS AS THEY FLOCK AROUND LITTER. Parrots, on the other hand, are among the most attractive of birds, with their vivid colours of scarlet, emerald and turquoise, their beady eyes, and their ability to mimic our voices and "talk". But pigeons and parrots have several features in common. Both eat mainly seed and fruits. Both are bold and curious, but also placid and easy-going. And both have long associations with people. Parrots and doves live near or even in our villages, towns and cities. Many kinds, including the small members of the parrot group called parakeets, are kept as cage birds and pets. Pigeons and doves are entered for shows and competitions such as racing, and they are even used for carrying messages because of their amazing homing instincts.

The budgerigar is a small species of parrot from Australia. It is mainly green for camouflage. Flocks of budgies swoop and chatter around waterholes at dusk.

Besides familiar town pigeons, there are nearly 300 other pigeon species around the world, ranging from the large and spectacular crowned pigeons of New Guinea to tiny ground doves. In general, the larger and plumper types are called pigeons and the smaller, slimmer species are known as doves. All are mainly seed-eaters, and most build untidy stick nests in trees. Pigeons are also among the strongest-flying birds, and many migrate long distances. Most pigeons and doves have soothing, rather sad-sounding, cooing songs. These can often be heard in woods, parks and gardens, especially in early morning and evening.

The pigeons in our cities are not truly wild, but part-wild or feral. This means they are descended from domestic pigeons, which were kept widely in the past, both to carry messages and to eat! Those domestic pigeons, in turn, were descended from wild rock doves, whose natural habitats are sea cliffs and rocky crags.

◄ Lorikeets like the Australian varied lorikeet, have long beaks to reach nectar in flowers.

Pigeons and doves are the only birds that feed their young on "milk", like mammals. The parent produces a milky substance from the lining of its throat, to feed to the chicks.

PARROTS

Parrots are tropical birds with strong hooked beaks and bright plumage. They also have clinging feet, with two toes pointing forwards and two backwards. This design allows a parrot to clamber in trees, using its beak as a "third foot". The real foot can also hold fruits and nuts, to eat.

There are more than 300 species in the parrot group, including macaws, lories, lorikeets, cockatoos, lovebirds and parakeets. Many are inquisitive and investigate objects with great care, holding and pecking them to see if they are good to eat. Many of the larger species are also long-lived, surviving for 30, 40 or more years in captivity. These are further reasons why they are so popular as cage birds and even as pet "companions". Sadly, this popularity means thousands of parrots are illegally captured from the wild each year. And perhaps half suffer and die before they reach the pet shops. Several kinds of parrot are now endangered in the wild as a result of this cruel and unlawful trade.

BRUSH-TIPPED TONGUES

Lories and lorikeets are colourful parrots from Southeast Asia and Australia. Unlike most other parrots they feed not on seeds and fruits, but on pollen and nectar from flowers. They have brush-like tips on their tongues to lick up these foods.

CRESTED COCKATOOS

The cockatoos have feathered crests on their heads, which they fan out when excited, such as when a predator or rival approaches. Some species are white or pinkish. Largest is the palm cockatoo of New Guinea and northeast Australia.

▲ The crested cockatoo only erects its crest when aroused in some way.

THE REAL MACAW

Macaws are big, long-tailed parrots that live in the forests of Central and South America. They rest and nest in tree trunk holes. They are colourful even by parrot standards, in shades of brilliant blue, red, yellow and green.

Most parrots have few natural enemies, apart from hawks and eagles, and monkeys who may steal eggs and chicks. But continuing threats from the pet trade mean many are still endangered.

Parrots, cockatoos and lories
- 330 species
- strong hooked beak
- two toes face forwards, two backwards
- bright greens or reds
- mainly tropical or southern hemisphere

Pigeons and doves
- 300 species
- dumpy bodies
- tree-dwelling
- mournful calls

◄ The gold-and-blue macaw has a beak so strong that it can easily crack open Brazil nuts.

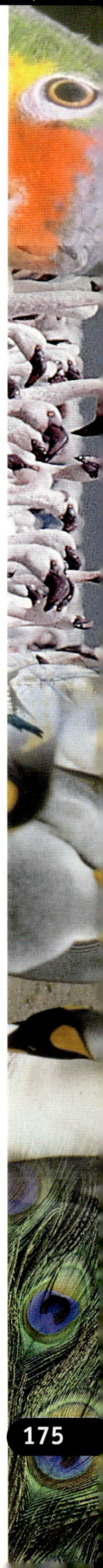

CUCKOOS AND TURACOS

Coucals are among the many colourful cuckoos living in the forests of the tropics. Unlike European and American cuckoos, they stay mostly on the ground.

IN EUROPE, A SOFT "CUCK-OO" CALL HERALDS SPRING, AS THESE BIRDS ARRIVE FROM SOUTHERN AFRICA OR ASIA TO BREED. The cuckoo is also known from its habit of laying eggs in the nests of smaller birds. The large cuckoo egg develops rapidly for its size, so that it hatches at the same time as the smaller eggs of the unknowing foster parents. The baby cuckoo is looked after by its foster parents – even though it grows far bigger than them. There are about 130 kinds of cuckoos, roadrunners and coucals all over the world. Many of the tropical species are large and colourful. The heavy-bodied turacos or plantain-eaters from the tropical forests of Africa are also colourful. They include the go-away bird, named for its persistent "g'way! g'way!" call.

Many birds have feathers in shades of green. But turacos are the only birds that actually make a green pigment, or colouring substance, in their feathers. In other birds, the green colour is due to tiny ridges on the feathers. These split up the white light of sunlight into the rainbow colours of the spectrum, and reflect only the green rays.

BASH!

The roadrunner kills its prey in a very simple way. When it catches a snake or lizard, it simply bashes the reptile to death by pecking, pounding and banging it with its beak. Then the roadrunner swallows its meal head-first.

About one third of all cuckoo species, including the common or European cuckoo, are brood parasites. Instead of hatching their own eggs, the male and female mate, and then the female lays her eggs in the nest of another bird species, such as a reed warbler, meadow pipit, dunnock or redstart. She chooses the foster parents carefully. Usually, they are the same species as the foster parents she had when she was a chick. She must also choose her moment with great care, otherwise the foster parents might abandon the nest and all the eggs. She must put her own egg into the nest as soon as the foster mother has laid her own eggs, in the brief interval that she is away feeding, but before she has started to incubate (sit on) her eggs.

The roadrunner of southwestern North America can fly, but prefers to run. It can do so at more than 30 km/h, outpacing most predators. Its diet includes insects, snakes and fruit.

A female cuckoo may lay more than 20 eggs, each in a different nest. When the cuckoo chick hatches, it tips out the other eggs or chicks. The foster parents feed it as if it were their own, desperately trying to keep up with the appetite of their giant baby. After six weeks the young cuckoo can fly and leaves its tiny, tired foster parents.

Some Eurasian or Old World cuckoos, like the common cuckoo, get other birds to rear their young. Most American or New World cuckoos, such as the black-billed and yellow-billed cuckoos, do not.

RUNNING THE ROADS

The roadrunner of desert scrub in Mexico and the southwestern USA is a type of ground cuckoo. It is about 60 cm long, but most of this is tail. It gets its name from its habit of racing along roads in front of cars, then quickly darting off into the bushes on the roadside. Roadrunners do not deliberately dice with death by dodging vehicles. They simply choose the road as an easy place to walk, and also as a source of injured animals which might be good to eat.

TROPICAL CUCKOOS

Coucals are mostly large, ground-dwelling members of the cuckoo group that live in the tropics. The pheasant coucal of New Guinea and Australia stalks through dense undergrowth for small insects and other prey. The buff-headed coucal of the Solomon Islands is one of the largest cuckoos, with a beak-to-tail length of 70 cm. It eats a wide variety of prey, including lizards, snakes and frogs.

The hoatzin of the Amazon region is one of the world's oddest birds. The chick clambers about in trees using its legs, beak and two claws, one halfway along the front of each wing. The adult hoatzin loses the claws, but is the most vegetarian of all birds, browsing only on certain types of leaves, such as arum and mangrove. This unique bird may be related to the cuckoo group.

FEEDING ON FRUITS

The turacos of Africa are forest birds with colourful, silky plumage. Many have bright flashes of yellow, red, green and blue on their wings and bodies. Some have bare areas of brilliantly coloured skin around the eyes or on the face. A few turacos eat a mixed diet of plants and small animals, but most are specialist fruit-eaters, feeding their chicks mainly on fruit pulp. The drabbest member of the group is the go-away-bird, which is grey all over apart from dark wingtip feathers.

Turacos such as the red-crested turaco are weak flyers. They prefer to climb and run along tree branches, almost like squirrels, hunting for fruit and insects.

Cuckoos and coucals
- 130 species
- most continents
- slim body, long tail
- most are grey or brown
- about one third of species are brood parasites
- mixed diet

Turacos
- 22 species
- Central and southern Africa
- mostly brightly coloured
- fruit-eaters

Hoatzin
- 1 species
- Amazon region of South America
- chicken-like with head crest
- leaf-eater

OWLS AND NIGHTJARS

MOST HUNTING BIRDS FLY BY DAY, BUT OWLS, NIGHTJARS AND FROGMOUTHS HUNT AT NIGHT. They rely on their amazing twilight vision and even more astonishing hearing to locate their prey in the dark. Owls have enormous eyes that take up over half of the skull. They can see in almost pitch darkness. Also their ears are four times more sensitive than a cat's ears. On a quiet night an owl can hear a mouse move 45 m away. It can also pinpoint the direction of sounds with incredible accuracy. Nightjars, too, have large eyes that see especially well at twilight. They feed mainly on moths and other night-flying insects. Frogmouths are also dusk-flying birds, but they tend to swoop from a perch onto prey on the ground.

The potc (left) is relative of th nightjar. Its nan comes from i ooo-ing call. Th frogmouth (belo hunts on the fore floor for beetles, snai and other small anima It has even been known take whole mice and sma birds into its gapir mouth, which surrounded l sensiti bristles feelir food the dar

Owls live in most parts of the world, from the tropics almost to the Arctic regions. There are some 135 species. They vary in size, but all are similar in appearance with a big, broad head, no obvious neck and a saucer-shaped ruff of feathers, called the facial disc, around the huge eyes. Both eyes face directly forward, unlike those of most birds, which look partly to the side.

THE WISE OLD OWL

The owl's intense forward stare has made it a symbol of wisdom since ancient times (although owls are no more intelligent than other birds). In fact the eyes fit so tightly in the skull bone that they cannot swivel in their sockets. To look to the side, an owl twists its neck and turns its whole head. It can do this to look directly behind!

The tiny elf owl from the southern USA and Mexico is one of the smallest owls. It measures only about 12 cm from beak tip to tail tip. Largest is the European eagle owl, which can be 70 cm long, with a wingspan of 1.5 m.

Most owls are mottled grey or brown. But the male snowy owl is almost pure white, the perfect disguise in its snowy Arctic habitat.

The nightjar's song is a mechanical "churring" that resembles the sound of a distant motorcycle.

The great horned owl does not have horns. Its ear-like tufts are simply extra-long feathers. It is one of North America's largest owls, standing almost 60 cm tall.

The short-eared owl is one of several owls that hunt by day as well as by night.

The oilbird of South America is a relative of the nightjars. It is unusual among the owl-like birds, in many ways. It spends all day deep in its breeding cave, then comes out at night to feed – not on insects, but on oily fruits. Oilbirds find their way in the total darkness of their cave in the way that bats do, by making loud clicking sounds and analyzing the echoes.

Owls are wonderfully adapted for night hunting. They have sharp sight and keen hearing, and their wing feathers have soft, almost furry, edges. This muffles the sound of the wings' beating and swooping, so the owl's prey is not disturbed. Smaller owls eat mostly insects. Medium-sized owls, like the barn owl and boobook (morepork), eat mice, rats, lizards and similar creatures. The biggest owls catch rabbits and squirrels. Eagle owls prey on other birds, including owls and hawks, and even carry away young deer. The fishing owls of Africa and Asia swoop on fish, frogs and crayfish, dipping just under the surface to grab prey with their sharp claws.

BIG-MOUTHED BIRDS

Nightjars glide gracefully after flying insects, which they snap up in their wide, gaping mouth. Like bats and the oilbird, they may use a type of sonar or echo-location to find their way and avoid obstacles in the dark. After the hunt, nightjars roost by day – but not hidden away in holes, caves or buildings, like owls. The nightjar rests in the open. It nestles against a tree branch or among leaves on the forest floor. This may sound risky, but its mottled plumage is such perfect camouflage that the bird is almost impossible to spot.

Frogmouths are named after their wide, gaping mouths. They are not very agile in flight. Instead, they catch their prey by dropping onto the ground from a twig or rock. Like nightjars, frogmouths rest by day in the open, relying on their camouflaged plumage for protection.

The little owl has the dished face typical of all owls. The dish shape acts as a sound trap to funnel the faintest noises towards the owl's super-sensitive ears, under the feathers on the sides of its head.

Owls
- 135 species
- most are nocturnal
- soft feathers
- large, flat face
- huge eyes
- hooked beak
- sharp claws
- camouflaged plumage

Nightjars and frogmouths
- 100 species
- nocturnal
- sleek and graceful
- large eyes
- gaping mouth
- camouflaged plumage

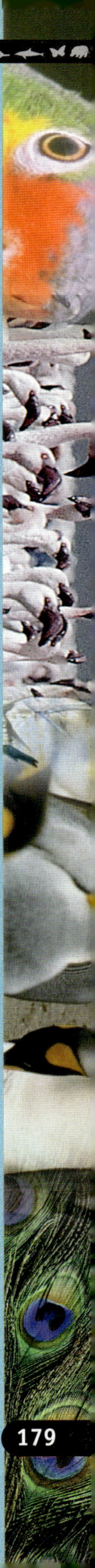

SWIFTS AND WOODPECKERS

Hummingbirds like this violet crowned hummingbird beat their wings up to 80 times every second. This produces the bee-like humming sound of their name.

A WALK THROUGH A TROPICAL RAINFOREST REVEALS A HOST OF SMALL BIRDS, CHATTERING IN THE TREETOPS AND DARTING BETWEEN THE BRANCHES. They include hummingbirds, jacamars, toucans, barbets, bee-eaters and many more. Most have such startlingly brilliant colours that they seem to have little in common with the drabber birds of temperate woodlands. Yet many of them are closely related. Hummingbirds belong to the same group of birds as swifts. Toucans and jacamars are cousins to the woodpecker. Kookaburras and hornbills are related to the kingfishers, bee-eaters, rollers and hoopoes. Most of these birds have large beaks compared to their body size.

Few birds have a beak that is as distinctive as the toco toucan's. The beak is as big as the bird itself, and strong and stiff. But it is made of a very light, spongy, horny substance, so the toucan has no problem flying, balancing or moving its beak to peck at fruits.

Woodpeckers like the downy woodpecker hammer at trees to find wood-boring grubs and also to make nest holes.

The kingfisher sits on its perch above a stream, watching for food. When it sees a fish or frog, it dives like a flash into the water, swims below with its wings and bobs up with its catch. Back on its perch, it swallows the meal whole.

The white-fronted bee-eater is a tropical bird related to hornbills and kingfishers. It catches bees and wasps in mid-air, and bashes them on a branch to kill them and so reduce the risk of being stung.

The alpine swift wheels over mountains, uplands and cliffs across southern Europe, Africa, the Middle East and Asia. It flies even faster than the common swift.

Most birds spend some time in the air. But swifts are so well adapted for flight that they rarely settle on a perch. They are on the wing nearly all the time, swooping, hovering, soaring, diving, courting and resting, and, of course, feeding. As a result, their legs and feet have become quite weak. Swifts and hummingbirds belong to the same bird group, the Apodiformes, which means "footless ones". They are not actually footless, but the legs and feet are certainly tiny.

The kookaburra of Australia is a type of kingfisher, yet it is quite at home in dry scrub far from water. It eats mainly insects and reptiles. Its cackling call has earned it the nickname of the laughing jackass.

SWIFT BY NAME AND NATURE

Swifts really live up to their name. They are among the fastest flying birds. The spine-tailed swifts of eastern Asia have been timed at over 200 km/h in level flight. Swifts catch insects on the wing, swooping through swarms of gnats with their gaping mouths wide open. They often fly through the night without landing. When they do touch down, they cling clumsily to upright surfaces such as cave walls, tree trunks and brickwork.

The male crested tree swift has a red-brown eye patch; the female's eye patch is green.

SIPPING NECTAR

Hummingbirds are the helicopters of the bird world. They are brightly coloured and sip nectar as they hover close to flowers. They are incredibly agile, flap their wings faster than we can see, and hover in mid-air, fly sideways, go straight up or down, or even fly backwards. The long, thin, curved beak probes deep into flowers for the sugary nectar that fuels their high-energy life. There are more than 300 species of hummingbirds, mostly in tropical America. In the 19th century, millions were killed and made into feathered jewellery such as brooches. Luckily the fashion died out before the birds did.

UNUSUAL FEET

Woodpeckers, toucans, barbets, jacamars and honeyguides all have the same type of feet. Each foot has two toes pointing forwards and two backwards (rather than three forwards and one backwards as in most other birds). A woodpecker uses its feet to cling to the tree while hammering at the wood with its large, powerful beak, to search for insects below the bark. The toucans of tropical South and Central America have massive, brightly coloured bills, which they use to feed on berries, fruit and soft-bodied insects.

The hornbill is mainly black and white. It uses its enormous beak for picking fruits.

SMALLEST... !

The world's smallest bird is the bee hummingbird of Cuba. Its body is hardly larger than a bumblebee's, with a total length of 5 cm—including its beak and tail!

The honeyguide of Africa eats mainly beeswax—but it cannot obtain the wax for itself. Instead, it perches near a wild bees' nest, and calls out. The sound draws honey-eating mammals, such as the honey badger, which break open the nest to get at the honey. The honeyguide then feasts on the wax.

Woodpeckers	• 200 species	Rollers	• 16 species
Hornbills	• 45 species	Barbets	• 78 species
Toucans	• 38 species	Honeyguides	• 15 species
Kingfishers	• 86 species	Swifts	• 74 species
Bee-eaters	• 24 species	Hummingbirds	• 315 species

CROWS, SHRIKES AND BOWERBIRDS

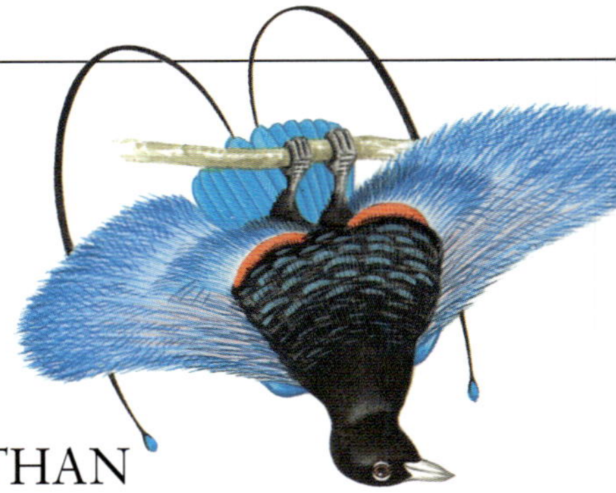

A male blue bird of paradise shows off his plumage.

MORE THAN TWO THIRDS OF BIRDS – MORE THAN 5,000 DIFFERENT SPECIES – BELONG TO THE GROUP KNOWN AS PERCHING BIRDS OR PASSERINES. Of course, many kinds of bird perch. But passerines have a special design, a four-toed foot, with three toes pointing forwards and one facing backwards. This allows them to cling securely to a twig, branch or other perch, but not to swim easily or run fast on the ground. So passerines tend to live in or near trees and bushes, where they can hop among the branches and find places to build nests. Most passerines are small. Crows, shrikes, bowerbirds and the lyrebird are among the biggest species.

White-cheeked bulbul

LARGEST... !

Ravens are the largest perching birds. These powerful members of the crow family can reach 65 cm beak-to-tail length. They can kill prey as large as a rabbit, but they usually scavenge on dead animals.

There are more than 100 species in the crow group, including rooks, jackdaws, jays, magpies and the largest type, ravens. Most are noisy, bold, aggressive birds, which bully other bird species and are not especially afraid of other animals or even people. Jays screech and squawk all year except during the breeding season, when they go quiet so as not to give away their nests. Most crows collect and hoard bits of food and other items. European jays even "steal" shiny objects such as bottletops and rings. Most crows have black or drab plumage, except for jays such as the blue jay, and also some magpies, which are quite colourful.

A black cuckoo shrike feeds its chicks.

A male lyrebird courts the female from the top of an earthen mound about 90 cm across, which he builds himself.

THE BUTCHER BIRDS

Shrikes are like birds of prey, but smaller. They lack sharp talons, but they do have a fierce-looking hooked beak, used to catch large insects, mice, lizards and frogs. A shrike usually sits in a bush or similar lookout, watching for prey. It may store surplus food by impaling the carcasses on long thorns, to eat later. This gruesome "larder" has earned the shrike the name of butcher bird.

The male satin bowerbird waits in his decorated bower.

MIMICS!

Many perching birds mimic sounds, including the songs of birds, human voices, engines and machines. Members of the starling family, which includes mynahs, are some of the most skilled. They learn animal noises, whistles and even words, but of course they do not understand what they say. The superb lyrebird of southeast Australia copies the calls of local birds, and even imitates car sirens, telephones and chainsaws.

STARLINGS

Starlings are active, noisy birds that often gather together in huge flocks to feed or roost. In winter a starling roost may number thousands of birds. As dusk falls they gather somewhere such as a clump of evergreen trees or the ledges of a building. Mynahs, bulbuls and mockingbirds, which live in the Americas, are related to starlings. Mockingbirds mimic human laughter, hence their name. Their songs are loud, clear and musical.

COME INTO MY BOWER

Bowerbirds take courtship to an amazing extreme. These medium-sized birds from the forests of New Guinea and Australia build elaborate bowers. These are places where the male bird displays to his mate. Each male decorates his bower with flowers, shells, pebbles, berries, leaves and moss. He may even use natural coloured plant juices to "paint" some of the bower's decorations.

▲ Blue jays frequent parks and gardens in eastern North America.

PARADISE

Perhaps the most spectacular of the larger passerines are the birds of paradise. They inhabit tropical forests, mainly in Southeast Asia. The males are adorned with amazing coloured plumes and perform elaborate dances to attract females during the breeding season. The male lyrebird of southeast Australia also sings and displays to attract a female. He fans out and tips forward his lyre-shaped tail streamers, while producing a rich, melodious song that includes sounds like car engines and burglar alarms!

◄ The hill mynah, from India, is sometimes kept as a cage bird for its skill in imitating noises, especially the human voice.

▼ The male Baltimore oriole sings his courtship song for a female.

► The male spotted bowerbird builds an elaborate courting area, or bower, of twigs and grass decorated with fruits, seeds and pebbles. The bower helps to attract a female.

SOME PERCHING BIRD GROUPS:

Bulbuls
• 118 species
Crows
• 116 species
Starlings and mynahs
• 106 species
Birds of paradise
• 43 species
Shrikes
• 70 species
Mockingbirds
• 30 species
Orioles
• 28 species
Bowerbirds
• 18 species
Lyrebirds
• 2 species

SPARROWS, FINCHES AND WEAVERS

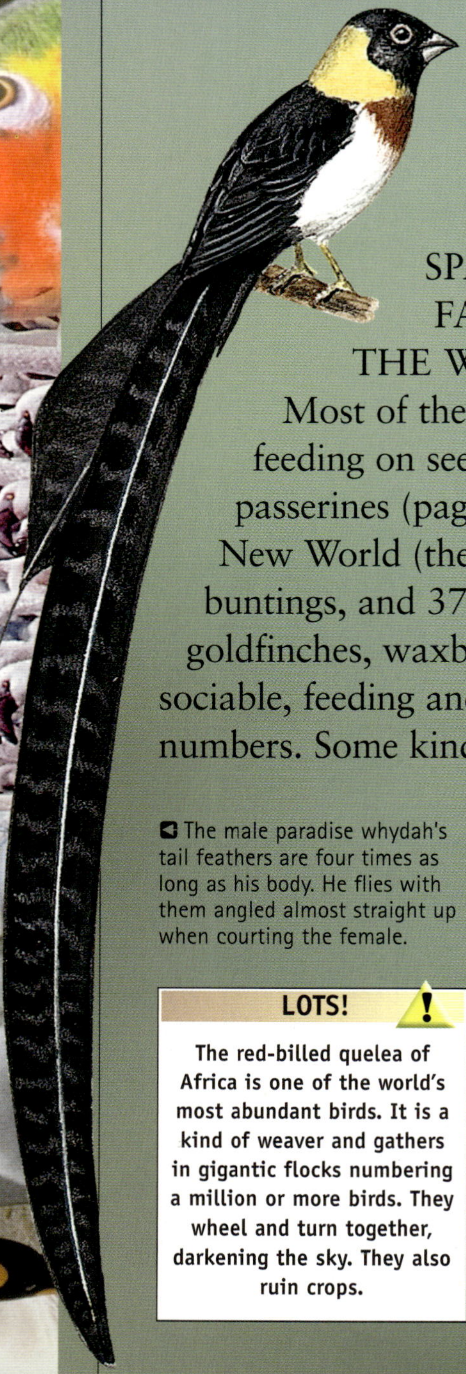

SPARROWS, FINCHES AND WEAVER BIRDS ARE FAMILIAR IN GARDENS AND COUNTRYSIDE AROUND THE WORLD. Many species migrate from Europe to Africa in winter. Most of these birds have short, strong, stubby, pointed beaks designed for feeding on seeds. They are sometimes called seed-eating passerines (page 182). There are some 315 species in the New World (the Americas), including cardinals and buntings, and 375 in the Old World, including goldfinches, waxbills and weavers. They tend to be sociable, feeding and roosting in flocks so as to gain safety in numbers. Some kinds, especially weavers, even breed in groups or colonies. Weaver birds get their name from their nests, woven like baskets from plant stems, twigs, grass and strips of leaves.

Male village weaver

The male paradise whydah's tail feathers are four times as long as his body. He flies with them angled almost straight up when courting the female.

LOTS!

The red-billed quelea of Africa is one of the world's most abundant birds. It is a kind of weaver and gathers in gigantic flocks numbering a million or more birds. They wheel and turn together, darkening the sky. They also ruin crops.

Most sparrows are stocky, active birds with drab brownish plumage. Few birds are more familiar in towns and cities, and their chirruping song is a common garden sound. House sparrows nest under the eaves of buildings even in the centre of a busy city. Other sparrows occupy a huge range of habitats – swamp sparrows in swamps, fox sparrows in forests, sage sparrows in deserts, and song sparrows in scrubland. Some sparrows are called buntings and these tend to be more brightly coloured, especially the male indigo bunting, painted bunting and lazuli bunting.

NUTCRACKER BEAKS

Finches of various kinds, with their powerful seed-cracking beaks, are found throughout the world. They often visit bird tables for extra food, especially in winter. The chaffinch is one of Europe's most common birds, nesting in a wide range of wooded habitats. Goldfinches, with their attractive red, gold and black plumage, often feed in small flocks on the seed heads of thistles or teasels. The powerful bill of the hawfinch can even crush cherry stones with ease. The tips of the crossbill's beak actually cross over at the tip. This allows the bird to extract seeds from pine cones.

The snow bunting nests further north than any other land bird. It also breeds on high mountains, where its black and white plumage gives good camouflage among the rocks and ice.

The snow bunting ranges into the Arctic Circle, and also up near the summits of the world's highest mountains. A species of bunting is found almost everywhere in the world, from the Equator nearly to the Poles.

INSIDE A BIRD

No birds have teeth, so they cannot chew their food. This means the inner parts must grind and mash the food into a pulp. This happens in a muscular, strong-walled section of the digestive system called the gizzard. First, the swallowed food enters a stretchy storage bag in the chest region, called the crop. A bird can feed very fast, fill its crop, and then digest its food more slowly later. It can also carry food back to its nest in the crop, and bring it up (regurgitate it) for its young.

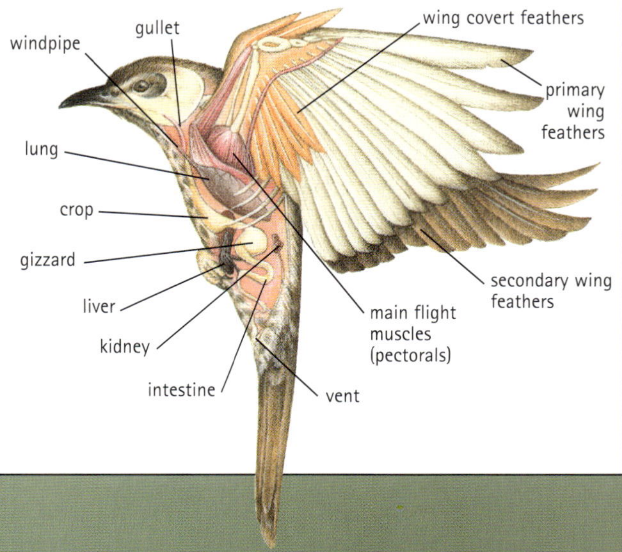

Hawfinches are big, orange-brown finches that live in broadleaved trees, such as beech or hornbeam, across most of Europe and Asia. The thick, strong beak can crack open nuts and even the seed stones of fruits such as cherries. The hawfinch is very shy. It is often only glimpsed in the treetops when it is feeding or when it makes its loud "tik" call.

EXPERT WEAVERS

Weaver birds are related to sparrows and are similar in body shape. But most are larger and more colourful than sparrows, with yellow, black and red plumage – especially in the males. Weavers make the most complex nests of any bird. Even the simplest designs have long funnels or tubes at the nest entrance to keep out predators (and cuckoos).

The song of the corn bunting sounds like a bunch of jangling keys. This bird is found in farmland and similar open areas.

The sociable weavers of Africa work together to build the most elaborate constructions in the bird world. Their huge colonial nest looks like the thatched roof of a cottage, transported to the branches of a tree. Each pair of weavers has its own entrance on the underside of the nest. The whole multi-nest may measure more than 7 m across. Village weavers also build a colonial nest from intertwined grass stems, with up to 100 nest compartments inside.

MORE PERCHING BIRDS:

Buntings
• 552 species
Finches
• 155 species
Weavers
• 95 species
Sparrows
• 35 species

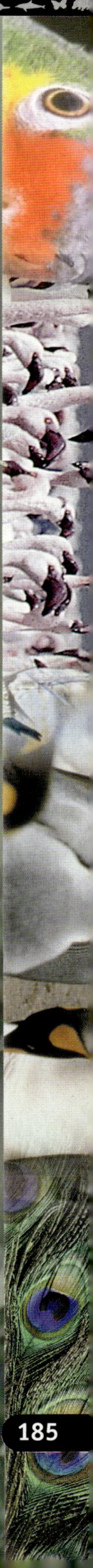

WARBLERS, THRUSHES AND FLYCATCHERS

Antbirds are forest-dwellers from South America. Not all feed on ants. Some eat beetles and other animals escaping from marching army ants.

MOST BIRDS MAKE THEIR OWN DISTINCTIVE NOISES OR CALLS. But perching birds or passerines (page 182) do not simply call, they sing. Perching birds admired for their beautiful songs include thrushes, warblers and nightingales. Indeed, these species are sometimes known as songbirds. Songs have a different purpose to the simpler, shorter calls. A call is designed to communicate a brief message. Chicks call to tell their parents they are hungry. A bird makes an alarm call to warn of possible danger. But the songs of songbirds are usually made only by the males, and only in the mating season. The male flits from twig to twig around his own patch of land, or territory, and sings loudly at each stop. He is warning off rival males of the same or competing species. He may also be trying to attract a breeding partner of his own species.

The cock-of-the-rock, from Colombia, is one of 90 species of tropical perching birds called cotingas.

Many warblers have drab plumage in shades of yellow, green and brown. This makes them hard to see as they dart among the leaves and twigs. But they make up for this with their loud, melodic songs, which are such a feature of temperate regions in late spring and summer. Most warbler species are visitors to these temperate regions.

In spring, the male redwing blackbird sings a rich, short, warbling song that sounds like a flute, with short pauses between phrases.

They time their breeding to fit in with the huge increase in caterpillars, flies and other insects each summer. They snap up the food in their narrow beaks as they flit about, rarely coming into the open. Most then fly south to warmer climates in the autumn, to avoid the cold of winter.

THRUSHES

The thrush group includes redstarts, wheatears, chats and the European blackbird.

The male Asian paradise flycatcher shares the task of sitting on the eggs to keep them warm. This species has two distinct types, or phases, of males. Both have blue heads. But a white phase male has a white body and tail, while the rufous male (shown here) is reddish.

Most thrushes have loud songs that carry well through trees and bushes, and even better across gardens and parks. The nightingale often sings at night. Its loud, rich voice echoes through the darkened woods in spring. This shy bird usually stays on or near the ground, where there is plenty of undergrowth.

European robin

The American redstart is a small perching bird with a loud, reedy song. Its warning alarm call sounds like a rattly ticking clock.

Thrushes feed on a mixed diet of worms, insects, fruits and berries. Some adults have bright plumage, but most are dull and mottled for camouflage. Exceptions are the red-breasted European robin and the similar but slightly larger American robin. Robins are also unusual because they sing in the autumn and winter, as well as in spring. One of the world's rarest birds is the Seychelles magpie-robin. Only about 50–100 survive on a couple of Seychelles islands.

SING!

Most songbirds have their own distinctive songs (which often help us to recognize them). But the marsh warbler produces "song samples" from perhaps 100 other bird species. It even copies species that it hears only while migrating.

CATCHING FLIES

Flycatchers like to sing from tree stumps. Most catch insects in mid-air. But the pied flycatcher of Europe and Asia uses its singing perch to watch for food. It waits patiently, then darts out to snap up a fly.

Monarch flycatchers are found in Africa, Asia and Australia. They have bold, bright plumage, especially the paradise flycatcher. The male's long tail streamers measure 15 cm, about twice as long as the bird's head and body. The African paradise flycatcher is rich chestnut brown with a black head. The Seychelles paradise flycatcher is similar in shape, but the male is glossy black with a deep blue sheen. Fantail flycatchers include the willy wagtail of Australia. This bold little bird is not afraid of larger animals, and often hitches a ride on the back of a sheep!

This is an Australian pied monarch flycatcher at its nest. Most perching birds build small, neat, cup-shaped nests in the branches of trees and bushes. The inside is lined with moss and grass, or perhaps with soft mud, to protect the eggs from draughts. The cup shape reduces the risk of the eggs falling out even if the nest rocks in a high wind.

The song thrush lives up to its name, producing a loud and beautiful song that lasts for five minutes or more. This thrush is seen hopping across the garden, head cocked on one side, listening for worms. It also eats snails, which it smashes on a stone "anvil" to break the shell and expose the juicy flesh.

MORE PERCHING BIRDS:

Flycatchers
- 156 species
- Europe, Africa, Australasia

Monarch flycatchers
- 133 species
- Africa, southern Asia, Australasia

Fantail flycatchers
- 38 species
- India, Southeast Asia, Australasia, New Zealand

Old World warblers
- 340 species
- mainly Europe, Africa and Asia

New World warblers
- 120 species
- Americas only

Australian warblers
- 60 species
- Southeast Asia, Australasia

Thrushes
- 304 species
- worldwide

LARKS, SWALLOWS AND TREECREEPERS

SOME OF THE SMALLEST PERCHING BIRDS, OR PASSERINES (PAGE 182), ARE SOME OF THE MOST FAMILIAR BIRDS IN TOWNS AND VILLAGES. The wren is one of the tiniest birds, but it makes its presence known with its loud, shrill warble. Blue tits are only slightly larger. They display lively, acrobatic behaviour, often coming to bird tables for food. Swallows and house martins build their nests under the eaves of houses. The American purple martin often uses a nest box. Treecreepers hop slowly up the trunks of trees in gardens and parks. The small, drab brown skylark makes a loud, trilling song as it flies, a well-known sound of European fields, meadows and moors.

White-eyes live mainly in southern Asia, with some species in Africa and others on Pacific islands. They eat nectar, fruits and insects.

The pied wagtail often lives near stables and farms, where there are plentiful flies and other insects to eat. It nests in any suitable hole.

Barn swallow

The wallcreeper searches for insects in crevices in cliffs and walls.

Barn swallows are summer visitors to temperate regions, and in the autumn can often be seen gathering in large numbers on wires ready for their winter migration.

Some swallows nest in holes pecked and dug out of cliffs and riverbanks. Others build nests of mud under a cliff—or its modern equivalent, a bridge or building.

BUSY BIRD!

The birds called tits (titmice) are busy and adaptable, always finding new ways of obtaining food. In the 1700s, French kings had them trained to perform tricks. In Japan, the varied tit is a fortune teller at shrines and festivals. It selects a fortune cookie for the person and tears off the paper top to reveal the message inside. Tits have also learned to peck into milk or juice bottles or cartons.

Sunbirds are the African and Asian versions of the American hummingbirds. A sunbird sips nectar from flowers with its long, probing beak and tongue. It also eats some insects and other foods.

Dippers are highly unusual perching birds. They feed underwater in fast-flowing rivers and streams. The dipper walks upstream along the gravel riverbed, pressed onto the bottom by the current flowing over its sloping head and tail.

Many smaller perching birds have loud songs which they make in flight, rather than from a perch. The skylark is a brownish, well-camouflaged lark that spends much time in the undergrowth, looking for insects. But when the male skylark soars upwards on a clear morning, he pours out a cascade of song as he hangs in the air for minutes at a time. At last he descends, first gently, then quickly as he dives into vegetation.

The nuthatch or "nut-hack" is named after its habit of wedging nuts into a crevice, to hack open with its beak.

Pipits, too, have a distinctive song flight that echoes through the air as they drop to the ground. Pipits are a kind of wagtail, named because they bob their tails up and down as they walk. But they have shorter tails than other wagtails. They are mostly dull, streaked browns, or greys, which makes them hard to see at rest in meadows or dry grassland.

Most wagtails have long tails and slender bodies. They feed on insects near marshes and ponds. Their striking plumage is either black and white, or combinations of green, yellow and blue. They have sharp, metallic calls and quieter songs.

The meadowlark of American grasslands is not a true lark but a cousin of the blackbird.

DRINKING IN FLIGHT

Swallows and martins are graceful in flight, and swoop over fields and water after flying insects. They can even drink on the wing, dipping the beak into a stream as they zoom over the surface. These birds look like swifts (page 180), but fly lower and more jerkily. Each year, swallows migrate from temperate lands to the tropics for winter. They return in spring to build cup-shaped nests, often on rafters in a roof. Sand martins scratch nest burrows in sandy banks.

A BEAK FOR INSECTS

Birds that pick up insects from the ground or from crevices in trees, like the treecreeper, need especially long, thin, tweezer-like beaks. The curve helps to lever off flakes of bark.

UNDERGROWTH AND UNDERWATER

Wrens and dippers are both tiny, dumpy birds with short tails, but they live in very different habitats. Wrens skulk in thick undergrowth, camouflaged by their brown plumage – but identified by their loud, musical songs. Dippers live around mountain streams and walk underwater as they search the stones and gravel on the bed for insects, worms and water snails. They even dive into rapids.

TITS AND TREECREEPERS

Tits are common garden birds in many regions. They nest in tree holes and feed largely on insects. Nuthatches and treecreepers both live around trees. The treecreeper climbs up from the base of the tree in a spiral, searching cracks for insects. The nuthatch can climb about the tree trunk moving upwards, sideways, or even downwards.

MORE PERCHING BIRDS:

Larks, wagtails and pipits • 130 species	Tits • 62 species
Swallows and martins • 74 species	Nuthatches • 21 species
Dippers and wrens • 64 species	Treecreepers • 14 species
	Sunbirds • 116 species
	White-eyes • 85 species

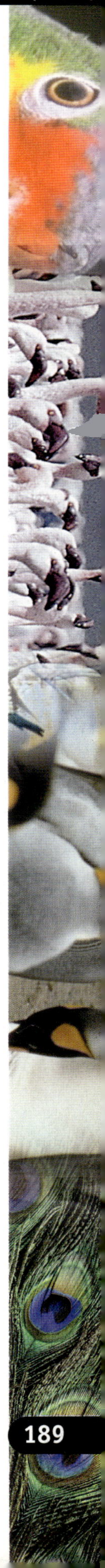

Blue whales emit ear-splitting, low-pitched grunts that are the loudest noises made by any animal.

SECTION 7
MAMMALS

FOR MANY PEOPLE, THE MOST FAMILIAR GROUP OF ANIMALS IS THE MAMMALS. This is partly because we keep many kinds of mammals as pets and on farms, including dogs, cats, rabbits, horses, cows, sheep and pigs. Also, the best-known animal in the world, and one of the most numerous, is a mammal – the human being.

A mammal is warm-blooded and has a body covering of fur or hair. Most mammal babies grow in their mother's womb, and are born quite well developed. But in marsupial mammals, such as kangaroos, the babies are born tiny and hardly developed at all. They continue their growth in the safety of the mother's pouch. Monotreme mammals do not give birth to babies at all. They lay eggs, like birds, and the eggs hatch into babies. But all female mammals make milk to feed their babies. This is produced by special glands called mammary glands – which is how the group got its name.

There are some 4,000 kinds, or species, of mammal. They include the largest creature ever to live on Earth, the blue whale. Most mammals walk and run on land. However, the whales, dolphins, porpoises and sea cows spend all their lives in water. Another group of mammals, the bats, have taken to the air. Others, such as moles and mole rats, tunnel underground and rarely see the light of day.

EGG-LAYING MAMMALS

PERHAPS THE ODDEST OF ALL MAMMALS ARE THE MONOTREMES, OR EGG-LAYING MAMMALS. There are only three kinds – the platypus and two species of echidnas or spiny anteaters, the short-beaked and long-beaked echidnas. They all live in Australia or nearby New Guinea. The platypus is also called the duck-billed platypus, because its mouth is shaped like a duck's beak. These highly unusual mammals do not give birth to babies, like the other 4,000-plus mammal species. The females lay eggs, like a bird or reptile.

The short-beaked echidna grows to about 35 cm in length. Both long- and short-beaked echidnas have strong claws for digging up their prey and excavating nest burrows.

STICKY TONGUE

The echidnas look similar to porcupines, being covered with long, sharp, protective spines. They use their powerful front claws to dig into soil, or ant or termite nests. Then they lick up the prey using their long, sticky tongue.

The long-beaked echidna grows to about 28 inches (70 cm) in length.

INSIDE A MAMMAL

All mammals have the same basic parts inside. The body has an internal skeleton made of bones, which give strength and support. In the chest are the heart and lungs. The abdomen contains the digestive, waste-disposal and reproductive parts.

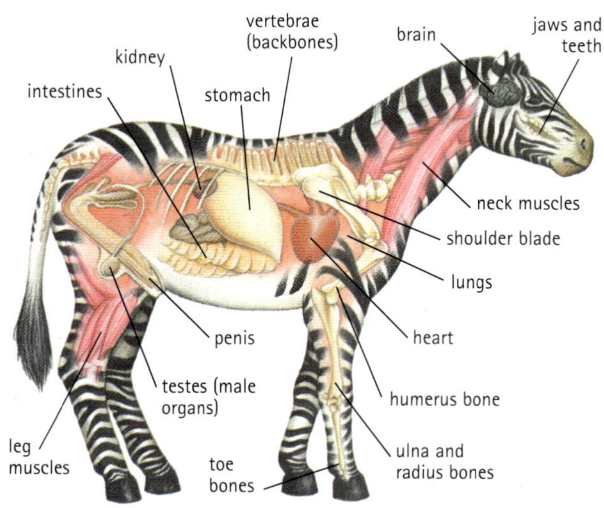

The female echidna keeps her single egg in a temporary brood pouch which develops on her belly. The egg hatches after about ten days. Then she feeds the tiny, helpless baby on her milk, as other mammals do.

The short-beaked echidna is quite common in Australia and New Guinea. It is found in a wide range of habitats, from dry deserts to cold uplands, scrubland and forest. The long-beaked echidna is found only in the highlands of New Guinea. It is larger than its short-beaked cousin, with fur longer than the spines, and a longer, down-curved snout. Despite its name of spiny anteater, this echidna feeds mostly on earthworms, which it catches using the tough spines on its tongue.

THE PLATYPUS

The platypus lives in eastern Australia, including Tasmania. It is one of the strangest of all mammals. When a preserved platypus body was first studied by scientists in 1798, they thought it was a fake made of several animals sewn together. The platypus has a wide beak like a duck, a flattened tail like a beaver and webbed feet like an otter.

The female platypus digs a very long breeding burrow, 18 m or more into the riverbank. At the end of the burrow she makes a nest of dry leaves and grass.

The male platypus has a poison spur hidden in the fur on each hind leg. If threatened, he kicks out and causes the attacker great pain.

WOW!

The mouth of a long-beaked echidna is just a small slit at the end of the snout. The tongue can poke out 18 cm beyond the snout tip. The echidna has no teeth. It squashes its tiny prey between its tongue and the roof of its mouth.

These body features make it ideally suited to swimming, and a platypus spends up to half its time nosing and grubbing in the water for food. It uses its tail as a rudder and to store a reserve of fat for the winter, when food is often scarce.

ELECTRIC BILL

Platypuses are not often seen since they live along creeks, rivers and lakes, and are usually active at night. They have an extraordinary method of feeding. They hunt at night along the stream or lake bed, detecting prey hidden in the mud by the tiny electrical impulses given out by the muscles in the prey's body. The platypus does this using its wide, leathery bill. This is very sensitive to touch and movements, and also has tiny pits which can detect electricity, like some fish (page 107). As it hunts, the platypus keeps its eyes and nostrils tightly closed.

The platypus catches mainly insect grubs, worms, little shrimps and similar small freshwater creatures. It stores them in its cheek pouches and eats them later, when it returns to its burrow in the bank. Then the platypus grinds up its food using horny ridges in its jaws since, like the echidnas, it has no teeth.

The platypus catches small creatures including frogs and fish, and even water plants. Each dive lasts about one minute. The head and body are about 45 cm long, and the tail 15–20 cm. Once very rare, platypuses are now protected by law and have become more common in some regions.

MAMMALS

Mammals	First major sub-group of mammals: Monotremes
• 4,150 species	• 3 species, platypus and 2 echidnas
• young fed on mother's milk	• only mammals that lay eggs
• body with fur or hair	• adults have no teeth
• warm-blooded	• found only in Australia and New Guinea
• most have four limbs	

MARSUPIAL MAMMALS

MARSUPIALS ARE POUCHED MAMMALS, NAMED AFTER THE POUCH (MARSUPIUM) OF THE FEMALE. She gives birth to babies that are at a very early stage of development, tiny and helpless. The babies crawl to the pouch and continue to develop there in safety, feeding on her milk. There are about 120 species of marsupial in Australia, 50 species in New Guinea and 90 species in South and Central America. One species, the Virginia opossum, has spread through southern North America. The largest marsupials are kangaroos and wallabies. They have big, muscular hind legs and bound along at great speed.

The Virginia opossum is an agile climber and usually lives in trees. But it has adapted to life in towns, clambering over fences and scavenging for food in dustbins and tips.

The marsupial mole has shiny golden fur.

The female red kangaroo is smaller than the male, weighing less than 30 kg. The young in the pouch is called a joey.

The babies of marsupial mammals are born tiny and undeveloped. At birth, a baby kangaroo is hardly larger than a grape, and its legs have only just begun to grow. Even so, it can crawl from the birth opening to its mother's pouch, where its mouth latches onto her nipple to suck her milk. The baby lives like this for six months. As it grows larger, it begins to leave the pouch for short periods. Meanwhile another tiny, newborn baby arrives. Even when a youngster is more than a year old, it may dash back to the safety of its mother's pouch if danger appears, and still pokes its head in to feed on her milk. Most kangaroos and wallabies eat leaves, stems and shoots. And the smaller, shorter-legged tree kangaroos really do live in trees!

The Tasmanian devil has a body length of about 60 cm. It lives on the Australian island of Tasmania. Its massive teeth and jaws easily crunch bones.

THE APPEALING KOALA

The koala is one of the most appealing marsupials, looking like a teddy bear soft toy. In fact it has very sharp claws to cling on to the branches of the gum (eucalyptus) trees where it lives. So it can give a deep scratch if threatened. Koalas spend much of their lives either sleeping or munching on gum leaves. They get all their nourishment and moisture from these, so they rarely come down to the ground. Another bear-like marsupial is the wombat. It lives in a complex system of burrows and chambers, which it digs using its powerful, large-clawed feet.

Wombats feed on roots, shoots and other plant material. They sometimes raid farm crops.

MARSUPIAL VERSIONS

There are many other kinds of marsupial. Some resemble mammals living on other continents. For example, there are marsupial mice and marsupial cats or quolls.

The brushtail possum once lived in forests, but has now spread to Australian suburbs, where it eats food scraps.

There are also marsupial shrews or planigales, rat- and rabbit-like marsupials called bandicoots, and even marsupial moles. The pouches of tunnelling marsupials, such as the wombat and marsupial mole, open backwards, so they do not fill with earth as the female digs her way through the ground.

One of the smallest marsupials is the honey possum. It is about the same size as a house mouse and lives on nectar and pollen from flowers. The possum licks up its food using its long, bristly, brush-tipped tongue.

MARSUPIAL GLIDERS

Several species of marsupials can swoop from tree to tree, using wing-like flaps of skin stretched between the front and rear limbs. These include various types of gliders, and the pygmy possum or feathertail glider. The greater glider, which weighs 1.4 kg, can travel as far as 91 m in a single burst of "flight".

Creatures very similar to marsupial gliders are the colugos or flying lemurs. There are only two species, living in the forests of Malaysia and the Philippines. They swoop through the air in a similar way to marsupial gliders, but with better flight control, covering more than 150 m. However, these animals are not marsupial mammals, they are placental mammals.

About 20 species of Australian marsupials have become extinct during the last 200 years. Dozens more are threatened, mainly by habitat loss or competition from introduced animals. The mahogany glider, however, was believed to be extinct, but has been rediscovered in the forests of North Queensland.

The second major sub-group of mammals:

Marsupials
- about 270 species
- tiny young raised in mother's pouch
- live mainly in Australia, New Guinea, South and Central America

Marsupial groups include:

American opossums
- 75 species

Marsupial mice
- 53 species

Kangaroos and wallabies
- 50 species

Bandicoots
- 17 species

Ringtail possums
- 16 species

Brushtail possums and cuscuses
- 14 species

Rat kangaroos
- 10 species

Gliders
- 7 species

Pygmy possums
- 7 species

Shrew *(rat)* opossums
- 7 species

Wombats
- 3 species

Bilbies
- 2 species

Honey possum
- 1 species

Koala
- 1 species

Marsupial mole
- 1 species

Monito del monte
- 1 species

Numbat
- 1 species

Koalas look peaceful and quiet. But they can defend themselves with their sharp claws, and the bellowing call of the male koala can be heard over a distance of several kilometres. Koalas are a threatened species and are fully protected.

INSECT-EATERS

THE INSECT-EATING MAMMALS, OR INSECTIVORES, ARE MAINLY SMALL AND VERY ACTIVE. They include shrews, hedgehogs and moles, and also tenrecs, solenodons, moonrats and desmans. Most types eat mainly insects, from soft caterpillars and grubs, to hard-cased beetles and biting ants. But they consume other small prey too, from juicy worms and slugs to spiders and woodlice. Insect-eating mammals are generally nocturnal (active at night). They sniff and feel for food with their sensitive noses and whiskers. Some shrews are so small and busy that their bodies soon run out of energy and they must eat every few hours to survive.

▲ The common shrew's small eyes and little rounded ears are almost hidden in its fur. Its main senses are smell and touch.

▲ Desert hedgehog

Many insect-eating mammals resemble rodents such as mice or rats. But rodents have long, chisel-like front teeth (page 206). Insectivores have sharp, pointed teeth, almost like a miniature cat. They are fierce hunters and, despite their size, if threatened they leap at the enemy in a frenzy of bites and squeals.

GOING COLD

The biggest problem faced by tiny and active mammals such as shrews is that they are warm-blooded. Being so tiny, the surface area of the body is very large compared to the volume of the body. So huge amounts of body heat are lost through the body surface, compared to larger mammals. To keep its body temperature up, a shrew must "burn" lots of energy, which it gets from food. So it must eat – or go cold and die.

The pygmy shrew is one of the smallest mammals, with a head-and-body as small as your thumb. It hunts for 2–3 hours, has a short rest, hunts again, and so on. It may starve to death after 12 hours without food.

PRICKLY BALL

The prickles of a hedgehog are long, thick, extra-sharp hairs. A fully grown European hedgehog has about 5,000 of them covering its body.

▶ The desman has a long, flattened tail for swimming.

▼ The tail-less tenrec is from Madagascar.

▼ Tree shrews live in the forests of Southeast Asia. They are not insectivores, but are similar in their habits and food, except that they are perfectly at home in the trees.

The prickles normally lie flat, but the hedgehog can raise them by tensing muscles just under its skin. With its back arched, head and legs tucked in and spines pointing out, the hedgehog then becomes a spiny ball. This deters most predators, but is no defence against road traffic.

LIVING UNDERGROUND

Moles are well suited to life in the earth. The cylindrical body, short limbs and soft, thick fur allow a mole to slide through the soil, as it digs tunnels using its flattened, strongly clawed front paws. Here and there the mole heaves loose soil to the surface through an upright tunnel, making a molehill. A mole's tunnel network may stretch more than 150 m. It feeds on animals like worms that fall in through the sides.

Golden moles are only found in southern and central Africa. They have shiny fur with a golden sheen, and their eyes are covered by hairy skin. Like other moles, they spend most of their lives in tunnel systems below the ground.

A shrew tackles a lizard almost its own size. Shrews have poisonous saliva (spit), which helps to paralyse victims when the shrew bites them.

MORE INSECTIVORES

Tenrecs are another group of African insectivores. Some resemble large shrews, others have spines like a hedgehog's. The most unusual tenrecs are the otter shrews of West Africa. They swim well and hunt for water insects, small fish and frogs. Solenodons are like giant shrews. There are only two species, both from the West Indies region and both rare. One is found just on the island of Cuba. The other lives only on nearby Hispaniola (Haiti and the Dominican Republic).

The moonrat (top left), with its striped face, is one of the largest insect-eaters. Its head and body length is 40 cm. It is active at night and has a hairless, scaly tail like a rat, hence its name. The golden mole (near left) often comes to the surface to feed. The Cuban solenodon (below left) is 30 cm long. It tackles animal prey as large as rats. The pygmy white-toothed shrew (bottom left) is the smallest of the insectivores.

The third major sub-group of mammals:

Placentals
- about 3,880 species
- unborn develop in the womb, nourished by the placenta (afterbirth)
- worldwide, in all habitats, mountain to deep sea

Placentals include:

Insect-eating mammals *(insectivores)*
- 345 species
- eat insects, worms, slugs and similar small animals
- small and active
- long snout, small eyes and ears

Insect-eating groups include:

Shrews
- 246 species

Tenrecs and otter shrews
- 33 species

Moles and desmans
- 29 species

Golden moles
- 18 species

Hedgehogs and moonrats
- 17 species

Solenodons
- 2 species

Tree shrews
- 18 species
- resemble squirrels

Elephant shrews
- 15 species
- small with pointed shrew-like face
- long nose, almost like an elephant's trunk in some species

Another group of placentals:

Colugos *(flying lemurs)*
- cat-sized gliders
- live in Southeast Asian forests

BATS

ABOUT ONE-QUARTER OF ALL MAMMAL SPECIES ARE BATS. They are the biggest mammal group, after rodents. About 960 different species are found throughout the world, except in the coldest regions. Although some mammals can glide, bats are the only mammals that can truly fly. There are two main kinds of bats. One is the fruit bats and flying foxes. These are mostly large, with a body the size of a small dog and wings about 1.8 m across. They eat fruits, flowers, leaves and other plant parts. The other main kind is the insect-eating bats. These are much smaller, with a body the size of a mouse or rat. Surprisingly, some insect-eating bats not only eat insects, but also mice, voles, frogs and fish.

The vampire bat has four razor-like canine teeth. It makes only a tiny slit in its victim's skin. It usually chooses a furless or featherless part of the body, such as the ankle. It feeds for about half an hour each night. In some areas vampire bats spread diseases such as rabies.

Most bats are nocturnal, or active at night. Apart from flying foxes, they find their way by a sound-radar system called echo-location. Most smaller bats feed on night-flying insects such as moths. But some bats specialize in finding other foods. The fisherman bat of Central and South America swoops over rivers and lakes, and hooks up fish from just under the surface.

The pipistrelle is one of the smallest bats, with a head and body 4 cm long and a wingspan of 20 cm.

The mouse-eared bat's high-pitched squeaks of sound emerge from its mouth. Some bats emit sounds through the nose.

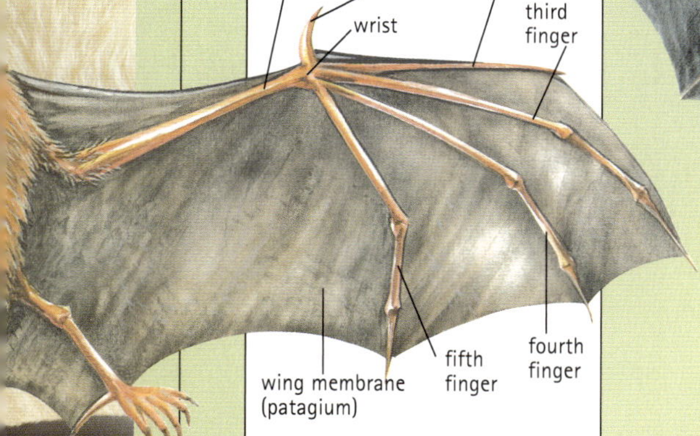

A BAT'S WING

The wing (arm) of a bat is different from the wing of a bird. It is a thin, skin-like membrane, the patagium, stretched between hugely long arm, hand and finger bones. The patagium is a thin layer of blood vessels and elastic threads sandwiched between two layers of skin.

It uses its long, curved claws to spear the fish. Mastiff bats catch bees and wasps. Greater horseshoe bats, named after their horseshoe-shaped noses, dive onto beetles and other ground-dwelling insects. Other bats catch night-flying birds such as nightjars and even small owls.

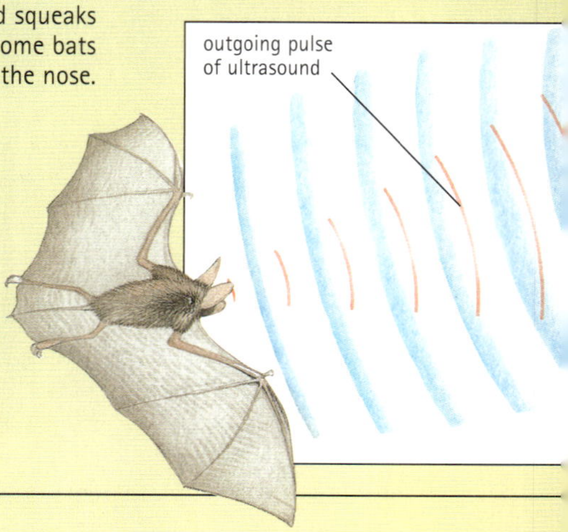

The huge ears of long-eared bats can turn and swivel with great accuracy, like radar dishes. They catch the returning echoes of sound, which a bat uses to find its way in the dark.

Resting, or roosting, bats hang upside down by their foot claws. They wrap their wings around the body to keep in warmth.

Flying foxes like the common long-tongued fruit bat have dog- or fox-like faces. They roost by day in trees, often making chattering noises.

World Watch

In some parts of the world, especially the tropics, bats are among the most common mammals. In other areas, such as Europe, they have become extremely rare. Modern farming methods using pesticides mean that their insect prey is scarcer now. The old hollow trees that they roost in have been felled, or their caves have been blocked up. In some countries, such as Britain, all bat species are protected by law.

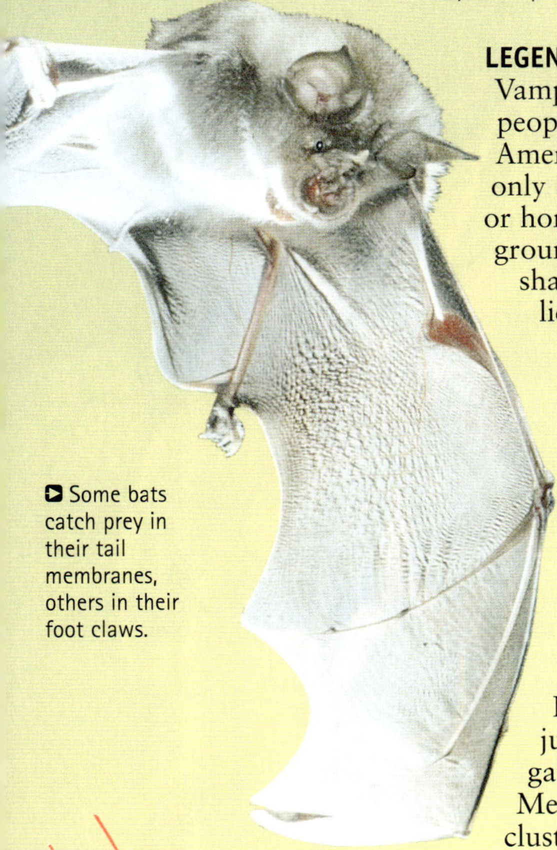

Some bats catch prey in their tail membranes, others in their foot claws.

LEGEND OF A VAMPIRE

Vampire bats feed on blood. But they are not dangerous to people, as the legends say. Vampire bats live in Central and South America, and are quite small, with a head and body length of only 8 cm. They usually feed on the blood of sleeping cattle, pigs or horses. The vampire bat lands near its victim, crawls over the ground and makes a small slit-like wound in the animal with its sharp teeth. Then it dribbles spit to stop the blood clotting and licks up the oozing blood.

Many bats roost together in colonies, in caves or hollow trees, and also inside modern "caves" such as church towers and mine shafts. In tropical areas bats are active all year. In temperate lands, most bats hibernate through the winter, emerging from their deep sleep when the weather warms up again in spring.

The biggest group of bats is the common or vesper bats. It includes common European species such as the pipistrelle, long-eared bat and noctule. The smallest mammal is a bat – Kitti's hog-nosed bat from Thailand. Its head and body are just 3 cm long and it weighs 1.5 g. And one of the biggest gatherings of mammals is of bats. Some colonies of the Mexican free-tailed bat contain up to 10 million bats, all clustered together in a single cave.

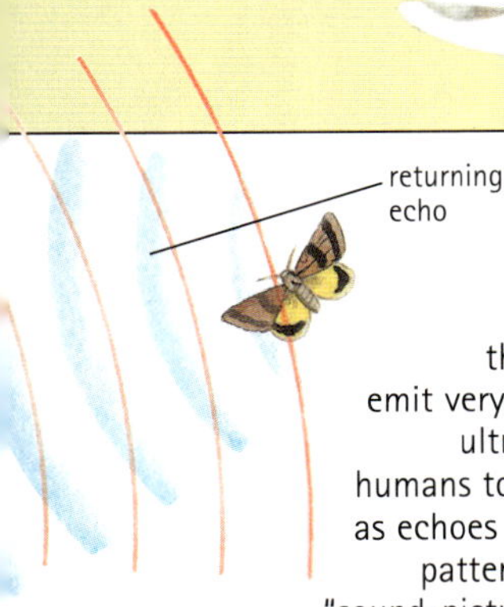

HOW BATS FLY IN THE DARK

Most bats use echo-location to find their way, even in total darkness. They emit very high-pitched pulses of sound, called ultrasound, which are too high for most humans to hear. The sound pulses bounce back as echoes off nearby objects. The bat hears the pattern of echoes and analyses it to give a "sound-picture" of the surroundings. Flying foxes and fruit bats have good eyesight and smell, and fly mainly at dusk and dawn. Most do use echo-location.

BATS

- 960 species
- the only mammals with true, powered flight
- front limbs are wings
- most are nocturnal

Some groups of bats:

Flying foxes, fruit bats
- 175 species

Common or vesper bats
- 320 species

Spear-nosed bats
- 140 species

Free-tailed bats
- 90 species

Horseshoe bats
- 70 species

Leaf-nosed bats
- 60 species

Sheath-tailed bats
- 50 species

Slit-faced bats
- 12 species

Ghost-faced bats
- 8 species

Vampire bats
- 3 species

Bulldog bats
- 2 species

Hog-nosed bat
- 1 species

A sloth is so well suited to hanging around that it can hardly walk on the ground. It has to drag its body along with its curved claws.

ANTEATERS, SLOTHS AND ARMADILLOS

SOME MAMMALS LIVE AT A SLOW PACE. They include anteaters, armadillos, pangolins and especially sloths. These creatures share other features too, such as long, sharp claws and very small teeth, or none at all. They feed on soft or tiny food items that do not need much biting or chewing. For defence, armadillos and pangolins have a covering of bands or scales made from tough bone and horn, like a suit of armour. Sloths rely on staying still and unnoticed. Anteaters slash at enemies with their claws.

The nine-banded armadillo is the most common and widespread type. Like the others, it feeds mainly at night.

LARGEST...!

The largest armadillo is the giant armadillo of Brazil and Peru, at 1.5 m long. It is endangered by the loss of its dense forest habitat.

An anteater eats not only ants. It also licks up termites and small grubs with its very long, sticky tongue, which emerges from the small mouth at the end of the long snout. The anteater digs out or rips open the ant nest or termite mound with its large front claws, and licks up the milling insects in their hundreds. But it does not eat them all. It soon moves on, leaving the nest to be repaired as a larder for the future.

The tongue of the giant anteater is 60 cm long. It can collect hundreds of termites or ants with a single lick. One anteater may eat 20,000 ants in a single day!

The giant anteater is the largest of the four anteater species. It is 200 cm long, but much of this is its long, down-curved nose and brush-like tail. It also has a shaggy coat and an awkward, rolling way of walking. Giant anteaters roam forests and scrub in Central and South America. The other three species are smaller and stay mainly in trees, using the strong tail as an extra limb to clasp branches.

The tree pangolin has a gripping or prehensile tail. A rough, scaleless patch of skin on the underside near the tip helps to give extra grip.

Most of the armadillo's body is protected by bony plates. However, a predator may succeed in flipping the armadillo onto its back, to get at the soft underside.

SLOW AS THE SLOTH

The sloths of South American rainforests are named after their very slow movements. They spend most of their lives hanging upside-down from tree branches, either munching leaves, crawling slowly along or staying perfectly still, asleep. A sloth relies on its stillness and camouflage to escape detection. The hairs of its fur have furrows where microscopic plants (algae) grow, giving the animal a greenish tinge among the leaves.

ARMOURED ARMADILLOS

The most obvious feature of an armadillo is the hard, protective covering over its back, like armour plating. Each plate or band has a hard, bony core covered by a tough, horny substance (like our fingernails). Flexible skin between the bands allows the armadillo to hunch up its body and tuck its legs underneath when a predator comes near. Some armadillos can roll up into a tight ball, for greater protection. Most armadillos eat ants, termites and similar small animals. Some are also fond of fruit. They live in South and Central America, and the nine-banded armadillo ranges into southern North America.

A sloth feeds mainly on fruit and leaves, hanging by its long, hooked claws. Even its digestion works slowly. It can take as long as a month for a meal to pass through its body. Most sloths come down from their trees about once each week, to leave their droppings on the ground. They spend about two-thirds of their time asleep!

MAMMAL "PINE CONES"

Pangolins, like armadillos, are protected by hard, bony plates. The plates consist of flat, point-edged scales that overlap like the scales on a pine cone. Most pangolins lick up ants and termites, using their long tongue in the same way as an anteater.

A pangolin sheds a few of its scales each month, and new ones soon grow. As it licks up ants with its strap-shaped tongue, the pangolin closes its eyes and nostrils so the ants cannot bite them.

EDENTATES (SMALL-TOOTHED OR TOOTHLESS MAMMALS)

- 36 species
- slow-moving
- most have long claws
- small simple teeth, or toothless

Groups include:

Armadillos
- 20 species
- South and Central America

Pangolins
- 7 species
- Africa, India and Southeast Asia

Sloths
- 5 species
- South and Central America

Anteaters
- 4 species
- South and Central America

RABBITS, HARES AND PIKAS

EVER ALERT TO DANGER, RABBITS AND HARES ARE ALWAYS READY TO DASH FOR SAFETY. They live in open, grassy country, and have large eyes and huge ears to look and listen for predators. Their back legs are long and muscular, ideal for running at high speed from danger. Although they resemble rodents such as squirrels and rats, rabbits and hares belong to a different mammal group, the lagomorphs. This name means "leaping shape", which is what these creatures do to survive. The lagomorph group also includes pikas. These are like small, dumpy rabbits with shorter ears and little legs. They also lack the rabbit's bobtail.

The winter fur of Arctic and snowshoe hares is white, for camouflage in snow and ice. It moults in spring. The summer fur is brown.

The volcano rabbit lives only on grassy mountain slopes in Mexico. It has short ears and a small tail. It is a very rare species, and protected by law.

There is no exact difference between rabbits and hares. Generally, the larger types with longer legs and longer ears are known as hares, or jackrabbits in North America. The smaller species with shorter ears are usually called rabbits. Hares that live in the far north, such as the Arctic and snowshoe hares, moult into a white coat during the snowy winter season. The numbers of snowshoe hares living in the northern forests of North America vary on a fairly regular cycle.

The hare's prominent eyes allow it to see above and even behind itself, so it can spot predators such as eagles from almost any direction.

"Mad March hares" are usually males battling for a female at breeding time in spring. Or the pawing and boxing hare may be a jill (female) chasing away an unwanted jack (male).

They reach a peak roughly every ten years, then fall again. Why this is so is not clear. But it affects the populations of lynx, snowy owls and other predators in the same way, since they depend on the hares for food.

The large ears of a rabbit or hare not only pick up the faintest noises, like an elephant's ears; they also help to lose body heat into the air during very hot weather. If a rabbit or hare detects danger, it races away, propelled by great leaps of its large back legs. It may thump the ground first with its rear feet to warn others nearby, and it can zigzag at great speed. Some hares sprint at more than 80 km/h. However, they do not have great stamina, and predators such as wolves soon tire them out with chasing.

GNAWING TEETH

Rabbits and hares have strong teeth for gnawing grasses, stems, seeds, roots, bark and other plant foods. Some rabbits live in groups or colonies in networks of underground tunnels, called warrens, which they dig in the soil of hedges and banks. Most hares live alone and rest in the open, in shallow bowl-like areas in the grass or scrub, called forms. They also have their babies in these forms. For this reason, young hares (known as leverets) can run and hide almost as soon as they are born.

BREEDING LIKE RABBITS

Baby rabbits born in the safety of the breeding chamber or "stop", are blind and helpless at first. Their eyes open at a week old and they venture out of the nest at three weeks. But at only four months of age they can breed. Since one female may have up to 20 babies each year, rabbits have a deserved reputation of increasing numbers very quickly.

HAY FOR WINTER

Pikas look like a combination of rabbit and guinea pig or vole. They live in mountainous country in Asia, with one species also in northwest North America. Most pikas prefer rocky slopes. The large-eared pika of the Himalayas and nearby mountains is one of the highest-living mammals, found at heights of more than 6,000 m. Pikas graze on a range of plants, mostly grasses, flowers and young stems. In the autumn, they pull hay, soft twigs and other stores of food into their burrows to eat during the long, cold winter.

The American black-tailed jackrabbit is actually a type of hare. It uses its large ears to listen for danger and also to keep cool in the great heat of summer.

The running hare kicks off with its long back legs, and cushions its landing on the two front legs with paws held together. Then it thrusts its rear legs forwards on either side of the front paws and makes another leap.

Most pikas, like the northern pika, are about 20–25 cm long.

Rabbits and hares
- 44 species
- large ears
- long back legs
- eyes face sideways
- very short "bob" tail
- slit-like nostrils
- eat plants

Pikas
- 14 species
- rounded ears
- almost tailless
- eat plants

HYRAXES AND THE AARDVARK

The tree hyrax climbs nimbly, even on damp, slippery branches. Hyraxes are long-lived for fairly small plant-eating mammals. Some survive for more than 12 years, compared to 2–3 years for most rabbits.

HYRAXES (ALSO CALLED HYRACES) ARE SMALL PLANT-EATING MAMMALS ABOUT THE SIZE OF RABBITS. They also resemble rabbits in appearance, but with shorter ears and legs, and a short, stumpy tail rather than a "bobtail". Hyraxes are found over much of Africa, and also in parts of the Middle East. Most types live in rocky country and sit on boulders or outcrops, sunning themselves as they rest. Rock hyraxes are commonly known as dassies, and some types are also called conies. The aardvark is another African mammal, and quite unlike any other – it is the only member of its group, the tubulidents.

COUSINS!

Hyraxes look similar to rabbits and hares (lagomorphs), or to rodents such as rats and guinea pigs. But scientific studies show that their closest mammal relatives are elephants! Hyraxes and elephants, and also aardvarks, share similarities in their teeth, jaw bones, muscles and other internal body parts.

Rock hyraxes form family groups. The adult male defends the territory against neighbouring groups of the species.

Hyraxes are stocky, well-built mammals suited for clambering over rocks or climbing trees. Their small feet have thick, rubbery, moist soles to give a firm grip even on smooth rocks and branches. The feet are also equipped with nail-like hooves rather than proper claws, and are not designed for digging burrows or scraping up food. So hyraxes make their nests in caves or cracks between rocks, under tree roots, or inside hollow trees.

Rock hyraxes make their homes on rocky outcrops or hills known as kopjes (koppies). They usually live in colonies of about 10–30, including adults and young. Rock hyraxes eat a wide variety of plants, especially grasses, even when dry and tough. Bush and tree hyraxes prefer softer leaves and fruits.

A hyrax has a small face and an upturned mouth that always seems to "smile". But this is only our own interpretation, based on human facial expressions.

THE "EARTH PIG"

There is only a single species of aardvark, a name that means "earth-pig" in the Afrikaans language. This strange animal is quite unlike any other mammal, especially its teeth and claws (right). Its teeth are covered not with hard white enamel as in most mammals (including ourselves), but with a soft, grey substance called cementum. The aardvark is also something of a mystery. Although it is the size of a large pig, it is hardly ever seen by day, since it hides in one of its many burrows. At night, it roams in search of its food, ants and termites. But it is extremely shy and secretive, and darts away into the darkness if it senses danger.

THE AARDVARK'S ODD CLAWS

The aardvark is a very efficient burrower. If a predator threatens, it can dig itself into even hard ground in just a few minutes. It also digs for food, and it excavates several burrows around its home territory for shelter and safety. The main breeding burrow of the female may be 12 m long. The aardvark does all this digging using its powerful feet with their unusual curved claws. There are four on each front foot and five on each rear foot. They jab into the hard soil even through matted grass roots.

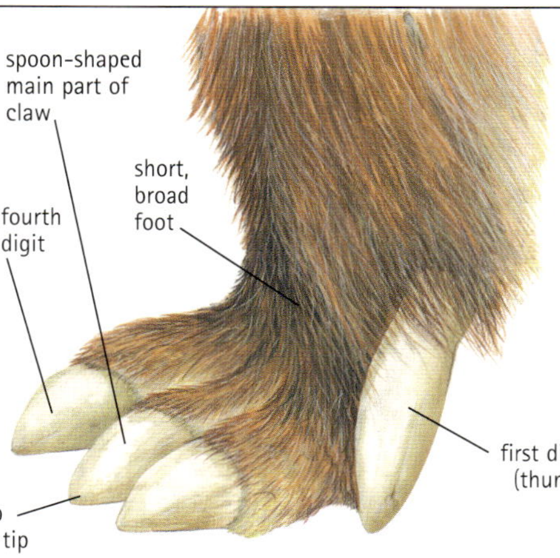

Aardvarks live in open woodland, scrub and grassland across much of central and southern Africa. They find their food by nosing about, sniffing and listening. After digging out the tiny prey, the aardvark gathers them using its long, sticky tongue. It may need to hunt for several hours each night, covering 15 km or more to find food.

The aardvark has a head-body length of about 1.2 m, with a tail of 50 cm. Its head is narrow, with long ears and a long, flexible snout tipped by a pig-like nose.

Hyraxes
- 11 species
- soft, moist pad on sole of foot
- flattened claws, like tiny hooves
- eat plants

Rock hyraxes *(Dassies)*
- live among rocks
- Africa, Middle East

Tree hyraxes
- live mainly in forests
- Africa

Bush hyraxes
- live among rocks or in hollow trees
- mainly east Africa

Aardvark
- 1 species
- large, pig-like
- prefers woodland and scrub
- central and southern Africa

MICE, RATS AND CAVIES

The jerboa has huge back feet that work like sandshoes, stopping it from sinking into the desert surface.

THE RODENTS OR GNAWING MAMMALS ARE BY FAR THE LARGEST MAMMAL GROUP. The 1,700 species mean that almost one of every two mammals is a rodent. About seventy-five per cent of these are types of mice and rats, and their South American relatives, cavies – the best-known being the guinea pig. The rodent's key feature is its four long, sharp, chisel-like incisor teeth at the front of the mouth. These can chew even the hardest foods, such as nuts or tree bark. Some small rodents, including mice, rats, hamsters, gerbils and guinea pigs, are often kept as pets. (More rodents are described on pages 208 to 211.)

A dormouse may hibernate for up to eight months, depending on the climate of the region.

The cavy group of rodents includes guinea pigs, porcupines, spiny rats and mole rats.

Mice and rats range in size from the pygmy mouse, at less than 10 cm long including its tail, to rats that reach a total length of 80 cm. The harvest mouse is one of the smallest, with a body hardly larger than a thumb. It is a very agile climber and uses its long tail as an extra limb to grasp grass stems. It spread rapidly when people began to plant wheat and similar crops. But then it suffered as machines took over harvesting from people. It could not escape from its ball-shaped nest as the combine harvester approached.

Some mice and rats have taken to living near people, especially in our houses, farms and food stores. They cause damage and also spread diseases. The fleas that live on certain rats may bite people and spread plague. House mice get into kitchens and food cupboards. Brown and roof rats are a nuisance in grain stores.

Lemmings have blunt noses, small ears, rounded bodies and thick fur. These features help them stay warm in their cold northern homelands. They live among grasses and bushes on the ground, feeding on roots and shoots. When conditions are good and food is plentiful, lemmings breed so fast that they end up eating all of the available food.

The yellow-necked mouse is common in farmland and woods across Europe. It may even come into houses in the autumn, to escape the cold and look for food. It eats mainly seeds, berries and insects.

Once the food supplies have gone, many lemmings set off on a mass migration to find new places to live. During these "lemming years", they become bold and aggressive. At first they travel only at night. But soon they journey by day too. The urge to move on is so strong that they enter towns and cross streets, and even dive into rivers or tumble off cliffs. These migrations have led to legends that the lemmings really want to die!

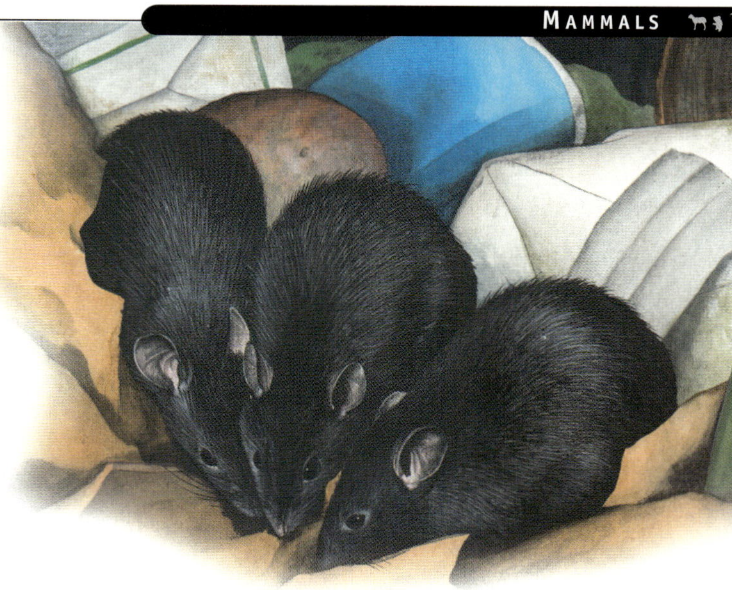

Black or ship rats have spread around the world, from their original homeland of tropical Asia. They travel on ships, being agile enough to climb aboard along the mooring ropes.

BIG CHEEKS

The hamster is a familiar pet, yet it is rarely seen in the wild. Its original home was the steppe grasslands of eastern Europe, but it has now spread into central Europe too. Hamsters eat many foods. They carry what they cannot consume back to the nest, filling their stretchy cheek pouches. In the wild, many hamsters hibernate during winter. But they wake up every few days to nibble at their store of nuts, berries and other food.

Another group of small rodents is the jerboas. They have very long back legs and jump exceptionally well, using the long tail to balance.

Naked mole rats work together for the good of the colony, like bees or ants. Only the chief female, or queen, can have babies. The rest are "workers" and do specific jobs.

Jerboas live in the deserts of North Africa, the Middle East, and Central Asia. They feed mainly on seeds and insects. Gerbils are similar to jerboas, but they have shorter back legs and smaller ears. Like jerboas, they spend the day in their burrows, to avoid predators and also the intense desert heat.

When lemmings become too numerous in an area, they have a strong instinct to set off and look for less crowded places.

SLEEPING MICE

Common dormice are about the same size as house mice. But they have soft, light brown fur and a furry tail. They are well known for their long winter sleep or hibernation. The name "dormouse" comes from the French word *dormir*, "to sleep". In summer they eat flowers, shoots, nuts, berries, insects and spiders.

African naked mole rats have hardly any fur and live entirely underground, in large colonies. They chisel through the soil with their huge front teeth. Members of the colony have different jobs. Some are diggers, some gather food, and some guard against intruders. Only one female, the queen, can produce young. Apart from certain insects, this type of colony is unique in the animal world.

Jumping mice bound along like miniature kangaroos. They can cover more than 1.8 m in a single leap. Fast reactions and speed help small rodents elude their many predators.

RODENTS
- 1,700 species
- long, sharp gnawing front teeth
- most are small and nocturnal

Some groups of small rodents:

Old World rats and mice
- 480 species

New World rats and mice
- 365 species

Pocket mice
- 65 species

Spiny rats
- 55 species

Jerboas
- 31 species

Jumping mice and birch mice
- 14 species

Dormice
- 10 species

African mole rats
- 9 species

Cane rats
- 2 species

Chinchilla rats
- 2 species

Rock rat
- 1 species

LARGE RODENTS

PORCUPINES, BEAVERS, CHINCHILLAS AND COYPUS ARE ALL LARGE RODENTS, BUT THE BIGGEST OF ALL IS THE CAPYBARA OF SOUTH AMERICA. The size of a sheep, the capybara lives in forests near lakes and rivers, and feeds on waterside vegetation. It has partly webbed toes and spends much of its time wading and swimming. The American beaver is another huge rodent, with a head and body about 1m long, and webbed feet suited to life in water. The crested porcupine of Africa is large too, with a head and body about 80 cm long. Like other porcupines, it is protected by spines which are thicker, sharper versions of normal mammal fur.

The tree porcupine has long toe claws and a muscular, curly, prehensile tail for gripping branches.

In the wild, chinchillas live in multi-family groups of about 50–100. They eat almost any kind of plant food.

Young capybaras can run and swim a few hours after birth. Capybaras live in family groups and feed mainly at dusk and dawn. They are preyed on by large cats, especially jaguars, and big snakes such as anacondas.

BEAVERS

Beavers gnaw through trunks to fell trees. They feed on the soft, sap-rich bark. They also use the logs and branches to build a wall or dam across a stream. Then they construct their home or lodge in the pool that forms behind the dam. The lodge gives protection against winter weather and predators such as wolves. Both dam and lodge are strengthened and cemented with stones and mud. The lodge has several tunnels leading from the living quarters down into the water. It also has a "chimney" leading upwards for fresh air. In cold weather, the beaver family stays in the lodge. They feed on twigs, bark and leaves which they have stored in the lodge or jammed under stones in their pool.

Inside a beaver's lodge, a mother suckles her young. When they reach two years of age, they will leave and build their own lodges.

Coypus can cause damage because they raid farm crops and dig burrows in the banks of drainage channels.

The beaver has a unique feature among rodents: its flat, scaly, paddle-like tail. This has two main uses. When the beaver swims with its webbed back feet, the tail is used as a rudder for steering. If the beaver senses danger, it slaps its tail onto the water's surface with a loud splash, to warn others of its family group.

PORCUPINES

There are two main groups of porcupines. The American or New World porcupines live mainly in trees and most have prehensile tails. They feed on leaves, fruits and shoots, feeding mostly at night. The Old World porcupines of Europe, Africa and Asia are ground-dwellers. At night they grub about in the soil for roots and other plant food. They also feed on fruits and berries, and can damage crops. By day, they sleep in their burrows.

Porcupines cannot "shoot" their spines, or quills, at enemies. Instead, they rush at an attacker and turn around to jab in the spines. If the spines pierce the skin, they come away from the porcupine's body and work into the flesh.

The biggest spines on the crested porcupine's back are 30 cm long. This rodent rattles special hollow tail spines as a warning that it may charge backwards at an attacker.

MAIN GROUPS OF LARGER RODENTS
(continued from page 207):

Porcupines • 21 species	Pacas • 2 species
Beavers • 2 species	Degus • 8 species
Mountain beaver • 1 species	Tuco-tucos • 33 species
Springhare • 1 species	Gundis • 5 species
Agoutis • 13 species	Chinchillas • 6 species
Hutias • 13 species	Capybara • 1 species
Pacarana • 1 species	Coypu • 1 species

CAVIES

Maras are active by day. They search for any type of plant material to eat, including grass, shoots, leaves and fruits. They can run almost as fast as a hare, bounding along in a similar manner using their strong back legs.

Among the South American cavy group there are several large species. The mara of Argentina has a head and body up to 75 cm long, and very long legs. It grazes in open grassland and can outrun most predators, sprinting at 45 km/h. Agoutis are also large cavies. They look like giant, tailless rats. They feed by day on plants and rest at night in burrows. An agouti can leap over 2 m straight upwards to avoid danger.

OLDEST... !

Porcupines are among the longest-lived rodents. The oldest known individual was at least 27 years of age when it died in a zoo. Since porcupines are so well protected by their spines, they may live almost as long in the wild.

Another group of cavies is the chinchillas and viscachas. The chinchilla itself is now rare in its natural habitat, the rocky uplands of the Andes mountains. But it is commonly kept as a pet, and some are still farmed for their fur, which is the finest and softest of any mammal. In the wild, this fur keeps the chinchilla warm in the bitter Andean winter, and is kept in good condition by regular dust baths.

The coypu is another large rodent of the cavy group. Swimming, it looks similar to a beaver, but has a rat-like tail. It eats water plants and rests by day in tunnels.

The beaver's sharp gnawing teeth, the incisors, can cut down a small tree in a few minutes.

SQUIRRELS AND CHIPMUNKS

European red squirrel

SQUIRRELS ARE BRIGHT-EYED, PERT-EARED, SHORT-NOSED, BUSHY-TAILED RODENTS THAT LEAP AROUND IN TREES AND FEED ON NUTS. Actually, this is true of most squirrels, but not all. Some members of the squirrel family live on the ground and hardly ever venture into trees In fact, rather than climb above the surface, they tunnel beneath it and live in underground burrows. These ground squirrels include marmots, chipmunks, prairie dogs and sousliks. But most squirrels stay high above ground in the branches, and flying squirrels can even glide from tree to tree.

Tree-dwelling squirrels are skilled climbers and leapers. They cling onto the bark with their sharp claws, and use the long, bushy tail as a balance when running along a branch, and as a rudder when leaping to another bough. The claws grip so firmly that a squirrel can race head-first down a tree trunk.

Thirteen-lined ground squirrel

The familiar grey squirrel lived originally in eastern North America. It has spread to Europe and southern Africa. Like its cousin the European red squirrel, it builds a main nest, or drey, from twigs and leaves. About the size of a soccer ball, the drey is usually anchored high in the fork of a tree branch. It has a soft lining of grasses and moss. Smaller dreys are used as temporary shelters. A larger, stronger drey is built to rear the young and as a winter refuge. In cold weather, tree squirrels stay in their dreys and sleep. Unlike some ground squirrels, they do not go into the very deep sleep of true hibernation. They emerge from time to time and search for food, especially in mild weather.

Some ground squirrels sleep very deeply, or hibernate, in their nests during the cold season. The Arctic ground squirrel of Alaska and northern Canada is perhaps the record-holder. It hibernates for up to nine months of the year.

The groundhog or woodchuck is one of the largest marmots, with a head-body length of 80 cm.

Eastern chipmunk

Many squirrels store food, mainly seeds and nuts, when it is plentiful. This happens especially in the autumn, as the squirrel prepares for the cold season. Grey squirrels regularly bury acorns or beech mast (nuts) in the soil, returning to dig them up later. But they lose or forget about many of the nuts. However, in doing this, they act as tree planters. This helps to offset the damage that some squirrels do in woodlands and timber plantations. They nibble bark and injure or even kill trees.

There are at least 50 species of flying squirrels, most from Asia. They glide on furry flaps of skin stretched between front and back legs.

Marmots and prairie dogs are stout-bodied, short-tailed or tailless ground squirrels. Most dwell in underground burrows. In Europe, Alpine marmots scamper over high meadows and rocky slopes. Many family groups live close together, their burrow entrances dotted over the ground. The burrows may go down 3 m, ending in a hay-lined sleeping chamber. In the autumn, the marmots collect grass, seeds, nuts, fruits and other plant food. Then they retreat underground, sealing the entrances with soil and hay, and hibernate huddled together. North American prairie dogs live in bigger colonies called townships, some with thousands of members.

The rat-sized European souslik inhabits warm, dry grasslands, where it digs deep tunnels in the soil.

The scaly-tailed squirrels of West African forests are not true squirrels, but they are rodents and have a similar lifestyle. They glide like flying squirrels and feed mainly on fruits and nuts. The pocket gophers of North America are expert diggers, using their large front claws and chisel-like teeth. Both grow about 1 mm each day to replace the wear.

Golden-mantled ground squirrel

MAIN GROUPS OF SQUIRREL-LIKE RODENTS (continued from page 207):

Squirrels and marmots
- 267 species
- includes tree squirrels, ground squirrels such as prairie dogs, chipmunks, marmots, sousliks

Pocket gophers
- 34 species

Scaly-tailed squirrels
- 7 species

Pocket mice
- 65 species

Prairie dogs are named for their dog-like, yapping "barks". Shown right is a black-tailed prairie dog.

DEER, CAMELS AND PIGS

MAMMALS WITH HOOVES RATHER THAN CLAWS ON THEIR FEET ARE CALLED UNGULATES. There are 203 species, all plant-eaters, in two main groups. The larger group is the even-toed ungulates, with two or four hoofed toes on each foot. They include deer, cattle, antelopes, giraffes, hippos, pigs, camels and llamas. The odd-toed ungulates have one, three or five hooves per foot (page 216). All even-toed ungulates, except pigs and peccaries, have a special form of digestion. The stomach is divided into several chambers. Food goes into the first chamber, the rumen, where it is part-digested. Then the animal brings it up and "chews the cud" before swallowing it again for the rest of digestion.

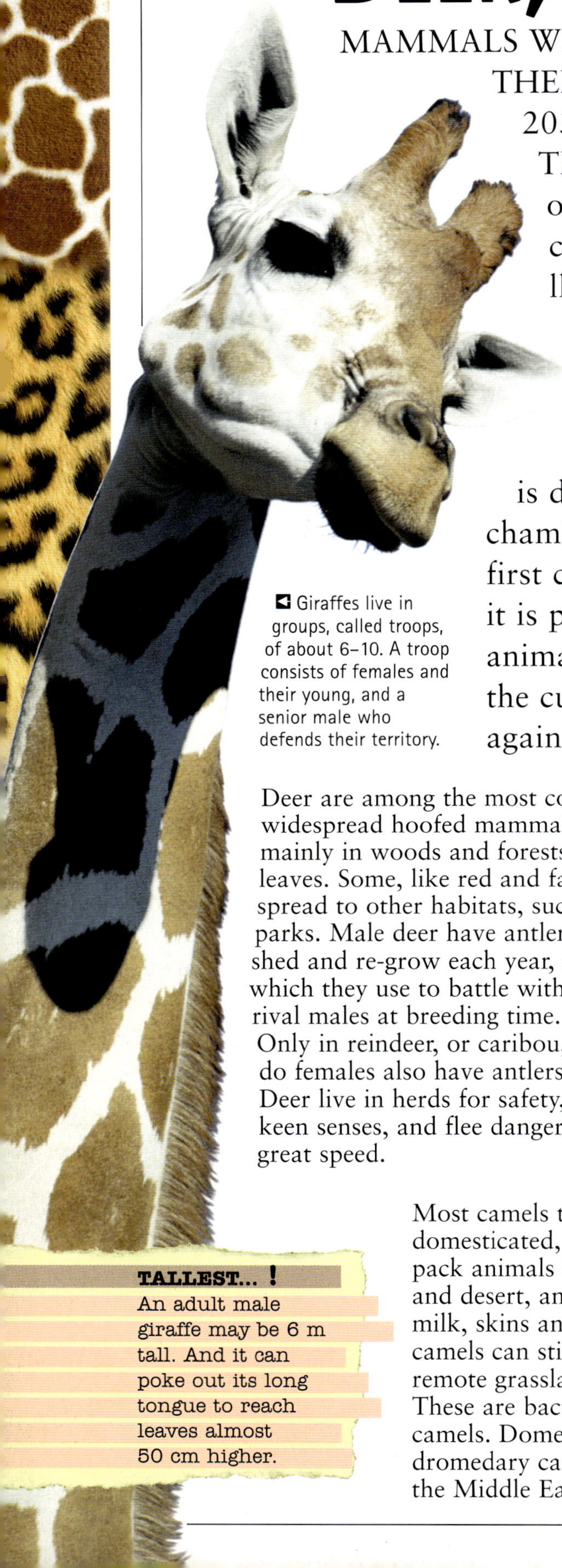

◄ Giraffes live in groups, called troops, of about 6–10. A troop consists of females and their young, and a senior male who defends their territory.

▲ During the breeding season, male deer like this wapiti bellow and threaten rival males for control of the herd. This is called the rut.

Deer are among the most common and widespread hoofed mammals. They live mainly in woods and forests, browsing on leaves. Some, like red and fallow deer, have spread to other habitats, such as moors and parks. Male deer have antlers, which they shed and re-grow each year, and which they use to battle with rival males at breeding time. Only in reindeer, or caribou, do females also have antlers. Deer live in herds for safety, have keen senses, and flee danger at great speed.

Most camels today are domesticated, used as pack animals in dry scrub and desert, and to provide meat, milk, skins and hair. But some wild camels can still be found in the remote grasslands of Mongolia. These are bactrian or two-humped camels. Domestic one-humped or dromedary camels live throughout the Middle East and North Africa. Some dromedaries were taken to Australia, as pack animals for the inland deserts, and now live wild in the outback.

WOOLLY COUSINS

The llama, alpaca, guanaco and vicuna of South America are close relatives of camels. They live mainly on the slopes of the Andes mountains and have thick, woolly coats. Llamas and alpacas are domesticated, kept as pack animals and for their fine wool. The vicuna is a protected species.

◄ Camels survive for days without food and weeks without a drink. They obtain some moisture from food, and also make water in their bodies because of their specialized body chemistry. A camel can gulp 50 litres in a few minutes.

TALLEST... !

An adult male giraffe may be 6 m tall. And it can poke out its long tongue to reach leaves almost 50 cm higher.

▶ Wild pigs like the warthog use their tusks and strong snouts to grub in the soil for their varied food of roots, bulbs and small animals.

Giraffes are so tall they are easy to spot in their homeland of the African savanna (grassland). They use their great height to reach tasty buds, leaves and fruits in the tree tops. The okapi is a close relative of the giraffe. This extremely shy forest dweller is seldom seen in the wild. It stands almost 1.8 m tall and has a giraffe-like head, neck and body, although the neck is not quite as long in proportion to the body as the giraffe's. It also has striped legs like a zebra.

▲ A fallow deer youngster, or fawn, feeds on its mother's milk.

WILD PIGS

The wild ancestor of our domestic pigs is the wild boar. It has thick fur and a large, powerful head. Wild boars are common in woods and forests in many parts of Europe and Asia. There are another seven species of wild pigs, including the African warthog and the very rare, protected babirusa of Sulawesi in Southeast Asia. Most have tusks formed from their up-curved canine teeth. Peccaries are very similar to wild pigs but have tusks in the upper jaw that grow downwards. They live mainly in South and Central America.

▲ Llamas are South American relatives of camels. They eat mainly grass.

The hippopotamus is the largest even-toed ungulate. Hippos live in Africa, in groups of 10–15. They spend the day lazing in rivers, lakes or water holes. They emerge at night to graze waterside plants, moving along regular pathways. The much smaller pygmy hippo is a rare animal of swampy forests in west and central Africa. It is an endangered species, with just a few thousand left.

UNGULATES
- 203 species
- hoofed feet

Even-toed ungulates:

Deer
- 36 species including red, fallow, sika, roe, caribou (reindeer), elk (moose), muntjac

Camels and llamas
- 6 species

Giraffe and okapi
- 2 species

Wild pigs
- 8 species

Peccaries
- 3 species

Hippos
- 2 species

Chevrotains
- 4 species

Musk deer
- 3 species

▼ The tusks of a hippo are really large canine teeth. They may be 50 cm long. Male hippos sometimes fight each other for females or territory and can inflict nasty wounds with their tusks. Hippos are the third largest land animals. A big male may reach a length of 4 m and weigh well over 3 tonnes.

ANTELOPES, WILD CATTLE AND SHEEP

Wild goats live from Greece and Turkey across to India. They are the ancestors of farmyard goats.

CATTLE, SHEEP, AND GOATS WERE PROBABLY TAMED FROM ABOUT 9,000 YEARS AGO, MAKING THEM SOME OF THE FIRST DOMESTICATED ANIMALS. The many breeds of cows today are descended from the wild aurochs, which roamed the forests of Europe and Asia, but which finally died out in the 17th century. Like antelopes, cattle have horns that grow throughout their lives and are not shed, unlike the antlers of deer. Most antelopes and gazelles are fairly large, long-legged, fast-running grazers and browsers of grasslands and open scrub.

The wild cattle group, known as bovids, includes the American bison or buffalo and European bison. Both species became rare due to hunting by humans. American buffalo are now protected in sanctuaries in the open plains and Canadian woodlands. European bison were almost extinct, but now live in several forest sanctuaries, especially in Poland and Russia.

There are two varieties of American buffalo. The wood buffalo is larger and darker than the plains buffalo, which lives further south.

The yak is another species of cattle. It lives on the high plains of Tibet, at altitudes of 6,000 m. Few wild yaks survive, but there are many domesticated yaks, which are kept by local people for their meat, milk, skins and hair.

North American mountain goats live high on snowfields and along edges of glaciers.

Another domesticated species of cattle is the water buffalo, which came originally from India and Southeast Asia. It has the largest horns of any living animal, with a record tip-to-tip spread of more than 4 m. Water buffalo have been taken to Africa, South America and Australia, where some have returned to the wild.

SHEEP AND GOATS

As with cattle, there are various species of wild sheep and goats, and some have been domesticated. Wild species include the wild goat of eastern Europe and Asia, the chamois and mouflon of Europe and the Middle East, and the American bighorn sheep. Chamois are very agile and sure-footed, leaping over high mountain crags. Their hooves have soft pads with hard edges, to help them grip even on smooth, slippery wet rocks. The ibex of eastern Europe, north Africa and Asia is another mountain dweller, normally found above the timber line. It climbs to even higher levels to avoid the summer heat, then descends to sheltered lower slopes for the winter.

Wild water buffalo survive in a few parts of Africa and Asia, mainly in swampy areas.

THE LONGEST COAT

Musk ox from northern North America look like wild cattle, but they are members of the sheep and goat group. They stand about 1.4 m tall at the shoulder and have the longest hair of any wild mammal, reaching 90 cm on the neck and flanks. This thick coat protects them from fierce Arctic storms. Like most cattle, sheep, goats, antelopes and gazelles, they live in herds. If danger or bad weather threatens, the adults huddle together and face outwards to protect the young in the middle.

KEEN SENSES

Antelopes and gazelles are known for their speed and agility. Keen senses give them early warning of predators. Most antelopes live on the African savanna (grassland). Several species, such as springbok, Thomson's gazelles and Grant's gazelles, gather in huge herds. Some antelopes, such as hartebeest, have short horns. Others, such as the sable antelope and gemsbok, have longer horns. The largest antelope species is the giant eland of Africa, at 3 m long and 1.8 m at the shoulder.

Some antelopes and gazelles, like springbok, leap straight up more than 3 m. This is called pronking. It shows predators such as lions that they are fit and difficult to catch.

Male cattle, sheep, goats, antelopes and gazelles use their horns to battle with rivals at breeding time. In Thomson's gazelles, the male has much larger, thicker horns than the female.

MORE GROUPS OF EVEN-TOED UNGULATES (continued from page 213):

Cattle
- 23 species, including domestic cattle, yak, water buffalo, African buffalo, American and European bison, kudus, elands, bongo, nyala

Sheep and goats
- 26 species, including saiga, musk ox, chamois, ibex, markhor, mountain goat, Barbary sheep, mouflon, bighorn sheep

Duikers
- 17 species

Gazelles and dwarf antelopes
- 30 species, including Grant's gazelle, Thomson's gazelle, dikdik, blackbuck, springbok, gerenuk

Grazing antelopes
- 24 species, including waterbuck, wildebeest (gnu), impala, sable antelope, oryx, lechwe, addax

Pronghorn
- 1 species

HORSES, ZEBRAS AND RHINOS

An adult tapir has a dark brown coat.

THE HOOFED MAMMALS CALLED ODD-TOED UNGULATES ARE A MUCH SMALLER GROUP THAN THE EVEN-TOED UNGULATES (PAGE 212). They include wild horses, asses and zebras, which are very similar in general body size and shape, and also rhinos and tapirs. Horses and zebras have long legs for fast running in open country. Like cows and sheep, horses have been domesticated and there are now many breeds of different sizes and colours. Rhinos are huge mammals – the white rhino is the third-largest land animal, after the two kinds of elephants. Tapirs are smaller, pig-like animals of South America, with one species in Southeast Asia.

Horses, donkeys, asses and zebras are all known as equids. All domestic horses belong to the species *Equus caballus*. They are probably descended from horses that looked very similar to Przewalski's horse, *Equus przewalskii*, of the Mongolian steppe (grassland) in Central Asia. There are no longer any truly wild members of this species. It was rescued from extinction by being domesticated by local Mongolian people, and being bred in various wildlife parks. It may be possible to re-establish wild herds of Przewalski's horses in their Mongolian homeland.

A baby Brazilian tapir is born with spots and stripes, but these fade and disappear when it becomes an adult.

There are two species of wild ass, one in Africa and one in Asia. Domestic donkeys are descended from a form of the African wild ass. Asses are smaller than horses and have longer ears, a more uneven mane and a tufted tail.

All rhinos are very similar in appearance. The white or square-lipped rhino (below) has a small hump on its back, just in front of the hips. The exceptionally thick skin of the Indian rhino is creased into deep folds at the shoulders and hips. Rhinos are usually peaceful but if they are threatened they will charge.

STRIPED HORSES

Zebras are "striped horses". The three species live mainly on the plains of east and southern Africa. Like all equids, zebras live in herds.

No one knows why zebras have such vivid stripes. Each zebra's stripe pattern is unique, so perhaps herd members use the markings to recognize each other.

Zebras use their speed to flee from large predators such as lions, hunting dogs and hyenas.

All equids have just one large hoofed toe on each foot. Rhinoceroses – rhinos for short – have three hoofed toes per foot. They are bulky animals with very thick skin, almost like armour plating. Unlike horses, rhinos generally live alone and have small eyes and poor sight. But their large ears can pick up the faintest sounds and they also have an excellent sense of smell.

Like all odd-toed ungulates, rhinos are plant-eaters. They graze on tough grasses and scrubby bushes. Both males and females have horns, but these are not true horn or bone, they are made of very tightly packed hairs. The white rhino reaches 4.3 m in head–body length, stands over 1.8 m tall at the shoulder and weighs over 3 tonnes. Smallest of the five species is the Sumatran rhino, which is just 2.5 m in length.

World Watch

All rhino species are hunted for their horns. Some people believe that the powdered horn has medicinal or magical powers. Horns are also made into trinkets and traditional dagger handles. White rhinos have increased in recent years in protected areas of southern Africa. But the other four species are all very rare. Most threatened is the small Javan rhino. Just a few dozen survive in one or two forest wildlife reserves.

TAPIR "TRUNK"

Tapirs live deep in the tropical forests and swamps of South America and Southeast Asia. They resemble pigs, but without the flat-ended snout. A tapir has a long, flexible upper lip, which it uses to gather food. The South American tapirs are reddish-brown; the Malayan tapir is black and white. All are about 2.5 m in length.

In many parts of the world, horses have escaped from captivity to run free on plains and hills. They grow up wild, but they can usually be caught and tamed.

ODD-TOED UNGULATES (continued from page 213):

Horses, asses and zebras
- 7 species, including domestic horse, Przewalski's horse, African ass, Asiatic ass, Grevy's zebra, mountain zebra, plains zebra

Rhinos
- 5 species, including black rhino, white rhino, Indian rhino, Javan rhino, Sumatran rhino

Tapirs
- 4 species, including Malayan tapir, Brazilian tapir, Baird's tapir, mountain tapir

ELEPHANTS

ELEPHANTS ARE THE LARGEST LAND ANIMALS. AFRICAN ELEPHANTS, WITH THEIR HUGE EARS AND LONGER TUSKS, ARE BIGGER THAN ASIAN ELEPHANTS. These great mammals are famed for their size, strength and stamina, and also for their long lives and complex herd behaviour. People have long trained elephants, especially in Asia, for farming, logging, hunting, warfare and ceremonies. Sadly, people also threaten their survival, especially in Africa, mainly through killing them for their ivory tusks.

World Watch

Elephant tusks are made mainly of a hard, white substance called ivory. This has been treasured through the ages for making tools, ornaments, weapons and decorative carvings. Despite wildlife laws and patrolling wardens, many elephants are still killed illegally for their tusks. However in a few areas where elephants are common, limited legal hunting may be allowed in future.

ELEPHANTS

- 2 species
- African elephant scattered across central, east and southern Africa, common in a few small areas
- Asian elephant found in India, Sri Lanka, southern China and Southeast Asia (rare in wild)

African elephants live mainly south of the Sahara Desert in a wide range of habitats including grassland, forests and dry, thorny scrub. Asian elephants are found mainly in the forests of India, Sri Lanka and Southeast Asia. Most Asian elephants are kept and trained by people. Fewer than 50,000 live in the wild, in hilly and remote jungle.

▲ Elephants sniff and caress each other when they meet, to make sure that they are from the same herd, not intruders.

▼ The Asian elephant has a more domed forehead and humped back than the African elephant. It squirts water, mud or dust over itself to keep cool and to get rid of irritating skin pests.

In each species, a small family group lives together. They move slowly and steadily, feeding mainly on grasses, bark, leaves and twigs. They spend up to 18 hours feeding and consume about 180 kg of food each day. An elephant walks at an average speed of 5 km/h. However, if it senses danger, it can sprint away or charge at the attacker at up to 40 km/h – which is faster than a human could run away.

Elephants keep in touch with their herd members in several ways. They have a simple language of deep growls and rumbles which carry for hundreds of metres in open country. They also sniff the air with their trunks, and they touch other herd members with their trunks too. In fact the elephant's trunk, an extra-long nose with a flexible tip (one lip in Asian elephants, two in African), has many jobs. It is used for grasping food, squirting water or dust, greeting other elephants and guiding babies or calves.

▶ As drinking holes shrink in the dry season, the herd relies on the long memory of the matriarch (senior female), who may be more than 60 years old. She knows places where there may still be water. The elephants gouge a hole with their tusks and sip the water that collects in it.

ELEPHANT ANATOMY

Elephants are some of the most specialized of all mammals. Their tusks, trunks, ears and feet are different from those of most mammals.

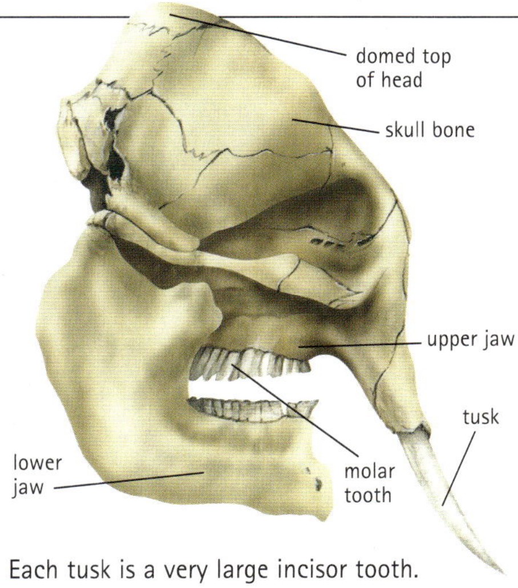

Each tusk is a very large incisor tooth.

The foot rests on a broad pad of tough fibres and fat that works as a cushion to spread the animal's weight.

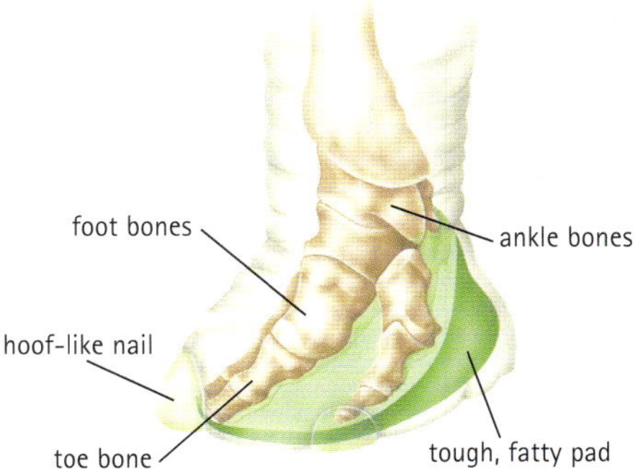

The Asian elephant has a single, flexible "nose-lip" at the end of its trunk. The African elephant has a double nose-lip.

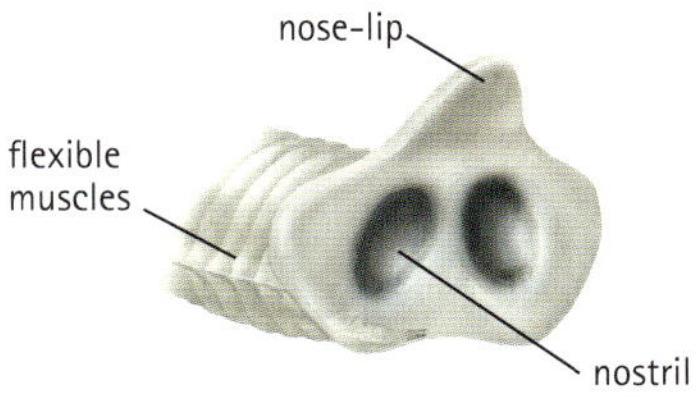

KEEPING COOL

An elephant cannot drink through its trunk. But it sucks water into the trunk and then squirts the water into its mouth – or over its back for a cooling "shower". Elephants also keep cool by bathing in mud and flapping their ears. The ears work like radiators to lose excess body heat into the air.

OVERSIZED TEETH

An elephant's tusks are its incisor teeth. They start to grow at about two years of age, and continue to grow throughout the animal's life. Both males and females have them, but usually in female Asian elephants they are short and hidden by the trunk and the lower lips.

LARGEST... !

The largest African male elephants stand 4 m tall at the shoulder, measure 10 m from trunk tip to tail tip, and weigh over 6 tonnes. The tusks can be over 3 m long.

An elephant herd is led by the matriarch. She remembers the location of seasonal feeding places.

CATS

"CARNIVORE" MEANS "MEAT-EATER". The Carnivora group includes mammals with long, sharp claws to catch prey and long, sharp teeth to rip it up. This group is described over the next ten pages, starting with the most carnivorous of all – the cats. Some carnivores scavenge or eat the occasional fruit or berry. But the cats are active hunters of living prey, with large eyes to see in the dark, and claws which (except for the cheetah) can be pulled back into the toes to keep them sharp. The carnivore group also includes wolves and wild dogs, hyenas, bears, raccoons, pandas, civets, genets, weasels, mongooses and, in the sea, seals and sea lions.

▲ The lynx lives in all northern continents. It is similar to the bobcat (opposite, top right), but larger, with bigger ear and cheek tufts. It takes larger prey such as hares and young deer.

▲ The cheetah is the fastest land animal over short distances. It can reach speeds of more than 95 km/h. But it gives up after about 180 m if the prey seems to be getting away.

Cats are found around the world in many habitats, from cold mountains to moist tropical forests. They combine strength and stealth with speed and agility, using their excellent eyesight, hearing and smell.

Cats are a uniform group, which means they are very similar in overall body shape and features – and also in their hunting methods. Most live alone and prowl at night. They stalk their prey quietly, keeping low near the ground. Then they make a quick dash to grab the victim, holding it down with their hooked claws and biting it with their long, sharp canine teeth. The large, sharp-edged cheek teeth or carnassials can shear through tough skin, sinews and gristle.

Lions are the only cats that live and hunt in groups, called prides. The large, shaggy-maned chief male patrols the pride's territory, roaring and leaving scent marks to warn off other prides. The lionesses do the hunting, often as a team to bring down a zebra or wildebeest. One or two lionesses walk towards the victim, to drive it towards the others who are waiting in ambush.

▲ Ocelots range from southern North America down to South America. They are expert swimmers and climbers, catching birds in the trees and frogs in the water.

▼ A lion pride is led by the chief male. Females or lionesses lack the long neck mane. Cubs lose their spots as they grow.

THE DOG-LIKE CAT

The cheetah is built more like a greyhound than a cat, with a long, flexible back, long slim legs and a relatively small head. It hurls itself after its prey with an amazing burst of speed, rather than stalking. The serval is a smaller version of the cheetah, but has larger ears. It also lives in Africa, hunts by day and races after prey such as hares.

Leopards often drop onto their prey from a branch, then drag the corpse back up to keep it safe from other animals, before indulging in a treetop feast.

The bobcat can climb, but it prefers to hunt on the ground for rats, rabbits and running gamebirds such as grouse.

Tigers are the biggest cats, and the rare Siberian tiger is the biggest of the tigers. It measures 3 m long and weighs over 300 kg.

THE BLACK "PANTHER"

The most adaptable of the seven species of big cat is the leopard. It has short legs and a muscular body, and swims or climbs after its prey. It often prowls near towns and villages and may lie on a branch, ready to drop silently on a victim passing below. Some leopards are born with almost black fur, and are called black panthers. The snow leopard or ounce is slightly smaller than the leopard and has very thick fur, to keep out the cold in its Asian mountain home. It can easily leap across an icy ravine 3 m wide.

SMALLER CATS

There are smaller cats on almost every continent. Most are about 80–110 cm long, including the tail. They live in trees, using the tail to help them balance, and hunt birds, snakes, lizards, squirrels and small monkeys. The pampas cat of South America is at home on grassland, where it pursues rodents and ground birds.

TAME CATS?

The many types of domestic cat were probably bred from the African wild cat, beginning in Egypt some 4,000 years ago. These first domestic cats probably caught mice in grain stores. Pet cats have the night-prowling, hunting instincts of their wild ancestors. In some areas, they have returned to live and breed in the wild, and are called feral cats.

Cats *(felids)*

Big cats
- 7 species
- sharp teeth and claws
- can roar loudly

Lion
- Africa

Tiger
- South and East Asia

Jaguar
- Central and South America

Leopard
- Africa, South Asia

Snow leopard
- Central Asia

Clouded leopard
- Southeast Asia

Cheetah
- Africa, Middle East

Small cats
- 28 species
- resemble big cats, but smaller
- most cannot roar loudly

Small cats include the cougar (puma or mountain lion, the largest small cat), lynx, bobcat, caracal, ocelot, margay, leopard cat, African wild cat, European wild cat, black-footed cat (the smallest small cat)

DOGS, FOXES AND HYENAS

▲ The fennec fox of North Africa hunts small prey such as termites and other insects, mainly by sound, so it has very large ears.

THE DOG FAMILY INCLUDES WOLVES, FOXES AND JACKALS, AS WELL AS THE FAMILIAR DOMESTIC DOG, WHICH WAS PROBABLY BRED FROM THE GREY WOLF. All of these carnivores (page 220) are strong and agile, with long legs for distance running, muscular bodies, powerful sharp-toothed jaws, and keen senses of sight, hearing and especially smell. They differ from cats mainly in that they have longer muzzles, they cannot pull their claws into their toes, and most live in pairs or larger groups called packs – apart from foxes, which dwell alone. Hyenas are also dog-like carnivores, but they are not members of the dog family.

▲ The coyote, with its mournful howl, may live alone but also gathers in packs to hunt.

Dogs have a different hunting technique from that of cats. Their long, powerful legs enable them to run well for long distances. They can track prey for many kilometres, following the scent until the prey tires and is caught.

▲ The grey wolf's strength, stamina and cunning are famed in myth and legend.

THE BIGGEST DOG

The grey wolf is the largest of the dog family, with a head–body length of 56 inches (130 cm).

▲ A male, or dog, red fox and a female, or vixen, chase in courtship before mating.

▼ The Arctic fox has thick fur that turns white in winter, matching its snowy surroundings.

It is found in remote scrub, forest, tundra and mountains – mainly because people have driven it away. Wolves eat a wide range of meat, from deer to mice, voles and lemmings. They also scavenge, and even take berries and fruits. The coyote is common in parts of North America, and resembles a smaller version of the wolf.

The maned wolf lives in tall grassland in parts of South America. It has red-brown fur and such long, slim legs that it looks like a "wolf on stilts".

The African wild dog is an endangered species. There are only about 5,000 left, mainly in one Tanzanian wildlife reserve. They are the most efficient of all pack hunters.

THE DOMESTIC DOG

All domestic dogs, from huge great danes to tiny chihuahuas, belong to one species, *Canis familiaris*. The first dogs were probably tamed from a type of grey wolf, as long as 10,000 years ago. The dingo of Australia may once have been an even earlier, part-domesticated form of the wolf. But dingoes now roam wild across large areas of Australia. The most carnivorous dogs are the African wild dogs, whose teeth are particularly large and sharp. They feed mainly on large mammals brought down by a pack of up to 20 members.

The striped hyena has a horse-like mane that extends from head to tail. It searches at night for carcasses of large animals already part-eaten by big cats.

WILY CUNNING

Most foxes are agile and stealthy, using a combination of stalking and running to catch prey. The red fox has a legendary reputation for cunning. It adapts to most habitats and foods, including those provided by people, so it has become one of the most widespread of all mammals. In spring and summer it feasts on eggs, young birds and rodents. In the autumn it fattens itself on fruits and berries and takes young rabbits and hares. In winter it raids rubbish bins and tips. Other foxes have similar wide tastes, ranging from crabs and dead fish along the water's edge to worms, beetles, snails, berries and fungi.

Most dogs bark, yip or yelp. But the dingo of the Australian outback rarely makes a sound.

Jackals are similar to foxes, although slightly larger, with a head–body length of 70–100 cm. They eat a wide range of foods, too. Unlike foxes, jackals live in family groups of four to six members. They hunt as a pack to catch prey such as small gazelles and antelopes.

Jackals, like most wild dogs, convey different messages to pack members by the positions of their ears, mouth, legs and tail.

THE MASTER SCAVENGERS

Hyenas do not belong to the dog family. But they are similar powerful carnivores. Far from slinking away like cowards, hyenas are very aggressive and successful pack-hunters. The hyena has one of the strongest sets of jaws and teeth in the animal kingdom. It is an expert scavenger, helping vultures to clear the remains of dead animals from the African plains. The hyena eats skin, chews gristle and cracks bones with ease. Some hyena groups do hunt and kill more than half their victims. Even lions are wary about trying to take a kill from a pack of hyenas.

Dogs *(canids)*

- large, sharp canine teeth
- long snouts
- claws cannot be pulled into toes
- most can bark or yelp

Larger wild dogs
- 4 species

Grey or timber wolf
- All northern lands

Red wolf
- Southeast North America

Coyote
- North and Central America

Dingo
- Australia, Southeast Asia

Other wild dogs
- 5 species including dhole, African wild dog, maned wolf, raccoon dog, bush dog

Jackals
- 4 species
- Africa, Middle East, India

Foxes
- 21 species
- worldwide

Hyenas
- 4 species
- Africa, Middle East

BEARS, RACCOONS AND PANDAS

The tree-dwelling sun bear of Southeast Asia is the smallest bear. It has a head-body length of only 1.2 m.

BEARS ARE NOT ESPECIALLY CARNIVOROUS. They catch prey such as deer, birds and fish. But they also scratch up worms and grubs, raid wild bees' nests for honey and eat buds, fruits, seeds and roots. However, like other carnivores, they have sharp teeth and strong jaws. They are big and muscular, with powerful limbs and huge paws. Raccoons are much smaller and look like a combination of bear and dog. They live across North, Central and South America. The red panda is similar to a raccoon and dwells in eastern Asia. Its cousin is one of the world's rarest yet best-known creatures – the giant panda.

Asian black bear

Red panda

Brown bears feast on salmon as they try to leap up waterfalls on their way to their spawning places upstream.

◘ The giant panda is a member of the carnivore group, but it hardly ever eats meat. It consumes mainly stems and leaves of bamboos.

Bears may look friendly and cuddly. But the larger species are massive, powerful animals, and sometimes dangerous to people – especially a mother bear protecting her young. If a bear is disturbed, it may charge as its main method of self-defence. Bears were once hunted for their fur, to protect farm animals and for "sport". Today most species are rare and live in remote places. Because of their unpredictable nature, they are best left undisturbed.

◘ The kinkajou lives in Central and northern South America. It rests in a tree hole by day and comes out at night to feed on small animals and fruits. Its tail is prehensile, working like a fifth limb to grasp branches.

The creamy white fur of the polar bear blends in well with its snowy, icy habitat in the far north. This camouflage helps it to stalk seals on the ice without being detected. As well as very thick fur, polar bears have a thick layer of fat under their skin to keep out the cold. A polar bear can run fast and even catch young or sick reindeer. Like other bears, it has poor eyesight and relies mainly on smell. It can scent a seal or walrus carcass 3 km away.

VARIABLE BEARS

The Asian (Himalayan) black bear has a silky coat with a white V-shaped chest mark and large, rounded ears. It is an expert climber, eats ants and grubs as well as fruits and nuts, and often rests in the branches. The small sun bear lives in the forests of Southeast Asia, where it feeds on fruits, termites, small birds and mammals. The brown bear species is very variable and includes the grizzly, Kodiak and Alaskan bears. The smallest variety is the European brown bear, now very rare, found in a few mountainous regions as far south as Italy and Spain.

◘ The grizzly or brown bear shows its long canine teeth in a warning snarl that few animals will ignore.

The giant panda of China is easily recognized and extremely rare – with perhaps only 1,000 left in the wild. It looks like a bear, but it is not closely related to bears. There is so little goodness in its bamboo food that it eats for up to 15 hours each day. The red panda is related to the giant panda, but is much smaller, fox-like in shape, and with deep red fur.

ABOUT AT NIGHT

The common raccoon, with its "bandit" face mask, is a well-known night-time scavenger in North America. It eats fish, frogs, small birds and mammals, eggs, fruits, nuts, seeds – in fact, almost anything. The raccoon group includes coatis, from the forests of South and Central America. The coati's flexible, elongated nose sniffs out insects and similar small prey on the forest floor.

◘ The common raccoon, like the red fox, is adaptable and comes into cities to scavenge in rubbish. It can climb and swim well, and handles food delicately in its front paws.

Bears *(Ursids)*

- 7 species
- large head, wide face
- poor sight but keen smell
- bulky, sturdy body
- big paws and claws
- very short tail

Polar bear
- Arctic Ocean and far north

Brown bear
- all northern lands, southern Europe

American black bear
- North America

Asian black bear
- Central and South Asia

Sun bear
- Southeast Asia

Sloth bear
- India, Sri Lanka

Spectacled bear
- South America

Raccoons and pandas
- 17 species
- mostly long-bodied, bushy-tailed
- alert, agile and adaptable
- live mainly in trees
- Americas, apart from 2 panda species

Main groups of raccoons and pandas:

Raccoons
- 6 species including crab-eating raccoon

Coatis
- 4 species including ringtailed coati, white-nosed coati

Olingos
- 2 species

Ringtail and cacomistle
- 2 species

Kinkajou
- 1 species

Pandas
- 2 species, giant and red

WEASELS, MONGOOSES AND CIVETS

The smallest mammal carnivore is the least (dwarf) weasel of North America, a variety of common weasel. It is less than 20 cm long, including the tail.

THE SMALLEST OF THE MAMMAL CARNIVORES (PAGE 220) ARE WEASELS, STOATS, SKUNKS, BADGERS, MINK, OTTERS AND THEIR RELATIVES, KNOWN AS MUSTELIDS. They are mostly long and slender, with low-slung bodies and short legs, keen eyes and sharp teeth. They may be small, but when out hunting they are some of the most fearless and aggressive of all animals. However, they are otherwise shy and secretive, seldom seen in the wild except when they bound across the road. Mongooses, civets and genets are also small carnivores; mongooses resemble stoats, while civets, genets and linsangs are cat-like animals with bushy tails, found in southern Europe, Africa, and southern and Southeast Asia.

The spray from the striped skunk's glands at the base of its tail is so foul-smelling, it can stop the enemy breathing.

The wolverine or "glutton" lives in all northern lands, but is rare in many areas. It is so strong that it can drag prey as large as a deer for several kilometres.

Each type of mustelid takes different prey, according to its size. Weasels are specialist hunters of mice and voles, but they occasionally eat birds, frogs and baby rabbits. The weasel's small head and narrow body allow it to follow mice into their burrows. Stoats are larger, have a black tail tip, and hunt rats and rabbits. Pine martens are bigger still, and such skilled climbers that they can catch squirrels. The sable of Siberian forests has a head–body length of 40 cm and very thick, soft fur. It stays mainly on the ground, eats hares and similar animals, and also fruits and berries.

The sea otter of north and east Pacific coasts floats on its back to prepare food.

Wolverines are the largest members of the weasel family. They live in northern forests and tundra, and move quickly over loose snow with their broad feet. They scavenge on carrion, but also kill prey as large as reindeer, covering up to 40 km in search of food.

Meerkats often stand upright near their burrows to peer across the African grassland and bush, watching for danger.

The common genet is indeed common in some areas, but shy and nocturnal, so rarely seen.

The black-footed ferret of North America is one of the world's rarest mammals. It became extinct in the wild in the late 1980s, but has been bred in captivity, and may become re-established in its habitat.

Badgers are mainly nocturnal and eat many foods – worms, insects, small mammals, roots, seeds and fruits. Eurasian badgers live in family groups, in extensive burrows called setts. American badgers are fiercer and live in western North America.

AT HOME IN THE WATER

Otters are beautifully adapted to swimming at the water's surface and below it. They paddle with their webbed feet and swim faster by swaying the whole body and tail from side to side. Otter fur is waterproofed by plentiful oil made in the skin. The thick underfur traps tiny bubbles of air. These prevent waterlogging and also keep the otter warm. The giant otter of South America has a head–body length of up to 1.5 m.

Skunks live only in the Americas. The 13 species are all very similar, with black and white fur and bushy tails. They feed on insects, lizards, fruits and berries. They are known for spraying a horrible-smelling liquid if disturbed.

THE HELPFUL MONGOOSE

Mongooses live mainly in dry country, hunting a variety of mice, insects and other small animals, and occasionally eating fruit. Some species may tackle rats and even poisonous snakes. For this reason, people allow them to stay around towns and may even feed them. Most live alone, but banded mongooses and meerkats live in large family groups. Meerkats post sentries that stand upright looking out for enemies.

Civets, genets and linsangs are cat-like in build and habits. They stealthily hunt small animals at night, camouflaged by their spots and stripes. Most species live in Africa, India or Southeast Asia, with a few in southern Europe. Civets produce a powerful musky-smelling substance that was once collected for perfumes.

A mongoose avoids a snake's deadly bite by its agility and lightning-quick reactions.

WEASELS AND STOATS
(MUSTELIDS)

- 67 species
- small to medium size
- long, slim, flexible body
- short legs, medium tail
- very active predators
- all regions except Australia, Madagascar

Groups include:

Weasels, stoats and martens
- 33 species, including:

Common weasel (North America, Europe, Africa, Asia)
Stoat (North America, Europe, Asia, New Zealand)

Other species include American, pine and stone martens, fisher, polecat, grison, mink, sable, zorilla, wolverine (largest), black-footed ferret (rarest)

Skunks
- 13 species, including:

Striped skunk (North America)
Spotted skunk (North, Central America)

Otters
- 12 species, including:

Eurasian otter (Europe, Asia, Africa)
Cape clawless otter (Africa)
Giant otter (South America)

Badgers
- 9 species, including:

Eurasian badger (Europe to China)
American badger (North America)
Honey badger or ratel (Africa to India)

Mongooses, civets and genets
- 66 species
- long, flexible body
- active, agile predators

Mongooses
- 31 species
- Africa, southern Asia
- resemble weasels or stoats

Species include Egyptian mongoose, banded mongoose, meerkat (suricate), cusimanse

Civets and genets
- 35 species
- Europe, Africa, southern Asia
- cat-like
- large eyes and ears
- bushy tail

Species include African civet, common genet, African linsang, binturong, fanalouc, fossa

SEALS, SEA LIONS AND SEA COWS

Like all sea mammals, the manatee must come to the surface to breathe.

SEALS, SEA LIONS AND THE WALRUS ARE SUPERBLY ADAPTED TO LIFE IN THE WATER. Unlike whales and dolphins, however, they rarely venture into the open ocean. They usually stay near land because they must come ashore to breed, typically on rocky, isolated coasts or on ice. These mammals are all meat-eaters, taking prey such as fish and squid. Sea cows are large, slow-moving mammals that graze on water plants.

A seal swims by bending its body and pushing with its rear flippers, like a fish uses its tail. The front flippers are held by its sides or used to steer and brake.

Seals, sea lions and sea cows are all marine mammals – they live in the oceans. They all have limbs that are paddle-shaped for rowing themselves through the water. True or earless seals form the largest group, with 19 species. They do have ears, but these lack ear flaps and so are not noticeable on the outside. On land, seals are clumsy and can only slide or hump along slowly. Their rear flippers trail uselessly behind. But in water, few animals can match their speed and grace.

NO CRABS TO EAT

The most abundant seal by far, and one of the world's most numerous large wild mammals, is the crabeater seal. Some 20 million live on and around the pack ice of Antarctica. But it does not eat crabs!

A Galapagos sea lion mother prepares to feed her youngster. Baby seals are called pups.

Walruses live all around the seas and oceans of the far north. A 4-cm-thick layer of fatty blubber under skin keeps out the intense cold.

Crabs do not live in this habitat. Instead, the crabeater, like the great whales, feeds mainly on shrimp-like krill.

SEAL-EATING SEAL

Three other seals in the same region are the Weddell seal, the smaller Ross seal and the larger leopard seal. The first two dive to great depths, the Weddell seal descending to 450 m after fish and squid. The leopard seal, in contrast, is a sleek, fast and fierce surface predator. It grows to 3.5 m long and pursues mainly penguins, but it will eat large fish and even kill other seals.

The baby harp seal is one of the most appealing of all animals. It gradually loses its fluffy baby fur and develops the dark head, dark side stripes and pale grey background colour of the adult.

FRONT FLIPPER POWER

The eared seals have much more noticeable ear flaps on the sides of the head. They include fur seals and sea lions. They have torpedo-shaped bodies like true seals, but their rear flippers are longer and more mobile, and their front ones larger and more powerful. They swim mainly by "rowing" with these long front flippers. On land, they can shuffle about by tucking their rear flippers under the body and propping themselves up on their front pair. They rest and breed on land at traditional sites called rookeries.

THE SEAL WITH TUSKS

The huge walrus is more than 3 m long. It has a very fat, blubbery body and extra-long upper canine teeth known as tusks. Both males and females have tusks, which can be 60 cm long. They use the tusks for grubbing in the sea bed for shellfish and other food, and to help pull themselves out from the water.

The Mediterranean monk seal is one of the rarest seals, with just a few hundred left. They live in remote sea caves in scattered colonies, in the Mediterranean Sea and Atlantic Ocean.

The male dugong munches sea grass, its body scarred from fights with male rivals at breeding time. A dugong has notched tail flukes like a whale; the manatee's tail is rounded.

GENTLE PLANT EATERS

Manatees and dugongs are sometimes called sea cows, because they are peaceful, slow plant-eaters, like cows on land. They graze on water plants in shallow tropical seas and estuaries. The dugong lives in the southwest Pacific Ocean, one species of manatee lives near the Amazon River, another around the West Indies, and a third off the coast of West Africa. These bulky animals grow 3–4 m long. Sea cows bobbing half-seen through ocean mists may have given rise to sailors' legends about mermaids (magical women with fish tails).

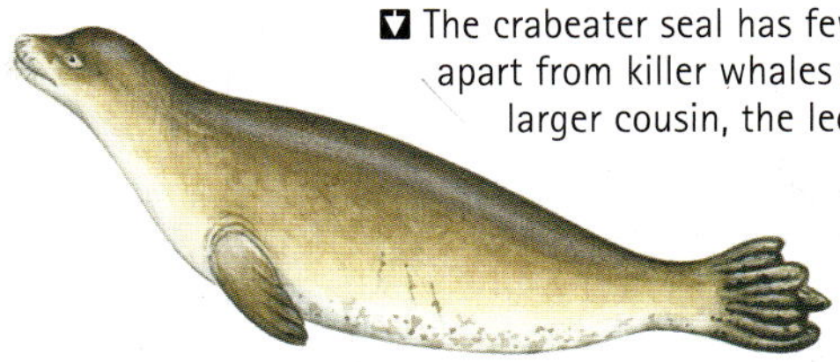

The crabeater seal has few enemies, apart from killer whales and its larger cousin, the leopard seal.

Sea lions and seals *(pinnipeds)*
- 34 species
- smooth, streamlined head and bulky body
- paddle-like limbs
- sharp teeth

True or earless seals
- 19 species
- no visible or external ear flaps
- cannot tuck rear flippers under body
- inshore waters of all seas and oceans but less common in tropics
- include grey seal, common (harbour) seal, harp seal, northern elephant seal, leopard seal, Mediterranean monk seal

Eared seals (fur seals and sea lions)
- 14 species
- ear flaps (may be hidden in fur)
- can tuck rear flippers under body
- inshore waters of most seas and oceans, ice floes
- include northern fur seal, Californian sea lion, Galapagos fur seal

Walrus
- 1 species
- long tusks
- Arctic and northern oceans

Manatees and dugong *(sea cows)*
- 4 species
- plant eaters
- include Amazonian manatee, West Indian manatee, West African manatee, dugong

GREAT WHALES

WHALES AND DOLPHINS ARE PERFECTLY ADAPTED TO LIFE AT SEA. In fact, they never come ashore – unless beached by accident, when they usually die. Great whales differ from toothed whales such as dolphins and porpoises (page 232) because they have comb-like baleen in their mouths, for filter-feeding. Great whales were once hunted in huge numbers for their meat, fat, oil and baleen (whalebone). The slaughter drove some species almost to extinction. Laws now prevent them from being killed in large numbers, and most whale populations are slowly recovering. Great whales show complicated behaviour and communicate with a wide variety of sounds and calls.

World Watch

For centuries, small numbers of great whales were hunted with spear-like harpoons from sailing or rowing boats. But in the 19th century, whaling ships were equipped with steam engines. Then came faster diesel engines and explosive harpoons. The whales could not escape. Thousands were killed yearly. By the 1950s their numbers had plummeted. In the mid 1980s mass whaling ceased at last.

Blue whale

Baleen whales have huge and very unusual mouths. Their jaws lack teeth. Instead, the mouth contains rows of baleen plates. These are strap-like or curtain-like structures that hang down from the roof of the mouth. They have fringed edges like brushes or combs. They work as filters to sieve the small animals of the plankton from the water.

Humpback whales open their vast mouths and swim up to the surface, trapping small creatures inside.

HOW GREAT WHALES FEED

These vast animals feed in different ways. Right whales cruise along with their mouths open at the surface. Blue and humpback whales take a massive mouthful of sea water, then press the huge tongue upwards inside the mouth to force the water out through the baleen plates.

The grey whale grubs in the mud of the sea bed and does the same. In all of these whales, food items such as krill and small fish get trapped in the combs or bristles of the baleen, which are tough and springy, like plastic. The whale then licks the food off the baleen plates and swallows it.

The grey whale feeds on small creatures in the mud, leaving great holes and furrows in the sea bed.

Over millions of years of evolution, a whale's front legs have become flippers, used for swimming slowly and steering in the water. The rear legs have disappeared, while the tail has developed wide flukes. These swish up and down to drive the mammal through the water with the power of a racing car engine.

Grey whales feed mainly in the shallow coastal waters of the Arctic, between North America and Asia. They dive down to 90 m, scoop up a rich mixture of mud and filter the small animals living in it. When the whale has a mouthful of food it surfaces to strain off the water, swallows its meal and dives for another load.

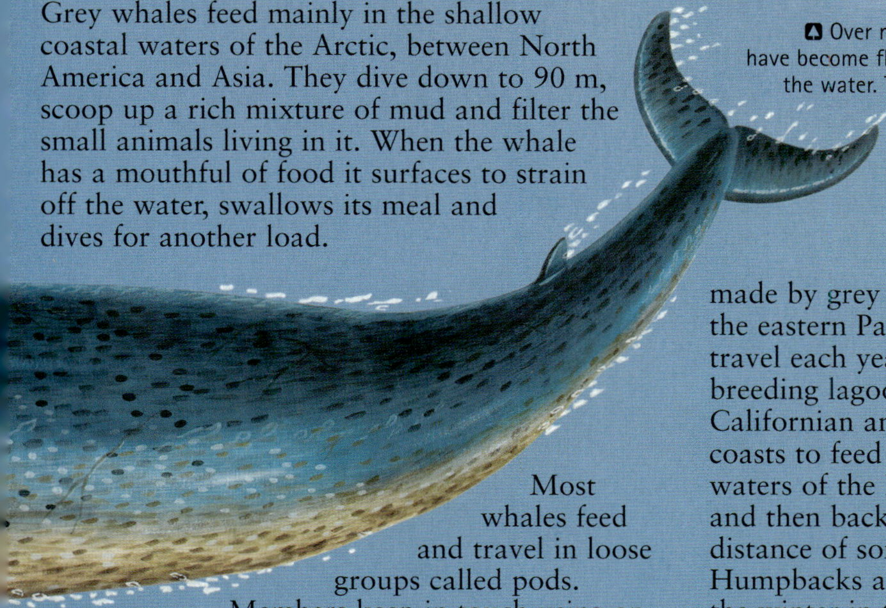

Most whales feed and travel in loose groups called pods. Members keep in touch using an amazing variety of sounds, many too low or high for us to hear. Blue and fin whales emit ear-splitting, low-pitched grunts that are the loudest noises made by any animal. Such sounds travel for hundreds of kilometres through the seas.

THE SONG OF THE HUMPBACK WHALE

Even more extraordinary are the songs of the humpback whale. These eerie, plaintive sounds plunge from high squeaks to deep wails, in a sequence that lasts half an hour or more, making it the longest, most complicated song of any animal. Usually, the singer is a male trying to attract a female at breeding time. Humpbacks also make acrobatic leaps almost right out of the water, then splash back in with an enormous crash.

WHALE MIGRATIONS

Many whales travel or migrate long distances between their main feeding places and the waters where the females give birth to their young, known as calves. Most great whales tend to feed in polar waters during the brief Arctic or Antarctic summer, then return near to the tropics for winter. The longest migrations are made by grey whales in the eastern Pacific. They travel each year from the breeding lagoons off the Californian and Mexican coasts to feed in the rich waters of the Bering Sea, and then back again – a distance of some 15,000 km. Humpbacks are also great travellers. Some spend the winter in the Caribbean and the summer near Greenland and Iceland.

LARGEST EVER... !

The largest animal that ever lived on Earth is the blue whale. An adult female blue whale can measure more than 30 m long, weigh over 150 tonnes and eat 4 tonnes of krill each day.

Great whale calves stay with their mothers for up to a year. Like all mammals, they feed at first on her rich milk, but gradually they learn to filter-feed for themselves. A newborn blue whale calf weighs 3 tonnes and measures 7 m long. Each day it drinks 200 litres of milk. Female great whales usually have only one calf every two years – one reason why their numbers take so long to recover.

Minke whales are the smallest great whales, at 10–11 m in length.

Dolphins and whales *(Cetaceans)*
- 76 species
- entirely aquatic, most in the sea
- long, submarine-shaped body
- front limbs are flippers
- tail flukes

The largest whales:

Baleen or great whales
- 10 species
- comb-like baleen in mouth
- worldwide, mainly colder oceans

Rorquals
- 6 species including blue whale (largest living animal), fin whale, humpback whale, minke whale, sei whale, Bryde's whale

Grey whale
- 1 species

Right whales
- 3 species including right whale, pygmy right whale, and bowhead

DOLPHINS AND PORPOISES

ON GUARD!

The narwhal grows to 5 m long and has mottled brown colouring. It also has a long tusk! Only the male has a tusk – a greatly lengthened upper left incisor tooth with a twisted spiral surface pattern. It grows up to 2.5 m long. Rival males "fence" with their tusks at breeding time.

TOOTHED WHALES INCLUDE MANY KINDS OF PORPOISES AND DOLPHINS, AND ALSO SPERM WHALES, BEAKED WHALES AND TWO WHITE WHALES – THE NARWHAL AND BELUGA. These all have more normal mouths and teeth than great whales (page 230). However, unlike land carnivores, a toothed whale's teeth are all similar in size and shape, designed to grasp slippery fish and squid. The largest species of toothed whale is the sperm whale. Males or bulls are up to 20 m long and weigh 50 tonnes – making them the largest carnivores on Earth.

▼ The common or harbour porpoise finds its prey of fish, such as herring or mackerel, using a sonar system of sound clicks and listening to the echoes.

Dolphins range in length from only 1.2 m in Heaviside's dolphin to 7 m or more in the huge and powerful killer whale, or orca. Killer whales are among the fiercest predators of the sea, though they rarely pose a threat to people. With immense speed and power, they pursue their prey of fish, seals, seabirds, dolphins and even larger whales. They hunt in groups and sometimes work together to herd a school of fish into shallow water to feed at their leisure.

▲ Narwhal

Like the other dolphins, killer whales are regarded as "intelligent" animals. This is partly because they can be taught to do tricks. But in the wild they also show great curiosity and adaptable behaviour, working out how to eat new and unfamiliar foods.

◄ The killer whale is the largest dolphin. It feeds mainly on seals and other sea mammals, as well as penguins and fish. It is a very fast swimmer, reaching a speed of 55 km/h.

All of the dolphins are active, even playful creatures. They are sleek, powerful swimmers, and sometimes follow ships – perhaps to feast on any leftovers thrown over the side, or to save energy by swimming in the ship's wake. Most dolphins live in groups and communicate with each other using a great variety of squeals, buzzes, clicks and grunts. They also use these sounds for echo-location or sonar, like bats (page 198) but underwater, to find prey and navigate through cloudy water. Like all whales, they breathe through their nostrils, which are joined together on the top of the head as the blowhole.

SNUB-NOSED WHALES

▼ River dolphin

A dolphin has a protruding beak-like snout and a curving sickle-shaped back fin. Porpoises are similar, but lack the dolphin's beak and have a snub nose instead. They are also generally smaller than dolphins, growing to about 2 m in length. Most species are dark grey and feed, like dolphins, on fish and squid.

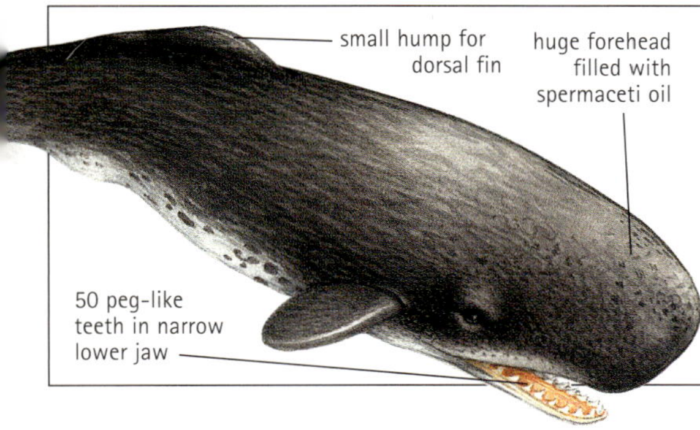

GIANT CARNIVORE
The massive sperm whale is the largest predator on the planet, and also the deepest-diving of all mammals. It reaches depths of 3 km in search of its prey, which includes the fearsome giant squid.

Porpoises tend to stay inshore, usually in small groups of about 10 or 15, and seldom leap clear of the water.

▲ The northern bottlenose whale is a toothed whale—but it only has two teeth. These are in the lower jaw, and they may never grow above the gum.

BIGGEST TOOTHED WHALES

Sperm whales feed mainly on large squid, which they catch deep in the ocean. The sperm whale is gigantic, but the dwarf sperm whale is more dolphin-sized, at about 2.6 m long. These whales are named for the waxy, oily substance, spermaceti, that takes up most of their bulging foreheads. It may help the whale to dive very deep and also to focus the sound waves it uses for echo-location.

BEAKED WHALES

The beaked whales are mysterious creatures that resemble overgrown dolphins. There are 18 species, but they spend most of their time diving to immense depths and so are seen much less often than other whales. They eat mainly squid. The largest is Baird's beaked whale, at about 13 m long.

The two kinds of white whales are the narwhal and beluga. The narwhal's sword-like tusk may have inspired legends about the mythical unicorn. The beluga is tuskless and is pure white when adult. It also has a flexible neck, so it can turn its head to each side. Belugas live in all Arctic and northern seas. They make such loud chirps, trills and squeaks that these can be heard above the water, earning them the nickname of "sea canary".

River dolphins live in fresh water and estuaries. Their echo-location is very sensitive, helping them find their way in muddy water. They include the very rare whitefin dolphin. There are perhaps only 150–200 left, in the Yangtze river in China.

Continued from page 231:

Dolphins and other toothed whales
- 66 species
- mostly smaller than great whales
- short, sharp teeth

Groups include:

Dolphins
- 32 species
- worldwide, mainly offshore in warm seas
- beak-like snout
- includes common, bottlenose and spinner dolphins, melon-headed whale, pilot whales, killer whale (orca)

Porpoises
- 6 species
- northern coastal waters
- lack dolphin's "beak"
- includes common and Dall's porpoises

River dolphins
- 5 species
- fresh water
- Amazon, La Plata, Indus, Ganges and whitefin dolphins

Sperm whales
- 3 species
- blunt forehead
- includes sperm and pygmy sperm whales

Beaked whales
- 18 species
- resemble large dolphins with beak-like snout
- includes northern bottlenose whale and Cuvier's beaked whale

White whales
- 2 species
- whitish colour
- narwhal and beluga

▲ Many dolphins, like these bottlenoses, make spectacular leaps into the air, sometimes up to 3 m clear of the sea. One species, the spinner dolphin, leaps high into the air and spins like a top at the same time.

LEMURS AND BUSHBABIES

ALONG WITH MONKEYS AND APES, THE LEMURS AND BUSHBABIES BELONG TO A GROUP OF MAMMALS KNOWN AS PRIMATES. The main primate features include a relatively large brain for the size of the body, well-developed hands with thumbs that can grasp and manipulate small items and large, forward-facing eyes. The lemurs and bushbabies, plus the pottos, lorises and tarsiers, are prosimians, which means "early-monkeys". They resemble animals that appeared on Earth before the later primates, the monkeys and apes.

The potto can grasp twigs between its fingers and thumb, and also between its big toe and other toes. It has a head–body length of about 35 cm.

Ring-tailed lemur mother and baby

Lemurs are found only in Madagascar. They resemble a combination of monkey and squirrel, and range in size from lesser mouse-lemurs smaller than your fist, to the large indri with a head–body length of 70 cm. Most lemurs feed mainly at night on fruits, seeds, flowers and leaves, which they gather as they move through the trees. They see and hear well at night with their large eyes and ears. Most species have long tails for balancing.

The ring-tailed lemur's tail is brightly patterned with alternate rings of black and white. This species is active by day. It wipes its large tail on scent glands under its arms and chin, then waves the tail aloft to send sight and smell signals to its troop members. However, most lemur species are much less noticeable, as they hide by day and creep through the shadowy trees at night.

Bushbabies have such precise hearing and fast reactions that they can hear a moth flutter past and reach out and grab it, all in total darkness.

Mouse lemurs are the smallest lemurs, and also the smallest primates. Yet they are long-lived for such small mammals. Some have survived 12–15 years in captivity.

The slow loris is well named, since it hardly seems to move as it creeps through the thickest rainforest. It can grip a twig and hang by just one foot.

PRIMATES
- 180 species
- large, forward-facing eyes
- manipulative hands
- mostly tree-dwelling

Prosimians
- 36 species
- mostly smaller than monkeys
- simple teeth with few points (cusps)

Main groups of prosimians:

Lemurs
- 10 species
- Madagascar only

Sifakas
- 4 species
- Madagascar only
- resemble large lemurs

Dwarf lemurs and mouse lemur
- 8 species
- Madagascar only

Aye-aye
- 1 species
- Madagascar only
- long, thin middle finger

Bushbabies
- 6 species
- Africa
- enormous eyes

Lorises and pottos
- 4 species
- Africa and Asia

Tarsiers
- 3 species
- Southeast Asia (Borneo, Sumatra, Philippines)

Bushbabies live mainly in eastern Africa. Like lemurs, they prefer dense forests. They are small and agile, and find insects at night with their huge eyes and keen hearing. The tailless lorises and pottos of Africa and Asia are much more slow-moving than bushbabies. They creep slowly along branches as they feed on a range of items, from fruits and tree sap to insects, snails, and even a small bird or shrew. Huge-eyed tarsiers watch the forest floor from a low bough. When a lizard or insect ambles past, they pounce.

The aye-aye of Madagascar has bat-like ears, large front teeth and an extraordinary long middle finger to pick grubs out of wood. It is an endangered species.

The indri is the largest type of lemur. It has a head and body up to 60 cm long, and weighs as much as 10 kg. It also lacks the typical lemur's long tail, having a short stump.

The tarsier leaps extremely well using its muscular back legs and long, strong rear feet. It keeps its body upright as it springs from one branch to another.

AFRICAN MONKEYS

White-cheeked mangabey

ABOUT 40 SPECIES OF MONKEYS LIVE IN AFRICA, IN HABITATS RANGING FROM DENSE TROPICAL FOREST TO OPEN WOODLAND AND SAVANNA, TO DRY ROCKY SCRUB. Most common are the guenons, with long tails. They inhabit mainly forests, travelling and feeding in groups. One of the most abundant and widespread guenons is the vervet monkey, equally at home on the ground or in trees. When feeding on the ground, vervets are always wary, and quickly rush to safety in the trees if danger threatens. Many of these African monkeys have colourful markings with different patterns of red, brown, grey, black and white, especially around the face. These colours change to show the sex and age of each troop member.

Colobus monkeys have four fingers on each hand. Their thumbs are tiny or missing.

Colobuses are some of the most beautiful and graceful of all monkeys, with their long, glossy coats and sweeping, tufted tails. They stay mainly in trees along the forest edge, and rarely come down to the ground except to feast on fallen fruits. Unfortunately, many colobus monkeys are killed for their fur, and several species are now rare or endangered. Another great threat to all monkeys is habitat loss—the clearance of their forest homes for farmland, buildings and roads.

Olive baboons live in troops of 100 or more. The troop has a social order with leading males and females. Young males patrol the edges and act as scouts to check for danger.

LARGEST... !
The mandrill and drill are the largest monkeys. Males can grow to 90 cm tall and weigh as much as 50 kg.

The adult male mandrill has a bright red nose, with vivid or pale blue patches at each side, and yellow-orange fur on the chin. Mandrills live in troops of 30–40 in the forests of west Africa. They sleep in trees, but feed mainly on the ground.

World Watch

The "Barbary apes" that scamper around and entertain tourists on the Rock of Gibraltar, at the west end of the Mediterranean Sea, are not true apes. They are a type of baboon-like, tailless monkey called the Barbary macaque (page 238). They were taken to Gibraltar from their natural home in North Africa, where they have now become rare. Yet some are still captured to keep up the numbers on Gibraltar.

DOG-FACED MONKEYS

Baboons are large, mainly ground-dwelling monkeys with dog-like faces and sharp teeth. They are powerfully built with muscular shoulders and arms, and can run and clamber with great skill. This group includes the forest-living mandrill with its vividly coloured face, and the drill with its equally colourful rear end.

Vervet monkeys can run, climb and swim well, and eat most kinds of food.

Most baboons live in large groups called troops, and have close-knit social behaviour. Olive baboons live in extended family groups within the larger troop. Each family usually includes offspring and also the offspring's offspring as well. The family tends to stay together and help each other if one is sick or injured. Some species of baboon even live in desert habitats with hardly any trees. Chacma baboons, a shaggy, dark grey variety of the savanna or common baboon species, can survive even in the almost waterless wastes of the Namib Desert in southern Africa.

Mangabeys are closely related to baboons. They too have strong jaws and especially powerful incisor teeth, used to crack open tough nuts and seeds. They also eat fruits, leaves, fungi, insects, lizards and baby birds. They are more lightly built than baboons, with tails longer than their bodies, to help balance in the treetops. Since they live among dense forest foliage, they communicate not by visual signs, like baboons, but by loud whoops and cries, like most other monkeys. Mangabeys are mainly black, grey or brownish.

PRIMATES
(continued from page 235):

Old World monkeys
- 133 species
- forward-facing eyes
- nostrils close together
- manipulating hands
- most have long tails

Groups of African monkeys:

Guenons
- 17 species
- slender body
- several are colourful
- mainly forests

Colobus monkeys
- 9 species
- graceful and agile
- black and white or red-brown
- woodland and forest

Baboons
- 5 species
- mainly African
- heavy body, dog-like face
- some have short tails
- spend time on the ground

Mangabeys
- 4 species
- medium-sized
- graceful and agile
- forests

ASIAN MONKEYS

THE LARGEST GROUP OF ASIAN MONKEYS IS THE LEAF MONKEYS AND LANGURS. They are found mainly in southern Asia, but some live in North Africa and others in China. This group contains many species that dwell in forests, like most other monkeys. But there are also some which survive high in mountains, where it is snowy and treeless. The Hanuman (or common) langur is one of the most adaptable, ranging from gardens and towns to remote, rocky uplands. It is regarded as sacred in the Hindu faith. Even though it often raids crops, it is seldom harmed. Most leaf monkeys and langurs feed on leaves, fruits, nuts, buds and flowers. They rarely drink, obtaining most of the water they need from their juicy food. Due to loss of their forest home, some of these monkeys are rare and a few are on the official "Red Lists" of threatened species.

Hanuman langurs are bold monkeys and soon become used to people. They sometimes raid picnic sites, shops and houses to look for food.

WAAAH!

In some langurs, a young monkey is cared for by "baby-sitters" as well as by its own mother. These other females may even give their own milk to the baby. However, they may also simply put it down and walk off! The abandoned baby cries out, and its mother soon comes back.

Most primates only enter water if they must, to escape danger. Proboscis monkeys are the best swimmers in the group. They often cross rivers, even diving below the surface.

Many macaques have hairless faces with red skin.

Macaques are the most widespread monkeys, found from North Africa across the Middle East and Asia, including the Philippines and Indonesia. The habitats they occupy are equally varied, including rainforests, mangrove swamps, scrub and even buildings such as shrines and temples. The rhesus and Japanese macaques can survive winter snow and ice, feeding on roots and tree sap.

Like many monkeys and other primates, rhesus macaques groom each other and their young. The monkey searches through the fur with its nimble fingers for bits of dirt, and for pests like fleas and lice, that it pops into its mouth. This mutual grooming helps to strengthen relationships within the family and the troop.

The crab-eating macaque was named because early scientific observers watched it eat crabs. But like many monkeys, it has a mixed diet of insects and similar small animals, eggs, fruit, buds, leaves and almost anything else.

SNUB-NOSED MONKEYS

These large monkeys take their name from the flat, short nose set back from the rounded muzzle. They also have strong arms, which are almost as long as their legs. They are found mainly in forests and bamboo jungles in China, Tibet and Southeast Asia, some species inhabiting the cloud forests high on mountain slopes. At least two species are rare or endangered, with populations of just a few hundred. These species will survive only if their forest habitats are protected from human encroachment.

PROBOSCIS MONKEYS

The proboscis monkey is named for the male's prominent, protruding nose, which droops down over the mouth. The female has a shorter, more normal monkey nose, as do both sexes of the related pig-tailed monkey. Both of these species are rare and live in restricted areas.

The snub-nosed monkeys of China migrate in spring up the mountain slopes, and come back down as cold autumn mists cloak the uppermost forests.

The proboscis monkey lives in Borneo, and the pig-tailed monkey on the Mentawai Islands off Sumatra.

The favourite habitats of the proboscis monkey are mangrove swamps along the coast, where they feed mainly on the young shoots and leaves of mangroves and the fruits of other trees, such as pedadas. Occasionally they swim across stretches of water and even dive from heights of 15 m into the sea to avoid danger. The proboscis monkey's leafy food is poor in nutrients, so it must eat large amounts. After a good meal, about half of the monkey's body weight of 15–20 kg is the leaves in its enormous stomach.

Japanese macaques live high in mountains, where it becomes cold and icy in winter. They sometimes warm themselves by bathing in natural hot springs.

Old World monkeys differ from New World or American species in various ways, including their nostrils being close together.

OLD WORLD MONKEYS
(continued from page 237)

Asian groups include:

Leaf monkeys and langurs
- 20 species
- India, China, Southeast Asia
- long limbs and tail
- some have crest-like hairs on head
- various habitats

Macaques
- 15 species
- mostly Asian
- bulky, sturdy build
- often live on the ground

Snub-nosed monkeys
- 6 species
- China and Southeast Asia
- broad face with snub nose
- forest and bamboo groves

Proboscis monkeys
- 2 species
- Borneo, Sumatra
- bulky, rotund body
- prominent floppy nose
- rainforest and mangroves

AMERICAN MONKEYS

NEW WORLD OR AMERICAN MONKEYS ARE FOUND MAINLY IN TROPICAL FORESTS. Most are agile and acrobatic, leaping easily through the treetops, but they are difficult to study and little is known about some species. There are two main groups, the small tamarins and marmosets, and the larger howler and woolly monkeys. They may be hard to see, but they can certainly be heard since they communicate by very loud calls. Their howls, hoots and whoops are some of the most characteristic rainforest noises.

Howler monkeys live mainly in the Amazon region, in small troops of up to ten. Their large throats work as resonance chambers to make their calls extremely loud.

Howler monkeys live in forests, from the steamy tropical lowlands to the slopes about 900 m above. The six species feed mainly on fruits and young leaves. As their name suggests, they are very noisy animals. Their howling cries carry for hundreds of metres through the forest. Most of the howling happens as dawn breaks, and for the same reason that birds sing their dawn chorus. The sounds allow rival howler troops to tell each other where they are, and that their home areas or territories are occupied. This helps to avoid direct fights.

SHAGGY SAKIS

Saki monkeys have shaggy fur coats, and the males tend to have bright markings around the face. Their main food is fruits, berries and seeds, gathered as they move in small groups through the forest canopy. Some types of sakis eat small animals like bird chicks, mice and bats, as well as eggs and the honey of wild bees.

The owl monkey, or douroucouli, is the only monkey which is active during darkness. Its large eyes are adapted for night vision.

Squirrel monkeys are lively and bold, and sometimes raid fields of crops. They live in groups of 30–40 and move in the branches with great ease. Like other monkeys, they use the long, thin tail as a balancing aid.

SPIDERS IN THE TREES

Spider monkeys are the most expert climbers of all monkeys. They are named for their long, furry legs and grasping tail, which stick out at all angles, making them look like hairy five-legged spiders. Some species can even pick up small objects with the tail. They dangle in the highest branches, run and leap with breathtaking skill, and also swing along using their hands as hooks, like gibbons. They feed on ripe fruits.

PARTLY PREHENSILE

Capuchin monkeys are medium sized, with a head and body length of 30–35 cm, and a tail up to 50 cm long. They are found in most parts of Central and South America, in a wide range of forest types. They have arms shorter than their legs, and the tail is less grasping or prehensile than most other American monkeys. Their varied diet includes insects and frogs, as well as fruits and leaves. Capuchins often come down to the ground to feed – which is another unusual feature of the New World monkeys.

The tail of the spider monkey is so muscular and grasping that it can hold the creature's entire body weight, leaving the hands and feet free to gather food.

SMALL FAMILIES

Titi monkeys are small, with long, bushy fur. Unlike most other American monkeys, they live in small family groups rather than large troops. Sitting side by side on a branch, they sometimes twist their dangling tails together for extra support and security. They are usually quiet, but make loud dawn calls that last for several minutes, to defend their territory.

WOOLLY COATS

Woolly monkeys live mainly in the Amazon region. Like spider monkeys, they have a long, strong prehensile tail, which they use to hang from forest branches. They are large monkeys with a head and body length of 60 cm and a tail even longer. They have thick, dense fur and feed mainly on fruits and leaves.

The red uakari is one of the oddest-looking of all monkeys. Its fur is white or chestnut, but its face and forehead are bald and the pale skin goes bright red in sunlight, almost as if sunburned. This monkey also has a relatively short tail. Uakaris prefer damp lowland forests, clamber rather than leap through the branches and feed mainly on fruit.

The woolly spider monkey, or muriqui, is the symbol of Brazil's conservation movement. This is the largest American monkey species, and also one of the rarest. Just a few hundred are left in the country's southeast coastal forests.

SMALL AND SQUIRREL-LIKE

Tamarins and marmosets are small, squirrel-like monkeys, found mostly in the Amazon region. Tamarins are generally bright in colour, and some have long "whiskers" or a ruff of hair around the face. They eat mainly fruit and insects. Marmosets are slightly smaller than tamarins, and less brightly patterned. They use their large front teeth to bite small holes in the bark of certain forest trees. They then feed on the nutritious, sugary sap or gum that oozes out.

IN GRAVE DANGER

Several species of tamarin and marmoset are in danger of extinction, often because they are restricted to a particular kind of forest with certain tree species. The lion tamarin, with its golden mane of silky fur, has almost disappeared from the wild. Several zoos around the world are trying to save this species.

The chief male of the brown capuchin troop follows just behind the younger males as they forage. In this position, he receives plenty of food, but he is also safe since those in front are more likely to encounter any predators.

NEW WORLD MONKEYS

- about 50 species
- nostrils far apart
- many have prehensile tails

Howler monkeys and spider monkeys
- 29 species
- flat faces
- most live in forests
- includes howler monkeys (6 species), saki monkeys (6), spider monkeys (5), capuchin monkeys (4), titi monkeys (3), woolly monkeys (2), uakaris (2), night monkey (1), squirrel monkey (1)

Tamarins and marmosets
- 21 species
- most live in forests of Amazon area
- small and squirrel-like
- long, furry tail
- thumb and fingers cannot hold or manipulate items as well as larger monkeys
- feed on fruit, sap and insects
- includes tamarins (12 species), marmosets (9)

GIBBONS

APES ARE LARGER THAN MONKEYS, HAVE ARMS THAT ARE LONGER THAN THEIR LEGS, AND LACK TAILS. They also have large heads and strong jaws with big teeth. The ape group includes gibbons or lesser apes, and orangs, gorillas and chimps, known as great apes. There are nine species of gibbon, all in the forests of Southeast Asia. They are incredibly agile climbers, using their hook-like hands and long, muscular arms to swing around. They also leap with great ease and walk upright on their back legs, even along narrow branches, holding their arms out for balance.

▲ The lar gibbon is also known as the common or white-handed gibbon. Its main coat colour varies according to where it lives. Almost black individuals are from the Thailand region (see map opposite).

Like many tree-dwelling primates, gibbons are almost entirely vegetarian. Their favourite food is ripe fruit, which accounts for about two-thirds of their diet, and which they travel great distances to find. They also eat flowers, buds, shoots and leaves, and the occasional insect or other small animal. Fruit provides most of the water they need, but they also lick raindrops or dew from leaves. In a typical day, a gibbon spends about three hours searching for food, some four hours eating, and the rest of the time resting, sleeping, grooming, playing and calling.

ARMS AND SHOULDERS

The gibbon's main method of moving is almost unique among primates. Most forest monkeys have long tails to help them balance and perhaps to grasp branches. But the gibbon is tailless. Instead, it has long, muscular arms and very broad shoulders. It uses these to hang from branches and swing hand-over-hand with amazing speed and skill. This way of moving is called brachiation.

▲ Siamangs make their calls louder by inflating their throat pouches like balloons.

The gibbon's shoulder and arm joints are very flexible, and a gibbon can hang by one arm and turn its body in a complete circle.

GIBBON DUETS

Gibbons are also famed for their loud, sometimes musical calls. These echo through the forest, especially during the dawn chorus. Gibbons use these calls to communicate with each other and with neighbouring groups. Usually the female starts the call. Her mate then adds his own cries in the gaps between her sounds, so the result is a duet. The song of a gibbon usually follows a regular pattern. It begins with a "tuning up" period where the pair practise and loosen their throats and mouths. The next stage consists of alternating sequences, as the female and male take turns. Then comes the main part – the "great call" of the female.

▶ On Sumatra and the Malay peninsula, most lar gibbons have brownish fur. These two sites are colour-coded blue and red on the map (opposite), while the Thai area is coded green.

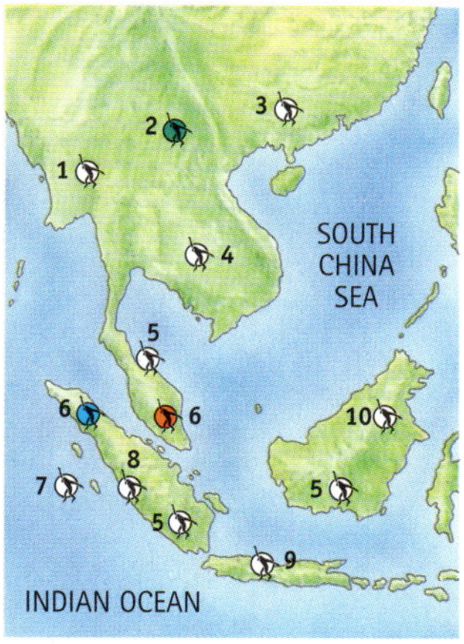

WHERE GIBBONS LIVE

Each species of gibbon lives in a different region of Southeast Asia. This is called geographic separation. It means that they do not compete for food, since all species have similar diets. The exception is the siamang, which is considerably larger than the other species and takes larger food items.

1 Hoolock gibbon
2 Lar gibbon
3 Concolor gibbon
4 Pileated gibbon
5 Agile gibbon
6 Lar gibbon
7 Kloss gibbon
8 Siamang
9 Moloch gibbon
10 Muller's gibbon

Gibbons, along with the orang, have the longest arms in relation to their body size, of any primate. The largest gibbon, the siamang, has an "armspan" of more than 1.5 m. Yet its head and body are only about 80 cm long.

PARTNERS FOR LIFE

The duet of a female and male gibbon helps to maintain their partnership, because they pair for life. They live as a small family group with their two or three young. Baby gibbons are born about every two years, and they cling tightly to their mother's fur even as she swings at speed through the trees. In some species, such as the siamang, the male takes over the care of the older offspring, until they are perhaps five years old. Gibbons are long-lived animals for their size, reaching about 40 years of age in the wild.

GOING SOLO

In one species, the kloss gibbon, male and female sing separately rather than together. The male produces a loud and musical solo in the morning, for as long as two hours. The female's song is usually shorter, but even more impressive. Every three or four days she climbs to the top of a tree to perform. Her song has some 20 different phrases, each lasting about half a minute, with long notes rising and falling. She ends with a flourish and her "great call" – during which she launches herself into the air, then rushes about tearing off leaves and snapping twigs.

APES

- 13 species
- resemble large, tailless monkeys
- Africa and Southeast Asia

Gibbons *(lesser apes)*
- 9 species

Agile gibbon
- Malaya, Sumatra, Borneo

Concolor gibbon
- Laos, Vietnam, S. China

Hoolock gibbon
- Assam, Bangladesh, Burma

Kloss gibbon
- Mentawai Islands (Sumatra)

Lar gibbon
- Thailand, Malaya, Sumatra

Moloch gibbon
- Java

Muller's gibbon
- Borneo

Pileated gibbon
- Thailand, Cambodia

Siamang
- Malaya, Sumatra

Compared to other mammals, baby apes are cared for by their mothers for a long time. The young lar gibbon feeds on its mother's milk for up to two years.

ORANGS AND GORILLAS

THE ORANG, GORILLA, CHIMP AND PYGMY CHIMP ARE THE FOUR KINDS OF GREAT APES, AND THE LARGEST OF THE PRIMATES. They are also the closest living relatives of ourselves, the human species. The mysterious orangs live deep in the forests of Borneo and Sumatra, in Southeast Asia. They are difficult to spot because they are rare, very shy and live mainly on their own rather than in family groups or troops. Gorillas, the largest apes, dwell in a few restricted areas of West and Central Africa. They live in small groups. They are massive, muscular and powerful animals, yet also peaceful and gentle – unless threatened.

The female gorilla is pregnant for just over nine months. When the baby is born, it cannot walk or climb, but only cling to her fur. By about three months of age the youngster is sitting up, and by six months old, it is able to climb and walk. The mother feeds it on her milk for up to 18 months.

The name "orang-utan" means "man of the woods". This second-largest ape has bright reddish-brown fur, which is long and shaggy. Despite their size and weight, orangs are skilled at clambering around in the trees, spreading their weight using all four limbs. They are very fond of fruit and spend many hours feasting on a tree of ripe figs or mangoes. They also eat leaves and shoots. Their big teeth and strong jaws help them to tear open even hard nuts, and pull off strips of bark to get at the sap-laden soft wood beneath. Orangs also eat insects and the occasional egg, chick, small bird, lizard or mouse.

World Watch

Gorillas are the largest primates. A mature male is 1.8 m tall and weighs over 150 kg. But their size and power have not helped them survive. Rather, it has partly led to their plight. Gorillas have been shot for "sport". Their hands and feet are cut off for "trophies". They are among the most endangered of all animals, especially the mountain gorilla. Human conflicts where they live have not helped.

LARGEST... !

The orang-utan is the largest tree-living mammal. Males grow to 1.5 m tall and weigh 90 kg.

The massive head, neck, shoulders and arms of the gorilla make it the strongest primate. Large males weigh up to 180 kg.

Gorillas usually sleep in nests that they make by bending and interlocking twigs and branches. Babies sleep with their mothers up to the age of about three years. These are mountain gorillas, with longer fur than the two lowland varieties.

The lowland gorillas have shorter, less shaggy fur than the rarer mountain gorillas.

THE LONG CALL

Orangs live in similar lowland rainforest habitats to gibbons (page 242). And like gibbons, orangs make loud calls to communicate with each other. However, it is only the male orang that does this, uttering what is known as his "long call", which lasts for a minute or two. The call starts with a series of roars, getting louder, then dying away to end with bubbling sounds. The call is not to keep in touch with family members, since orangs live solitary lives, except for a mother with her baby. The male probably makes the call to attract a female or to warn rival males off his territory.

Gorillas are very heavily built, with a broad chest, long arms and a large, tall-domed head (especially in adult males) with massive jaws and teeth. The nose is black, leathery and flattened. The fur and skin is mostly black, except in older adult males, which develop a silvery-white patch on the back and flanks, giving them the name of silverbacks.

Orangs seem to make no distinction between their arms and legs, using all of them for both climbing and feeding.

THE MOST VEGETARIAN APE

Gorillas are strong and muscular enough to overpower any animal in their dense forest habitat. Yet they are almost entirely vegetarian. They feed mainly on leaves, shoots, stems and ferns, and occasionally ripe fruits. Their main feeding periods are early morning and mid-afternoon, with long rests in between.

In the early evening, gorillas climb into trees to weave nest platforms where they sleep at night. Younger gorillas spend part of the day in trees too. They weigh much less than the adults and so find climbing easier – and there are more branches that will bear their weight. But most older members of the gorilla group prefer to feed and travel on the ground. They amble along on all fours, using the soles of the feet and the bent knuckles of their hands.

Gorillas live in groups of about 5 to 35 animals. A typical group consists of one silverback male, one or two junior males, and several females with their offspring. Unlike most other monkeys and apes, gorillas are mostly silent, except when rival adult males meet. Then they may threaten each other. They beat their chests, thrash branches and make barking, roaring and hooting calls.

Old male orangs develop long, shaggy fur especially over the shoulders and back, and loose, wrinkled skin on the chest and belly. They are also bigger and heavier, with larger cheek flaps than the females.

APES (continued from page 243):

Great apes
- 4 species
- largest primates
- tailless
- fingers and thumb can manipulate small items

Gorilla
- 1 species
- tropical rainforests
- 3 varieties or subspecies:

Western lowland gorilla (Cameroon, Central African Republic, Congo, Gabon, Equatorial Guinea)
Eastern lowland gorilla (eastern Congo)
Mountain gorilla (Congo, Rwanda, Uganda)
- eats plant material, berries, fruits

Orang *(orang-utan)*
- 1 species
- tropical rainforests
- Sumatra and Borneo

CHIMPANZEES

CHIMPANZEES HAVE THE MOST COMPLICATED SOCIAL LIVES OF ALL THE APES. They have a huge range of facial expressions, body postures, gestures, signs and sounds. They can work out how to solve simple problems, in the wild and in captivity. They make and use simple tools. In many ways, they seem to be a link between the world of animals and our human world. Their body structure and genes, their behaviour and intelligence, and their evolution as shown by fossils, mean that chimps are our closest relatives.

A mother chimp cares for her youngster for up to three years.

The pygmy chimp, or bonobo, is only slightly smaller than the common chimp, with a head-body length of 55–65 cm.

There are two species of chimpanzee. These are the chimp or common chimpanzee, and the bonobo or pygmy chimpanzee. The chimp is covered with black or grey hair, except for the ears, face, hands and feet. The face is usually pink, turning darker brown or black with age. The pygmy chimp is slightly smaller, with a lighter build and smaller teeth, and a darker face. It also has sideways tufts of hair over its ears.

Both species of chimps are long-lived. Some reach 50 years of age. More than any other animals, they show degrees of human-like attributes. These include care for their kin, teamwork during hunting, sharing out food, long-lasting bonds or "friendships", the ability to learn through their lives as they acquire skills, use tools and work out problems, with a good long-term memory for individuals, places and events. A chimp also shows self-awareness. Unlike other animals, it recognizes that the reflection in a mirror is itself, not another chimp.

THE TWO CHIMPS

There are several differences between the common chimp and the pygmy chimp. But these are quite minor, even in overall size. Some experts suggest that the two chimps are really varieties, or subspecies, of the same species.

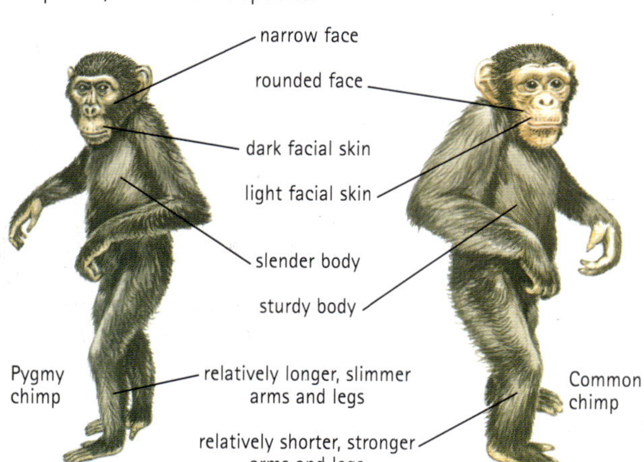

However, chimps can also show aggression and violence that is not directed towards catching food or in self-defence against rivals, as it is in other animals. In humans, this type of aggression might be described as "mindless".

Chimps spend many hours grooming others in their family or group. They remove old hairs, bits of dirt and pests such as fleas from each other's fur and skin. Apart from improving hygiene, this mutual grooming helps to strengthen the relationships within the troop.

THE CHIMP'S DAY

Chimpanzees are mainly active during the day. They rise at dawn to search for food, and spend time feeding and resting.

MAKING FACES

Chimpanzees use a kind of language to tell each other important information about their surroundings and intentions. They use many facial expressions and utter various shouts and grunts. Tame chimps have learned our own sign language, using their hands to communicate with people.

thoughtful pleased angry

When they move on, they travel (like gorillas) mainly on the ground rather than in trees, knuckle-walking on all fours. At night, each adult makes itself a nest platform, like the gorilla's. The chimp bends and weaves together branches, twigs and leaves, and rests and sleeps until the morning.

THE CHIMP'S HABITAT

Ideal chimp habitat includes areas with fruit trees, since fruit is their major food and they eat it for at least 4–5 hours each day. Other favoured foods are young, freshly sprouted leaves, seeds and also soft bark, sap, juicy pith wood and flowers. They sometimes use rocks to smash open hard-cased fruits and nuts, such as those of oil palms.

Chimps also eat termites, ants and caterpillars. A chimp may use a stick to probe inside a termite mound. The insects crawl onto the twig, and the chimp pulls it out and licks them off. Groups of chimps occasionally work together to catch and eat young pigs, monkeys and antelopes.

An adult male chimp is far stronger than an adult human, with a broad chest and very muscular arms. Male chimps, especially, get into fights or territorial disputes. They pick up and hurl large boulders or branches with great ease. Most chimp troops number about 20–50 individuals, with one or two large, leading males, various younger males and the rest females with their young.

Chimp numbers have fallen rapidly in recent years. The main causes are habitat destruction and illegal trapping. Many of the remaining populations are small and separated, and so at risk of extinction.

APES (continued from page 245):

Chimpanzees
- 2 species

Common chimpanzee
- West and Central Africa, from Senegal to Tanzania, mainly in Congo, Gabon, Cameroon
- forest, patchy woodland
- fruits, seeds, soft bark and other plant parts, also insects, eggs, small mammals

Pygmy chimpanzee *(bonobo)*
- Central Africa, only in Congo
- rainforest
- fruits, shoots, leaves, buds

Many facial expressions made by chimps look similar to our own. However, we must be very careful about assuming that a chimp's expression that looks like our own, means the same as our version. A chimp who appears to be in a good mood and laughing (right) is really fearful, baring its teeth in defence to a threat. Chimps learn much during their long "childhood".

GLOSSARY

Abdomen The region of an animal's body that contains mainly the parts or organs for digestion, reproduction and excretion (getting rid of waste products).

Antenna A "feeler", a long and thin part, usually on or near the head, that detects touch—and perhaps smells and tastes as well.

Arthropod An invertebrate animal that has a hard outer body casing (exoskeleton) and jointed limbs, such as an insect, crab, spider, centipede or millipede.

Asexual reproduction Producing offspring without sex (see Sexual reproduction). For example, some simple animals simply split in two (fission). Some grow "buds" that detach to form new individuals (vegetative reproduction). Some female animals produce eggs that develop into young without being fertilized by the sperm from a male (parthenogenesis).

Camouflage When an animal is shaped, coloured and patterned to blend in with its surroundings, so that it is less likely to be noticed, especially by its predators or prey.

Canine teeth Long, sharp teeth, like spears or daggers, near the front of the mouth of a mammal. They are well developed in meat-eaters such as dogs and cats.

Carapace A large, hard, shield-like covering over an animal's body. The upper part of the shell of a turtle is a carapace. So is the top part of the shell of a crab.

Carnivore An animal that eats the meat or flesh of other animals. Most carnivores are predators.

Carrion "Dead meat"—the dead and dying bodies or carcasses of animals, which are usually eaten by scavengers.

Cilia Microscopic hair-like parts that coat many outer surfaces and inner linings of animals and their body parts, such as the body surface of a tiny worm or the inside of the intestine. Cilia wave to-and-fro like tiny oars to cause movement.

Compound eye An eye made up of many separate light-detecting units, like a mosaic, rather than one larger unit, like our own eye. Insects have compound eyes.

Courtship behaviour The movements, actions, sounds and scents made by a male and/or female animal of the same species, when they come together to mate.

Detritivore An animal that feeds on detritus—the dead, dying and rotting bits of animals, plants and other once-living things.

Digestion Breaking down bits of food into tiny pieces by squeezing and squashing them, and pouring powerful chemical juices onto them. The pieces or nutrients are small enough to be taken into body tissues for growth and life processes.

Digit A toe, finger or similar part on the end of a limb.

Dorsal On the top, upper side or back of an animal, like a fish's dorsal fin.

Echo-location A system of sending out sounds, listening to the echoes that bounce back and working out the position of nearby objects. Bats, dolphins, shrews and some birds use echo-location.

Egg A single living cell produced by a female animal for reproduction. Some eggs are microscopic. Birds' eggs are large and enclosed in a hard shell.

Endoskeleton A strong supporting framework on the inside of the body, such as our own bones.

Evolution The changes in living things through time, due to changing conditions. New species appear, and existing species that are not suited or adapted to the conditions, and which cannot change or evolve, die out or become extinct.

Exoskeleton A strong supporting framework on the outside of the body, such as an insect's body casing.

Extinction When all the members of a particular group of living thing, usually a species, die out so that the species disappears forever.

Eye A body part that detects light rays and produces nerve signals that go to the animal's brain. (See also Compound eye.)

Filter-feeding When an animal feeds by filtering or sieving lots of tiny particles, usually from water, using body parts shaped like combs, brushes or feathers.

Flagellum A long, whip-like part sticking out from a microscopic cell. It lashes to-and-fro to cause movement.

Food chain and web The links between different living things, according to how they obtain their food. A simple food chain is when a rabbit eats some grass, and a fox eats the rabbit:
Grass > Rabbit > Fox

In nature, many animals eat a variety of foods, so the food chains link into a complex network known as a food web.

Genes Instructions or blueprints to make living things, in the form of chemical codes of the substance DNA (deoxyribonucleic acid), found inside cells. A living thing develops in shape, size and colour, and carries out its digestion and other body processes, according to the genes it is born with.

Gills Body parts specialized for absorbing oxygen dissolved in water. They are usually delicate and feathery.

Gland A body part that makes a certain product, usually a liquid, for use by the animal. A salivary gland, for example, makes saliva (spit), a venom gland makes poison and a mucus gland makes slimy mucus.

Habitat A type of natural place with characteristic plants and animals, such as a pond, an oak wood or a rocky seashore. Some animals, such as penguins, live only in one habitat. Others, such as the red fox, range across many habitats.

Herbivore An animal that eats mainly plants or their parts and products, such as leaves, fruits or roots.

Hermaphrodite An animal that has both female and male sex organs, which allow it to produce both eggs and sperm for reproduction.

Hibernation When a warm-blooded animal goes into a "deep sleep" during adverse conditions. Its body temperature falls drastically and its heartbeat, breathing and other body processes almost stop.

Incisor tooth Long, sharp-edged, chisel-like teeth at the front of the mouth of a mammal. They are well developed in rodents (gnawing animals) such as mice, rats and beavers.

Insectivore An animal that eats mainly insects, especially ants or termites, and often other small prey items too, such as worms, spiders, slugs and snails.

Invertebrate An animal without a backbone, or more accurately, without a vertebral column (see Vertebrate). The vast majority of animals, both in numbers of individuals and numbers of species, are invertebrates (eg insects, starfish and worms).

Kingdom One of the five main groups of living things. Animals make up the biggest kingdom, Animalia.

Larva The active growing and feeding stage in the lives of certain animals. It usually follows the egg stage. A larva does not look like its parent.

Lungs Body parts specialized for absorbing oxygen from air.

Metamorphosis When an animal changes its body shape dramatically as it grows. For example, a butterfly begins life as an egg, hatches into a caterpillar (larva), then turns into a chrysalis (pupa), and finally into the adult butterfly.

Migration A long journey to find food or more suitable conditions. Some migrations are regular, to-and-fro along the same route, at the same time each year. Others are occasional, as when lemmings run out of food and set off in almost any direction.

Molar teeth Wide, flat teeth at the back of the mouth of a mammal, for chewing. They are well developed in herbivores such as zebras, antelopes and elephants.

Mucus A slimy, usually sticky substance made by many animals, for uses such as protection, trapping bits of food, deterring enemies or easing movement.

Muscle A body part of an animal specialized to get shorter, or contract. Muscles make movements.

New World Term used for the continents and nearby islands of North and South America. They are separated from the Old World by the Atlantic and Pacific Oceans.

Nutrients Substances such as minerals that a living thing takes in as food, so it can grow, maintain and repair its body, and use energy for life processes.

Old World Term used for the continents and main islands of Europe, Africa, Asia and Australia. They are separated from the New World by the Atlantic and Pacific Oceans.

Omnivore An animal that eats many kinds of food, including meat and plants.

Oxygen An invisible gas, with no taste or smell, that makes up one fifth of the air around us. Oxygen is needed by living things because it is a vital part of the chemical process that breaks down food to get energy. Most animals obtain oxygen through their gills or lungs, or by absorbing it through the body's surface.

Parasite A living thing that exists on or in another living thing, known as the host. The parasite gains something, such as shelter or food, and usually causes harm to the host it lives on.

Parthenogenesis See Asexual reproduction.

Pheromone A chemical substance, like a scent, that an animal releases into the air or spreads on the ground. Each pheromone causes a certain reaction in others of its species, such as getting ready to breed, or following the pheromone trail to food.

Predator An animal that hunts or actively pursues other, usually smaller, creatures—its prey—for food.

Prehensile A body part that is flexible and muscular, and which can be used for grasping and holding. Some monkeys have prehensile tails for gripping branches.

Prey Any animal that is pursued or hunted as food by a predator.

Proboscis A movable stalk-like part on the head of an animal, usually with the mouth on it or near it.

Pupa The seemingly inactive, resting stage in the lives of certain animals, such as insects. It usually follows the larva stage and is sometimes called a chrysalis or cocoon.

Sexual reproduction When a sperm cell joins with an egg cell to make a fertilized egg, which develops into a new individual. This usually involves a female and male of the same species mating (having sex). (See Asexual reproduction.)

Species A kind or type of living thing, such as the tiger, the golden eagle, the African elephant or the common octopus. Members of a species can breed with each other, but not with members of another species.

Sperm A single living cell, usually shaped like a microscopic tadpole, produced by a male animal for reproduction. (See Sexual reproduction.)

Symbiosis When two different kinds or species of living things exist closely together and benefit each other in some way, such as giving protection to the other creature from potential predators, or sharing food. Sea anemones and clown fish have a symbiotic relationship. The fish's thick coating of slime protects it against the anemone's stings.

Territory An area that an animal occupies and defends against rivals of its species. Some territories are for feeding, some are for breeding and some are for both. A tiger's territory covers dozens of square kilometres of forest. A limpet's territory is just a few square metres of seashore rock.

Thorax The region of an animal's body that contains mainly the parts for moving, such as legs or wings, and often those for breathing and pumping blood (the heart). In the human body it is called the chest.

Torpor When a cold-blooded animal becomes inactive, usually because the temperature falls, as at night or in winter.

Vegetative reproduction See Asexual reproduction.

Ventral On the underside or belly of an animal, like a fish's ventral fin.

Vertebrate An animal with a backbone or, more accurately, a vertebral column—a row of bones or cartilages called vertebrae. The main groups of vertebrates are fish, amphibians, reptiles, birds and mammals.

Viviparous When a female animal gives birth to babies ("live young"), rather than laying eggs.

Warning colours Bright colours and patterns on an animal's body, which warn others that it is dangerous or harmful in some way. It may have a sting, or a poison bite, or a horrible taste. Red and black or yellow and black are common warning colours, found on bees, wasps, beetles, frogs, snakes and various other animals.

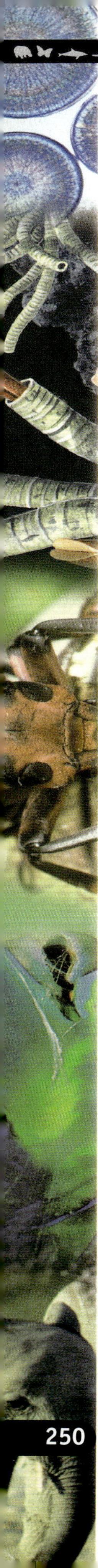

INDEX

Page numbers in **bold** refer to spread titles.

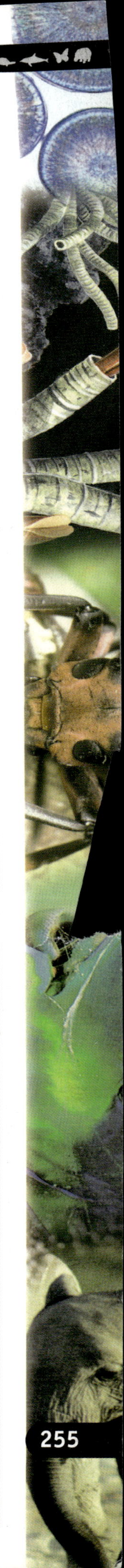

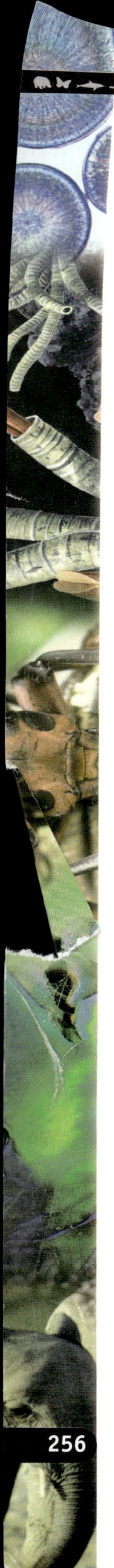

Acknowledgements

The publishers wish to thank the following artists who have contributed to this publication:

Janet Baker (Julian Baker Illustrations), Andy Beckett (Illustration), John Butler, Kuo Kang Chen, Wayne Ford, Chris Forsey, Roger Gorringe (Illustration), Ron Hayward, Roger Kent (Illustration), Stuart Lafford (Linden Artists), Mick Loates (Linden Artists), Alan Male (Linden Artists), Matt Nicholas (David Lewis Agency), Jane Pickering (Linden Artists), Terry Riley, Mike Saunders, Sarah Smith (Linden Artists), Christian Webb (Temple Rogers), David Webb (Linden Artists), Martin Wilcock (Illustration).

The publishers wish to thank the following photographic sources for the use of their photographs in this publication:
OSF = Oxford Scientific Films; NHPA = Natural History Photographic Agency

Page 12/13 (C) Peter Parks/OSF; 14 (C/L) Peter Parks/OSF; 17 (B/R) Karen Gowlett-Holmes/OSF; 16 (C/L) Harold Taylor/OSF; 18 (L) Peter Parks/OSF; 18/19 (C) M.I. Walker/NHPA; 22 (B) Richard Herrmann/OSF; 26 (B) Frederik Ehrenstrom/OSF; 29 (T/R) A.N.T./NHPA; 30/31 (C) Peter Parks/OSF; 34 (B/L) Norbert Wu/NHPA; 37 (T/R) A.N.T./NHPA; 38 (B) David B. Fleetham/OSF; 45 (T/L) David Fox/OSF, (B) Rodger Jackman/OSF; 46/47 (B) G.I. Bernard/NHPA; 49 (C/B) London Scientific Films/OSF; 50/51 (C) London Scientific Films/OSF; 52/53 (C) Image Quest/NHPA; 55 (C/R) Peter Parks/OSF; 56 (T/L) Colin Milkins/OSF; 56 (T/R) Rudie H.Kuiter/OSF; 58 (C/R) H.L. Fox/OSF; 62 (B/R) Norbert Wu/NHPA; 67 (T/L) Peter Parks/OSF; 68 (B/L) Frederik Ehrenstrom/OSF; 69 (T/L) Pam & Willy Kemp/OSF; 75 (L/T) Kjell B. Sandved/OSF; 76 (B/R) London Scientific Films/OSF; 79 (B/L) D.M. Shale/OSF; 82 (B/L) Bob Fredrick/OSF; 84 (T/L) Colin Milkins/OSF; 86 (B) Alastair Shay/OSF; 88 (B) Alastair Macewan/OSF; 91 (C) Jan Aldenhoven/OSF; 93 (R) J.A.L. Cooke/OSF; 95 (B/L) A.N.T./NHPA; 96 (B/L) Peter Parks/OSF; 99 (T) Michael Fogden/OSF; 106/107 (T/C) Hellio & Van Ingen/NHPA; 108/109 (C) Kathy Tyrrell/OSF; 110 (B/R) Agence Nature/NHPA, (T/L) Peter Parks/OSF; 112 (B) D. Heuclin/NHPA; 115 (B) B. Jones & M. Shimlock/NHPA; 117 (R) David B.Fleetham/OSF; 118 (B) Richard Herrmann/OSF; 119 (B/L) Kathie Atkinson/OSF, (T/L) Max Gibbs/OSF; 120/121 (C) NHPA; 122 (B) Tobias Bernhard/OSF; 122 (T/L) G.I. Bernard/NHPA; 125 (B/R) A.N.T./ NHPA; 128/9 (B/C) Dr. Ivan Polunin/NHPA; 135 (B/L) Robert Erwin/NHPA; 136 (B/R) G.I. Bernard/NHPA; 136 (B/L) Stephen Dalton/NHPA; 139 (T/R) Martin Harvey/NHPA; 143 (B) Jany Sauvanet/NHPA; 145 (T/L) Daniel Heuclin/NHPA; 146-147 (T/C) Stan Osolinski/OSF; 148/149 (B) Stephen Dalton/NHPA; 149 (T/L) Stephen Dalton/NHPA; 151 (T/R) Haroldo Palo Jr./NHPA; 155 (T/L) Jany Sauvanet/NHPA; 156 (B) Daniel Heuclin/NHPA; 158/159 (B) Stephen Dalton/NHPA; 163 (R) Tui de Roy/OSF; 168-169 (B) David C. Fritts/Animals Animals/OSF; 173 (B) Roger Tidman/NHPA; 174/175 (C) L. Hugh Newman/NHPA: 176 (B) Martyn Chillmaid/OSF; 180 (T/R) Robert Tyrrell/OSF; 183 (B/R) Michael Morcombe/NHPA; 185 (B) Maurice Tibbs/Survival Anglia/OSF; 187 (R) Ralph & Daphne Keller/NHPA; 193 (R) A.N.T./NHPA; 197 (T/R) Raymond A. Mendez/Animals Animals/OSF; 198 (T/L) Richard la Val/Animals Animals/OSF; 199 (C) Stephen Dalton/NHPA; 201 (T/R) Michael Fogden/OSF; 203 (C/R) Manfred Danegger/NHPA; 204 (B/L) Survival Anglia/OSF; 206 (B/L) Andrew Thomson; 207 (C/L) Raymond A. Mendez/Animals Animals/OSF; 211 (T/R) Nick Bergkessel/Photo Researchers/OSF; 215 (C) Anthony Bannister/NHPA: 223 (T/L) Peter Pickford/NHPA; 226/227 (B) Daniel Heuclin/NHPA; 229 (T/R) A.N.T./NHPA; 233 (B) Konrad Wothe/OSF; 236 (B/C) Brian Hawkes/NHPA; 238 (C) Norbert Wu/NHPA; 240 (L) Stephen Dalton/NHPA; 242 (C/R) Martin Harvey/NHPA; 245 (T/C) Martin Harvey/NHPA; 246 (C/R) Martyn Colbeck/OSF.